Lecture Notes in Computer Science 6583

Commenced Publication in 1973
Founding and Former Series Editors:
Gerhard Goos, Juris Hartmanis, and Jan van Leeuwe

Claus Vielhauer Jana Dittmann
Andrzej Drygajlo Niels Christian Juul
Michael Fairhurst (Eds.)

Biometrics and ID Management

COST 2101 European Workshop, BioID 2011
Brandenburg (Havel), Germany, March 8-10, 2011
Proceedings

Springer

Volume Editors

Claus Vielhauer
Brandenburg University of Applied Sciences
14737 Brandenburg an der Havel, Germany
E-mail: claus.vielhauer@fh-brandenburg.de

Jana Dittmann
Otto-von-Guericke-University Magdeburg
39016 Magdeburg, Germany
E-mail: jana.dittmann@iti.cs.uni-magdeburg.de

Andrzej Drygajlo
Swiss Federal Institute of Technology Lausanne (EPFL)
1015 Lausanne, Switzerland
E-mail: andrzej.drygajlo@epfl.ch

Niels Christian Juul
Roskilde University, 4000 Roskilde, Denmark
E-mail: ncjuul@ruc.dk

Michael Fairhurst
University of Kent
Canterbury CT2 7NT, United Kingdom
E-mail: m.c.fairhurst@kent.ac.uk

ISSN 0302-9743
e-ISSN 1611-3349
ISBN 978-3-642-19529-7
ISBN 978-3-642-19530-3 (eBook)
DOI 10.1007/978-3-642-19530-3

Springer Heidelberg Dordrecht London New York
Library of Congress Control Number: 2011921816

CR Subject Classification (1998): I.5, J.3, K.6.5, D.4.6, I.4.8, I.7.5, I.2.7

LNCS Sublibrary: SL 6 – Image Processing, Computer Vision,
Pattern Recognition, and Graphics

Typesetting: Camera-ready by author, data conversion by Scientific Publishing Services, Chennai, India

Printed on acid-free paper

Springer is part of Springer Science+Business Media (www.springer.com)

Preface

This volume of Springer Lecture Notes in Computer Sciences (LNCS) constitutes the final publication of the EU COST 2101 Action "Biometrics for Identity Documents and Smart Cards," which has been successfully running during the years 2006-2010. One of the many valuable outputs of this initiative is the realization of a new scientific workshop series, dedicated to the project's goals: the "European Workshop on Biometrics and Identity Management (BioID)." This series started in 2008 with the first workshop at Roskilde University, Denmark (BioID 2008) and continued with a second event, hosted by the Biometrics Recognition Group (ATVS) of the Escuela Politécnica Superior, Universidad Autónoma de Madrid, Spain in 2009 (BioID_MultiComm 2009). From the very beginning, the research papers of BioID workshops have been published as Springer LNCS volumes; vol. 5372 (2008) and vol. 5707 (2009).

Continuing the series, this present volume collects together the submitted research papers accepted for the Third European Workshop on Biometrics and Identity Management (BioID 2011), taking place during March 8–10, 2011 at Brandenburg University of Applied Sciences, Germany. The workshop Call for Papers was open to the entire research community and all submissions underwent a double-blind review process by the workshop Scientific Committee. Readers will see that the event attracted an interesting mix of papers, with the wide-ranging topic coverage which is to be expected from a field as diverse as that addressed by this workshop.

In addition to the peer-reviewed papers, two contributions were invited by the workshop Chairs. As this volume constitutes a final project output, it begins with an invited introductory paper by the COST 2101 Action Chair, summarizing the scientific experiences from the overall project and lessons learned from it. Secondly, the Action Chair contributes an invited paper in the domain of ageing face recognition.

The remainder of the papers in these proceedings are dedicated to further original work covering different research topics within biometrics. These topics can be categorized in the following groups:

1. Face Modalities
2. Handwriting Modalities
3. Speech Modalities
4. Iris Modalities
5. Multibiometrics
6. Theory and Systems
7. Convergence of Biometrics and Forensics.

Face recognition has proved to be the most popular strand represented in the submissions to this workshop, with seven individual papers. These propose

About COST

COST – the acronym for European Cooperation in Science and Technology – is the oldest and widest European intergovernmental network for cooperation in research. Established by the Ministerial Conference in November 1971, COST is presently used by the scientific communities of 36 European countries to cooperate in common research projects supported by national funds.

The funds provided by COST – less than 1% of the total value of the projects – support the COST cooperation networks (COST Actions) through which, with EUR 30 million per year, more than 30,000 European scientists are involved in research having a total value which exceeds EUR 2 billion per year. This is the financial worth of the European added value which COST achieves.

A "bottom–up approach" (the initiative of launching a COST Action comes from the European scientists themselves), "à la carte participation" (only countries interested in the Action participate), "equality of access" (participation is open also to the scientific communities of countries not belonging to the European Union) and "flexible structure" (easy implementation and light management of the research initiatives) are the main characteristics of COST.

As precursor of advanced multidisciplinary research, COST has a very important role in the realization of the European Research Area (ERA) anticipating and complementing the activities of the Framework Programmes, constituting a "bridge" toward the scientific communities of emerging countries, increasing the mobility of researchers across Europe and fostering the establishment of "Networks of Excellence" in many key scientific domains such as: biomedicine and molecular biosciences; food and agriculture; forests, their products and services; materials, physical and nanosciences; chemistry and molecular sciences and technologies; earth system science and environmental management; information and communication technologies; transport and urban development; individuals, societies, cultures and health. It covers basic and more applied research and also addresses issues of pre-normative nature or of societal importance.

Web: http://www.cost.eu

EUROPEAN SCIENCE FOUNDATION

ESF provides the COST Office through an EC contract

COST is supported by the EU RTD Framework programme

Organization

BioID 2011 was organized by the COST 2101 Action "Biometrics for Identity Documents and Smart Cards."

General Chairs

Claus Vielhauer	Brandenburg University of Applied Sciences, Germany
Jana Dittmann	Otto von Guericke University Magdeburg, Germany

Co-chairs

Andrzej Drygajlo	EPFL, Switzerland
Niels Christian Juul	Roskilde University, Denmark
Michael Fairhurst	University of Kent, UK

Program Chairs

Claus Vielhauer	Brandenburg University of Applied Sciences, Germany
Jana Dittmann	Otto von Guericke University Magdeburg, Germany

Scientific Committee

Akarun, L., Turkey
Alba Castro, J. J., Spain
Ariyaeeinia, A., UK
Bigun, J., Sweden
Campisi, P., Italy
Correia, P.L., Portugal
Delvaux, N., France
Dorizzi, B., France
Gluhchev, G., Bulgaria
Greitans, M., Latvia
Harte, N., Ireland
Hernando, J., Spain
Humm, A., Switzerland
Keus, K., Germany
Kittler, J., UK
Kotropoulos, C., Greece
Kounoudes, A., Cyprus
Kryszczuk, K., Switzerland
Kümmel, K., Germany
Lamminen, H., Finland
Leich, T., Germany
Majewski, W., Poland
Moeslund, T.B., Denmark
Ortega-Carcia, J., Spain
Pavesic, N., Slovenia
Pitas, I., Greece
Ribaric, S., Croatia
Richiardi, J., Switzerland
Salah, A.A., The Netherlands
Sankur, B., Turkey
Scheidat, T., Germany
Schouten, B.A.M., The Netherlands
Soares, L.D., Portugal
Staroniewicz, P., Poland
Strack, H., Germany
Tistarelli, M., Italy
Uhl, A., Austria
Veldhuis, R., The Netherlands
Zganec Gros, J., Slovenia

Organizing Committee

Jana Dittmann	Otto von Guericke University Magdeburg, Germany
Silke Reifgerste	Otto von Guericke University Magdeburg, Germany
Claus Vielhauer	Brandenburg University of Applied Sciences, Germany
Karl Kümmel	Brandenburg University of Applied Sciences, Germany
Tobias Scheidat	Brandenburg University of Applied Sciences, Germany

Local Organizing Committee (from Brandenburg University of Applied Sciences, Germany)

Sylvia Fröhlich
Stefan Gruhn
Robert Fischer
Christian Arndt

Sponsors

- COST Action 2101 "Biometrics for Identity Documents and Smart Cards"
- European Science Foundation (ESF)

Table of Contents

Introductions of the COST Action Chair

Theory and Systems

Handwriting Authentication

Speaker Authentication

Face Recognition

Multibiometric Authentication

Convergence of Biometrics and Forensics

Biometrics for Identity Documents and Smart Cards: Lessons Learned

Andrzej Drygajlo

Speech Processing and Biometrics Group
Swiss Federal Institute of Technology Lausanne (EPFL)
CH-1015 Lausanne, Switzerland
andrzej.drygajlo@epfl.ch
http://scgwww.epfl.ch

Abstract. This paper presents advances of biometrics and their future development as identified during the COST 2101 Action "Biometrics for Identity Documents and Smart Cards". The main objective of the Action was to investigate novel technologies for unsupervised multi-modal biometric authentication systems using a new generation of biometrics-enabled identity documents and smart cards, while exploring the added-value of these technologies for large-scale applications with respect to the European requirements in relation to storage, transmission and protection of personal data. At present, we can observe that identifying people is becoming more challenging and more important because people are moving faster and faster and digital services (local and remote) are becoming the norm for all transactions. From this perspective, biometrics combined with identity documents and smart cards offer wider deployment opportunities and their application as enabling technology for modern identity management systems will be more important in the near future.

Keywords: biometrics, identity documents, smart cards.

1 Introduction

Although considerable research had been conducted into biometrics before the start of the COST 2101 Action in 2006, there had not been much evidence of any established knowledge about the implementation of such techniques into the identity documents and smart cards. As a result, it appeared from the beginning that the problems and issues associated specifically with the use of biometrics in identity documents and smart cards were not very well known.

In 2011, at the end of the COST 2101 Action, biometric systems are increasingly deployed in practical smart card applications but are currently mainly driven by government-led initiatives from electronic passports (e-passports) to national identity cards, with increasing social and legal impact on everyday life [2]. While technological aspects of biometric systems will continue to be key to such developments, legal, cultural and societal issues will become increasingly

C. Vielhauer et al. (Eds.): BioID 2011, LNCS 6583, pp. 1–12, 2011.

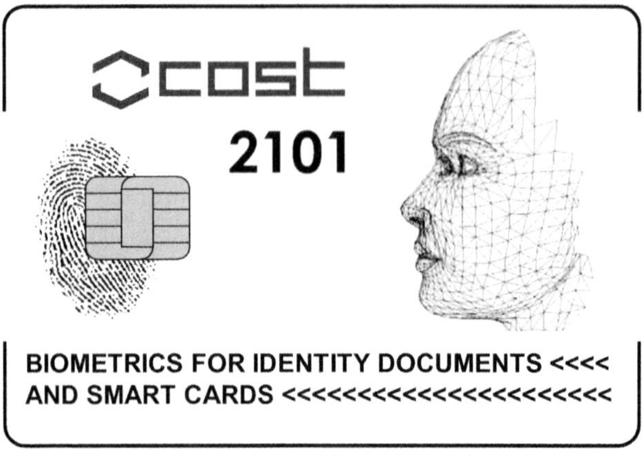

Fig. 1. COST 2101 logo

important in addressing the shortcomings of current delivery and in preparing for future applications. Biometric technology will only be successful in a wide range of identity documents and smart cards applications if it is convenient, privacy friendly, and, at the end, accepted by the wide majority of the population.

Increasing movement of people is a further challenge [3]. Migratory pressure, as well as the prevention of entry of persons seeking to enter European countries for illegitimate reasons, are obvious challenges facing the continent and, therefore, also its policies on borders. Technology developments and scientific progress in areas such as biometrics are paving the way for new solutions to meet these challenges. Biometrics help strengthen identity solutions by integrating biological or behavioral characteristics (for example, face, fingerprint, iris, hand palm/geometry/veins, dynamic signature and voice) with biographic identity information. Biometric technology is being integrated into identity credentials such as travel documents (e-passports and visas) and smart cards for frequent travelers to reduce the threat of a criminal assuming a fake identity or committing identity theft while also improving the facilitation of people movements.

The combination of biometric technology, high storage and processing capacity chips, secure transmission technology and new authentication tools supports border management agencies in making decisions about identity and risk and strengthens the processes to rapidly facilitate known, low-risk travelers while improving security. It is notably possible to perform automatic identity verification using e-passports and automated gates. In such scenarios the gate has the ability to read the e-passport biometric information, capture the biometrics of the traveler, perform the identity verification, check the authenticity of the document and connect to watch list databases.

Recently, the world has rapidly and largely moved from being paper-based to a digital services world. In the digital world the absence of written and visual proof that characterizes physical exchanges has given rise to a demand for secure identification and authentication of parties and transactions. The very first electronic identity cards, called electronic identity (e-ID) cards, were produced in 1997 and then deployed widely in Europe. Securing these cards for e-Services is still a critical issue. Statistics show that identity fraud is increasing spectacularly and all the European countries must have a coordinated plan to fight this type of fraud. Generally, people are identified by three basic means: by something they have, something they know, or something they are. e-ID cards - things they have - are tools that permit the bearers to prove, to some degree of certainty, that they are who they say they are. The security features of these documents vary widely and some are easily duplicated. There is always the risk that Personal Identification Numbers (PINs) - something they know - for securing their cards, are compromised. Fraudulent use is common. The use of biometrics - something they are - can create a more reliable link between the e-ID card and the bearer.

On the Internet trusting the identity of the users and fighting cyber-criminality is particularly challenging. If e-banking is to truly evolve as e-Service on the Internet, it is essential to reliably identify parties and authenticate transactions for internet payments. Unfortunately, passwords fail to protect efficiently online services. Combination of e-ID cards, passwords or PINs and biometrics to grant access to the card information is a solution. The smart card is able to augment the biometric identity verification system, providing a secure container for the biometric template and having the ability to compute the biometric match within the card rather than on external equipment. Already in use in several European countries, this combination is a secure and user-friendly means to prove ones identity in the digital world, at low cost, and for all applications. This provides a level of control in identity management that has never been reached before by any other technology and therefore, the trust in the identity management systems is dramatically increased both for the users and the e-service providers.

A global breakthrough by biometrics in security technology is imminent in terms of its use in identity documents and smart cards and, in particular, corresponding biometrically based controls. All over the world, states and groups of states are creating the political and legal conditions for this. Biometrics will surely proliferate in society, extending from initial government use (e.g., e-passports) to civil and commercial applications. As an enabler of identity verification systems, biometrics can play a role in most modern online public services, such as e-government, e-learning and e-health, in particular in the development of e-Government cards, registered traveler cards, driver licence cards and medical insurance cards, as well as several forms of commercial services like ATM cards, credit cards, tickets issued on name, hotel registration, car rental, time (e.g., annual) tickets and a variety of physical and logical access applications. However, we can see that there are areas that remain to be improved if we are to avoid undermining the strength of biometric systems for identity documents and smart cards. There is strong expectation of all stakeholders that fundamental and applied research will be conducted on national and European levels into the future practices and systems of establishing and using biometrics-enabled identity documents and smart cards and to evaluate their effectiveness.

2 Biometrics Challenge

A better fundamental understanding of the distinctiveness of human individuals would help in converting the fundamental dogma of biometrics ("An individual is more likely similar to him- or herself over time than to anyone else likely to be encountered") into grounded scientific principles [4]. Such an understanding would incorporate learning from biometric technologies and systems, population statistics, statistical techniques, systems analysis, algorithm development, process metrics, and a variety of methodological approaches. However, the distinctiveness of biometric characteristics used in biometric systems is not well understood at scales approaching the entire human population, which hampers predicting the behavior of very large scale biometric systems.

Biometric person identity verification (biometric authentication) is a multimodal technology in its own right, with many potential applications. Every biometric modality has some limitations. Authentication systems built upon only one biometric modality may not fulfil the requirements of demanding large-scale applications in terms of universality, uniqueness, permanence, collectability, performance, acceptability and circumvention. A biometric system using single modality may not be able to acquire meaningful biometric data from a subset of users, for example visually handicapped or disabled people. One possible solution to these problems is the endemic use of multiple biometrics. Multi-modal biometric systems hold the promise of flexible and robust person authentication avoiding person exclusion or discrimination. Thanks to the advances in fusion techniques, multi-modal biometric systems have many benefits such as being more fit for purpose, improve accuracy, increase security, improve efficiency, increase user comfort by more accurate checks.

All of the modalities used contain both physiological and behavioural components. Currently, existing supervised multi-modal biometric interfaces (first generation) take no or little advantage of a behavioural study of the user. The presentation of any biometric characteristic to the sensor introduces a behavioural component to every biometric method. Interactive biometric systems can be designed to facilitate proper presentation by providing feedback to users during the presentation process. Such a technology is an essential component in developing autonomous (unsupervised), intuitive biometric interfaces and contributes towards stronger but user-oriented non-invasive automatic multi-modal authentication. The demand for new generation autonomous, interactive multimodal biometric systems is increasing dramatically because of security pressures and the need for successful deployment of such unsupervised systems worldwide.

Autonomous interactive person authentication interfaces integrating several sources of possibly corrupted biometric data (e.g. noisy, incomplete or inconsistent), represent without doubt one of the most challenging problems in the field of multi-modal interfaces. Acquiring biometric data of sufficient quality and suitability and using it for reliable decision making is of critical importance for automatic biometric authentication. If quality can be improved, either by sensor design, by user-interface design or by standards compliance, better performance can be realised. For those aspects of quality that cannot be designed into the system, an ability to analyse the quality of live biometric data is needed.

It is necessary to study, develop and assess unsupervised multimodal biometric authentication interfaces in the context of identity documents and smart cards, plus provide a diagnosis of the quality of biometric data and decision support for efficient interaction with identified persons.

The biometric enhancement of identity documents and smart cards and their global use in identity controls constitute a task on such a scale that experience to date (e.g. with e-passport pilot projects and registered travelers on border controls with limited number of participants) can, at best, provide only a rough estimate of the outcome. In view of the volume of international travel and migration and the complexity of the necessary technical, administrative and legal implementation, our present state of knowledge and experience is still limited. People may hold electronic identity documents while the legal infrastructure is neither adopted nor deployed. E-Passports are a good example: they are already deployed in Europe even though border controls are not able to verify such an electronic document. The verification is almost always visual. A similar situation can also be considered with e-ID cards. Many countries in Europe have already started to issue e-ID cards but these cards are not used as widely as they could. The principal reason for that is probably the lack of interoperability among countries.

It is expected that once the public becomes accustomed to using biometrics at frontier borders, a diffusion effect in commercial applications will be likely to follow. Consequently, there is an obvious need for fundamental research in the domain of a global system for biometric authentication using identity documents and smart cards.

By definition, biometrics is multidisciplinary and the involved research issues are intertwined. Therefore, one must distinguish between the technological, operational and security aspects, and the privacy and legal issues. Today more than ever, technology is an important means to enhance the efficiency of identity documents. When deploying a technology for this purpose, it must strike the right balance between security, user convenience and privacy. In doing so, one has to carefully assess the potential impact of the technology on the individual's fundamental rights and society. Creation of a common, scientifically founded methodology for automatic collection and processing of sensitive biometric data in identity documents should be determined by the application of the principles of the Council of Europe Convention for the Protection of Individuals with regard to Automatic Processing of Personal Data. There is no doubt that the decisions taken today will have a long-lasting impact on citizens. This is certainly the key challenge that has to be tackled with biometric technology - a fairly young, still evolving technology. The deployment of biometrics in large-scale applications (identity documents and smart cards such as passports, visas, national identity cards, driver's licences, health insurance cards etc.) must, therefore, be preceded by a thorough multidisciplinary analysis.

These can be achieved by having signal processing, pattern recognition, cryptography, multi-sensory processing, human-machine interface, and legal experts working and collaborating together. The impact of such collaboration is multiple, as each partner is expected to benefit from the experience of the others either in their own activity domain, or in closely related disciplines, by the integration of new ideas and visions in their own research. As such, the collaboration of industrial, academic partners and government agencies brings to the table a well-balanced portfolio of needed competencies.

One of the European goals is to converge on the common technologies in unsupervised interactive multi-modal biometric systems dedicated to convenient services using identity documents and smart cards. In order for this to happen, the country-specific cultural and legal issues have to be understood and implemented.

3 COST 2101 Action

The main objective of the European COST 2101 Action [1] was to investigate novel technologies for unsupervised multi-modal biometric authentication systems using a new generation of biometrics-enabled identity documents and smart cards, while exploring the added-value of these technologies for large-scale applications with respect to European requirements in relation to the storage, transmission, and protection of personal data.

Over the last four years, COST 2101 operated as a valuable and effective platform for close collaboration of European researchers in Europe and with researchers all over the world in the field of investigation. A main outcome of this has been the continuous advances achieved in various classes of biometrics and their implementations in the identity management domain. These contributions to knowledge have been disseminated through the First European Workshop on Biometrics and Identity Management (BioID 2008) organized in Roskilde, Denmark on 7-9 May 2008 [5], the Third International Conference on Biometrics (ICB 2009) held in Alghero, Italy on 2-5 June 2009 [6], the Joint COST 2101 and 2102 International Conference on Biometric ID Management and Multimodal Communication held in Madrid, Spain on 16-18 September 2009 [7], and the Third European Workshop on Biometrics and Identity Management (BioID 2011) organized in Brandenburg, Germany on 8-10 March 2011.

The Action has already benefited the European community, individual European states, the providers of technology for biometrics, identity documents and smart cards, providers of public and private services, various security organizations wishing to use biometrics authentication. The Action studied, developed and assessed multi-modal biometric authentication systems in the context of automated situation awareness, diagnosis of the quality of biometric data and decision support for efficient interaction with persons who use identity documents and smart cards. It was focused on the development of novel, second generation multimodal biometric systems using unsupervised, interactive interfaces and third generation multi-modal biometric systems using transparent authentication. Its goal was to develop and integrate advanced techniques for robust, multi-modal biometric authentication interfaces based on the combinations of selected biometric modalities among face, fingerprint, iris, hand palm/geometry/veins, dynamic signature and voice which are subject to behavioral changes in person presentation and in ambient environments.

4 Research Focus

The overall task of the COST 2101 Action [1] was to investigate current and novel technologies of identity documents and smart cards for unsupervised multi-modal biometric authentication that feature robust and ergonomic interaction, to recognise user reactions and respond to them intelligently and naturally, while exploring the added-value of these technologies for large-scale applications. By integrating research components into a real application, this Action helped to further identify research priorities in the important area of multi-modal biometric interfaces, within the scope of an increasingly important worldwide application domain of biometric authentication using identity documents and smart cards. It aimed at delivering original and innovative research in four main areas:

1. Biometric data quality and multi-modal biometric templates,
2. Unsupervised interactive interfaces for multi-modal biometrics,
3. Biometric security challenges,
4. Standards and privacy issues for biometrics in identity documents and smart cards.

In all cases, the focus of the Action was on user convenience, intuitiveness and comfort of biometric sensing, through multi-modal interfaces that are autonomous and capable of learning and adapting to user intentions and behavior, in dynamically changing environments. It has become obvious that a specific fundamental research effort is needed in the trans-disciplinary domain of adaptation of the state-of-the-art biometric techniques to the real-world environmental conditions and to user behavior when using identity documents and smart cards. Since biometric recognition systems are inherently probabilistic, this Action contributed to extending theoretical and applied experience in the very important area of statistical and probabilistic modeling and, in particular, provided evaluation of the practical feasibility of new multi-modal biometric techniques for unsupervised systems.

4.1 Biometric Data Quality and Multi-modal Biometric Templates

Biometric data quality limits the accuracy of biometrics. Poor data quality is responsible for many or even most recognition errors in biometric systems and may be the greatest weakness of some implementations. The factors influencing biometric quality mainly have to do with four issues: the individual itself, the sensor used in the acquisition, the user-sensor interaction, and the system used for processing and recognition. The performance of biometric systems is strongly correlated with the discriminatory information of biometric signal. This discriminatory information depends on how faithfully the signal represents the biometric characteristics of the user. Any distortion of the measurement introduced by various degradation factors may compromise the discriminatory information content and consequently the ability to confirm or determine the identity of the person. The need to measure quality of biometric signals and use them in biometric pattern recognition has emerged from the disappointing results of the application of classical classification paradigms to biometrics.

One of the biggest challenges in constructing biometric systems is making them robust to variations in biometric data quality. The term quality normally refers to the degree biometric signal is free of corrupting degradations. Quality measurement algorithms are increasingly deployed in operational biometric systems and there is now international consensus in industry, academia and government that a statement of a biometric sample's quality should be related to its recognition performance. Biometric data quality is also one of the subjects of ongoing international standardization efforts. Current multi-modal biometrics-based recognition methods tend to be very sensitive to the quality of biometric data. Slight changes in the operating environment (e.g. illumination and composition in face recognition, fingerprint image quality) can produce disproportionately large reductions in the recognition rates. In order to dampen the impact of changing environmental conditions on the accuracy of biometric authentication researchers have proposed a row of automatic quality assessment algorithms. Algorithms for quality assessment of fingerprint images are probably the most advanced. Much less advanced are the existing techniques for automatic quality measures of face and iris images, which are heavily impacted by external illumination conditions. It is well-known fact that the individual physical characteristic features change with time. In particular, aging changes person's face at a slow rate, albeit irreversibly. Nowadays, digital face images are becoming prevalent in government issued e-passports and e-ID cards. Developing face verification systems that are robust to age progression would enable the successful deployment of face verification systems in those large-scale, long-term applications. The Action members specifically identified a possible way of using age information as a class-independent quality metadata, which in combination with other quality measures can further improve the biometric verification performance. Generally, this Action aimed at increasing the robustness and reliability of multi-modal biometric interfaces including quality and reliability measures of biometric modalities. It assessed current quality and reliability measurement capabilities and identified technologies, factors, operational paradigms and standards that could measurably improve quality and reliability of multi-modal biometrics.

4.2 Human Behaviour and Unsupervised Interactive Interfaces for Multi-modal Biometrics

The main research themes of this area are the development of statistical and probabilistic integration models based on multivariate approaches. Investigations cover a number of ways in which the raw data, feature streams and recognizers being developed, might interact. The essence of multi-modal biometric recognition is in the monitoring of data and its quality, models and modalities and in combination of recognizers for several feature streams. The analysis of the behavior can provide the system with additional information that can help to directly identify the person, but as well to help the process of interactive data collection. For example the knowledge which behavioral patterns can deteriorate the collected data and in what way, can help in the automatic guidance of the user in the process of data acquisition. Human factors directly impact error rates, and error rates directly impact the perceived recognition performance of the system.

Certain biometric modalities differ from the others in the way the quality of the data depends on the behavior of the person whose identity is to be recognized. In particular, the way of placing oneself in the field of view of the camera and placing the finger on the scanning device determines to a large extent the quality of the data that the system operates on. It must be noted that low quality input data is likely to render even the most sophisticated feature extractor useless. In on-line applications, where the identity recognition must be done in a very short time after the biometric data have been collected, it is at least just as important to have reliable data as it is important to employ a reliable feature extraction and classification engine. Therefore, the integration of quality and reliability measures in multi-modal, multi-classifier biometric recognition systems is very important.

The goal of this area is also to focus on user convenience and on the speed-up of multi-modal biometric sensing in large-scale applications. Consequently, the problem of transparent biometric authentication, that is, not requiring specific user actions, as a means to enhance user convenience, has been addressed. Biometric data used for transparent authentication has a greater variability and a reduced quality, which may result in a loss of recognition performance.

It became obvious that particular fundamental research effort is still needed in the domain of adaptation of the state-of-the-art interactive and transparent multi-modal biometric authentication to user behavior using quality and reliability measures.

4.3 Biometric Security Challenges

Security considerations are critical to the design of any recognition system, and biometric systems are no exception [4]. When biometric systems are used as part of authentication applications, a security failure can lead to granting inappropriate access or to denying access to a legitimate user. The protection of personal information is not the only reason for protecting biometric data. As in all systems, it is important to consider the potential for a malicious attacker to subvert proper operation of the system. Further, biometric data are exposed not only when data leak from un-encrypted or poorly protected databases. They can, at least in principle, be derived from publicly observable human traits. In this case, encryption and database protection, however, are insufficient to protect against identity theft by an attacker impersonating an individual by mimicking his or her biometric traits.

Liveness detection is a key mechanism to prevent spoofing using fake biometric samples. Liveness detection techniques can be based on intrinsic properties of a living body, involuntary signals of a living body and bodily response to external stimuli. As more and more biometric systems are built to avoid requiring a human presence, the liveness detection techniques will become more and more crucial to the success of biometric deployments. Human surveillance should be considered as a transitional solution as long as the anti-spoofing techniques are not fully satisfactory.

While academic research becomes abundant in biometric recognition, only a small percentage of it is dedicated to embedded biometric recognition. A new type of middleware for biometric identification is emerging in the form of software embedded on smart cards [3]. These applications offer a lot of opportunities especially in terms of scalability of the biometric systems. One approach which will gain momentum in the coming years consists of match-on-card (MoC), where the biometric template (e.g., fingerprint) is only stored and encrypted inside the integrated circuit (IC) chip of a smart card. The rights and privileges of the user are based on a public-key infrastructure (PKI) and stored on a server, but no biometric data reside on a server. In these solutions, the matching is done on the embedded software itself. This solves part of the security and privacy issues. Furthermore, as the enrolled template does not have to be retrieved from a central database this solution is also faster. Match-on-card (MoC) has the privacy advantage of storing the biometric template (e.g., of fingerprint) within the card, making it unavailable to external applications and the outside world. In addition, the matching decision is securely authenticated internally by the card itself. It has the security advantage of being far more secure than matching on a server, as the biometric template never leaves the secure environment of the card and no biometric data ever has to be transmitted over an open network. It has the inter-operability advantage of being an open system: the MoC process does not require any special capabilities of the biometric or smart card reader. It is also fully scalable, offering a good solution to remote biometric identity verification (authentication) without the need for a large infrastructure. This means there is no limit to the number of possible users when rolling out match-on-card. It also reduces the security requirements on the infrastructure itself. Furthermore, there is no need for network resources, server processing, and operator supervision during authentication. For all these reasons, MoC is cost effective.

By adopting MoC, users have a secure way of adding biometric template to smart cards. MoC makes it possible for biometric technology to be used in non-government applications, as it does not require strong certification of the matching infrastructure. Government e-ID cards using biometric MoC present several advantages to the private sector. They offer stronger security than PIN-based cards, and private sector organizations can accept government-issued MoC cards for local identity verification without having to connect to government systems, thus protecting privacy. The technology could also be deployed with many benefits to open systems. For example, an e-ID card can be used to identify the cardholder for many Web based applications, including retail applications, tax payments, and voting.

In the health care sector, which often involves both public and private partners, there is a growing trend towards issuing smart cards to patients so they can enjoy more convenient and secure access to services. Security could be further improved by the addition of MoC, ensuring that only those entitled to treatment receive it. MoC can also be performed with multiple biometric traits, enlarging the potential application fields and scaling different strengths of the identification systems.

4.4 Standards and Privacy Issues for Biometrics in Identity Documents and Smart Cards

The COST 2101 Action contributed widely to fundamental and applied research and advancing the state-of-the-art, but standardization in itself did not play the central role in it. The active participation of the Action members in the CEN Biometrics Focus Group allowed for establishing a road map for short/medium follow-up activities in relation to European biometrics standardization needs [2]. This way the Action participated in reinforcing the European progress in the standardization process.

With the development of biometrics a certain fear of "losing" control of one's identity has appeared. The argument is that the objectives of the systems can change and then the biometric data can be used for an additional purpose (different from the original), so the systems should also be able to guarantee the usage, share or cession of biometric data. An enhancement should be that when a biometric data is collected, it is to associate the usage. Consequently, an important question to be answered is whether biometrics can be revoked, i.e., if a person needs to change identity or finds that his/her biometric data has been compromised, what can be done to revoke that person's biometrics. This question will assume even greater importance as biometrics diffuse into everyday life. When the public becomes aware of the risks to their privacy and the potential for identity theft, without recourse, they will demand revocability. No one serious about security would use a password or identity card, which could not be changed or revoked.

The risks associated to the use of electronic identities (eIDs), including biometric identities, will grow at least proportionally to their level of ubiquity. In particular, it will be increasingly important to adequately address privacy issues if eID-solutions need to be widely accepted. Proposing a practical solution to the issue of template revocability was an important aspect of the Action activities within the framework of the European FP7 project TURBINE (TrUsted Revocable Biometric IdeNtitiEs) [8]. Research was dedicated to the definition and implementation of a technology solution that allows revoking a protected biometric identity and processing a fingerprint sample to generate different protected biometric identities. For an individual, when his/her protected biometric identity is revoked, a new protected biometric identity should be possible to issue. Only a system offering MoC, protected templates, and revocable templates can satisfy the demand for privacy-protective biometrics needed in private and public sectors.

5 Conclusions

Many biometric technologies have evolved and there are many new products that have been or are about to be launched. This recent market success, however, has created greater challenges, as government and industry are more dependent than ever on robust biometric identity verification tools and identity management principles. There are both a market pull and a technology push that continuously bring the combination of identity documents/smart card technology and multi-modal biometrics to the next level of maturity. In considering the possibility of a global biometrics-based identity verification and management system, European countries should think of electronic identity as infrastructure, like a railway, electricity or transportation system.

References

1. COST 2101 Action.: Biometrics for Identity Documents and Smart Cards. Memorandum of Understanding, COST Office, Brussels (2006)
2. Schouten, B.: A roadmap for short/medium follow-up activities in relation to European biometrics standardization needs. Report 3 of Biometrics Focus Group, European Committee for Standardization (CEN), Brussels (2009)
3. European Security Research and Innovation Forum: Working Group: Identification of People and Assets. In: ESRIF Final Report, Brussels, pp. 171–193 (2009), `http://www.esrif.eu`
4. Pato, J.N., Millett, L.I. (eds.): Biometric Recognition: Challenges and Opportunities. Whither Biometrics Committee, National Research Council. The National Academies Press, Washington (2010)
5. Schouten, B., Juul, N.C., Drygajlo, A., Tistarelli, M. (eds.): BIOID 2008. LNCS, vol. 5372. Springer, Heidelberg (2008)
6. Tistarelli, M., Nixon, M.S. (eds.): ICB 2009. LNCS, vol. 5558. Springer, Heidelberg (2009)
7. Fierrez, J., Ortega-Garcia, J., Esposito, A., Drygajlo, A., Faundez-Zanuy, M. (eds.): BioID MultiComm 2009. LNCS, vol. 5707. Springer, Heidelberg (2009)
8. Yang, B., Busch, C., Gafurov, D., Bours, P.: Research findings for standardisation. Deliverable D2.3.3., FP7 ICT project TURBINE (TrUsted Revocable Biometric IdeNtitiEs) (2010)

Biometric Authentication Based on Significant Parameters*

Vladimir B. Balakirsky and A.J. Han Vinck

Institute for Experimental Mathematics, 45326 Essen, Germany
American University of Armenia, 0019 Yerevan, Armenia
v_b_balakirsky@rambler.ru, vinck@iem.uni-due.de

Abstract. We analyze the model where the outcomes of biometric measurements of a person are expressed by a ternary vector whose components equal to a special symbol $*$ are considered as information that the corresponding parameters are non–significant. The 0 and 1 components show the types of significant parameters.

The authentication of a person on the basis on significant parameters is reduced to the decoding of data transmitted over a binary–input and ternary–output channel. A special authentication algorithm that differs from the maximum likelihood decoding and forces an attacker to use the so–called "fair gambling strategy" is proposed.

1 Introduction

One of basic setups of applied cryptography is as follows [1]. There is a fixed string ("I am a plane belonging to your air forces", "I am user A", etc.), which is encoded and sent to the receiver over a noisy channel. An attacker wants to substitute some data that will be recognized as a corrupted version of the transmitted data. The setup is directly relevant to biometrics where the encoded version of the string represents the outcomes of biometric measurements of a person at the enrollment stage. These data are stored as sample data in the database under the name of the person. When some person appears at the verification stage, he presents the name (therefore, the verifier knows the sample data) and offers the outcomes of his biometric measurements. If the identity claim is true, then they represent the corrupted version of sample data.

We consider the setup above under the assumption that the outcomes of biometric measurements at the enrollment and at the verification stages are expressed by ternary vectors

$$\mathbf{a}^* = (a_1^*, \ldots, a'_{n^*}),\ \mathbf{b}^* = (b_1^*, \ldots, b_{n^*}^*) \in \{0, *, 1\}^{n^*},$$

respectively. Each component of the vectors gives information about the corresponding biometric parameter of the person in such a way that the $*$ symbol

* This work was partially supported by the DFG.

C. Vielhauer et al. (Eds.): BioID 2011, LNCS 6583, pp. 13–24, 2011.

located at the t^*-th position says that the t^*-th parameter of the person is non–significant. Otherwise, the t^*-th parameter is significant and it has type 0 or 1.

The procedure for constructing the vectors $\mathbf{a}^*$ and $\mathbf{b}^*$ should be oriented to a particular application. For example for the DNA data [2], $n^* = 28$ and the outcome of the measurements of the t^*-th parameter is an integer belonging to the set $\mathcal{S}_{t^*} = \{i_{t^*}, \ldots, i_{t^*} + k_{t^*} - 1\}$, where the numbers i_{t^*}, k_{t^*} are associated with the t^*-th allele and the probability distribution over the set $\mathcal{S}_{t^*}$ is known. A possible mapping of the outcomes of the measurements, x_{t^*}, y_{t^*}, received at the enrollment and at the verification stages, to the components $a_{t^*}, b_{t^*} \in \mathcal{S}_{t^*}$ is as follows: we fix $i_{t^*}^{(0)}, i_{t^*}^{(1)}$ and set

$$a_{t^*} = \begin{cases} 0, \text{ if } x_{t^*} < i_{t^*}^{(0)}, \\ *, \text{ if } x_{t^*} \in [i_{t^*}^{(0)}, i_{t^*}^{(1)}], \\ 1, \text{ if } x_{t'} > i_{t^*}^{(1)} \end{cases} \quad b_{t^*} = \begin{cases} 0, \text{ if } y_{t^*} < i_{t^*}^{(0)}, \\ *, \text{ if } y_{t^*} \in [i_{t^*}^{(0)}, i_{t^*}^{(1)}], \\ 1, \text{ if } y_{t^*} > i_{t^*}^{(1)}. \end{cases}$$

The description of the algorithm above stays an abstract description until the values of $i_{t^*}^{(0)}, i_{t^*}^{(1)}$ are specified for all $t^* = 1, \ldots, n^*$ and "an analysis of the scheme is given". Nevertheless, we follow the lines of [3], [4] where the significant components were defined as components whose values deviate from the average values by certain thresholds fixed in a way that the fraction of significant components to the total number of components n^* is "large enough" and the probability that the observation noise changes the 0 component to the 1 component and *vice versa* is "small".

In the following considerations, we assume that the verifier's decision is made only on the basis of significant components, formed at the enrollment stage, and transform the vector $\mathbf{a}^*$ to the binary vector $\mathbf{a} = (a_1, \ldots, a_n) \in \{0,1\}^n$ of some length n by puncturing the non–significant components. The puncturing of the corresponding components of the vector $\mathbf{b}^*$ transforms it to the ternary vector $\mathbf{b} = (b_1, \ldots, b_n) \in \{0, *, 1\}^n$. An example of the transformations is given below,

$$\left.\begin{array}{l} \mathbf{a}^* = 0 * * 1 0 1 * 1 1 * \\ \mathbf{b}^* = 0 1 * * 1 1 0 1 * * \end{array}\right\} \to \left\{\begin{array}{l} \mathbf{a} = 0 1 0 1 1 1 \\ \mathbf{b} = 0 * 1 1 1 * \end{array}\right.$$
$$n^* = 10 \to n = 6.$$

We will also assume that the stochastic description of the transformation $\mathbf{a} \to \mathbf{b}$ in the case, when the biometric observations belong to the same person, is specified by the conditional probability

$$V(\mathbf{b}|\mathbf{a}) = \prod_{t=1}^{n} V(b_t|a_t), \tag{1}$$

where

$$V(b|a) = \begin{cases} 1 - \xi - \theta, & \text{if } (a,b) \in \{(0,0),(1,1)\}, \\ \xi, & \text{if } (a,b) \in \{(0,*),(1,*)\}, \\ \theta, & \text{if } (a,b) \in \{(0,1),(1,0)\} \end{cases} \tag{2}$$

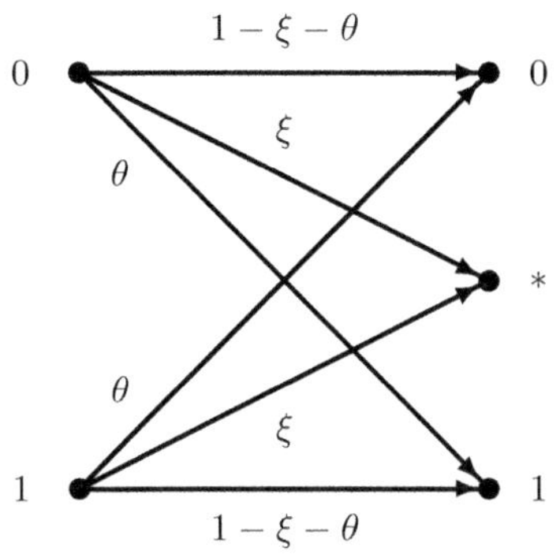

Fig. 1. Transition diagram of a symmetric binary–input and ternary–output channel with errors $0 \to 1, 1 \to 0$ and erasures $0 \to *, 1 \to *$

and the values of ξ, θ are given in such a way that $1 - \xi - \theta, \xi, \theta \in [0, 1]$. Thus, the transmitted bit a is inverted with probability θ, erased with probability ξ, and noiselessly given to the verifier with probability $1 - \xi - \theta$. The transition diagram of the channel is depicted in Figure 1.

One of the main differences of the scheme under our considerations from "conventional schemes" [3], [4], [5] is the point that we do not allow any hidden randomness included into the authentication procedure. As a result all probabilities are computed over the ensemble of the observation noise and the ensemble introduced by an attacker, who is allowed to use a randomized strategy. More precisely, we assume that the value of n, the positions of the significant components and the Hamming weight np of the binary vector $\mathbf{a}$ of length n are known to the attacker. The sublect of the paper is the decoding algorithm for the symmetric binary–input and ternary–output channel with errors $0 \to 1, 1 \to 0$ and erasures $0 \to *, 1 \to *$, which makes the possibilities of the attacker very limited. The algorithm can be considered as an extended version of the procedure described in [6] for a binary–input and binary–output channel where we noticed that the procedure, which is based on the maximum likelihood decoding for the given channel can have a poor security performance meaning that the attacker has good chances to generate a vector $\mathbf{b}$ that will be accepted as a corrupted version of an unknown vector $\mathbf{a}$. Furthermore, we assume that the attacker has rather high requests: for any fixed vector $\mathbf{a}$ of length n and weight np, the probability of successful attack has to be large. Such a request, together with the absense of the input probability distribution, forces the attacker to use a memoryless probability distribution while generating the substitution vectors. The parameters of an optimum distribution essentially depend on the values of n and p for the maximum likelihood authentication and they are independent on these values for the proposed authentication algorithm.

2 The Authentication Scheme and Summary of the Results

Let us consider the scheme in Figure 2. The pair of vectors $(\mathbf{a}, \mathbf{b})$, where $\mathbf{a} \in \{0,1\}^n$ and $\mathbf{b} \in \{0,*,1\}^n$, is given to the verifier. The output of the verifier is a binary variable taking values Acc and Rej. Let the authentication be formalized as the mapping

$$(\mathbf{a}, \mathbf{b}) \rightarrow \text{Decision} = \begin{cases} \text{Acc, if } \mathbf{b} \in \mathcal{D}_{\mathbf{a}}, \\ \text{Rej, if } \mathbf{b} \notin \mathcal{D}_{\mathbf{a}}, \end{cases}$$

where $\mathcal{D}_{\mathbf{a}}, \mathbf{a} \in \{0,1\}^n$, are the acceptance sets. These sets have to be fixed in advance in such a way that the verifier can reliably distinguish between the following cases.

Acc: the vector $\mathbf{b}$ is received as a result of transmission of the vector $\mathbf{a}$ over the V channel defined in (1), (2);

Rej: the vector $\mathbf{b}$ is generated by a memoryless source with the probability

$$Q(\mathbf{b}) = \prod_{t=1}^{n} Q(b_t), \tag{3}$$

where the probability distribution

$$(Q(0), Q(*), Q(1)) = (q_0, 1 - q_0 - q_1, q_1) \tag{4}$$

is unknown to the verifier.

The probabilities of the verification errors, called the false rejection and the false acceptance rates, are expressed as

$$\text{FRR}_{\mathbf{a}} = \sum_{\mathbf{b} \notin \mathcal{D}_{\mathbf{a}}} V(\mathbf{b}|\mathbf{a}), \quad \text{FAR}_{\mathbf{a}}(Q) = \sum_{\mathbf{b} \in \mathcal{D}_{\mathbf{a}}} Q(\mathbf{b}), \tag{5}$$

and the problem under consideration is formulated by the R_0–R_A–R_R requirements.

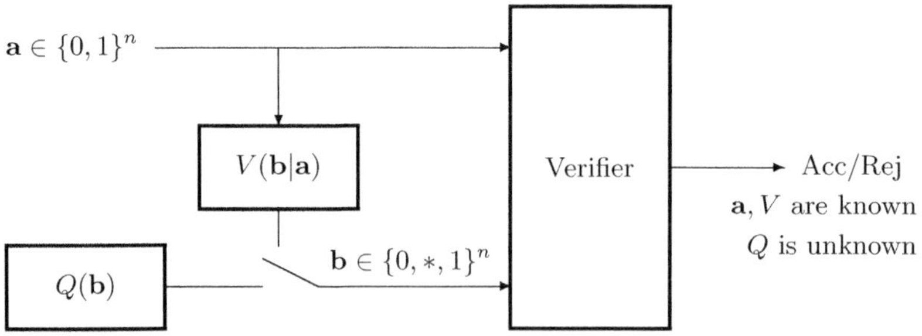

Fig. 2. The authentication scheme for binary–input channels with errors and erasures

R$_0$: *Find a regular construction for the acceptance sets* $\mathcal{D}_{\mathbf{a}}$, $\mathbf{a} \in \{0,1\}^n$.

A regular construction is understood as the threshold–type set

$$\mathcal{D}_{\mathbf{a}} = \Big\{ \mathbf{b} \in \{0,*,1\}^n : m(\mathbf{a},\mathbf{b}) < T \Big\}, \tag{6}$$

where the function $m(\mathbf{a},\mathbf{b})$, called the metric between the vectors $\mathbf{a}$ and $\mathbf{b}$, is defined as an additive extension of the component–wise metric,

$$m(\mathbf{a},\mathbf{b}) = \frac{1}{n}\sum_{t=1}^{n} m(a_t,b_t). \tag{7}$$

Notice that the R$_0$ requirement implies the complexity constraints on the specification of the acceptance sets, which is important for a practical use when n is large enough.

R$_R$: *For all vectors* $\mathbf{a} \in \{0,1\}^n$,

$$\mathrm{FRR}_{\mathbf{a}} \leq \varepsilon. \tag{8}$$

The R$_R$ requirement is also oriented to practical applications of the verification scheme. For example, the scheme should guarantee a certain false rejection rate for biometric measurements of an arbitrary chosen person.

R$_A$: *Given a* $p \in \{0/n, 1/n, \ldots, n/n\}$,

$$\max_{Q} \min_{\mathbf{a}\in\{0,1\}^n_{np}} \mathrm{FAR}_{\mathbf{a}}(Q) \;\rightarrow\; \min, \tag{9}$$

where

$$\{0,1\}^n_{np} = \Big\{ \mathbf{a} \in \{0,1\}^n : \mathrm{wt}(\mathbf{a}) = np \Big\} \tag{10}$$

denotes the set of binary vectors of weight np *and the maximum is taken over the probability distributions (3), (4).*

In the minimization problem stated above, we assume that the attacker knows the weight of the vector $\mathbf{a}$, which is equal to np. By the memoryless assumptions and the restriction of the metric between any pair of vectors to an additive extension of the component–wise metric, the value of $\mathrm{FAR}_{\mathbf{a}}(Q)$ is the same for all vectors $\mathbf{a} \in \{0,1\}^n_{np}$. Therefore, instead of taking the minimum over $\mathbf{a} \in \{0,1\}^n_{np}$ in (9), we can equivalently require the minimum value of $\mathrm{FAR}_{\mathbf{a}}(Q)$ for any vector $\mathbf{a}$ having the weight np.

The ideas developed in our approach to the authentication problem can be explained using the following game. Suppose that there is a sample binary vector $\mathbf{a}$ containing n_0 zeroes and n_1 ones. The values n_0 and n_1 are known to an attacker, who submits a binary vector $\mathbf{b}$. If $a_t = 0$, then the attacker receives n_1 coins when $b_t = 0$ and losses n_1 coins when $b_t = 1$. If $a_t = 1$, then the attacker receives n_0 coins when $b_t = 1$ and losses n_0 coins when $b_t = 0$. Thus, the presentation of the all–zero or the all–one vector brings a balance when the attacker does not finally receive or lose any coin (in case of the all–zero vector, he gets n_1 coins n_0 times and lose n_0 coins n_1 times). Let the attacker be successful if he finally receives T coins. We notice that the best chance to succeed is reached by the submission of a vector chosen by a Bernoulli source with the probabilities of zeroes and ones equal to 1/2 (the fair coin tossing strategy). "The chance" is understood by the following underlying random experiment. The attacker submits a vector **b**, and the outcome of the verification, i.e., the answer to the question whether the trial is successful or not, is put on a storage and unknown to the attacker. Then the attacker makes the 2-nd, ..., the k-th trial under the same rules. If k' trials were successful, then k'/k is an estimate of the probability of success.

It also turns out that the fair coin tossing strategy is the best one for any T and n_0, n_1, provided that the values of parameters are not very small. Moreover, it is true when the attacker's alphabet is extended by the $*$ symbol with the update of the rules of the game in such a way that $b_t = *$ means that the attacker does not receive or lose any coin at the t-th time instant.

The conclusion about the optimality of the fair coin tossing strategy seems to be very important in the following sense. Any cryptographic system allows the blind attack when the attacker uses this strategy without any knowledge about the scheme. In our case, after the attacker becomes informed about the authentication algorithm and the weight of the sample vector, he cannot include this knowledge into the attack to improve its performance, i.e., the scheme has the so–called the perfect algorithmic secrecy. Thus, *the main direction of our research is the design of an authentication algorithm that has a good performance and it is highly protected against the information leakage.*

3 The p-Authentication Algorithm

⊙ *Let* $\mathbf{a} \in \{0,1\}^n_{np}$*, where the set* $\{0,1\}^n_{np}$ *is defined in (10). The threshold* T *and the values of the component–wise metric* $m(a,b)$*,* $a \in \{0,1\}$*,* $b \in \{0,*,1\}$*, are assigned depending on* p *in such a way that*

$$m(0,b) = \begin{cases} -p, & \text{if } b = 0, \\ 0, & \text{if } b = *, \\ +p, & \text{if } b = 1 \end{cases} \quad m(1,b) = \begin{cases} -(1-p), & \text{if } b = 1, \\ 0, & \text{if } b = *, \\ +(1-p), & \text{if } b = 0. \end{cases} \tag{11}$$

The threshold T *is assigned to satisfy (8) when the metric is defined in (11).*

The authentication algorithm, where the rules above are used, will be referred to as the p-authentication algorithm. Notice that the dependence of the component–wise metric on p means that the value of the metric $m(\mathbf{a}, \mathbf{b})$ also depends on p, and (7) specifies a memory containing function.

Two examples of computing the component–wise metric are given below.

$$\begin{bmatrix} \mathbf{a} \\ \mathbf{b} \end{bmatrix} = \begin{bmatrix} 001111 \\ 10010* \end{bmatrix} \Rightarrow m(\mathbf{a},\mathbf{b}) = \frac{4/6 - 4/6 + 2/6 - 2/6 + 2/6 + 0}{6},$$
$$\begin{bmatrix} \mathbf{a} \\ \mathbf{b} \end{bmatrix} = \begin{bmatrix} 001110 \\ 10010* \end{bmatrix} \Rightarrow m(\mathbf{a},\mathbf{b}) = \frac{3/6 - 3/6 + 3/6 - 3/6 - 3/6 + 0}{6}.$$

Although the both examples contain the same pairs of symbols at the first 5 positions, but their contributions to the metric are different.

If $\mathbf{b}$ is the vector containing the values of a randomly chosen vector $B^n = (B_1, \ldots, B_n)$, then $m(\mathbf{a},\mathbf{b})$ is also the value of a random variable $m(\mathbf{a}, B^n)$. By (11) and the specifications of the probabilistic ensemble used to generate the vector $\mathbf{b}$ in the Acc and the Rej cases, the probability distribution of $m(\mathbf{a}, B^n)$ is the binomial–type distribution determined by all possible collections

$$\Big(k(a,b),\ a \in \{0,1\},\ b \in \{0,*,1\} \Big)$$

such that all entries belong to the set $\{0,\ldots,n\}$ and

$$\begin{aligned} k(0,0) + k(0,*) + k(0,1) &= n(1-p), \\ k(1,0) + k(1,*) + k(1,1) &= np. \end{aligned}$$

It is well–known that the binomial–type probability distributions are approximated by the Gaussian PDF with the high accuracy if the number of observations is not very small, i.e.,

$$\Pr\{m(\mathbf{a}, B^n) = \mu\} \approx \mathrm{Gaus}(\mu | \mathsf{E}, \mathrm{Var}), \quad \mu \in \mathsf{R}, \tag{12}$$

where

$$\mathsf{E} = \mathsf{E}[m(\mathbf{a}, B^n)], \quad \mathrm{Var} = \mathrm{Var}[m(\mathbf{a}, B^n)]$$

denote the expected value and the variance of the random variable $m(\mathbf{a}, B^n)$. We denote the pairs $(\mathsf{E}, \mathrm{Var})$ by $(\mathsf{E}_V, \mathrm{Var}_V)$ in the Acc case and $(\mathsf{E}_Q, \mathrm{Var}_Q)$ in the Rej case, where

$$\begin{aligned} \mathsf{E}_V &= \sum_{\mathbf{b}} V(\mathbf{b}|\mathbf{a}) m(\mathbf{a},\mathbf{b}), \\ \mathrm{Var}_V &= \sum_{\mathbf{b}} V(\mathbf{b}|\mathbf{a}) m^2(\mathbf{a},\mathbf{b}) - \mathsf{E}_V^2 \end{aligned}$$

and

$$\begin{aligned} \mathsf{F}_Q &= \sum_{\mathbf{b}} Q(\mathbf{b}) m(\mathbf{a},\mathbf{b}), \\ \mathrm{Var}_Q &= \sum_{\mathbf{b}} Q(\mathbf{b}) m^2(\mathbf{a},\mathbf{b}) - \mathsf{E}_Q^2. \end{aligned}$$

In particular, (12) imply the approximation of the false acceptance and the false rejection rates, defined in (5),

$$\mathrm{FRR}_{\mathbf{a}} \approx \hat{\mathrm{FRR}}_V, \quad \mathrm{FAR}_{\mathbf{a}}(Q) \approx \hat{\mathrm{FAR}}_Q,$$

where

$$\hat{\mathrm{FRR}}_V = \int_T^{+\infty} \mathrm{Gaus}\Big(\mu | \mathsf{E}_V, \mathrm{Var}_V\Big)\, d\mu,$$

$$\hat{\mathrm{FAR}}_Q = \int_{-\infty}^{T} \mathrm{Gaus}\Big(\mu | \mathsf{E}_Q, \mathrm{Var}_Q\Big)\, d\mu.$$

Proposition 1. *Suppose that* $\mathbf{a} \in \{0,1\}^n_{np}$ *and, for all* $q \in [0,1]$, *let*

$$\sigma_q^2 = q(1-q)$$

denote the variance of the random variable generated by a Bernoulli source having the probability of bit 1 *equal to* q. *Then*

$$(\mathsf{E}_V, \mathrm{Var}_V) = \Big(\, -2(1-\xi-2\theta)\sigma_p^2,\ (\sigma_\xi^2 + 4(1-\xi)\sigma_\theta^2)\frac{\sigma_p^2}{n}\,\Big),$$

$$(\mathsf{E}_Q, \mathrm{Var}_Q) = \Big(\, 0,\ (\sigma_{q_0}^2 + \sigma_{q_1}^2 + 2q_0q_1)\frac{\sigma_p^2}{n}\,\Big).$$

In particular,

$$\mathrm{Var}_Q \le \mathrm{Var}_{\overline{Q}} = \frac{\sigma_p^2}{n}, \tag{13}$$

where the probability distribution

$$\overline{Q} = (1/2, 0, 1/2). \tag{14}$$

specifies the $0:1$ *fair coin tossing strategy.*

Proof: The random variable $m(\mathbf{a}, B^n)$ can be expressed as

$$m(\mathbf{a}, B^n) = \frac{1}{n}\sum_{t\in\mathcal{T}_0} m(0, B_t) + \frac{1}{n}\sum_{t\in\mathcal{T}_1} m(1, B_t),$$

where $m(a_1, B_1), \ldots, m(a_n, B_n)$ are independent random variables. Therefore,

$$n\mathsf{E}[\, m(\mathbf{a}, B^n)\,] = \sum_{t\in\mathcal{T}_0} \mathsf{E}[\, m(0, B_t)\,] + \sum_{t\in\mathcal{T}_1} \mathsf{E}[\, m(1, B_t)\,]$$

and

$$n^2\mathrm{Var}[\, m(\mathbf{a}, B^n)\,] = \sum_{t\in\mathcal{T}_0} \mathrm{Var}[\, m(0, B_t)\,] + \sum_{t\in\mathcal{T}_1} \mathrm{Var}[\, m(1, B_t)\,],$$

where

$$\mathcal{T}_0 = \Big\{ t \in \{1, \ldots, n\} : a_t = 0 \Big\},$$

$$\mathcal{T}_1 = \Big\{ t \in \{1, \ldots, n\} : a_t = 1 \Big\}.$$

In the Acc case,

$$t \in \mathcal{T}_0 \Rightarrow m(0, b_t) = \begin{cases} -p, & \text{with probability } 1 - \xi - \theta, \\ 0, & \text{with probability } \xi, \\ +p, & \text{with probability } \theta, \end{cases}$$

$$t \in \mathcal{T}_1 \Rightarrow m(1, b_t) = \begin{cases} -(1-p), & \text{with probability } 1 - \xi - \theta, \\ 0, & \text{with probability } \xi, \\ +(1-p), & \text{with probability } \theta. \end{cases}$$

In the Rej case,

$$t \in \mathcal{T}_0 \Rightarrow m(0, b_t) = \begin{cases} -p, & \text{with probability } q_0, \\ 0, & \text{with probability } 1 - q_0 - q_1, \\ +p, & \text{with probability } q_1, \end{cases}$$

$$t \in \mathcal{T}_1 \Rightarrow m(1, b_t) = \begin{cases} -(1-p), & \text{with probability } q_1, \\ 0, & \text{with probability } 1 - q_0 - q_1, \\ +(1-p), & \text{with probability } q_0. \end{cases}$$

Simple calculations using the expressions above prove the statement.

Some important claims of Proposition 1 are listed below.

- ⊙ If $\xi + 2\theta < 1$, then the expected value of the metric in the Acc case is less than the expected value of the metric in the Rej case.
- ⊙ The expected value of the metric in the Rej case is equal to 0 independently of p and ξ.
- ⊙ If $p \notin \{0, 1\}$, then the variances of the metric decrease as the function of $1/n$ when n increases.
- ⊙ The variance of the metric in the Rej case is maximized when $Q = \overline{Q}$, which means that the attacker uses the fair coin tossing strategy and never generates the $*$ symbols.

Some examples of Gaussian approximations to the probability distributions of the metric for the p-authentication algorithm are illustrated in Figure 3. Notice that, *independently on p, ξ and the threshold T the Gaussian approximation of the false acceptance rate is the maximum when the variance of the probability distribution of the metric in the* Rej *case is maximized, and it is attained by using the fair coin tossing attacker's strategy.* The estimates of the false rejection and the false acceptance rates are given in the statement below.

Proposition 2. *Let us denote*

$$E_V(T) = \frac{(T/\sigma_p + 2(1 - \xi - 2\theta)\sigma_p)^2}{2(\sigma_\xi^2 + 4(1 - \xi)\sigma_\theta^2)},$$

$$E_Q(T) = \frac{(T/\sigma_p)^2}{2(\sigma_{q_0}^2 + \sigma_{q_1}^2 + 2q_0 q_1)}.$$

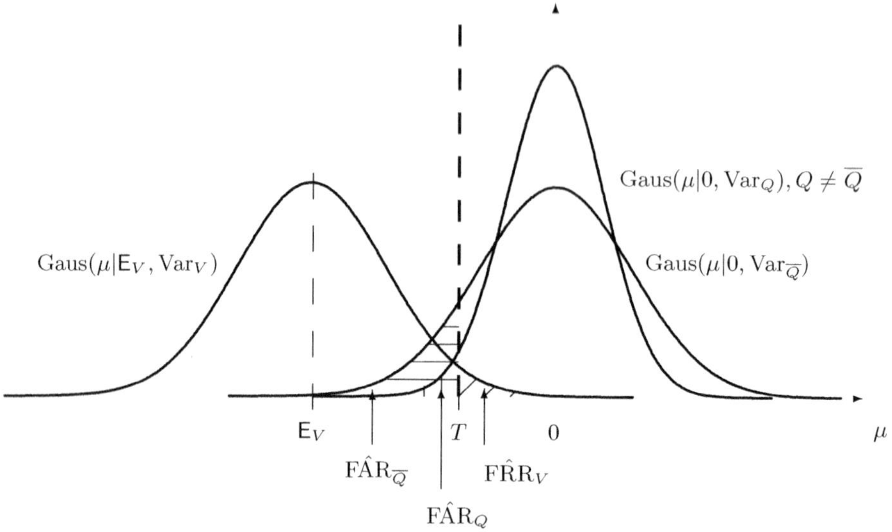

Fig. 3. Examples of Gaussian approximations to the probability distributions of the metric for the p-authentication algorithm

Then

$$\hat{\mathrm{FRR}}_V = \frac{1}{2} - \frac{1}{2}\mathrm{erf}\Big(\sqrt{E_V(T)n}\Big),$$
$$\hat{\mathrm{FAR}}_Q = \frac{1}{2} + \frac{1}{2}\mathrm{erf}\Big(\sqrt{E_Q(T)n}\Big)$$

and, if

$$-2(1-\xi-2\theta)\sigma_p < T/\sigma_p < 0,$$

then

$$\hat{\mathrm{FRR}}_V \le \exp\Big\{-E_V(T)n\Big\},$$
$$\hat{\mathrm{FAR}}_Q \le \exp\Big\{-E_Q(T)n\Big\}.$$

Corollary. *If* $q_0 = q_1 = 1/2$ *and*

$$E_V(T) = E_{\mathrm{FRR}}, \;\; E_Q(T) = E_{\mathrm{FAR}},$$

then, when θ *is small,*

$$E_{\mathrm{FRR}} \approx f(E_{\mathrm{FAR}}),$$

where

$$f(E_{\mathrm{FAR}}) = \frac{(-\sqrt{2E_{\mathrm{FAR}}} + 2(1-\xi)\sigma_p)^2}{2\sigma_\xi^2}.$$

The function $f(E_{\mathrm{FAR}})$ specifies the curve connecting points $(0, A_{p,\xi})$ and $(B_{p,\xi}, 0)$, where

$$A_{p,\xi} = \frac{2(1-\xi)\sigma_p^2}{\xi},$$
$$B_{p,\xi} = 2(1-\xi)^2\sigma_p^2.$$

Furthermore,

$$\frac{E_{\text{FAR}}}{B_{p,\xi}} = \alpha \Rightarrow \frac{E_{\text{FRR}}}{A_{p,\xi}} = (1-\sqrt{\alpha})^2 \tag{15}$$

for any p and ξ.

Table 1. Some values of $A_{p,\xi}, B_{p,\xi}$ attained by the p-authentication algorithm

	$\xi = 1/6$		$\xi = 1/3$		$\xi = 1/2$		$\xi = 2/3$		$\xi = 5/6$	
p	$A_{p,\xi}$	$B_{p,\xi}$	$A_{p,\xi}$	$B_{p,\xi}$	$A_{p,\xi}$	$B_{p,\xi}$	$A_{p,\xi}$	$B_{p,\xi}$	$A_{p,\xi}$	$B_{p,\xi}$
1/6	1.389	0.193	0.556	0.123	0.278	0.069	0.139	0.031	0.056	0.008
1/3	2.222	0.309	0.889	0.198	0.444	0.111	0.222	0.049	0.089	0.012
1/2	2.500	0.347	1.000	0.222	0.500	0.125	0.250	0.056	0.100	0.014

Some values of $A_{p,\xi}, B_{p,\xi}$ are given in Table 1. The claim (15) can be viewed as a universal law, which easily allows one to evaluate the performance of the p-authentication algorithm for any p and ξ, when the value of α is determined by the constraint for the false rejection rate given by the inequality (8).

4 Conclusion

The verification algorithm is an important cryptographic tool of any data transmission scheme. We demonstrated this point for the authentication setup where the vector generated by a legitimate user is transmitted to the verifier over a channel whose transition probabilities are defined in (2). If the p-authentication algorithm is used, then the generation of the input vector **b** by flipping a fair coin (the probabilities of zeroes and ones are equal to 1/2) is the attack, which maximizes the false acceptance rate. As a result, the attacker becomes equivalent to a blind attacker, who is ignorant both about the weight of the vector of the legitimate user and the parameters of the channel. These features make such a solution attractive when real biometric data are processed for the authentication and the identification purposes.

References

1. Schneier, B.: Applied Cryptography. Addison-Wesley, Reading (1996)
2. Balakirsky, V.B., Ghazaryan, A.R., Han Vinck, A.J.: Additive block coding schemes for biometric authentication with the DNA data. In: Schouten, B., et al. (eds.) BIOID 2008. LNCS, vol. 5372, pp. 160–169. Springer, Heidelberg (2008)
3. Linnartz, J.P., Tuyls, P.: New shielding functions to enhance privacy and prevent misuse of biometric templates. In: Kittler, J., Nixon, M.S. (eds.) AVBPA 2003. LNCS, vol. 2688, pp. 393–402. Springer, Heidelberg (2003)

4. Verbitskiy, E., Tuyls, P., Denteneer, D., Linnartz, J.P.: Reliable biometric authentication with privacy protection. In: Proc. 24th Benelux Symposium on Information Theory, Veldhoven, The Netherlands, pp. 125–132 (2003)
5. Maurer, U.M.: The strong secret key rate of discrete random triples. In: Blahut, R., et al. (eds.) Communication and Cryptography – Two Sides of One Tapestry, pp. 271–285. Kluwer, Dordrecht (1994)
6. Balakirsky, V.B., Han Vinck, A.J.: Performance of the verification for binary memoryless channels. In: Security and Communication Networks. Wiley, Chichester (2011) (to be published)

Attack against Robust Watermarking-Based Multimodal Biometric Recognition Systems

Jutta Hämmerle-Uhl, Karl Raab, and Andreas Uhl

Multimedia Signal Processing and Security Lab (WaveLab)
Department of Computer Sciences, University of Salzburg, Austria
uhl@cosy.sbg.ac.at

Abstract. Several multimodal biometric schemes have been suggested in literature which employ robust watermarking in order to embed biometric template data into biometric sample data. In case robust embedding is used as the sole means of security, tampering attacks can be mounted. The results of a corresponding attack against a multimodal iris recognition scheme show, that in this environment either semi-fragile watermarking or additional classical cryptographic means need to be applied to secure the system against the demonstrated attack.

1 Introduction

Biometric recognition applications become more and more popular. But eventually, biometric features can be stolen or adopted and there exist various other ways to circumvent the integrity of a biometric authentication system. Recent work systematically identifies security threats against biometric systems and possible countermeasures [15, 16].

Among other suggestions to cope with security threats like liveness detection or classical cryptographic encryption and authentication techniques, watermarking has been suggested to solve security issues in biometric systems in various ways. Dong et al. [3] try to give a systematic view of how to integrate watermarking into biometric systems in the case of iris recognition by distinguishing whether biometric template data are embedded into some host data ("template embedding"), or biometric sample data is watermarked by embedding some data into them ("sample watermarking").

Several contributions in literature on applying watermarks in biometrics combine both ideas in the multibiometric scenario, where biometric template data is embedded into biometric sample data (of different modalities) to enable multibiometric fusion. For most such schemes **robust** watermarks have been suggested. However, the motivations for applying this specific type of watermarks are not made clear and discussed superficially only in most papers. The usage of robust embedding schemes seems to indicate that both data need to be tightly coupled and that the entire transmitted data might be subject to various manipulations, since robust embedding is meant to make the embedded data robust against changes of the host data. Therefore it seems that an insecure channel between

C. Vielhauer et al. (Eds.): BioID 2011, LNCS 6583, pp. 25–36, 2011.

sensor and processing module is assumed in this context. In such an environment host data manipulations are to be expected, including even malicous tampering like cropping. While tampering is not a threat against the classical scenario when robust watermarks are being used (in fact, these watermarks are actually designed to be robust against this type of attacks), in the multibiometric scenario tampering can be used to fool the system. By demonstrating a corresponding attack we show that robust watermarking is not a suited technology for the purpose it is suggested for in this context.

While this specific attack is targeted against the security of robust embedding (and can be eventually resolved by using different types of watermarks), robust watermarking additionally introduces distortions into the sample data impacting on recognition performance [4]. A concatenation of data (sample data and "embedded" template data) plus additional cryptographic authentication seems to be an alternative without this undesired effect.

In this paper, we will demonstrate a tampering / cropping attack against a watermarking-based multimodal biometric system, where biometric template data stored on a smart-card (the watermark) is embedded into acquired iris sample data at the sensor site using robust embedding. This demonstrates that additional or other security measures need to be taken to make the scheme secure. Section 2 provides an overview of several techniques how to incorporate watermarking techniques into biometric systems. Emphasis is given to the discussion of several examples of multibiometric techniques, which are enabled by embedding template data into sample data using watermarking. In Section 3, we discuss the attack scenario and provide detailed experimental results of the conducted attack. Section 4 concludes the paper.

2 Watermarking in Biometric Systems

One of the first ideas to somehow combine biometric technologies and watermarking is "biometric watermarking" [20]. The aim of watermarking in this approach is not to improve any biometric system, but to employ biometric templates as "message" to be embedded in classical robust watermarking applications like copyright protection in order to enable biometric recognition after the extraction of the watermark (WM).

A second application case for robust WMs is to prevent the use of sniffed sample data to fool the sensor in order to complement or replace liveness detection techniques. During data acquisition, the sensor (i.e. camera) embeds a WM into the acquired sample image before transmitting it to the feature extraction module. In case an intruder interferes the communication channel, sniffs the image data and presents the fake biometric trait (i.e. the image) to the sensor, it can detect the WM, will deduce non-liveness and will refuse to process the data further. This idea may also be applied to biometric databases where e.g. Bartlow et al. [1] propose a framework that encodes voice feature descriptors in raw iris images stored in a database.

An entirely different aim of applying robust embedding techniques to sample data is proposed in [17]. Here, the embedded signature is used as an additional security token like an additional password, which basically leads to a two-factor authentication system, based on biometrics and the additionally embedded secret data.

A steganographic approach is to transmit biometric data (i.e. template data) hidden into some arbitrary carrier / host data or biometric samples of different biometric modalities. The idea is to conceal the fact that biometric data transfer takes place, e.g. Jain et al. [6] propose to embed fingerprint minutiae data into an arbitrary host image while Khan et al. [8] suggest to embed fingerprint templates into audio signals.

Questions of sensor and sample authentication using watermarks have also been discussed. During data acquisition, the sensor (i.e. camera) embeds a watermark into the acquired sample image before transmitting it to the feature extraction module. The feature extraction module only proceeds with its tasks if the WM can be extracted correctly. For example, fragile watermarking has been suggested to serve that purpose either embedding image-independent [22] or image-dependent data as WM [21]. Ratha et al. [14] propose to embed a response to a authentication challenge sent out by a server into a WSQ compressed fingerprint image in order to authenticate the sensor capturing the fingerprint image.

A significant amount of work has also been published in the area of using WMs to enable a multibiometric approach by embedding a biometric template into a biometric sample of different biometric modalities. There are two variants: First, there are two different sensors acquiring two biometrics traits. Since for one modality template data is embedded, these data need to be generated at the sensor site which makes this approach somewhat unrealistic, at least for low power sensor devices. In addition to that, besides the increased recognition performance of multimodal systems in general there is no further specific gain in security. The second variant is to store the template on a smart-card which has to be submitted by the holder at the access control site. The smart-card embeds the template into the host sample data. This in fact represents a two-factor authentication system which increases security by introducing an additional token-based scheme and also leads to higher recognition accuracy as compared to a single biometric modality.

Hoang et al. [5] embed fingerprint minutiae in facial images (with fragile watermarks), while Jain et al. [7] embed face data into fingerprint images using a technique classified as being robust. Chung et al. [2, 11] use the same watermarking technique as well to embed fingerprint templates into facial images and vice versa, and compare the recognition performance of the resulting systems. They also use this embedding technique as the fragile part of a dual watermarking approach [11, 10] so that doubts remain about the actual robustness properties of the scheme. Vatsa et al. employ robust embedding techniques: in [18], they embed voice features in colour facial images, the same group [12, 19] propose to embed facial template data (and additional text data in the first work) into fingerprint sample data using a robust (multiple) watermarking approach. Park et al. [13] suggest to use robust embedding of iris templates into face image data to enable various functionalities, Kim et al. [9] propose a blind and robust spread spectrum watermarking technique for embedding face template data into fingerprint samples.

Note that several contributions in literature focusing on the multibiometric scenario indeed propose robust WMs for embedding.

3 Attacking Two-Factor Multibiometric Iris Recognition

We focus on the watermarking approach as described before enabling multibiometric recognition using a smart-card with stored template to facilitate template embedding. In case of this two-factor authentication technique, we suppose the attacker can utilise a stolen smart-card to fool the system. Additionally, she is in possession of sniffed sample iris data of the person owning the smart-card (the legitimate user) which could have been acquired with a telephoto lens or cropped from his high-resolution personal Facebook image for example.

Even if the WM embedding algorithm uses secret key information stored on the smart-card for embedding (which is the case for all watermarking schemes considered later), the following attack can be mounted since it is not the watermark that is being attacked. The attacker uses the biometric system pretending to be a legitimate user: an iris sample is acquired, the (stolen) smart-card is inserted, and finally, the template of the second biometric modality (e.g. fingerprint minutiae data stored on the smartcard) is secretly embedded as robust watermark. Now the attacker exploits the unsecure channel and intercepts the transmission of the data to the matching module. She modifies the transmitted iris image such that the acquired attackers' sample data matches that of the sniffed sample data of the legitimate user while not destroying the embedded WM. We will show in the subsequent experiments, that it is in fact possible to tamper / crop the iris image in a very crude manner without destroying the embedded template of the legitimate user. The result of this attack is the incorrect (i.e. false-positive) authentication of the attacker.

Note that there is a big difference between watermarking and iris recognition techniques: while watermarking is applied to the entire rectangular image data, iris recognition only relies on the iris texture data, a small circular ring around the pupil. For our experimental data, iris texture covers about 30% of the entire image area. Robust watermarking techniques aim in keeping the signature information (i.e the biometric template in our case) even if image data undergoes significant manipulations. Especially in case the image content after manipulation is similar from a perceptual viewpoint, the WM is expected to remain intact. So it may be possible to replace only the iris texture, not affecting the watermark detection capability. We will investigate if this is indeed the case for certain schemes.

Figure 1 illustrates this attack. The iris texture of the left image (attackers' sample) is replaced by the iris texture of the right image (legitimate users' sniffed sample data), thus resulting in a new iris image as shown in the figure (eventually still watermarked with the legitimate users' template).

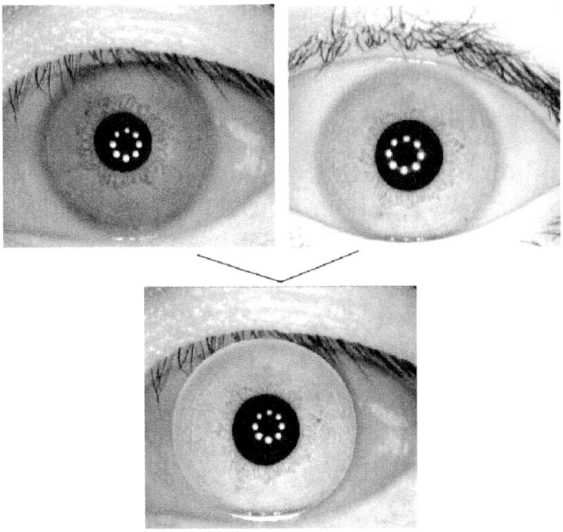

Fig. 1. Left: the original watermarked image with signature A, right: the image where the iris is copied out (with no signature or signature B), beneath: the resulting "attacked" image

3.1 Setting and Methods

In the experiments we select two randomly chosen rectangular iris images from the CASIA-IrisV3 interval database. The watermarked image (left in Fig. 1, with embedded signature A representing the legitimate users' template) will be attacked by the right image which can either contain

1. no watermark ("no signature")
2. a watermark embedded by the same algorithm but with different signature B ("other signature")
3. a watermark embedded by the same algorithm but with the same signature B ("same signature")

The different attacks correspond to different ways how the data to be inserted has been acquired. The first "no signature" attack can e.g. occur in case an iris image of a target person has been covertly acquired thus it contains no embedded WM. The second and third attacks ("other signature","same signature") can occur in case an intruder has sniffed transmitted images from the communication channel between sensor and feature extractor / matcher and intends to replace the iris of one image with the other one. If the sensor embeds the same image-independent signature in all images (not recommended), this results in the third attack ("same signature"), if the watermark is changed in every transmission being an image-dependent hash, the attack would be the second one ("other signature").

Since in any biometric application scenario there is no unmarked original image available to detect the WM in the marked image, only blind WM techniques are applicable in this context. We consider a variety of robust watermarking techniques in different flavours which have been also used to assess the impact of robust WM on iris recognition performance [4].

Spatial and DCT based algorithms

Bruyndonckx (shorthanded Bruyn) the Bruyndonckx algorithm operates on 8x8 blocks with modifications on the luminance values where each block is able to obtain one bit of information.

Koch Uses a random sequence of concrete image positions. At this positions the DCT coefficients of 8x8 blocks are used for embedding imposing a strict ordering.

Wavelet-based algorithms

Barni: 4-level decomposition. Additive embedding in the 3 finest detail subbands with visual masking.

Cao: Uses a redundant wavelet transform and embeds in the 3 finest detail subbands. Additive embedding by creating a significance mask is used.

Chen: Embedding is done in the approximation subband depending on the watermark length via a bit selection algorithm.

Dugad: 3-level decomposition. Additive embedding is applied only to a few significant coefficients above a threshold using an image sized watermark in the detail subbands.

Kundur (shorthanded Kund2): 3-level decomposition. Locations for embedding are pseudo-randomly selected in the detail subbands. A triple of coefficients at different subbands within the same spatial position is selected. The middle coefficient is then quantised.

Pla: Additive proportional embedding in significant trees of coefficients in the detail subbands by visual modelling.

Wu: 3-level decomposition. The quantisation based watermark is embedded in trees of coefficients.

Xie: Embedding only in the approximation subband. Selecting the middle of three coefficients by a sliding window. The middle coefficient is then quantised.

The experimental results are derived by examining 1000 random watermarks for each attack. For our tests, we trimmed the watermark embedding strength to achieve an average PSNR of about 42dB and 30dB to model medium and high embedding strength. In order to simulate differently sized templates being embedded, we chose either a "normal" standard signature length of 128 bits or 1000 Gaussian-distributed values, or a "long" signature length of 1024 bits or 32000 Gaussian-distributed values to check the signature length influence. For "Xie" the length is limited by the size of the approximation subband (here 80 bits), therefore for this algorithm only the "normal" signature length is available. The same applies to the other algorithms, where the signature length is dependent on the image size.

To decide if the watermark is present or not, a threshold on the detection results has to be determined. In literature often a threshold is selected which results in a false alarm rate of 10^{-8} which is derived by detector responses of images not containing the watermark (hypothesis H0) and is modelled by Generalized Gaussian distributions. In the plots the vertical line shows the calculated threshold, the x-axis shows the detector response value. All detector responses lying on the left side of the threshold line are interpreted as not indicating the watermark and on the right side as detecting the watermark.

3.2 Experimental Results

The following figures show histograms (i.e. discrete distributions where on the y-axis the number of responses with a certain x-value is shown) of detector response values for all three attacks (no signature, other signature, same signature) as well as for the not attacked image (the "left" image with signature A – the hypothesis H0), and for comparison a JPEG compression with quality 50.

Fig. 2 shows the only two algorithms / parameter settings where the watermark is not detected anymore in the attacked images. There is almost no difference among the results of the three attack types. Still, the effect of JPEG compression is different in the two cases: while in case of Kund2 compression removes the watermark entirely, Xie is able to detect the signature even with these compression settings. This difference is due to the entirely different embedding strategies used in the two schemes, the former embedding into detail subbands, the latter into the approximation subband which makes the scheme obviously more robust.

(a) Xie, 42dB (b) Kund2, 30dB

Fig. 2. Algorithms & parameters not detecting the WM

Changing the employed parameters however results in very different results as shown in Fig. 3 where we display detection results of Kund2 using 42dB with normal signature length and 30dB with long signatures.

In the case of 42dB, in roughly 50% of all considered cases the WM cannot be extracted. For 30dB and long signatures, all types of embedded marks could be extracted. The latter result is a rather typical one. However, it is clearly visible that detection values are clearly reduced for the attacked images as compared

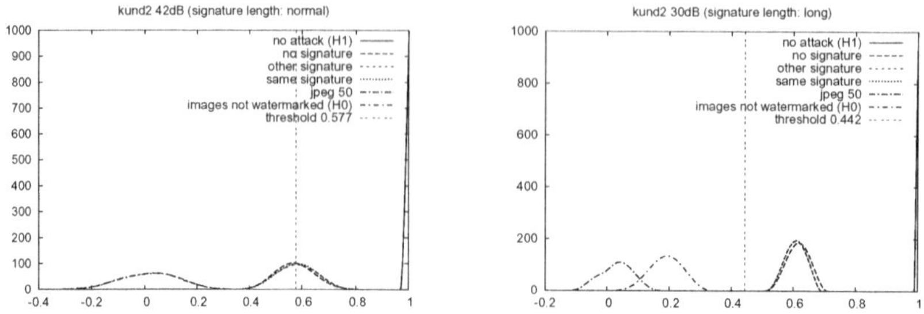

(a) 42dB, normal signatures (b) 30dB, long signatures

Fig. 3. Kund2 with parameters detecting the WM

to the not attacked ones (H1), which is true for all considered watermarking algorithms.

Fig. 4 provides more examples where detection results are clearly reduced for the attacked images, but still indicate the presence of the watermark using the threshold leading to a false alarm rate of 10^{-8}.

In order to provide a better overview, we have calculated the probability of missing the WM by modelling Generalised Gaussian distributions to the detector responses. A probability of zero means that each WM can be detected. A probability of e.g 0.5 means that in every second case the WM will be detected and 1 means that no WM will be detected. The results (for normal signature length) are shown in Table 1.

At 42dB, for Dugad and Xie the watermark will be destroyed with a probability of about 80% or higher (note that Dugad on the other hand exhibits a significant probability of miss for the H1 data). For Barni, Cao, Chen, Koch, Pla and Wu the attacks do not show significant influence, hence do not destroy the watermark. Using the higher embedding strength (30dB) the impact is quite similar. Only for Bruyn and Kund2 the detection miss probability raises from about 50% to 98% (where Bruyn again exhibits a significant probability of miss for the H1 data).

3.3 Impact on Security of the Multimodal Watermarking Approach

We have found that for most robust schemes, the embedded WM can be extracted although the iris texture has been changed. This is somewhat surprising at first sight since the iris texture covers about 30% of the watermarked image. However, when keeping in mind that robust WM schemes are intended to keep the WM in place even in case of cropping attacks, this result is not really entirely unexpected.

As a result of these experiments, we clearly find that robust watermarking techniques, although proposed in many watermarking-based multimodal biometric systems, are not appropriate as the only means of security in such schemes. While increasing the security in general due to the introduction of two-factor

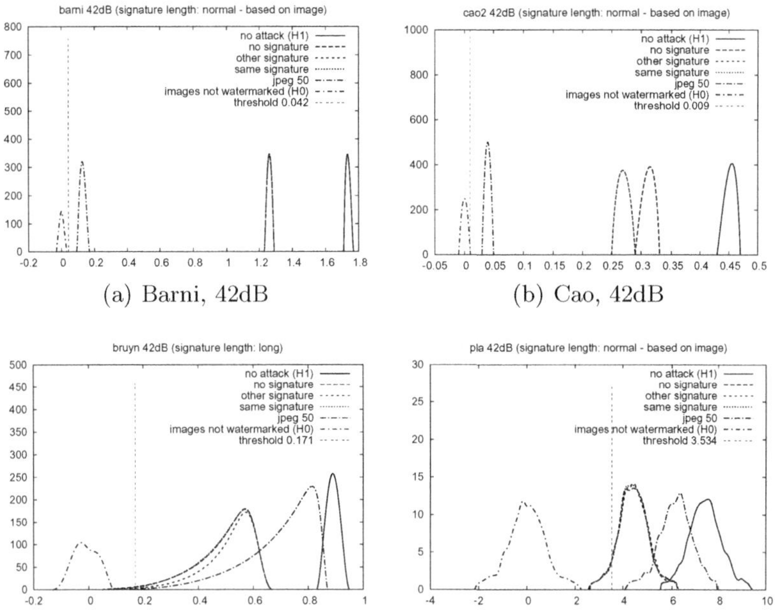

(a) Barni, 42dB (b) Cao, 42dB

(c) Bruyn 42dB, long signatures (d) Pla, 42dB

Fig. 4. Typical examples for detection behaviour

authentication, the issue of the protection of the sensor – matching module communication is not solved by just employing robust watermarking.

How can we resolve the issues identified in this work:

1. The method of choice for the target scenario is semi-fragile WM embedding. These schemes allow for some robustness against unintentional image modifications like compression but are fragile against more severe intentional tampering. Exchanging iris texture as in our attack would lead to a destruction of the embedded template raising manipulation alarm. Of course, all fragile techniques discussed before can also be used, however, sacrificing robustness entirely. Another solution would be to employ the dual watermarking technique as proposed by Kim et al. [10] where the fragile part would detect the manipulation as conducted in the attacks used in this paper.
2. Recent work by Zebbiche et al. [23] proposes a watermarking scheme for fingerprint images where WM data is embedded into the ridge area (region of interest) only. This scheme can be applied to iris imagery by selectively watermarking the iris texture areas. Exchanging the iris leads to a destruction of the embedded template as well.
3. Protection of the sensor module – processing module communication by classical cryptographic means including authentication might represent a superior alternative to using watermarking. The small data overhead when concatenating sample and template data (and securing this concatenation

Table 1. Probability of missing the WMs - normal signatures

		no attack	no signature	other signature	same signature	jpeg 50
barni	42dB	0	0	0	0	1.89e-39
	30dB	0	0	0	0	0
bruyn	42dB	1.69e-05	0.434	0.435	0.437	8.14e-20
	30dB	0.659	0.974	0.975	0.974	1.54e-05
cao	42dB	0	0	0	0	2.93e-66
	30dB	0	0	0	0	0
chen	42dB	0	5.71e-04	7.85e-04	4.41e-04	5.99e-29
	30dB	0	2.5e-05	1.11e-04	5.41e-05	1.6e-87
dugad	42dB	0.045	0.795	0.806	0.807	0.286
	30dB	0.033	0.913	0.964	0.957	0.071
koch	42dB	0	0.026	0.027	0.017	0
	30dB	0	0.014	0.009	0.014	0
kund2	42dB	0	0.540	0.479	0.482	1
	30dB	0	0.981	0.996	0.996	1
pla	42dB	5.25e-10	0.045	0.043	0.043	1.09e-05
	30dB	5.75e-54	1.15e-29	4.18e-24	2.07e-24	7.22e-56
wu	42dB	0	1.93e-116	1.42e-112	4.52e-110	4.04e-57
	30dB	0	9.38e-120	4.24e-106	2.17e-114	0
xie	42dB	4.22e-18	1	1	1	2e-19
	30dB	0.770	1	1	1	0.787

with a signed hash) can probably be tolerated, since on the other hand, employing such a strategy we do not suffer from recognition performance decrease as caused by watermarking. However, this decision and the eventual demand for the robustness property in watermarking depends on the application scenario.

It has to be noted that the situation is different for the multibiometric approach without smart-card being applied (which is on the other hand unrealistic due to required template generation at the sensor module as discussed before). Tampering the sample data to match these of a legitimate user does not represent a threat in this case, since still also the attackers' template would be embedded in the data.

4 Conclusion

We have demonstrated that, contrasting to several suggestions made in literature, the use of robust watermarking for embedding templates in the context of multimodal biometric systems is not suited to act as the sole means of security in such a scheme. This is in particular true when the scheme is used in connection with a two-factor authentication system where the template to be embedded is stored on a smart-card where tampering / cropping can be applied to forge the sample data while the embedded template keeps in place. Instead, fragile or even better, semi-fragile embedding techniques have to be used instead. As an alternative, classical cryptographic techniques to secure the sensor module – processing module channel might be considered useful.

References

[1] Bartlow, N., Kalka, N., Cukic, B., Ross, A.: Protecting iris images through asymmetric digital watermarking. In: IEEE Workshop on Automatic Identification Advanced Technologies, vol. 4432, pp. 192–197. West Virginia University, Morgantown (2007)

[2] Chung, Y., Moon, D., Moon, K., Pan, S.: Hiding biometric data for secure transmission. In: Khosla, R., Howlett, R.J., Jain, L.C. (eds.) KES 2005. LNCS (LNAI), vol. 3683, pp. 1049–1057. Springer, Heidelberg (2005)

[3] Dong, J., Tan, T.: Effects of watermarking on iris recognition performance. In: Proceedings of the 10th International Conference on Control, Automation, Robotics and Vision (ICARCV 2008), pp. 1156–1161 (2008)

[4] Hämmerle-Uhl, J., Raab, K., Uhl, A.: Experimental study on the impact of robust watermarking on iris recognition accuracy (best paper award, applications track). In: Proceedings of the 25th ACM Symposium on Applied Computing, pp. 1479–1484 (2010)

[5] Hoang, T., Tran, D., Sharma, D.: Remote multimodal biometric authentication using bit priority-based fragile watermarking. In: Proceedings of the 19th International Conference on Pattern Recognition, Tampa, Florida, USA, pp. 1–4 (December 2008)

[6] Jain, A.K., Uludag, U.: Hiding fingerprint minutiae in images. In: Proceedings of AutoID 2002, 3rd Workshop on Automatic Identification Advanced Technologies, Tarrytown, New York, USA, pp. 97–102 (March 2002)

[7] Jain, A.K., Uludag, U., Hsu, R.L.: Hiding a face in a fingerprint image. In: Proceedings of the International Conference on Pattern Recognition (ICPR 2002), Quebec City, Canada, pp. 756–759 (August 2002)

[8] Khan, M.K., Xie, L., Zhang, J.S.: Robust hiding of fingerprint-biometric data into audio signals. In: Lee, S.-W., Li, S.Z. (eds.) ICB 2007. LNCS, vol. 4642, pp. 702–712. Springer, Heidelberg (2007)

[9] Kim, W.-G., Lee, H.K.: Multimodal biometric image watermarking using two-stage integrity verification. Signal Processing 89(12), 2385–2399 (2009)

[10] Kim, W.-G., Lee, S.H., Seo, Y.-S.: Image Fingerprinting Scheme for Print-and-Capture Model. In: Zhuang, Y.-t., Yang, S.-Q., Rui, Y., He, Q. (eds.) PCM 2006. LNCS, vol. 4261, pp. 106–113. Springer, Heidelberg (2006)

[11] Moon, D., Kim, T., Jung, S.-H., Chung, Y., Moon, K., Ahn, D., Kim, S.K.: Performance evaluation of watermarking techniques for secure multimodal biometric systems. In: Hao, Y., Liu, J., Wang, Y.-P., Cheung, Y.-m., Yin, H., Jiao, L., Ma, J., Jiao, Y.-C. (eds.) CIS 2005. LNCS (LNAI), vol. 3802, pp. 635–642. Springer, Heidelberg (2005)

[12] Noore, A., Singh, R., Vatsa, M., Houck, M.M.: Enhancing security of fingerprints through contextual biometric watermarking. Forensic Science International 169, 188–194 (2007)

[13] Park, K.R., Jeong, D.S., Kang, B.J., Lee, E.C.: A Study on Iris Feature Watermarking on Face Data. In: Beliczynski, B., Dzielinski, A., Iwanowski, M., Ribeiro, B. (eds.) ICANNGA 2007. LNCS, vol. 4432, pp. 415–423. Springer, Heidelberg (2007)

[14] Ratha, N.K., Figueroa-Villanueva, M.A., Connell, J.H., Bolle, R.M.: A secure protocol for data hiding in compressed fingerprint images. In: Maltoni, D., Jain, A.K. (eds.) BioAW 2004. LNCS, vol. 3087, pp. 205–216. Springer, Heidelberg (2004)
[15] Ratha, N.K., Connell, J.H., Bolle, R.M.: Enhancing security and privacy in biometrics-based authentication systems. IBM Systems Journal 40(3), 614–634 (2001)
[16] Roberts, C.: Biometric attack vectors and defenses. Computers & Security 26, 14–25 (2007)
[17] Satonaka, T.: Biometric watermark authentication with multiple verification rule. In: Proceedings of the 12th IEEE Workshop on Neural Networks in Signal Processing, pp. 597–606 (2002)
[18] Vatsa, M., Singh, R., Noore, A.: Feature based RDWT watermarking for multimodal biometric system. Image and Vision Computing 27(3), 293–304 (2009)
[19] Vatsa, M., Singh, R., Noore, A., Houck, M.M., Morris, K.: Robust biometric image watermarking for fingerprint and face template protection. IEICE Electronics Express 3(2), 23–28 (2006)
[20] Vielhauer, C., Steinmetz, R.: Approaches to biometric watermarks for owner authentification. In: Proceedings of SPIE, Security and Watermarking of Multimedia Contents III, San Jose, CA, USA, vol. 4314 (January 2001)
[21] Wang, D.-S., Li, J.-P., Hu, D.-K., Yan, Y.-H.: A novel biometric image integrity authentication using fragile watermarking and Arnold transform. In: Li, J.P., Bloshanskii, I., Ni, L.M., Pandey, S.S., Yang, S.X. (eds.) Proceedings of the International Conference on Information Computing and Automatation, pp. 799–802 (2007)
[22] Yeung, M.M., Pankanti, S.: Verification watermarks on fingerprint recognition and retrieval. Journal of Electronal Imaging, Special Issue on Image Security and Digital Watermarking 9(4), 468–476 (2000)
[23] Zebbiche, K., Khelifi, F.: Region-based watermarking of biometric images: Case study in fingerprint images. International Journal of Digital Multimedia Broadcasting (March 2008)

Handwriting Biometrics: Feature Selection Based Improvements in Authentication and Hash Generation Accuracy

Andrey Makrushin[1], Tobias Scheidat[1,2], and Claus Vielhauer[1,2]

[1] Otto-von-Guericke University of Magdeburg, Universitätsplatz 2, 39106 Magdeburg, Germany
[2] University of Applied Sciences Brandenburg, Magdeburger Str. 50, 14770 Brandenburg an der Havel, Germany
makrushin@iti.cs.uni-magdeburg.de, {scheidat,claus.vielhauer}@fh-brandenburg.de

Abstract. Biometric cryptosystems extend the user authentication functionality of usual biometric systems with the ability to generate robust stable values (also called biometric hashes) from variable biometric data. This work addresses a biometric hash algorithm applied to handwriting data and investigates the performance of both user authentication and hash generation scenarios. In order to improve the hash generation performance, some feature selection approaches are proposed. The intelligent reduction of features leads not only to a better ratio of collision/reproduction rates, but also improves equal error rates in user authentication scenario. Additionally, the parameterization of biometric hash algorithm is discussed. It has been shown that different quantization parameters as well as different features should be selected to achieve better performance rates in both scenarios. For the best semantic, symbol, the EER is improved from 8.30% to 5.27% and the CRR from 11.20% to 6.32%. Finally, the almost useful and needless features are figured out e.g. only 2 features are selected for every semantic in both scenarios and 10 features are never selected.

Keywords: biometrics, handwriting, user authentication, biometric hashing, biometric cryptosystems.

1 Introduction

The usual biometric systems take a focus on reliable user authentication. In addition to the user authentication, biometric cryptosystems aim to securely preserve biometric templates and generate individual values (biometric hashes or biohashes) from biometric data. Therefore, two requirements can be formulated for biometric hash generation. Firstly, biometric hashes have to be irreversible. Secondly, biometric hashes have to be constant for each particular user and at the same time to be unequal for different users. While the user authentication performance is measured by the relationship between false accept/reject curves usually expressed in equal error rate (EER), the robustness of hash generation is determined by reproduction and collision rates, which represent the probabilities of hash reproduction in genuine and impostor

C. Vielhauer et al. (Eds.): BioID 2011, LNCS 6583, pp. 37–48, 2011.

trials correspondingly [7]. While the collision rate (CR) should be possibly low, the reproducibility rate (RR) should be possibly high. The biometric hash algorithm for dynamic handwriting (hereafter BioHash algorithm) has been described in [9] and aims to fulfill both requirements mentioned before, namely irreversible and robust hash generation, by means of user based quantization of feature values. Feature values are mapped to user-individual intervals resulting in the transformation of a feature vector to a vector of hash values. The hash vector can further be used either for user authentication or as seed for cryptographic key generation.

It is hard to parameterize the algorithm in the way that both, EER and CR/RR, become better. In this work the tuning of internal BioHash parameters as well as a selection of essential features is done to improve performances in both user authentication and hash generation scenarios. Since some features are not suitable for biometric hash generation because of very high intra-class variance or very low inter-class variance, the elimination of these features is required. The feature selection has been provided by means of five exemplary selected filters and three wrappers. The results based on these eight selection algorithms are compared to each other. Using the best feature selection approach, the most useful as well as needless features are determined. Experiments are based on handwriting data collected from 39 users. The samples used for enrollment, for parameters tuning and for actual tests are separated in time by at least one month. Experimental results are provided for five writing contents, so called semantics.

Hereafter the paper is organized as follows. The next section briefly introduces state-of-the-art in biometric hash generation and feature selection domains. The biometric hash algorithm is described in third section. Section 4 addresses several feature selection strategies. The test set up, evaluation methodology as well as the results of experimental evaluation are discussed in section 5. Section 6 provides conclusion and future work.

2 State-of-the-Art

The problem of secure preservation of user templates is probably one of most discussed issues in biometrics [3]. The general idea here is to facilitate the reconstruction of cryptographic key from user specific biometric data and to disable the cryptographic key generation from biometric data of other users.

Juels and Wattenberg in [5] combine ideas from the areas of error-correcting codes and cryptography, and provide the fuzzy commitment scheme. The very resembling scheme was suggested by Dodis et al. in [1] and called secure sketch. The sketch P and a template W are generated from a user enrollment data D. Using this sketch P and a test sample of the same user D', sufficiently similar to D, the template W can be exactly reconstructed. The sketch P is considered as public information and a secret template W alone does not allow the reconstruction of initial biometric data D. Sutcu et al. [8] propose a practical secure sketch generation scheme and apply it to face modality. Our work addresses the biometric hash algorithm for dynamic handwriting developed by Vielhauer [9]. Here, a user based quantization is applied for irreversible generation of a user's template.

The main problem of all practical template coding schemes is that some features, extracted from biometric data, are not suitable for that, which makes feature selection essential. The feature selection is a general problem of pattern recognition, which has been intensively discussed over the last years in different domains. The selection of biometric features is addressed for example by Kumar et al. in [6]. They applied the Correlation Based Feature Selection (CFS) for bimodal biometric system and investigated the classification performance. Moreover, feature level fusion used in combination with feature selection was addressed.

According to the common terminology originally provided in [4] the feature selection approaches are divided to wrappers and filters. Wrappers select the feature subset based on a particular classifier performance. Contrariwise, filters provide classifier independent quality criterion for features ranking. A comprehensive survey on feature selection is given in Guyon et al. [2]. Both approaches, filters and wrappers, were considered and two alternative ways for feature selection are suggested. These are the ranking using the correlation coefficient or mutual information and a nested subset selection with forward or backward selection or with multiplicative updates. Aforementioned ideas become practical in this work. Exemplary chosen feature selection strategies, which appear relevant for biometric handwriting features, are applied to biometric hash generation. The impact of these strategies on the performance of a given biometric hash algorithm is investigated.

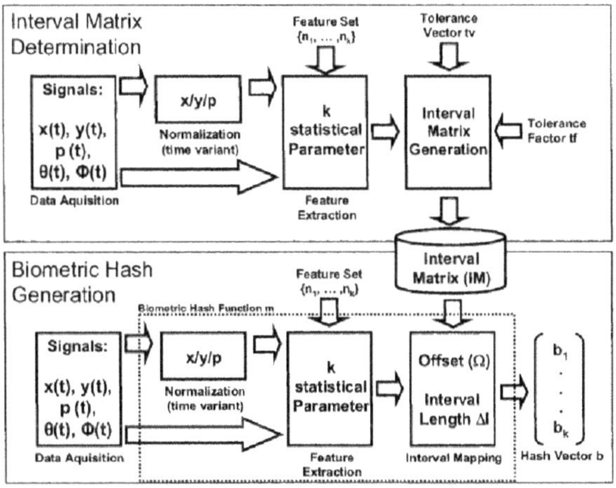

Fig. 1. Two stages of biometric hash generation process: determination of interval matrix (top) and generation of biometric hash vector (bottom). Taken from [9].

3 Biometric Hashing Algorithm

The biometric hash calculation consists of two stages: determination of interval matrix (IM) and biometric hash function to generate an actual biohash vector. Both stages are shown in figure 1. The calculation of IM together with generation of reference biohash vectors can be considered as an enrolment stage. The generation of biohash vectors from test feature vectors and subsequent matching of resulting vectors with reference ones can be considered as an authentication stage, shown in figure 2.

Both the IM determination and the biohash vector generation contain conventional signal processing steps: data acquisition, normalization and feature extraction. Five time dependent signals are recorded from an input device, namely pen positions x(t), y(t), pressure p(t), pen altitude θ(t) and pen azimuth Φ(t). After normalization the signal values are resided in appropriate range. The feature extraction process provides a k-dimensional feature vector $(n_1,\ldots,n_k)$. We will not concentrate here on these stages and refer an interested reader to the detailed description in [9].

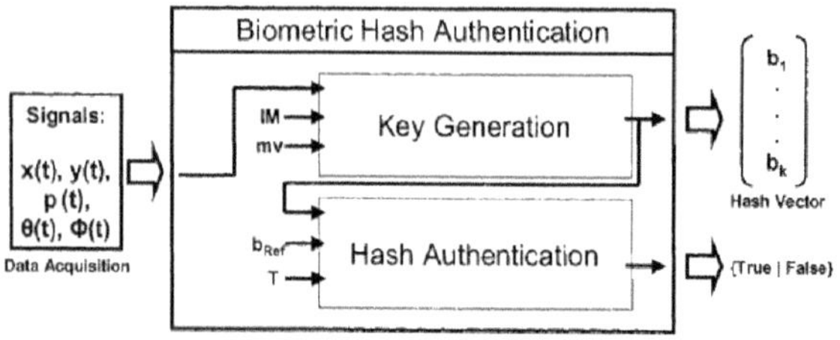

Fig. 2. Contradistinguishing of hash generation and user authentication. Taken from [9].

An interval matrix is generated for each user individually using his enrolment and two auxiliary parameters: a k-dimensional tolerance vector (*tv*), and a scalar tolerance factor (*tf*). IM consist of interval length vector ΔI and interval offset vector Ω. (see figure 1). Calculation of IM components is reflected in equations 1-4. The $I_{InitLow}$ and $I_{InitHigh}$ are vectors of minimums and maximums of feature values and ΔI_{Init} is the absolute difference between $I_{InitHigh}$ and $I_{InitLow}$.

$$I_{High} = \begin{pmatrix} \lceil I_{InitHigh,1} + tv_1 * \Delta I_{Init,1} * tf \rceil \\ \ldots \\ \lceil I_{InitHigh,k} + tv_k * \Delta I_{Init,k} * tf \rceil \end{pmatrix} \tag{1}$$

$$I_{Low} = \begin{pmatrix} \lfloor I_{InitLow,1} - tv_1 * \Delta I_{Init,1} * tf \rfloor & if & (\lfloor I_{InitLow,1} - tv_1 * \Delta I_{Init,1} * tf \rfloor) > 0, & 0 \ otherwise \\ & \ldots & & \\ \lfloor I_{InitLow,k} - tv_k * \Delta I_{Init,k} * tf \rfloor & if & (\lfloor I_{InitLow,k} - tv_k * \Delta I_{Init,k} * tf \rfloor) > 0, & 0 \ otherwise \end{pmatrix} \tag{2}$$

$$\Delta I = \begin{pmatrix} \Delta I_1 \\ \ldots \\ \Delta I_k \end{pmatrix} = I_{High} - I_{Low} = \begin{pmatrix} I_{High,1} \\ \ldots \\ I_{High,k} \end{pmatrix} - \begin{pmatrix} I_{Low,1} \\ \ldots \\ I_{Low,k} \end{pmatrix} \tag{3}$$

$$\Omega = I_{Low} \bmod \Delta I \tag{4}$$

After determination, the IM is connected with user's identity and persistently stored. The *tv* is conceived to reflect the world model information about the variance of features. If this knowledge is not available, the mapping intervals are entirely extracted from enrolment data and *tv*=(0,…,0). The *tv* could also be seen as adaptation parameter that dynamically regulates individual mapping interval lengths. However, if a synchronous adaptation of all mapping intervals is required, the *tv* have to be set to (1,...,1) and *tf* have to be used instead. The *tf* determines the global expansion level of mapping intervals. A feature vector $(n_1,\ldots,n_k)$ is mapped to the biohash vector by the interval mapping process, making use of a persistently stored user-specific IM. This mapping is given by equation 5.

$$m(n,IM) = m(n,\Delta I,\Omega) = \begin{pmatrix} m_{Scalar}(n_1,\Delta I_1,\Omega_1) \\ \ldots \\ m_{Scalar}(n_k,\Delta I_k,\Omega_k) \end{pmatrix} = \begin{pmatrix} \left\lfloor \frac{(n_1-\Omega_1)}{\Delta I_1} \right\rfloor \\ \ldots \\ \left\lfloor \frac{(n_k-\Omega_k)}{\Delta I_k} \right\rfloor \end{pmatrix} \tag{5}$$

In authentication mode the reference and test biohash vectors have to be compared. This is done using Hamming distance. Taking into account that only one reference biohash vector (b_{ref}) is generated for each user, the matching is done through one-to-one comparison. The verification decision is made based on predefined decision threshold (T). A user is accepted if the matching score is less or equal to T and rejected otherwise.

4 Feature Selection

Due to the physical capabilities of the digitizer tablets, not each of the currently considered features is appropriate for the hash value calculation. Some digitizer tablets, for instance, are not capable to record pen angle signals. Therefore, all angle dependent features result in a constant value of 0 in all samples. Some features are not suitable for biohash generation because of very high intra-class variance. They cannot be reproduced for some users. Other features have very low inter-class variance and are always reproduced in impostor trials. Thus, feature selection is required to eliminate all irrelevant features and to allow reliable hash generation.

According to the common terminology originally provided in [4] the feature selection approaches are divided to wrappers and filters. Wrappers select the feature subset based on a particular classifier performance. Contrariwise, filters provide classifier independent quality criterion for features ranking based only on intrinsic properties of the data.

Since the wrapper based feature selection is inherently connected with the applied classifier, the search is done through the repetition of classification trials with different feature subsets. However, an exhaustive search is required to find out the optimal subset. Given M features there are 2^M feature subsets possible. This exponential relationship between the number of features and the number of possible subsets makes an exhaustive search inapplicable. Moreover, the single evaluation trial implies the classification of the whole test set and, therefore, the computational complexity is closely related with the number of test samples as well. There are several strategies to avoid an exhaustive search. The easiest way is a classification with each single feature and selection of features with least classification error rates. This is a univariate kind of selection. That means no interaction between features is regarded. Another possibilities are forward and backward selections. The forward selection starts with an empty set and adds the best features one by one at each step. The best feature, in combination with already selected features, has the highest classification error decrease. The iterative process stops when the addition of a new feature does not decrease the classification error. The backward selection starts with the whole feature set and removes the worst features one by one at each step. The removal of the worst feature leads to the highest classification error decrease (or might even slightly increases it). The iterative process stops when the next removal increases classification error significantly. These two subset selections are multivariate, which means that an interaction between features is taken into account.

In order to be independent on classification algorithms, one should use filters. In contrast to wrappers the considered filter approaches are univariate. Here several heuristics have been suggested to define feature quality. The heuristics facilitate the ranking of features through the calculation of quality values. Filters are computationally simple, because the heuristics have to be calculated only ones. The actual filtering is done by elimination of low ranked features.

ANOVA. ANalysis Of VAriance test evaluates the relationship between within-class scatters and between-class scatter. Within-class scatter is intra-class variance and between-class scatter is the difference between mean values of classes. Equation 6 gives feature quality defined by ANOVA test for the case of two users. Here N_1 and N_2 denote the numbers of test samples of the first and second users correspondingly.

$$F = \frac{N_1 \cdot N_2 \cdot (\mu_1 - \mu_2)^2}{N_1 \cdot \sigma_1^2 + N_2 \cdot \sigma_2^2} \tag{6}$$

If more than two users are presented, there are two principal ways to calculate the feature quality (F-value). In the first case, we call it *anova-2class*, for each user k all other users are considered as only one non-user class and the value F_k can be calculated through the application of equation 1. The final F-value is given by the sum of F_k values. In the second case the multivariate ANOVA test is applied. The feature variation inside of a user is presented by the sum of deviations of user samples x_{kj} from a user mean value μ_k and the feature variation between different users is presented by the sum of deviations of user mean values μ_k from the global mean value μ. The feature rank is given by equation 7. Here K is the number of users, N_k is the number of test samples of the user k and N is the total number of samples.

$$F = \frac{\frac{1}{K-1}\sum_{k=1}^{K} N_k (\mu_k - \mu)^2}{\frac{1}{N-K}\sum_{k=1}^{K}\sum_{j=1}^{N_k} (x_{kj} - \mu_k)^2} \tag{7}$$

Correlation. The use of the correlation between features and class labels, as the quality criterion of feature, is described in [2]. Equation 8 provides the Pearson correlation coefficient R, whereby the μ_x and μ_y designate mean values of feature and class labels correspondingly. R becomes zero if no correlation between feature and labels is established. This means complete irrelevance of the feature. Contrariwise, R=1 designates maximal correlation and therefore absolute relevance of the feature.

$$R = \left| \frac{\sum_{x_j}\sum_{y_j}(x_j - \mu_x)(y_j - \mu_y)}{\sqrt{\sum_{x_j}(x_j - \mu_x)^2 . \sum_{y_j}(y_j - \mu_y)^2}} \right| \tag{8}$$

Entropy. Alternatively, the information theoretic ranking criteria could be used instead of correlation coefficient. The empirical estimation of the mutual information (joint-entropy) between features and class labels gives the quality of the particular feature. The equation for this approach could be found in [2]. Another way to build an entropy-based quality criterion (*entropy-2class-bha*) relies on the comparison of user and non-user distributions of the particular feature. In case of discrete features the probability distribution can be substituted by the histograms built from the evaluation data. The bigger difference, measured by means of Bhattacharyya distance, between user and non-user histograms designates better discrimination power of the feature. The final quality coefficient is the sum over all users. Suppose $H(A)$ is the histogram of feature values from the user A and $H(\bar{A})$ is the histogram of feature values from the remaining users. The aforementioned divergence is given by equations 9. N is the maximal feature value and K is the number of users.

$$R = \sum_{k=1}^{K}\left(- \ln \sqrt{\sum_{j=1}^{N} H_j(k) \cdot H_j(\bar{k})} \right) \tag{9}$$

5 Evaluation

The experimental data was captured from 39 users in three sessions with an interval of at least one month between two sessions in laboratory conditions by a Toshiba M200 Portege tablet PC. Each user was asked to provide 10 samples of 5 different semantics: public PIN (77993), secret PIN, pseudonym, symbol and an answer to the question “Where are you from?” (place). It was intentionally refrained from capturing of signatures, which were substituted by pseudonyms because of privacy reasons. The samples from the first session were used for enrolment. The samples from the second session were employed for *tf*-tuning and feature selection. The samples from the third session were applied for hash generation and user authentication tests. The tests were done in verification mode. An attempt of one user to be verified as another user is considered as an impostor trial. Thus, each test contains 390 genuine trials, which correspond to 39 users times 10 test samples, and 14820 impostor trials, which correspond to 38 user claims times 39 actual users times 10 test samples. Note that this protocol leads to a realistic situation where enrolment data has already undergone an aging of at least 2 months. The evaluation is provided relying on 131 features extracted from dynamic handwritten data and BioHash algorithm described in section 3. The feature extraction is based on 3 time dependent characteristics of raw data points: x- and y-coordinates and pressure.

5.1 Performance Measures

While the user authentication scenario requires only that genuine matching scores are less than impostor matching scores, the hash generation scenario requires exact reconstruction of biometric hash vector. Therefore, completely different performance measures have to be used. A traditional methodology for evaluation of authentication performance consist of calculating of FAR(T) and FRR(T) as functions of decision threshold (T). Further, the threshold (T_{EER}) is extracted where both functions take an equal value and this value, called equal error rate (EER), reflects the authentication reliability of a biometric system. In hash generation scenario the reproducibility rate (RR) and collision rate (CR) are used instead of EER. These values are relative sums of identically reproduced hashes in genuine and impostor trials correspondingly [7]. The CR and RR are reciprocal values. The tuning of the algorithm to improve RR automatically leads to worse CR and vice versa. Therefore, the collision reproduction rate (CRR), as defined by the equation 10, is selected as a hash generation quality criterion in our tests. Here CR and RR are weighted equally.

$$CRR = \frac{1}{2}(CR + (1 - RR)) \tag{10}$$

5.2 Tolerance Values

The tolerance vector (*tv*) facilitates feature based adaptation of mapping interval lengths. Since all features are considered equally this vector is set to (1,...,1). Given that *tv* contains constant values, the tolerance factor (*tf*) is the principal parameter for controlling CR and RR values. The *tf* value of 0.5, for instance, means that the margins of quantization interval are expanded left and right to the half of the interval length and the interval becomes double length (see equations 1 and 2).

The evaluation data from the second capturing session is used for the determination of *tf* values. These are defined for each semantic class dependent on the scenario. Figure 3 shows the relationship between CR and RR and also performance indexes CRR and EER dependent on *tf*. Small dark and big light areas identify the symbol semantic as a very good one, just as public PIN with very big dark area can be rather identified as a bad semantic. According to the results of *tf* -test with all 131 features the *tf* values are set to 1.5, 1.75, 2.5, 3.5 and 2.5 in hash generation scenario for public pin, secret pin, pseudonym, symbol and place, correspondingly. Presented values are selected with respect to the fact that CR should not exceed 5% margin (see figure 3). In the user authentication scenario the *tf* values are set to 1, 1, 1.25, 1.5 and 1.25 for public pin, secret pin, pseudonym, symbol and place, correspondingly, because of the best EERs and practically zero CR at these points.

5.3 Feature Selection

Since a realistic hash generation as well as user authentication scenario requires an a-priori size definition of the target feature set, the size was intuitively set to 60 features even if a smaller number of features leads to better performance during the evaluation. Table 1 provides the evaluation results of user authentication experiment for all semantic classes expressed in EER with specifying of appropriate decision threshold.

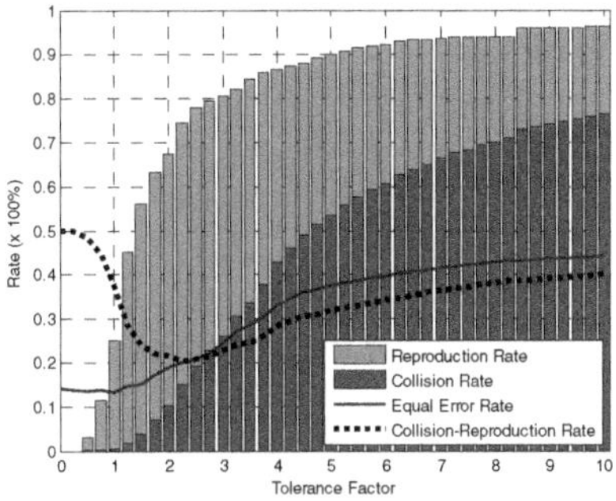

(a) public PIN (77993)

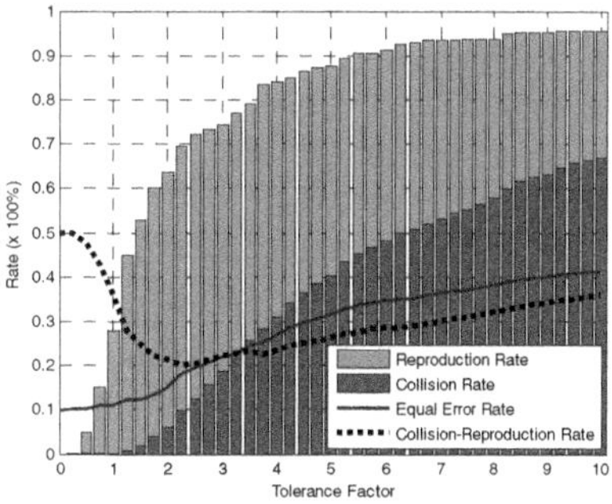

(b) secret PIN

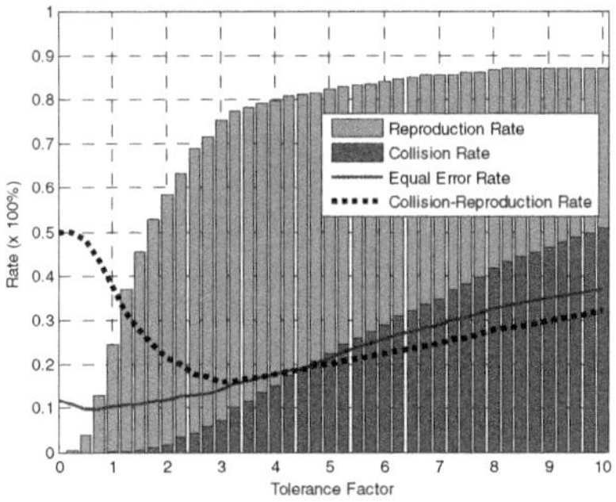

(c) pseudonym

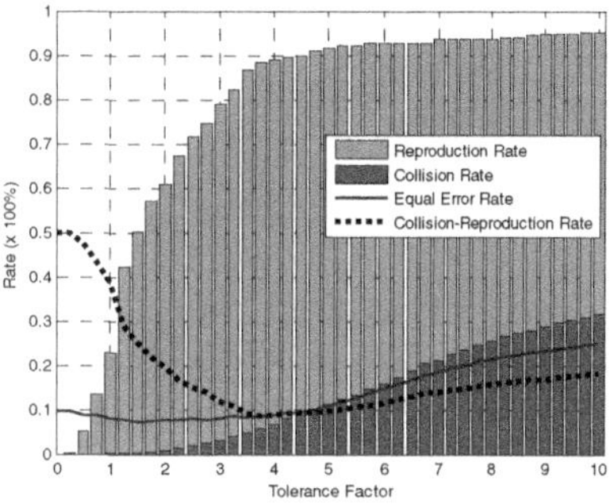

(d) symbol

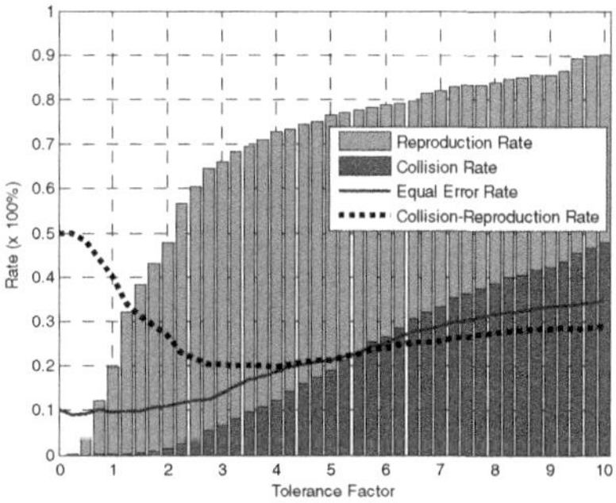

(e) place

Fig. 3. Dynamics of CR, RR, CRR and EER dependent on tolerance factor

The best user authentication performance is achieved with symbol and amounts to 5.27% EER with the best-first selection strategy. The worst EER, namely 14.88% for the best selection strategy, was calculated for public PIN.

The experiments have shown that *anova-2class* provides in almost each case the best EER for all semantics (except pseudonym) and could be pointed out as the best heuristic. The *anova-2class* has also better performance than simple wrapper. The more complex wrappers (*best-first*, *discard-worst*) invariably leads to significantly better EER, but the wrapper-based feature selection is intrinsically associated with classifier and can not be done a-priori before defining the classifier. The heuristics-based feature selection does not guaranty the improvement of EER, which can be seen comparing the second row in the table (raw) with heuristics rows (*anova*, *anova-2class*, *correlation*, *entropy-2class-bha* and *joint-entropy*). Hence, the *best-first* or the *discard-worst* wrapper is suggested to be used in case of predefined classifier. Otherwise the *anova-2class* is preferable.

Table 1. Results of user authentication experiment with different feature selection strategies. Target feature set is limited to 60 features.

	public PIN		secret PIN		pseudonym		symbol		place	
	EER	T_{EER}	EER	T_{EER}	EER	T_{EER}	EER	T_{EER}	EER	T_{EER}
reference (all 131 feat.)	16.55%	5.3895	13.42%	6.7085	10.96%	6.8164	8.30%	5.8032	9.79%	6.5830
raw (first 60 features)	19.98%	1.9843	16.84%	2.6543	13.84%	2.7070	11.60%	2.6149	11.13%	2.5325
anova	18.56%	3.1245	15.61%	3.8051	11.59%	4.2000	10.80%	3.9928	9.66%	3.3714
anova-2class	16.78%	2.6980	12.50%	2.9819	13.03%	3.3629	9.00%	2.3756	7.72%	2.9970
correlation	18.10%	2.9130	16.45%	3.4948	12.60%	3.8470	10.14%	3.0385	12.12%	3.2868
entropy-2class-bha	19.32%	2.9639	17.08%	3.9763	12.35%	4.2059	9.89%	3.4969	10.15%	3.7138
joint-entropy	20.12%	2.0637	17.03%	2.7537	12.33%	2.1728	11.69%	2.7806	12.06%	1.8401
simple wrapper	17.93%	3.5026	14.56%	4.5142	11.59%	4.6855	9.02%	4.2013	10.23%	4.1832
best-first	15.06%	2.4930	12.65%	3.2334	9.73%	2.8669	5.27%	1.9286	7.20%	2.7441
discard-worst	14.88%	3.0436	11.41%	3.6485	11.02%	4.0009	6.47%	3.0481	7.41%	3.5924

Table 2 provides the evaluation results of hash generation experiment for all semantic classes expressed in CR, RR and CRR. The best hash generation performance is also achieved with symbol and amounts to 6.32% CRR with the *best-first* selection strategy. The worst CRR, namely 15.94% for the best selection strategy, has public PIN. In this scenario the best heuristic is *anova* with the best CRR for all semantics except public PIN. As well as in case of user authentication, the single wrapper has worse performance than the best heuristic. The *best-first* and the *discard-worst* wrappers are still significantly better then all examined heuristics. The heuristics-based feature selection as before does not guaranty the improvement of CRR (comparing of the raw row in the table with heuristics rows: *anova*, *anova-2class*, *correlation*, *entropy-2class-bha* and *joint-entropy*).

Table 2. Results of hash generation experiment with different feature selection strategies. Target feature set is limited to 60 features.

	public PIN (77993)			secret PIN			pseudonym			symbol			place		
	CRR	RR	CR	CRR	RR	CR	CRR	RR	CR	CRR	RR	CR	CRR	RR	CR
reference (all 131 feat.)	27.81%	48.72%	4.33%	24.27%	55.64%	4.18%	18.57%	66.67%	3.80%	11.20%	82.31%	4.70%	19.15%	65.39%	3.68%
raw (first 60 features)	21.23%	71.28%	13.75%	19.98%	77.44%	17.40%	15.15%	81.80%	12.09%	7.90%	95.13%	10.94%	16.11%	77.95%	10.17%
anova	20.34%	72.05%	12.74%	17.83%	77.95%	13.62%	12.22%	85.39%	9.83%	7.89%	91.80%	7.58%	10.44%	88.21%	9.09%
anova-2class	19.51%	72.05%	11.07%	18.86%	74.36%	12.09%	13.92%	85.13%	12.97%	12.27%	89.49%	14.02%	13.50%	82.56%	9.57%
correlation	21.29%	69.49%	12.07%	20.02%	72.82%	12.85%	14.01%	83.85%	11.87%	10.72%	90.77%	12.20%	16.89%	77.69%	11.47%
entropy-2class-bha	21.53%	68.97%	12.04%	20.68%	70.26%	11.62%	13.74%	83.08%	10.55%	9.39%	91.03%	9.80%	14.42%	80.77%	9.62%
joint-entropy	23.22%	68.46%	14.91%	19.97%	76.67%	16.61%	14.63%	83.59%	12.85%	9.26%	91.03%	9.55%	14.59%	85.64%	14.81%
simple wrapper	21.83%	65.90%	9.56%	19.28%	69.23%	7.78%	15.22%	76.15%	6.59%	10.09%	86.15%	6.34%	18.44%	69.74%	6.62%
best-first	15.94%	81.54%	13.42%	15.28%	79.49%	10.05%	10.94%	87.44%	9.31%	6.32%	93.59%	6.23%	8.86%	91.28%	9.01%
discard-worst	17.72%	76.92%	12.36%	15.88%	80.51%	12.28%	10.18%	88.72%	9.08%	7.11%	92.05%	6.27%	9.41%	90.26%	9.08%

In further tests only the best feature selection approach is considered. Table 3 shows the user authentication performance (EER) calculated for the system tuned for better hash generation performance (CRR) and vice versa.

As can be seen from figure 3 the EERs are stable in the region of relatively small *tf*. Thus, the EERs in the table do not differ drastically in both scenarios. The highest difference is observed for secret PIN and amounts to 3.76%. The parameters of hash generation scenario can be hence applied for user authentication. In contrast to EERs, the CRRs in user authentication scenario are unacceptable poor. The difference between CRRs in user authentication and hash generation scenarios fluctuates from 13.12% to 20.78%. Therefore, the hash generation performance is very sensible to *tf* selection as well as to feature subset selection and parameters of user authentication scenario can not be applied for hash generation.

Finally, the features were discovered which are presented in resulting subsets of all five semantic classes in both scenarios. These are feature no. 26 (normalized average velocity in x-direction in pixels) and feature no. 30 (total number of sample values). Mentioned features can be considered as always suitable independent of scenario and semantic class. Features no. 55 (numeric integration of y-values for 4th one-fifth time period), 67 (path length of the convex hulls of segments vs. path length of the bounding box) and 76 (number of intersections within the sample itself) are included in resulting subsets of all semantics of hash generation scenario. Features no. 14 (maximum absolute pressure), 18 (horizontal azimuth of centroid from origin), 27 (normalized average velocity in y-direction in pixels), 73 (number of minimum points in the y-signal) and 83 (number of intersections of the horizontal line Y3 with the sample) are in all resulting subsets of user authentication scenario. The features no. 14, 18, 27 and 73 are presented in 9 of 10 subsets and, therefore, can be considered as almost always suitable for both scenarios independent on semantic class.

Table 3. Joint results of user authentication and hash generation experiments on the 60 features subsets created with in each case best feature selection strategy

	CRR	RR	CR	EER	T_{EER}
	public PIN (77993)				
user auth., ref. EER (131 feat.)	39.41%	21.80%	0.61%	16.55%	5.3895
user auth., opt. EER (discard-worst, 60 feat.)	33.37%	34.62%	1.35%	14.88%	3.0436
hash gen., ref. CRR (131 feat.)	27.81%	48.72%	4.33%	17.42%	1.7601
hash gen., opt. CRR (best-first, 60 feat.)	15.94%	81.54%	13.42%	16.58%	0.2224
	secret PIN				
user auth., ref. EER (131 feat.)	40.83%	18.46%	0.12%	13.42%	6.7085
user auth., opt. EER (discard-worst, 60 feat.)	36.06%	28.21%	0.32%	11.41%	3.6485
hash gen., ref. CRR (131 feat.)	24.27%	55.64%	4.18%	15.56%	1.5515
hash gen., opt. CRR (best-first, 60 feat.)	15.28%	79.49%	10.05%	15.17%	0.359
	pseudonym				
user auth., ref. EER (131 feat.)	32.91%	34.36%	0.18%	10.96%	6.8164
user auth., opt. EER (best-first, 60 feat.)	24.07%	52.56%	0.70%	9.73%	2.8669
hash gen., ref. CRR (131 feat.)	18.57%	66.67%	3.80%	12.20%	1.2674
hash gen., opt. CRR (discard-worst, 60 feat.)	10.18%	88.72%	9.08%	10.50%	0.109
	symbol				
user auth., ref. EER (131 feat.)	28.68%	42.82%	0.18%	8.30%	5.8032
user auth., opt. EER (best-first, 60 feat.)	19.44%	61.80%	0.67%	5.27%	1.9286
hash gen., ref. CRR (131 feat.)	11.20%	82.31%	4.70%	8.74%	0.6347
hash gen., opt. CRR (best-first, 60 feat.)	6.32%	93.59%	6.23%	6.34%	0.0123
	place				
user auth., ref. EER (131 feat.)	34.43%	31.28%	0.14%	9.79%	6.583
user auth., opt. EER (best-first, 60 feat.)	27.14%	46.15%	0.43%	7.20%	2.7441
hash gen., ref. CRR (131 feat.)	19.15%	65.39%	3.68%	11.49%	1.4626
hash gen., opt. CRR (best-first, 60 feat.)	8.86%	91.28%	9.01%	8.98%	0

All features, which posses some variance, are included to at least one of 10 resulting subsets. There are only three features discovered, which are included into only one subset and, therefore, can be considered as almost useless. These are features no. 38 (number of pixels in second row, third column), 107 (fmapped size of enclosed areas), and 130 (fmapped speed at the inflection point of the sample). All 10 features without any variance are automatically discarded as absolutely useless.

6 Conclusion

It has been shown that the wrong parameterization, or to be more precisely, false tolerance factor determination can drastically degrade a hash generation performance. Contrariwise the intelligent selection of tolerance factor and feature set reduction can significantly improve the performance of both hash generation and user authentication of the considered system. The comparison of different feature selection strategies has shown that forward and backward selection algorithms have always better results than considered heuristics. However, the anova test for hash generation and anova-2class test for user authentication show better results than simple wrapper and, therefore, are very useful for immediate estimation of particular feature quality in comparison to other ones. Through the best feature selection approach the EERs were improved, at an average, to 19.85% and the CRRs, at an average, to 44.44%. The most appropriate semantic symbol has the RR of 93.59% with CR of 6.23%, which is nearly sufficient rate to practically consider the generated biometric hash as a basis for cryptographic key generation. The EER for the same system configuration amounts 6.34% and even 5.27% for the configuration specified for user authentication scenario. This rate is very promising regarding the fact that handwriting samples used for enrollment, parameters tuning and tests are separated in time by at least one month. Further work will be devoted to the extraction of further features with immediate heuristics based evaluation of their quality and an investigation of key entropy. Another objective is to extend the BioHash algorithm by means of user based feature selection.

Acknowledgments. This work is partly supported by the Deutsche Forschungsgemeinschaft (DFG, German Research Foundation, project Writing Print). Our special thanks go to Prof. Jana Dittmann for fruitful discussions on biometric hashing.

References

1. Dodis, Y., Reyzin, L., Smith, A.: Fuzzy Extractors: How to Generate Strong Keys from Biometrics and Other Noisy Data. In: Cachin, C., Camenisch, J.L. (eds.) EUROCRYPT 2004. LNCS, vol. 3027, pp. 523–540. Springer, Heidelberg (2004)
2. Guyon, I., Elisseeff, A.: An Introduction to Variable and Feature Selection. Journal of Machine Learning Research 3, 1157–1182 (2003)
3. Jain, A.K., Nandakumar, K., Nagar, A.: Biometric Template Security. EURASIP Journal on Advances in Signal Processing, Article ID 579416 (2008)
4. John, G.H., Kohavi, R., Pfleger, K.: Irrelevant Features and the Subset Selection Problem. In: Proc. of the International Conference on Machine Learning, pp. 121–129 (1994)
5. Juels, A., Wattenberg, M.: A Fuzzy Commitment Scheme. In: Proc. of the ACM Conference on Computer and Communications Security, pp. 28–36 (1999)
6. Kumar, A., Zhang, D.: Biometric Recognition Using Feature Selection and Combination. In: Kanade, T., Jain, A., Ratha, N.K. (eds.) AVBPA 2005. LNCS, vol. 3546, pp. 813–822. Springer, Heidelberg (2005)
7. Scheidat, T., Vielhauer, C., Dittmann, J.: Advanced studies on reproducibility of biometric hashes. In: Schouten, B., Juul, N.C., Drygajlo, A., Tistarelli, M. (eds.) BIOID 2008. LNCS, vol. 5372, pp. 150–159. Springer, Heidelberg (2008)
8. Sutcu, Y., Li, Q., Memon, N.: Protecting Biometric Templates with Sketch: Theory and Practice. IEEE Trans. on Information Forensics and Security 2(3), 503–512 (2007)
9. Vielhauer, C.: Biometric User Authentication for IT Security: From Fundamentals to Handwriting. Springer, New York (2006)

Eigen-Model Projections for Protected On-line Signature Recognition

Emanuele Maiorana[1], Enrique Argones Rúa[2], Jose Luis Alba Castro[2], and Patrizio Campisi[1]

[1] University Roma Tre, Department of Applied Electronics
[2] University of Vigo, Department of Signal Theory and Communications

Abstract. The protection of the templates stored in a biometric recognition system represents an issue of paramount importance for the security and privacy of the enrolled users, and directly affects the successful deployment of the system itself. In this paper we propose a protected on-line signature recognition system where the properties of Universal Background Models are exploited to provide a small dimensionality and a limited intra-class variability signature representation. The reported experimental results show that the employed signature representation and protection scheme allow to reach high recognition accuracy while providing protection to the considered biometric data.

1 Introduction

Automatic people recognition by means of biometric data is nowadays employed in many applications and services due to the greater convenience, comfort and security they offer with respect to traditional authentication methods based on passwords or tokens. However, the use of biometrics also involves serious risks not affecting other approaches: if a characteristic is somehow stolen or copied, it can be hard to replace. Moreover, biometric data can contain sensitive information regarding the users health or habits, which can be used in an unauthorized manner for malicious or undesired intents [1]. Therefore, when designing a biometric recognition system, such possibilities have to be carefully considered, trying to provide countermeasures to the possible attacks which can be perpetrated at the system's vulnerable points [2].

In this paper we address the issue of biometric template security by proposing a protected on-line signature recognition system relying on Universal Backgroung Models (UBMs). Specifically, some approaches already proposed for the protection of biometrics are discussed in Section 2. Universal background modeling is introduced in Section 3, while the proposed protection scheme is presented in Section 4, and its security is discussed in Section 5. The experimental results proving the effectiveness of the proposed approach are then discussed in Section 6, while some conclusions are finally drawn in Section 7.

C. Vielhauer et al. (Eds.): BioID 2011, LNCS 6583, pp. 49–60, 2011.

2 Biometric Template Protection

The unauthorized acquisition of the templates generated from an original biometrics is widely recognized as one of the most dangerous threat regarding the users' privacy and security. In fact, although it was commonly believed that it would not be possible to reconstruct the original characteristics from the corresponding extracted templates, some concrete counterexamples, which contradict this assumption, have been provided in the recent literature [3].

In the recent past some techniques for template protection have been proposed. Roughly speaking, they can be classified as *feature transformation approaches* and *biometric cryptosystems* [4].

Transformation-based approaches have been introduced in [2]. When implementing a feature transformation approach, a function dependent on some parameters, which can be used as a key, is applied to the input biometrics. The protected templates are thus given by transformed versions of the original data. Invertible functions are employed in *salting* schemes, whose security therefore relies on the protection of the defining transformation parameters [5]. One-way functions are conversely employed in *non-invertible transform* approaches, thus producing templates from which it is computationally hard to retrieve the original data, even if the transform's defining parameters are known. A cartesian, a polar and a functional transform have been applied to fingerprints' minutiae in [6]. Three general non-invertible transforms designed for biometrics which can be expressed in terms of a set of sequences have also been described in [7]. However, it is in general difficult to quantitatively determine the actual hardness of the transformation's inversion process.

Biometric cryptosystems provide the means to integrate biometric recognition into cryptographic protocols, and can be classified as *key generation* schemes, where binary keys are directly created from the acquired biometrics, and *key binding* schemes, which store information obtained by combining biometric data with randomly selected keys. The main issues characterizing key generation approaches rely on the stability of the resulting cryptographic key, which typically results in recognition performances significantly lower than those of their unprotected counterparts [8]. A key binding system can be twofold: it can be used to protect a biometric template by means of a binary key, thus securing a biometric recognition system, or to release a cryptographic key only when its owner presents a specific biometric trait. In both cases a secret key, independent of the considered biometrics, is combined during enrollment with a reference template to generate the *helper data*, from which it should be impossible to retrieve information about both the original biometric trait and the secret. The helper data is then used during authentication in conjunction with a query biometrics to retrieve the key. Error-correcting codes are commonly employed to manage the intra-class variability of the considered templates. One of the most commonly employed key binding frameworks is the fuzzy commitment scheme [9], already applied to fingerprints [10], face [11], and iris [12], among others. The fuzzy commitment is employed in this paper to provide protection to the signature representation described in Section 3.

3 Universal Background Models

A UBM is a reference template which can be used to model general, person-independent biometric observations. Such general model should be estimated by processing a large number of biometric acquisitions, taken from as many different subjects as possible. The biometrics of a specific user could then be represented with a model obtained by updating the well-trained parameters in the UBM via a Bayesian adaptation to the characteristics of the acquired users traits. Since their first introduction in [13], UBMs have been extensively employed for biometric authentication purposes, as in [13] for speaker, in [14] for face, and in [15] for signature verification. In all these cases, a given biometric measurement can be expressed in terms of a set of F discrete-time sequences, as described for on-line signature in Section 3.1, and the acquired dataset can be modeled by means of hidden Markov models (HMMs).

Specifically, having collected a large database with sample acquisitions, an UBM can be trained by means of the Baum-Welch algorithm [16]. This procedure requires an initial estimate of the samples belonging to each of the S state of the HMM. In order to provide such information, the LBG algorithm [17] is commonly employed to cluster the available data. The estimated UBM is then characterized in terms of the triple $\lambda^{(\mathrm{UBM})} = \{A, B, \Pi\}$, where A is the state transition matrix, B is the set of state-dependent output probability density functions, while Π is the set of initial state probabilities. The state-dependent output probability density functions are usually modeled with Gaussian Mixture Models (GMMs), and can be therefore specified in terms of the weights $w_{i,j}$, the means vectors $\boldsymbol{\mu}_{i,j}$ and the covariance matrices $\boldsymbol{\Sigma}_{i,j}$, $i \in \{1, \ldots, S\}$, $j \in \{1, \ldots, M\}$, where S is the number of states in the HMM, and M is the number of Gaussian Mixtures in each state-dependent output probability density function.

In order to derive a template representing a specific user u, an adaptation of the UBM to the characteristics of a given set of acquisitions has to be performed. Specifically, such adaptation can be applied over the means $\boldsymbol{\mu}_{i,j}$ of the HMM [13]. When following the *maximum a posteriori* (MAP) adaptation [18] for this purpose, it is assumed that E acquisitions $\mathbf{O}^{(u)e}$, $e = 1, \ldots, E$, of the biometrics of a given user u are available during enrollment. Each considered observation consists of F sequences $\mathbf{o}_f^{(u)e}[l]$, with $f = 1, \ldots, F$ and $l = 1, \ldots, L_e$, being L_e the length of the e-th enrollment acquisition. Having indicated with $\boldsymbol{\varrho}_l^{(u)e} = \left[\mathbf{o}_1^{(u)e}[l], \ldots, \mathbf{o}_F^{(u)e}[l]\right]'$ a vector comprising the values of the F considered features at discrete time l, the *Maximum-Likelihood* (ML) estimates of the adapted model means for the j-th Gaussian of the i-th state of the user u can be calculated as

$$ {}^{\mathrm{ML}}\boldsymbol{\mu}_{i,j}^{(u)} = \frac{1}{q_{i,j}^{(u)}} \sum_{e=1}^{E} \sum_{l=1}^{L_e} \eta_{i,l}^{(u)e} \frac{w_{i,j} \mathcal{N}(\boldsymbol{\chi}|\boldsymbol{\mu}_{i,j}, \boldsymbol{\Sigma}_{i,j})\big|_{\chi=\boldsymbol{\varrho}_l^{(u)e}}}{\sum_{j=1}^{M} w_{i,j} \mathcal{N}(\boldsymbol{\chi}|\boldsymbol{\mu}_{i,j}, \boldsymbol{\Sigma}_{i,j})\big|_{\chi=\boldsymbol{\varrho}_l^{(u)e}}} \boldsymbol{\varrho}_l^{(u)e} \tag{1} $$

which represents a vector with F coefficients, where $\mathcal{N}(\boldsymbol{\chi}|\boldsymbol{\mu}_{i,j}, \boldsymbol{\Sigma}_{i,j})\big|_{\chi=\boldsymbol{\varrho}_l^{(u)e}}$ denotes a multivariate normal probability density function, with mean vector $\boldsymbol{\mu}_{i,j}$

and covariance matrix $\boldsymbol{\Sigma}_{i,j}$, evaluated at $\boldsymbol{\varrho}_l^{(u)e}$, $\eta_{i,l}^{(u)e}$ represents the probability of state i at the discrete time l for the enrollment observation $\mathbf{O}^{(u)e}$, while $q_{i,j}^{(u)}$ is the soft count of samples belonging to the j-th Gaussian mixture of the i-th state given by

$$q_{i,j}^{(u)} = \sum_{e=1}^{E}\sum_{l=1}^{L_e} \eta_{i,l}^{(u)e} \frac{w_{i,j}\mathcal{N}(\boldsymbol{\chi}|\boldsymbol{\mu}_{i,j}, \boldsymbol{\Sigma}_{i,j})\big|_{\boldsymbol{\chi}=\boldsymbol{\varrho}_l^{(u)e}}}{\sum_{j=1}^{M} w_{i,j}\mathcal{N}(\boldsymbol{\chi}|\boldsymbol{\mu}_{i,j}, \boldsymbol{\Sigma}_{i,j})\big|_{\boldsymbol{\chi}=\boldsymbol{\varrho}_l^{(u)e}}}. \tag{2}$$

The user's model is characterized by the MAP adapted means, denoted as $\widehat{\boldsymbol{\mu}}_{i,j}^{(u)}$, which can be calculated from ${}^{\mathrm{ML}}\boldsymbol{\mu}_{i,j}^{(u)}$ and $\boldsymbol{\mu}_{i,j}$ as described in [19]. According to the approach generally performed [13], the authentication phase then relies on the evaluation of the log-likelihood ratio of a new query acquisition between the stored user's model, and the UBM.

However, the MAP adaptation can be also performed for a single biometric acquisition, as if $E = 1$. It would be therefore possible to compute the adapted model means $\widehat{\boldsymbol{\mu}}_{i,j}^{(u)e}$, for all the enrollment acquisitions $e \in \{1, \ldots, E\}$, and then perform the matching process by resorting to a simple computation of the Mahalanobis distance between the MAP representations computed during enrollment and the one derived from the query biometrics.

Unfortunately, the MAP procedure can adapt only mixtures which are actually present in the enrollment data provided by a user, thus resulting in possible bad adaptations, characterized by a high intra-class variability. The authentication performance of a system employing the vectors $\widehat{\boldsymbol{\mu}}_{i,j}^{(u)e}$ as biometrics' feature-based representation would be therefore unacceptable, as empirically demonstrated in Section 6. It is then necessary to resort to a different adaptation process, that is, the *eigen-model* adaptation [20].

According to this approach, and having indicated as

$$\mathbf{m} = \left[\boldsymbol{\mu}'_{1,1}, \ldots, \boldsymbol{\mu}'_{1,M}, \ldots, \boldsymbol{\mu}'_{S,M}\right]' \tag{3}$$

the UBM means supervector composed by $S \cdot M \cdot F$ coefficients, it is assumed that the means supervector characterizing a given user u can be written as:

$$\mathbf{m}^{(u)} = \mathbf{m} + \mathbf{V}\mathbf{g}^{(u)}, \tag{4}$$

where $\mathbf{V}$ is a $(S{\cdot}M{\cdot}F){\times}T$ user independent projection matrix whose columns are eigen mean differences supervectors, and $\mathbf{g}^{(u)}$ is the eigen-model user-dependent projection vector with T coefficients. The dimension T of this projection vector is a system design parameter, and it is therefore possible to easily control the length of the user templates. Different approaches for obtaining both the projection coefficients and the projection matrix can be found in the literature, and the most of them is based on Principal Component Analysis (PCA) [20] and eigen-model MAP [21]. When following this latter approach, the matrix $\mathbf{V}$ is estimated by means of the Expectation-Maximization (EM) algorithm from a set of users $\mathcal{U}$ that may include the one used for the UBM training. From the acquisitions taken from a specific user, it is then possible to construct an $(F \cdot M \cdot S) \times (F \cdot M \cdot S)$ block-diagonal matrix $\mathbf{Q}^{(u)}$, whose $M \cdot S$ blocks are given by the $F \times F$ matrices $q_{i,j}^{(u)} \mathbf{I}_F$, $i \in \{1, \ldots, S\}$, $j \in \{1, \ldots, M\}$, where $\mathbf{I}_F$ is the $F \times F$ identity matrix. Let also $\boldsymbol{\Omega}$ be a $(F \cdot S \cdot M) \times (F \cdot S \cdot M)$ matrix built the same way as $\mathbf{Q}^{(u)}$, using the UBM covariance matrices $\boldsymbol{\Sigma}_{i,j}$, $i \in \{1, \ldots, S\}$ and $j \in \{1, \ldots, M\}$, as diagonal blocks. Let us define the $T \times T$ matrix $\mathbf{Y}^{(u)}$ as:

$$\mathbf{Y}^{(u)} = \mathbf{I}_T + \mathbf{V}' \boldsymbol{\Omega}^{-1} \mathbf{Q}^{(u)} \mathbf{V} \tag{5}$$

Having then defined the vector

$$\mathbf{s}_{i,j}^{(u)} = \sum_{e=1}^{E} \sum_{l=1}^{L_e} \eta_{i,j,l}^{(u)e} (\mathbf{o}_l^{(u,e)} - \boldsymbol{\mu}_{i,j}) \tag{6}$$

with size F, where $\eta_{i,j,l}^{(u)e}$ is the posterior probability of Gaussian mixture j in state i at discrete time l for the acquisition sequence $\mathbf{O}^{(u)e}$, let the vector $\mathbf{H}^{(u)}$ with size $F \cdot S \cdot M$ be the concatenation of the vectors $\mathbf{s}_{i,j}^{(u)}$ as in (3). As shown in [21], for any given person u, the posterior distribution of $\mathbf{g}^{(u)}$ is also Gaussian, with its mean expressed as:

$$\mathcal{E}\left\{\mathbf{g}^{(u)}\right\} = \bar{\mathbf{g}}^{(u)} = \left(\mathbf{Y}^{(u)}\right)^{-1} \mathbf{V}' \boldsymbol{\Omega}^{-1} \mathbf{H}^{(u)} \tag{7}$$

and covariance matrix:

$$\mathcal{E}\left\{\left(\mathbf{g}^{(u)} - \bar{\mathbf{g}}^{(u)}\right)\left(\mathbf{g}^{(u)} - \bar{\mathbf{g}}^{(u)}\right)'\right\} = \mathbf{Y}^{-1(u)} \tag{8}$$

The inter-class mean of the eigen-model's projection coefficients vectors $\mathbf{g}^{(u)}$ is zero [21].

From (7) and (4), it is trivial to derive $\mathcal{E}\left\{\mathbf{m}^{(u)}\right\} = \bar{\mathbf{m}}^{(u)} = \mathbf{m}^{(u)} + \mathbf{V}\bar{\mathbf{g}}'^{(u)}$ if the matching process has to be performed through log-likelihood ratio tests. Conversely, in the proposed system we directly exploit the low-dimensional mean eigen-model projections $\bar{\mathbf{g}}^{(u)}$ to compare different biometrics acquisitions. As already discussed for the MAP representation, also with the eigen-model approach it is possible to independently process each given biometrics, thus using the mean eigen-model projections as a feature-based representation. It is also worth specifying that the whole eigen-model adaptation can be performed separately for each HMM state, leading to representations characterized by an $R = S \cdot T$ coefficients. This is indeed the approach followed in the proposed systems.

3.1 Signature Observations

In order to apply the proposed eigen-model representation to on-line signature biometrics, it is assumed that the horizontal $x[l]$ and vertical $y[l]$ position trajectories of the signature, together with the signal pressure $p[l]$, the pen elevation

$\gamma[l]$ and azimuth $\phi[l]$, where $l = 1, \ldots, L$ is the discrete time index, can be acquired by means of a digitizing tablet. Additional dynamic features are derived from the aforementioned characteristics, namely the path velocity magnitude velocity $v[l]$ and its regularized logarithm $\log(v[l] + 1)$, the total acceleration magnitude $a[l]$, the path-tangent angle $\theta[l]$, the curvature radius $\rho[l]$ and the regularized logarithm $\log(p[l] + 1)$ of the pressure $p[l]$, are then derived. Having defined the row vector $\mathbf{w}_l$ as

$$\mathbf{w}_l = [x[l]\ y[l]\ p[l]\ \gamma[l]\ \phi[l]\ v[l]\ a[l]\ \theta[l]\ \rho[l]\ \log(1 + v[l])\ \log(1 + p[l])], \quad (9)$$

each signature acquisition is then defined in matrix notation as:

$$\mathbf{O} = \begin{pmatrix} \dot{\mathbf{w}}_1 & \ddot{\mathbf{w}}_1 \\ \vdots & \vdots \\ \dot{\mathbf{w}}_L & \ddot{\mathbf{w}}_L \end{pmatrix} \quad (10)$$

where the upper dot notation denotes the time-derivative operator. $F = 22$ sequences are therefore employed to represent the considered on-line signatures.

4 Proposed Protection Scheme

The architectures of the proposed enrollment and authentication schemes, derived from the application of the fuzzy commitment paradigm [9] to the signature representation $\bar{\mathbf{g}}^{(u)}$, are illustrated in Figure 1.

Specifically, during the enrollment a number E of biometric measurements are recorded for each user u. The acquired biometrics are then individually processed, in order to extract the eigen-model projection vectors $\bar{\mathbf{g}}^{(u)e}$, $e = 1, \ldots, E$. The vector $\mathbf{d}^{(u)} = \frac{1}{E}\sum_{e=1}^{E} \bar{\mathbf{g}}^{(u)e}$, containing the mean values of the evaluated projections, is then used to characterize the acquired data.

In order to binarize $\mathbf{d}^{(u)}$, a comparison with a threshold value has then to be performed. Specifically, it is possible to demonstrate that the eigen-model projections can be modeled with Gaussian distributions having an inter-class

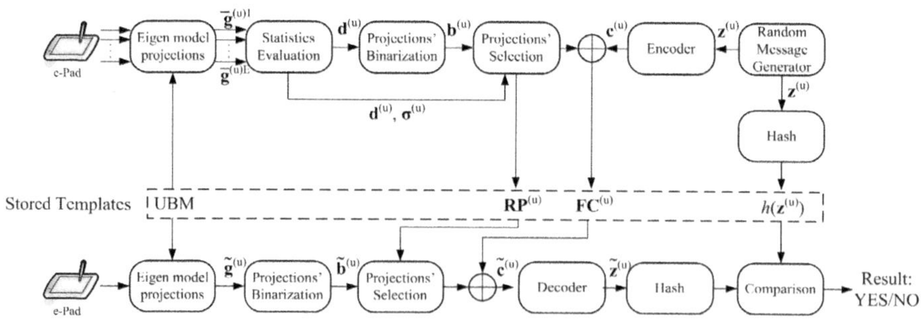

Fig. 1. Architectures of the proposed enrollment and authentication schemes

mean equal to zero, when evaluated over a large population of users. This value is therefore employed to perform the binarization of the coefficients as

$$\mathbf{b}^{(u)}[r] = \begin{cases} 0 \text{ if } \mathbf{d}^{(u)}[r] < 0 \\ 1 \text{ if } \mathbf{d}^{(u)}[r] \geq 0 \end{cases}, \quad r = 1, \ldots, R, \tag{11}$$

The extracted biometric information is then protected by means of error correcting codes. Specifically, a random binary message $\mathbf{z}^{(u)}$ with k bits, representing the secret key, is generated. An (n, k, t) encoder, taking k bit input strings, is then selected, and employed to generate a codeword $\mathbf{c}^{(u)}$ with length n. The error correcting capability t of the employed code is selected in order to take into account the intra-class variability of the system's users, and therefore directly affects the verification performance of the proposed system. In case the dimension R of the eigen-model projection vectors in (4) is selected to be equal to n, the system computes the fuzzy commitment $\mathbf{FC}^{(u)} = FC(\mathbf{b}^{(u)}, \mathbf{c}^{(u)}) = \mathbf{b}^{(u)} \oplus \mathbf{c}^{(u)}$. A hashed version $h(\mathbf{z}^{(u)})$ of $\mathbf{z}^{(u)}$ is then stored together with $\mathbf{FC}^{(u)}$.

If $R > n$, a procedure to select, for each user, the most relevant projections in the eigen-model space, is needed. Specifically, it would be highly desirable, for each user, to select the n projections with the greater stability, in order to provide a robust biometric representation when performing the binarization in (11). By taking into account that the considered features can be modeled with Gaussian distributions, and that the binarization process is performed by means of a threshold value set to zero, a reliability measure $\boldsymbol{\delta}^{(u)}[r]$ for the r-th projection of the biometric characteristics taken from user u is defined as

$$\boldsymbol{\delta}^{(u)}[r] = \frac{|\, \mathbf{d}^{(u)}[r] \,|}{\boldsymbol{\sigma}^{(u)}[r]} \tag{12}$$

where

$$\boldsymbol{\sigma}^{(u)}[r] = \sqrt{\frac{1}{E-1} \sum_{e=1}^{E} (\bar{\mathbf{g}}^{(u)e}[r] - \mathbf{d}^{(u)}[r])^2}, \tag{13}$$

is the standard deviation of the r-th projection, $r = 1, \ldots, R$, estimated during the enrollment.

For each user the projections of the eigen-model space are then ordered according to their estimated reliability, and only the n coefficients having the largest values of $\boldsymbol{\delta}^{(u)}[r]$ are selected. Their indexes are collected in a vector $\mathbf{RP}^{(u)}$, which is stored in the databes together with the fuzzy commitment $\mathbf{FC}^{(u)}$ and the hashed secret $h(\mathbf{z}^{(u)})$.

During the authentication phase, the biometric query provided by a user is first processed according to the system's UBM and projection matrix $\mathbf{V}$, in order to determine its eigen-model representation $\tilde{\mathbf{g}}^{(u)}$. The binarization described in (11) is then applied to $\tilde{\mathbf{g}}^{(u)}$ in order to generate the binary string $\tilde{\mathbf{b}}^{(u)}$, which is combined with the stored fuzzy commitment to reconstruct a possibly corrupted codeword $\tilde{\mathbf{c}}^{(u)} = \tilde{\mathbf{b}}^{(u)} \oplus \mathbf{FC}^{(u)}$. Having selected a decoder corresponding to the encoder used during enrollment, an attempt to recover the original message $\mathbf{z}^{(u)}$

from $\tilde{\mathbf{c}}^{(u)}$, which is affected by errors due to the intra-class variability of the user's biometrics, is performed. If the correction capability of the selected code is able to correct the differences between $\mathbf{c}^{(u)}$ and $\tilde{\mathbf{c}}^{(u)}$, the hash of the decoded message $\tilde{\mathbf{z}}^{(u)}$ matches the stored template $h(\mathbf{z}^{(u)})$, thus allowing the system to authenticate the presented user.

5 Security Discussion

As for the security of biometric cryptosystems, it is worth noting that an attacker can attempt a brute force attack to determine $\mathbf{z}^{(u)}$ by analyzing all the possible binary strings with length k. The parameter k characterizing the employed error correcting code therefore express the *key strength* [22]. The possibility that the fuzzy commitment stored in a system can be exploited by an attacker in order to leak some information regarding users biometrics has been analyzed in [23]. Specifically, the entropy loss due to the availability of the fuzzy commitment $\mathbf{FC}^{(u)}$ can be expressed as $\Lambda = n - k$, and therefore increases with the error correction capability t employed in the system, when keeping fixed the parameter n. More in detail, the expression $\Lambda = n - k$ for the entropy loss in a fuzzy commitment scheme is derived for biometric binary representations $\mathbf{b}^{(u)}$ with uniform distribution and maximum entropy. Therefore the security of a key binding scheme depends also on the characteristics of the employed biometric representation, and not only on the framework employed to protect them. The privacy and secrecy aspects of biometric cryptosystems have also been deeply analyzed and discussed in [24], where the secrecy leakage of a cryptosystem has been defined as the mutual information between the employed secret and the stored template, and the privacy leakage as the mutual information between the original biometric template and the stored data. These measures have been explicitly evaluated for a fuzzy commitment scheme in [25], where the same results presented in [23] have been obtained for a system characterized by a memoryless totally-simmetric distribution for the employed biometrics.

The representation an on-line signature in terms of its eigen-model projections is advantageous for the security characteristics of the proposed protection scheme, due to the fact that the mean projections $\bar{\mathbf{g}}^{(u)}[r]$, $r = 1, \ldots, R$, computed as in (4) are mutually uncorrelated. Moreover, by performing a binarization with the inter-class mean as in (11), the produced binary vectors $\mathbf{b}^{(u)}$ are characterized by high entropy. Therefore, the properties of the employed biometric representation allow characterizing the security and the privacy characteristics of the proposed system by the secret-key versus privacy-leakage rate regions described in [25].

6 Experimental Results

An extensive set of experimental results is performed using the public version of the MCYT on-line signature database [26], which includes 100 users. For each user, 25 genuine signatures and 25 skilled forgeries are made available. Each signature is encoded through the matrix $\mathbf{O}$ given in (10). It is assumed that $E = 10$ signatures are taken from each user for the enrollment phase, while the

Table 1. Comparison between the authentication performance of systems using the MAP signature representation and the eigen-model-based one in terms of the EER(%)

Log-likelihood measure		Mahalanobis distance	
MAP	Eigen-model	MAP	Eigen-model
3.45	4.95	31.47	7.15

remaining 15 signatures are used to evaluate the False Rejection Rate (FRR). The False Acceptance Rate (FAR) is computed by trying to authenticate the 25 forged signatures available for each enrolled user.

Table 1 reports a comparison, in terms of Equal Error Rate (EER), between the systems exploiting the characteristics of a MAP-based signature representation and those of an eigen-model-based system. The dimension R of the mean eigen-model projection vector $\bar{\mathbf{g}}^{(u)}$ is set to $S \cdot T = 4 \cdot 75 = 300$. Specifically, the comparison between the two biometrics representations takes into account two different matching strategies: in the first one the authentication phase relies on the classical log-likelihood ratio measure which can be computed from the model stored in the database and the acquisition provided during authentication. In this case the MAP representation outperforms the eigen-model approach. The usefulness of employing the eigen-model biometric representation becomes evident when comparing the recognition rates achievable when performing authentication by means of the Mahalanobis distance between the feature vectors in both the MAP and in the eigen-model space. Due to the high intra-class variability which characterizes the MAP modelization, this representation cannot be used to directly match the feature vectors generated with its application. On the other hand, the eigen-model features allow performing user verification with good recognition rates also when the matching process is performed directly by comparing the extracted vectors, instead of resorting to the log-likelihood available when using the entire modelization.

Such experimental evidence is fundamental to design the proposed protected biometric cryptosystem. In fact, it would be impossible to estimate the log-likelihood of a model which has to be protected by means of the fuzzy commitment. Conversely, the proposed protected scheme performs authentication by comparing the hashes of the two messages $\mathbf{z}^u$ and $\tilde{\mathbf{z}}^u$, which are different if the Hamming distance between the binary vectors $\mathbf{b}^u$ and $\tilde{\mathbf{b}}^u$ is greater than the error correction capability t of the employed code. According to the results presented in Table 1, comparing the binarized version of the MAP vectors would provide unacceptable verification rates, while it seems that the eigen-model representation can be employed for such task. Specifically, the results which could be obtained by selecting different thresholds for the maximum Hamming distance which have to separate $\tilde{\mathbf{b}}^u$ from $\mathbf{b}^u$ to let a user to be recognized, are reported in Figure 2. The procedure described in Section 4 for selecting the user's most reliable projections during the enrollment phase is employed to obtain the results in Figure 2.b, 2.c and 2.d, corresponding to systems using $n = 127$, $n = 63$ and $n = 31$ coefficients, respectively. The EER achievable when considering 300

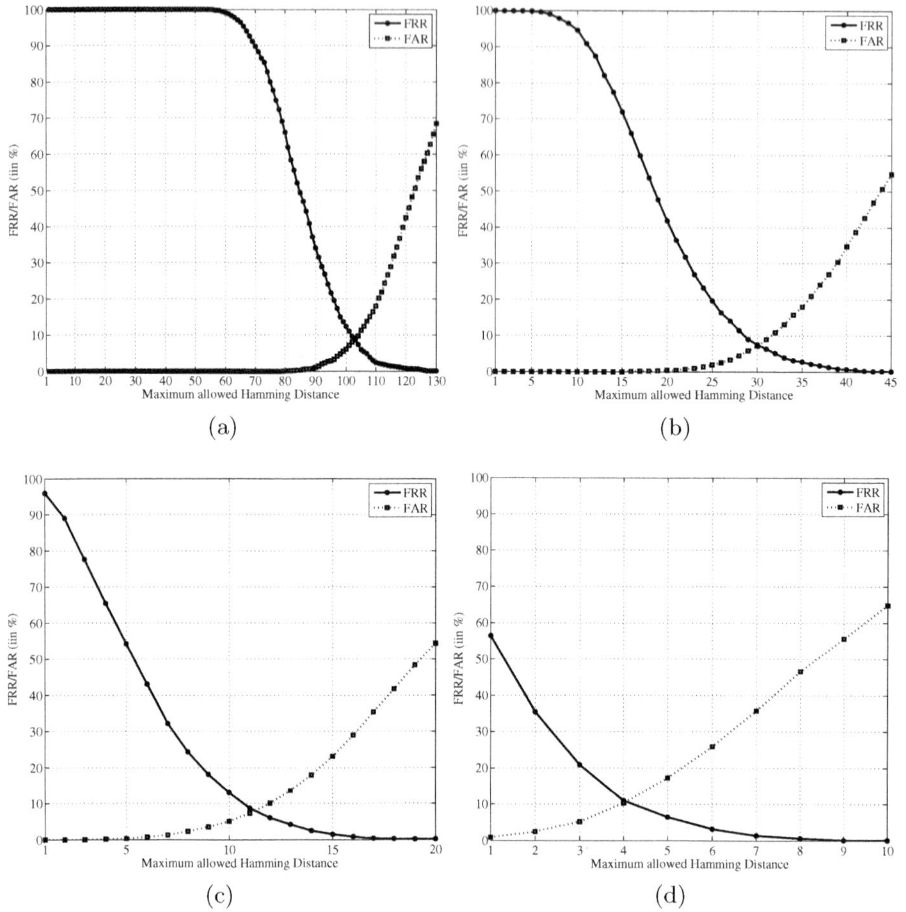

Fig. 2. Verification rates for different values n of considered eigen-model projections, with $R = 300$. (a): $n = 300$; (b): $n = 127$; (c): $n = 63$; (d): $n = 31$.

coefficients for signature representation is 8.79%. It becomes 7.65% and 8.07% when using respectively 127 and 63 coefficients, while EER = 11.80% for $n = 31$. However, it is worth remarking that only a limited range of error correction capabilities are in practice available when using a specific error correcting code in a protected system. Specifically, the verification rates achievable when employing BCH codes [27] in the proposed cryptosystem are given in Figure 3. As can be seen, increasing the number of projections considered in the employed signature representation reduces the amount of operating points working at low FRR. Although the best verification performances are obtained when the dimension of the employed feature vectors and of the BCH codeword is set to $n = 127$, this system configuration does not allow to work close to the EER as shown in Figure 3. However, by setting $n = 63$, it is possible to choose an operating point close to the EER (8.07%).

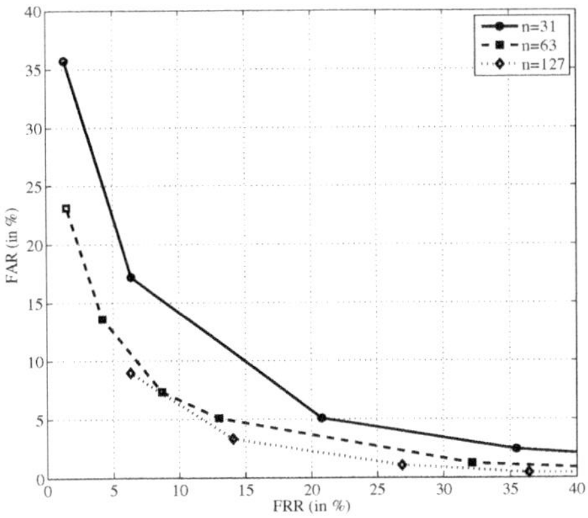

Fig. 3. ROC for the proposed protected recognition system, with $n \in \{127, 63, 31\}$

7 Conclusions

In this paper we have exploited the properties of UBM to derive an on-line signature representation relying on the mean eigen-model projections, which can be used to perform authentication in a protected system based on the fuzzy commitment scheme. The proposed eigen-model representation is characterized by an intra-class variability significantly lower than that the one shown by the MAP projections, and it allows expressing the considered biometrics using low-dimensionality feature vector. The obtained experimental results testify that the eigen-model representation provides a promising approach to perform on-line signature verification in a protected domain, allowing to reach good verification performances while providing security to the considered biometric templates.

References

1. Prabhakar, S., Pankanti, S., Jain, A.K.: Biometric Recognition: Security and Privacy Concerns. IEEE Security & Privacy Magazine 1(2), 33–42 (2003)
2. Ratha, N.K., Connell, J.H., Bolle, R.: Enhancing Security and Privacy of Biometric-based Authentication Systems. IBM Systems Journal 40(3), 614–634 (2001)
3. Cappelli, R., Lumini, A., Maio, D., Maltoni, D.: Fingerprint Image Reconstruction from Standard Templates. IEEE Transactions on PAMI 29(9), 1489–1503 (2007)
4. Jain, A.K., Nandakumar, K., Nagar, A.: Biometric Template Security. EURASIP Journal on Advances in Sign. Proc., Special Issue on Biometrics (2008)
5. Goh, A., Ngo, D.C.L.: Computation of Cryptographic Keys from Face Biometrics. In: Lioy, A., Mazzocchi, D. (eds.) CMS 2003. LNCS, vol. 2828, pp. 1–13. Springer, Heidelberg (2003)
6. Ratha, N., Chikkerur, S., Connell, J.H., Bolle, R.M.: Generating Cancelable Fingerprint Templates. IEEE Transactions on PAMI 29(4), 561–572 (2007)
7. Maiorana, E., Campisi, P., Fierrez, J., Ortega-Garcia, J., Neri, A.: Cancelable templates for sequence-based biometrics with application to on-line signature recognition. Transactions on System Man and Cybernetics Part A 40(3), 525–538 (2010)
8. Vielhauer, C., Steinmetz, R.: Handwriting: Feature Correlation Analysis for Biometric Hashes. EURASIP Journal on Applied Signal Processing, Special Issue on Biometric, 542–558 (2004)

9. Juels, A., Wattenberg, M.: A Fuzzy Commitment Scheme. In: 6th ACM Conf. Computer and Communication Security, Singapore (1999)
10. Tuyls, P., Akkermans, A., Kevenaar, T., Schrijen, G.J., Bazen, A., Veldhuis, R.: Practical biometric template protection system based on reliable components. In: Kanade, T., Jain, A., Ratha, N.K. (eds.) AVBPA 2005. LNCS, vol. 3546, pp. 436–446. Springer, Heidelberg (2005)
11. Van der Veen, M., Kevenaar, T., Schrijen, G.-J., Akkermans, T.H., Zuo, F.: Face biometrics with renewable templates. In: SPIE Conference on Security, Steganography, and Watermarking of Multimedia Contents (2006)
12. Hao, F., Anderson, R., Daugman, J.: Combining crypto with biometrics effectively. IEEE Transactions on Computers 55(9), 1081–1088 (2006)
13. Reynolds, D.A., Quatieri, T.F., Dunn, R.B.: Speaker verification using adapted gaussian mixture models. Digital Signal Processing 10(1-3), 1941 (2000)
14. Alba-Castro, J.L., González-Jiménez, D., Argones-Rúa, E., González-Agulla, E., Otero-Muras, E., Garcýa-Mateo, C.: Pose-corrected face processing on video sequences for webcam-based remote biometric authentication. Journal of Electronic Imaging 17(1) (2008)
15. Argones Rúa, E., Pérez-Piñar López, D., Alba Castro, J.L.: Ergodic HMM-UBM system for on-line signature verification. In: Fierrez, J., Ortega-Garcia, J., Esposito, A., Drygajlo, A., Faundez-Zanuy, M. (eds.) BioID MultiComm2009. LNCS, vol. 5707, pp. 340–347. Springer, Heidelberg (2009)
16. Baum, L.E., Petrie, T., Soules, G., Weiss, N.: A Maximization Technique Occurring in the Statistical Analysis of Probabilistic Functions of Markov Chains. The Annals of Mathematical Statistics 41(1), 164–171 (1970)
17. Linde, Y., Buzo, A., Gray, R.: An Algorithm for Vector Quantizer Design. IEEE Transactions on Communications 28(1), 84–94 (1980)
18. Gauvain, J.-L., Lee, C.-H.: Maximum A Posteriori Estimation for Multivariate Gaussian Mixture Observations of Markov Chains. IEEE Transactions on Speech and Audio Processing 2(2), 291–298 (1994)
19. Huang, X., Acero, A., Hon, H.: Spoken Language Processing: A Guide to Theory, Algorithm, and System Development, ch. 3, pp. 111–113. Prentice Hall PTR, Upper Saddle River (2001)
20. Kuhn, R., Nguyen, P., Junqua, J.C., Goldwasser, L.: Eigenfaces and Eigenvoices: Dimensionality Reduction for Specialized Pattern Recognition. In: IEEE Second Workshop on Multimedia Signal Processing (1998)
21. Kenny, P., Boulianne, G., Dumouchel, P.: Eigenvoice Modeling With Sparse Training Data. IEEE Transactions on Speech and Audio Processing 13(3), 345–354 (2005)
22. Li, Q., Guo, M., Chang, E.-C.: Fuzzy Extractors for Asymmetric Biometric Representation. In: IEEE CVPR (June 2008)
23. Dodis, Y., Reyzin, L., Smith, A.: Fuzzy extractors: How to generate strong keys from biometrics and other noisy data. In: Cachin, C., Camenisch, J.L. (eds.) EUROCRYPT 2004. LNCS, vol. 3027, pp. 523–540. Springer, Heidelberg (2004)
24. Ignatenko, T., Willems, F.M.J.: Biometric Systems: Privacy and Secrecy Aspects. IEEE Transactions on Information Forensics and Security 4(4), 956–973 (2009)
25. Ignatenko, T., Willems, F.M.J.: Information Leakage in Fuzzy Commitment Schemes. IEEE Transactions on Information Forensics and Security 5(2), 337–348 (2010)
26. Ortega-Garcia, J., et al.: MCYT baseline corpus: A bimodal biometric database. In: IEE Conference on Vision, Image and Signal Processing (2003)
27. Purser, M.: Introduction to Error-Correcting Codes. Artech House, Boston (1995)

Biometric Hash Algorithm for Dynamic Handwriting Embedded on a Java Card

Karl Kümmel and Claus Vielhauer

Brandenburg University of Applied Sciences, P.O. Box 2132,
14737 Brandenburg, Germany
{kuemmel,claus.vielhauer}@fh-brandenburg.de

Abstract. In some biometric verification systems smart cards are used to store personal biometric data of a person instead of storing them in a database. If smart cards are correctly authenticated such as with cryptographic signatures, attacks to biometric databases are reduced like template replacement or cross-matching of biometric databases. Furthermore, smart cards are used to match reference data with the actual data of a claimed identity (e.g. [1], [2] and [3]); these systems are called matching-on-card (MOC). In this paper we present a system which besides matching, storing and decision of biometric templates also implements the feature extractor on a smart card to increase the security level and therefore minimize attack possibilities. In this work a exemplary Java Card as widely deployed smart card environment in today business applications is used as implementation platform and a biometric hash algorithm for dynamic handwriting introduced in [4] as biometric user authentication method. Our goal is to evaluate the processing time performance and EER to show the overall tendency. Due to the limited hard- and software resources of a Java Card, a feature extractor with reduced features (9 features), selected based on uncomplex implementation and fast determination time, is deployed. First experimental results show that a biometric hash algorithm for dynamic handwriting, embedded on a Java Card including the feature extraction, is capable of biometric user verification. However, processing time measurements of the first experimental non-time-optimized test system show that real-time applications are not suitable. To show the verification performance we use 500 raw data sets. Test results show an average EER of 28.5%, whereas a reference biometric hash algorithm (103 features) executed on a standard computer achieves an average EER of 4.86%. Furthermore we compare the performance with an existing DSP (digital signal processor) implementation.

Keywords: biometrics, handwriting, on-card matching, java card.

1 Introduction

Biometric user authentication is an important field in IT security today. It relies on personal biological or behavioral characteristics of a person. The purpose of a generic biometric system is to identify and/or verify a person's identity based on at least one biometric modality (i.e. fingerprint, iris, voice etc.). A biometric system is basically composed of four main modules: (i) a *Sensor* to capture the biometrics, (ii) a *Feature*

C. Vielhauer et al. (Eds.): BioID 2011, LNCS 6583, pp. 61–72, 2011.

Extractor to determine and extract specific statistical and/or non statistical features, (iii) a *Matcher* to compare the reference and actual data and finally (iv) a *Decision* module to either confirm/deny a verification (verification mode) or display possible matches (identification mode). To ensure a secure authentication process of a biometric system, it is crucial to protect the system against external influence (e.g data manipulation). Ratha et al. shows in [5] eight different attack points on generic biometric systems, see figure 1. An ideal biometric system is at least immune against all of these attack possibilities. Actual research work deals with these threats and tries to minimize or eliminate them. Some of these attack points can be eliminated by implementing several modules on a secured environment, e.g. smart card.

For example, in typical biometric verification systems the templates are often stored in a central database. With the central storage of the biometric templates, possible threats like template replacement or cross-matching of biometric databases arise. One possible method among many others to prevent such threats is to decentralize the database into hundreds of smart cards. In this case the smart card is used only as a secure storage device to store the biometric template (Store-on-card system). The new electronic passport and identity card launched 2010 in Germany are only examples for Store-on-card (SOC) systems being introduced lately. Regarding to the decentralized storage of the biometric template, SOC systems minimize the possible threats on attack point 6 and 7 (figure 1). If the storage is also authenticated, spoofing attacks can be avoided.

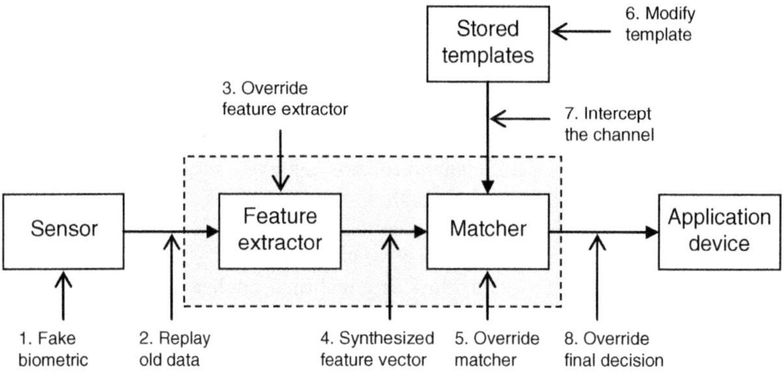

Fig. 1. Possible attack points on a generic biometric system (adapted from [5])

In order to reduce security threats on further attack points the SOC system can be extended. Because the matching process within a SOC system is done on an external system (terminal), the biometric reference data needs to be released into the terminal to be compared with the current verification data, which might offer several insecure states. In a lot of today's system setups, the matching is done on a not or not sufficiently protected environment; therefore the manipulation of the matcher is often possible (attack point 5). To eliminate/minimize this threat, the verification process should be performed in a secure environment, such as an in-card processor, not by the external terminal device. This extended SOC system is called a Match-on-card (MOC) system because the matching process is done on the smart card itself.

Struif et al. introduce in [1] a minutiae-based on-card matching algorithm for fingerprint. Henninger et al. presented in [2] an algorithm based on handwritten signature and Choi et al. suggested in [3] a SVM-based verification algorithm for speaker verification which can be used on a MOC system. These are some examples of Match-on-card (MOC) systems for different modalities recently introduced.

In this paper we go one step further and introduce a system which also includes the feature extractor on the smart card to improve attack resistance. Some authors call such a system also Match-on-card others describe it as a System-on-card. We call it a biometric-system-on-card (BOC) without sensor element. By integrating the feature extractor on a MOC system we also minimize the threats pointed out at attack point 3 and 4, due to the higher effort an attacker has to accomplish to manipulate a secured environment on a smart card. We choose the biometric hash algorithm for dynamic handwriting, introduced by Vielhauer in [4], as the biometric user authentication method and a Java Card (JC) as implementation platform for our BOC. Because of the rapid development capability of prototype smart card applications (see section 3), a Java Card is chosen. The main objective is to show and evaluate the overall tendency and the feasibility of implementing such a biometric hash algorithm on a Java Card. Therefore and with respect to the limited hardware resources, we choose only 9 features to be extracted from the raw data instead of the 103 features presented in an actual version of the algorithm in [6]. These 9 features are selected based on their simplicity and therefore are easy to implement and fast to determine in terms of process time.

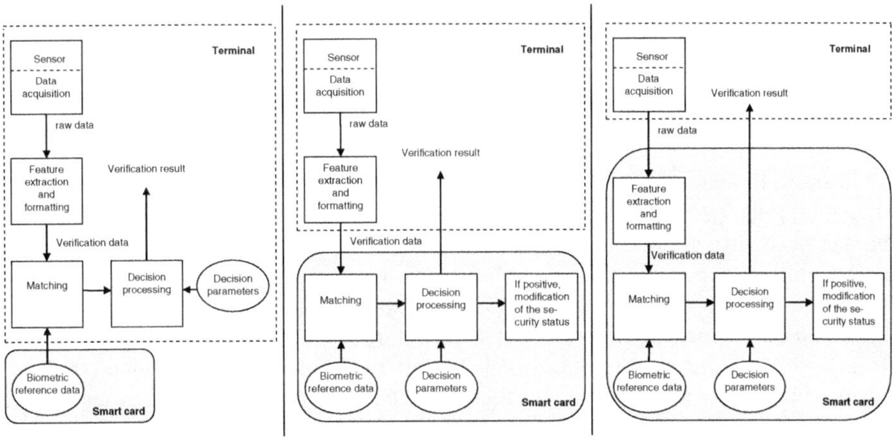

Fig. 2. Store-on-card (left), Match-on-card (center) and Biometric-system-on-card (right)

In this work we do not intend to present trustworthy communication protocols between smart cards and terminals, such as securing raw data or verification results exchange considering security aspects such as integrity, authenticity, confidentiality, non-reputation and availability. Only the possibility of implementing the BioHash algorithm with feature extraction, storage and matching of BioHash data (see Figure 2 right) on a Java Card and its experimental evaluation are focused. Figure 2 summarizes all three mentioned on-card methods (Store-on-card, Match-on-card and biometric-system-on-card without sensor element). The structure of the paper is composed as follows. Section 2 gives an overview to the biometric hash algorithm for dynamic handwriting. Information about the Java Card architecture and functionality are given in section 3. Section 4 gives an overview on the embedded BioHash algorithm and its feature extractor. Experimental results are shown and discussed as well as compared with a DSP (digital signal processor) implementation in section 5. The last section concludes the paper and gives a short outlook to future work in this area.

2 Biometric Hash Algorithm

A description on the BioHash algorithm for dynamic handwriting can be found in several contributions. This description and all containing figures and formulas are adapted from [7]. The basic idea behind the BioHash algorithm is to extract a set of statistical feature values from actual handwriting samples and to find a parameterized transform function for mapping of these values to a stable hash value space. Figure 3 shows a workflow on the algorithm.

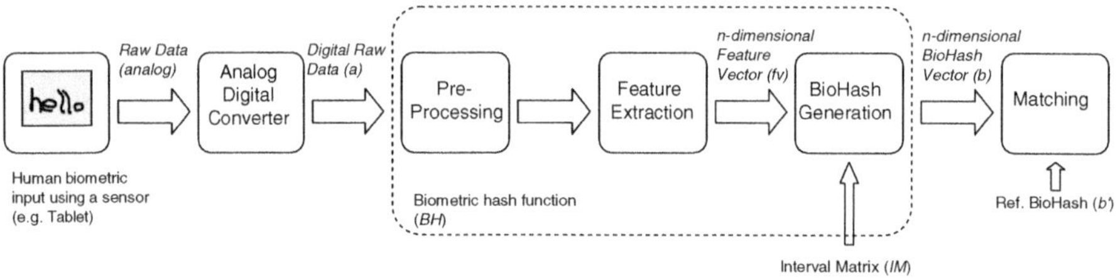

Fig. 3. General Workflow of the biometric hash generation [7]

In the following we briefly summarize the main steps from [4]. A sensor, which transforms pen positions and pressure into an analogous electrical signal, acquires a human handwritten input (e.g. a handwritten signature). This signal is converted by an analog-digital converter into a digital signal a, i.e. the digital raw data. In this work, we define such raw data a as digital signals, composed of time-dependent pen positions and corresponding pressure and angle (altitude and azimuth) values. Within the Biometric Hash generation process a feature extraction function determines statistical features based on the raw data a. Statistical features define characteristics such as *total-write-time*, *total-number-of-event-pixels* or *maximum-pressure* for example; a complete list of all actual used features can be found in [6].

All feature values are composed in a feature vector of a dimension of n, whereas n denotes the number of statistical features being used during the extraction process. In order to compensate intra-class variability, the biometric hash algorithm creates an Interval Matrix (*IM*) during the enrollment process based on at least 3 feature vector samples. Its basic function is to map a certain value range into one specific value. The Interval Matrix consists of an Interval Length Vector ΔI and an Interval Offset Vector Ω: $IM = (\Delta I, \Omega)$. Each feature possesses a related pair of Interval Length and Interval Offset, therefore the length of Interval Matrix and feature vector are equal. With help of the IM, the statistical features are mapped into a n-dimensional Biometric Hash vector (BioHash). The mapping for each feature element fv_i within a feature vector fv into a BioHash element b_i based on the Interval Matrix (Interval Length Vector and Offset Vector) is described in the following Equation 1, whereas i denote the index from 1 to n.

$$b_i = \left\lfloor \frac{fv_i - \Omega_i}{\Delta I_i} \right\rfloor \tag{1}$$

The result of a Biometric Hash generation process is an n-dimensional Biometric Hash vector b (BioHash). In verification mode this BioHash b is compared to a reference BioHash b_{ref}. The matching can be done, for example, by calculating the Hamming distance (amount of equal vector elements) between b and b_{ref}. Reference BioHash b_{ref} and Interval Matrix (IM) are stored for each user in a reference database.

A more detailed description on the BioHash algorithm is given in [4] and a further discussion in [8]. Note that the BioHash cannot only be generated out of personal handwriting such as signatures, it is also possible or even advised to use pass phrases, pseudonyms, symbols or Personal Identification Numbers (PIN). These alternative handwriting samples are called semantics or semantic classes. It has been observed in [4] that these kinds of semantics produce similar recognition accuracy as compared to handwriting signatures, without disclosing the true identity of the writer.

3 Java Card

Smart cards are plastic cards, which embeds a microprocessor, RAM, ROM, EEPROM and an encryption coprocessor. They provide only limited hardware resources compared to standard personal computers today. Typical specifications of currently available smart cards are approximately 160 Kbytes ROM, 4,5 Kbytes RAM, 72 Kbytes EEPROM and an 8-bit microprocessor with an external clock of 1-5 MHz (default clock rate: 3.712 MHz) [9]. Next generation architectures like Philips SmartXA controllers provide a 16-bit microprocessor and the Infineon SLE88 chip card series a 32-bit microprocessor. Additional features to common smart cards are i.e. PKI Crypto-Engine, DES/AES/CRC Engine and multiple 16-bit Timers.

A Java Card is a special smart card which includes an interpreter (Java Card Virtual Machine) capable of executing processor-independent byte code. This byte code is a subset of Java and Java development tools and therefore a subset of the Java language. Java Cards support in general only basic data types like *boolean*, *byte* and *short*; in addition only one-dimensional arrays are supported. Latest Java Card models (JCOP41) provide a garbage collector function to free occupied memory space from unused objects and arrays. The Java Card Virtual Machine in combination with specific APIs and the application manager are designated as the Java Card Runtime Environment (JCRE). APDUs (Application Protocol Data Units) are used to establish communication between the Java Card and the terminal (off-card application) which sends commands and receives responses from the card. Those APDUs are composed of a command identifier and a set of parameters. Executable Java Card applets are uploaded to the smart card by the off-card environment. After upload and successful verification of the applet's digital signature, the applet will be installed and creates an applet instance, which runs in a separate sandbox. Multiple applets can be installed on one single Java Card. By using the *select()* and *deselect()* method, the off-card environment is able to switch between all installed applets. Only one applet can be executed at a time and all received APDUs by the Java Card are relayed to it.

Today, Java Cards have been widely established as a pseudo-standard for smart card application development and an operating system. Because of the rapid development capability of prototype smart card applications, see for example in [2], we choose a Java Card to embed the biometric hash algorithm for dynamic handwriting into it.

4 BioHash Algorithm on a Java Card

Unlike standard MOC systems, we integrate the Feature Extraction module on the smart card as well as the Matcher and Decision module, see figure 2. As described in section 3, Java Cards provide only limited hardware resources compared to modern computers where a biometric system is usually executed. Therefore, in first experiments we choose only 9 features (from the actual 103 suggested in [6]) being extracted from the raw data to show the performance and the feasibility of implementing the BioHash algorithm for dynamic handwriting on such a limited hardware. These features are uncomplex compared to others, relatively simple to determine and need few resources (memory). All 9 selected features are shown in table 1.

Table 1. List of all features used in the Java Card BioHash algorithm

Feature (fv_i: i=)	Name	Description
0	Ttotal	Total writing time in ms
1	SampleCount	Total number of event pixels
2	AvgPressure	Average Writing Pressure relative to MaxPressure
3	MaxPressure	Maximum absolute pressure occurred during writing
4	AspectRatio	Image Width * 1000 DIV Height
5	VxAbsolute	Average velocity in x direction
6	VyAbsolute	Average velocity in y direction
7	SegmentCount	Number of consecutive pen-down segments
8	TpenUp	Absolute cumulated Pen-up time in ms

The Java Card implementation of the BioHash algorithm processes time-dependent pen position (horizontal *x* and vertical *y*) and corresponding pressure signals, no angle signals. The incoming raw data is transmitted from the off-card application, via APDU. Each sample point (time-, *x*-, *y*- and pressure value) is send by one single APDU. The feature extraction process starts after sending a specific command APDU. After the feature extraction is done, the received raw data is removed from the card. Depending on what operating mode is set (Enrollment or Verification, see fig. 4) the feature vector *FV* is processed differently.

In Enrollment mode the feature vector *FV* is stored together with all other feature vectors of the enrollment until the Interval Matrix determination and BioHash vector calculation are done. After reference Interval Matrix IM_{ref} and corresponding BioHash vector b_{ref} are calculated, all feature vectors are erased from the card. In verification mode the feature vector *FV* is mapped to a BioHash vector *b* using the reference

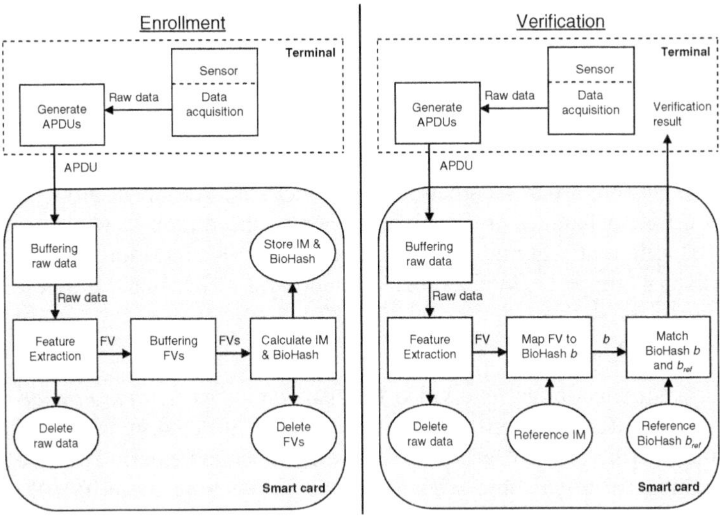

Fig. 4. Overview on the enrollment and verification process of the BOC

Interval Matrix IM_{ref} and then compared with the reference BioHash b_{ref} by calculating the Hamming distance between them. According to the preset threshold value and the actual calculated Hamming distance a positive or negative verification decision is made. An overview on the algorithm is given in figure 4. No considerations about time-optimization within the source code or APDU structure was made in our first implementation of the BioHash algorithm on a Java Card. The goal is to show the feasibility and performance of a BioHash algorithm on a Java Card including the feature extraction on it (BOC).

5 Experimental Evaluation

In this section we show our first experiments on the integrated BioHash algorithm on a Java Card. Our goal is to specify the processing time in enrollment and verification mode. Furthermore we compare error rates generated by the Java Card and by the original (reference) BioHash algorithm (103 features) using the same input data. First we define hardware specifications and the experimental settings. Secondly we introduce our methodology to provide a comparative study of the achieved results to the general verification performance. Thirdly, results are presented, discussed and compared to the DSP performance.

5.1 Hardware Specifications and Experimental Settings

We use a NXP P541G072V0P (JCOP 41 v2.3.1) Java Card with 72 Kbyte EEPROM in first experimental tests. The 8-bit microprocessor on this card uses the default clock rate of 3.57 MHz. The communication between Java Card and Terminal is established by a Fujitsu Siemens Lifebook T4210 built-in card reader. Its transfer rate is set by default to 9600 bit/s and can not be changed.

The biometric database of our initial tests consists of 10 subjects, which have donated 10 handwriting samples for 5 different semantics (500 samples overall). These semantics are "Free chosen Pseudonym" (Pseudonym), "Free chosen Symbol" (Symbol), "Answer to the Question: Where are you from?" (Place), "Fixed 5 digit PIN: 77993" (77993) and "Free chosen 5 digit PIN" (PIN). The first 4 samples are used for Interval Matrix determination and the 5th sample for BioHash generation (enrollment). The remaining samples 6 to 10 are used for verification. The Java Card feature extractor uses 9 different features (see table 1), whereas the reference BioHash algorithm extracts 103 different features. The reference BioHash algorithm is executed on a general personal computer (Intel Core2Duo P8600@2.4 GHz and 4 GByte RAM).

5.2 Methodology

Our evaluation methodology is divided into two major parts: *time measurement* and *error rates*. The idea behind the *time measurement* is to determine if a Java Card is capable of executing the BioHash algorithm within a suitable period of time, concerning the usability in a real time scenario (for example time to verify). Whereas the *error rate* part is used to determine the verification performance of a Java Card BioHash algorithm with limited extracted features (BOC) compared to the original reference BioHash algorithm. In addition, we compare this error rates to error rates (ERR) achieved by another verification algorithm embedded on a DSP (digital signal processor). The implementation of this algorithm on a DSP, which extracts 7 features (total time, numbers of sign changes in the x and y velocities and x and y accelerations, number of zero values in the x and y accelerations, pen-up time, total path length), is described in [10] and embeds also a feature extraction, storage and matcher.

In order to specify the processing time of the Java Card BioHash algorithm, we first measure the time between sending one sample point (single APDU) and receiving the response to it. Then we measure the processing time of the on-card feature extractor using raw data samples with different amounts of sample points (100, 200 and 300) without transfer time for each sample point. Then, BioHash generation time and Matching time (Hamming distance calculation) are measured.

To compare the performance of the on-card BioHash algorithm with the reference BioHash algorithm, biometric error rates FRR/FAR and EER are calculated. The false rejection rate (FRR) describes the ratio between the number of false rejections of authentic persons and the total number of tests. The FAR (false acceptance rate) is the ratio between number of false acceptances of non-authentic persons and the entire number of authentication attempts. For a comparative analysis of verification performance, the equal error rate (EER) is a common measurement in biometrics. EER denotes the point in error characteristics, where FRR and FAR yield identical value.

In the further discussion of our experimental results, we analyze processing time and error rate diagrams, which consists of error rates graphs for FAR and FRR for each semantic class to illustrate ERR. The Threshold in all error rate diagrams is determined by the Hamming distance.

5.3 Experimental Results

In table 2 we show the results of all recorded processing times for specific tasks of the embedded BioHash algorithm on a Java Card. All time values are stated in milliseconds.

Based on these results, a complete verification process using only 100 sample points will take 14.654 seconds (100*124ms (sending raw data) + 2114ms (calculating FV) + 105ms (mapping FV to BioHash) + 35ms (calculating Hamming distance)). Time for an entire enrollment process (sending raw data, calculating FVs, generating BioHash and IM) using 5 samples with an average of 100 sample points each is 72.926 seconds ([100*124ms + 2114ms]*5 + 356ms). To provide comparison for the embedded Java Card and reference algorithm we present in table 3 processing times for an entire enrollment and verification process of one user for both algorithms based on an average of 100 sample points.

Table 2. Processing times of the embedded BioHash algorithm on a Java Card

Task No.	Description	Result (time in ms)
1	Send one sample Point (single APDU)	124
2	Extract Features (Input data consist of 50 sample points)	1280
3	Extract Features (Input data consist of 100 sample points)	2114
4	Extract Features (Input data consist of 200 sample points)	3690
5	Extract Features (Input data consist of 300 sample points)	5277
6	Generate BioHash & IM (based on 5 Feature Vectors)	356
7	Map FV to BioHash using IM (verification mode)	105
8	Calculate Hamming distance	35

Processing times, shown in table 3, for the reference BioHash algorithm are only rough estimations due to included database transactions times.

Table 3. Enrollment and verification processing times of embedded and reference BioHash algorithm using 100 sample points, stated in milliseconds

Task	Embedded BioHash algorithm	Reference BioHash algorithm
Enrollment	72926 ms	905 ms
Verification	14654 ms	105 ms

The equal error rate for both BioHash algorithms (embedded and reference) are presented in table 4. Highest and lowest rates are marked in bold letters.

Table 4. EER of embedded and reference BioHash algorithm

Semantic class	EER (Embedded BioHash)	EER (reference BioHash)
Pseudonym	0.275 (27.5%)	0.066 (6.6%)
77993	0.275 (27.5%	**0.072 (7.2%)**
Free PIN	0.280 (28%)	0.038 (3.8%)
Place	**0.290 (29%)**	0.059 (5.9%)
Symbol	**0.170 (17%)**	**0.008 (0.8%)**

The embedded BioHash algorithm obtains an average EER of 25.8%. In comparison, the reference BioHash algorithm achieves an average EER of 4.86%.

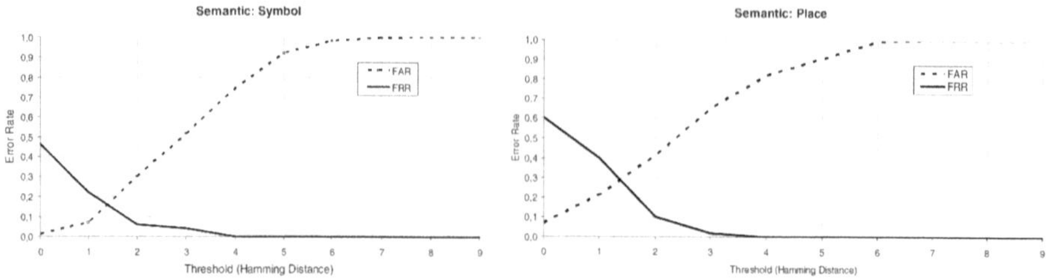

Fig. 5. Error rates of the embedded BioHash algorithm: Symbol (left), Place (right)

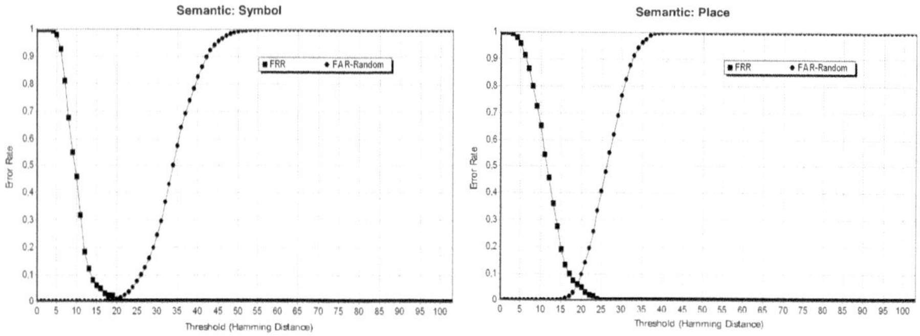

Fig. 6. Error rates of the reference BioHash algorithm: Symbol (left), Place (right)

In order to compare both algorithms, error rate diagrams (highest and lowest EER) of the embedded BioHash algorithm are shown in figure 5 left (lowest), respectively in figure 5 right (highest). In addition we present the error rate diagrams of the same semantic classes obtained by the reference BioHash algorithm (Figure 6).

5.4 Discussion of Results

First results show that processing time for enrollment and verification mode requires too much processing time, for real time scenarios a complete enrollment takes approx. 73 seconds and verification takes approx. 15 seconds. Transferring raw data to the Java Card is the most time consuming operation (approx. 12 seconds for 100 sample points). Modern sensors are capable of recording 500 sample points in a second (2ms sample rate), which increases transfer time dramatically. This transfer time has to be reduced so that it can be used in real-time applications. Compared to the transfer time, the feature extraction process is less time consuming but has also to be optimized for real-time applications, especially when modern sensors (high sample rate) are employed.

The verification performance of the embedded BioHash algorithm (EER of 25.8%) based on 9 features is poor in comparison to the reference algorithm (EER of 4.86%). This is not surprising as feature selection was done based on easy to compute features. A sophisticated feature selection strategy would be of course recommended. Results displayed in figure 5 reveal that the reproduction is below 60% (Threshold = 0) in our first tests. Besides high EERs, this also indicates that 9 features (used in this constellation) are possibly insufficient for stable reproduction and verification. Dullink et al. achieve in [10] an EER of approximately 7% using a simple dynamic handwriting verification algorithm implemented on a DSP, with 7 features. They recorded 10 samples from each user and achieved a feature extraction processing time of 100µs for 300 sample points. Even though the DSP approach from [10] has a higher computational power and the implemented biometric algorithm is different from the one embedded on a Java Card, the feature extraction time is faster by a factor of approx. 50.000 (5277ms vs. 100µs) and it also shows that a selection of 7 features can achieve a more acceptable verification performance (Java Card EER 25.8% vs. DSP EER 7%) then 9 features.

6 Conclusion and Future Work

In this paper we presented a biometric-system-on-card (BOC) without sensor element based on a Java Card. A simplified biometric hash algorithm for dynamic handwriting was used as biometric user authentication method. First experimental results show that this BOC is capable of biometric user verification, even if the verification performance is poor. It could be demonstrated that feature extraction for dynamic handwriting can be done on a Java Card. Due to the limited and not considered appropriate selection of features used in the first experimental test system, the verification performance of this system is not practicable. Based on the verification performance of the reference system, it can be assumed that by implementing more or select better features and/or a different constellation of them within the BOC a better verification performance can be achieved. By optimizing the source code for the embedded BioHash algorithm it is expected that the feature extraction time, BioHash generation time and Hamming distance calculation time can be reduced.

Motivated by this assumption, we will push our work forward to the development of a BOC system, which includes a sensor element and a more powerful microcontroller, in terms of higher computation performance and memory size. Requirements to this BOC are to process more features within an acceptable processing time and a higher verification performance so that it can be used in real-time applications. Parallel to this, we will optimize the source code of the Java Card BioHash algorithm as well as the transmitting format (APDU structure) in order to increase the overall processing time. The transferred data structure, for example, can be changed in a way that only the difference to the predecessor is send to the card instead of the whole value itself. Approaches for this can be derived, for example, from earlier work suggesting differential coding for handwriting samples [11]. We also intend to change system settings like transfer rate of the smart card reader and external clock frequency of the smart card to increase processing time.

Acknowledgements

This work is supported by the German Federal Ministry of Education and Research (BMBF), project "OptiBioHashEmbedded" under grant number 17N3109. The content of this document is under the sole responsibility of the authors. We also thank Stefan Malkwitz for doing most of the embedded java coding.

References

1. Struif, B., Scheuermann, D.: Smartcards with Biometric User Verification. In: Proceedings of IEEE International Conference on Multimedia and Expo 2002, vol. 2, pp. 589–592. Swiss Federal Institute of Technology, Lausanne (2002)
2. Henniger, O., Franke, K.: Biometric User Authentication on Smart Cards by Means of Handwritten Signatures. In: Zhang, D., Jain, A.K. (eds.) ICBA 2004. LNCS, vol. 3072, pp. 547–554. Springer, Heidelberg (2004)
3. Choi, W.Y., Ahn, D., Pan, S.B., Chung, K.I., Chung, Y., Chung, S.H.: SVM-based speaker verification system for match-on-card and its hardware implementation. Electronics and Telecommunications Research Institute Journal 28(3), 320–328 (2006)
4. Vielhauer, C.: Biometric User Authentication for IT Security: From Fundamentals to Handwriting. Springer, New York (2006)
5. Ratha, N.K., Connell, J.H., Bolle, R.M.: An analysis of minutiae matching strength. In: Bigun, J., Smeraldi, F. (eds.) AVBPA 2001. LNCS, vol. 2091, pp. 223–228. Springer, Heidelberg (2001)
6. Kümmel, K., Vielhauer, C.: Reverse-engineer methods on a biometric hash algorithm for dynamic handwriting. In: Proceedings of the 12th ACM Workshop on Multimedia and Security (MM&Sec 2010), Italy, Rom, pp. 67–72 (2010)
7. Kümmel, K., Vielhauer, C., Scheidat, T., Franke, D., Dittmann, J.: Handwriting Biometric Hash Attack: A Genetic Algorithm with User Interaction for Raw Data Reconstruction. In: De Decker, B., Schaumüller-Bichl, I. (eds.) CMS 2010. LNCS, vol. 6109, pp. 178–190. Springer, Heidelberg (2010)
8. Vielhauer, C., Steinmetz, R., Mayerhoefer, A.: Biometric Hash based on Statistical Features of Online Signatures. In: Proceedings of the IEEE International Conference on Pattern Recognition (ICPR), Quebec City, vol. 1, pp. 123–126 (2002)
9. Philips SmartMX Contact and Dual Interface PKI Controllers, `http://www.nxp.com/acrobat_download2/other/identification/smartmx_pki_controllers_0.18_um_line_card.pdf`
10. Dullink, H., van Daalen, B., Nijhuis, J., Spaanenburg, L., Zuidhof, H.: Implementing a DSP Kernel for Online Dynamic Handwritten Signature Verification Using the TMS320 DSP Family. In: DSP Solution Challenge 1995 European Team Papers, SPRA304, EFRIE, France (1995)
11. Croce Ferri, L., Mayerhöfer, A., Frank, M., Vielhauer, C., Steinmetz, R.: Biometric authentication for ID cards with Hologram Watermarks. In: Proc. of Security and Watermarking of Multimedia Contents IV, vol. 4675, pp. 629–640. SPIE, Bellingham (2002)

The Use of Static Biometric Signature Data from Public Service Forms

Emma Johnson and Richard Guest

School of Engineering and Digital Arts, University of Kent, Canterbury, UK
{ej45,r.m.guest}@kent.ac.uk

Abstract. Automatic signature verification/recognition is a commonly used form of biometric authentication. Signatures are typically provided for legal purposes on public service application forms but not used for subsequent biometric recognition. This paper investigates a number of factors concerning the use of signatures in so-called static form (an image of a completed signature) to enable the sample to be used as stand-alone or supplementary data alongside other biometric modalities. Specifically we investigate common sizes of unconstrained signatures within a population, assess the size of application form signing areas with respect to potential constraints and finally investigate performance issues of how constrained and unconstrained enrolment signature data from forms can be accurately matched against constrained and unconstrained verification data, representing the full range of usage scenarios. The study identifies that accuracy can be maintained when constrained signatures data is verified against other constrained samples while the best performance occurs when unconstrained signatures are used for both enrolment and verification.

Keywords: Signature biometrics, static feature analysis, form design.

1 Introduction

The human signature is a widely used and accepted form of personal authentication with application areas spanning a multitude of everyday domains (including retail and legal) [1],[2],[3]. Signature also has widespread use within automatic biometric analysis solutions alongside other modalities such as fingerprint, face and iris recognition [4]. Despite comparable performance in terms of verification error rates, signature does not enjoy the market share of other modalities within large scale deployment applications such as national identity cards or border documentation (for example passports or visas) for which face and fingerprint are often primary choices [5]. These modalities require specific capture and enrolment equipment often meaning that enrolees have to attend a specific site (in the case of fingerprints) or donate samples to a particular predefined specification (in the case of facial images). Applications for official identify documentation are almost always made using a paper form on which the applicant has to sign (usually for legal purpose regarding use of data and consent). Using this signature data in a static/image format may be fully integrated

C. Vielhauer et al. (Eds.): BioID 2011, LNCS 6583, pp. 73–82, 2011.

into the verification process as additional data readily available to enhance the biometric process alongside the primary biometrics collected for the application [6].

This study aims to assess several key aspects of the use of this "supplementary" static biometric signature data collected on application forms. Specifically, we firstly focus on the design of common application form signing areas with respect to the range of human signature sizes (both Western and non-Western) to investigate if constraints are imposed which will affect normal signature production. By using a specially collected signature dataset we will secondly investigate verification performance rates of constrained and unconstrained static signatures using a common static signature verification engine. This second experiment will lead to an understanding of performance issues as to how both constrained and unconstrained (enrolment) signature data from forms can be accurately matched against constrained and unconstrained verification data, representing the full range of usage scenarios.

2 Methodology

To investigate the effects of signature size, form-based constraints and verification performance, three separate stages to the experiment were conducted.

2.1 Stage 1 – Unconstrained Signature Size Analysis

Throughout the investigation a new dataset was used which comprised of 150 signers who were asked to donate four separate instances of their signature on individual blank A4 sheets of paper, which, when scanned, formed an unconstrained subset of static signature images. The data collection took signature samples in a single session, and the images were scanned using an HP Scanjet 8250 at a resolution of 600dpi and a bit depth of 24. The images were stored in jpeg format.

The signers donating to the dataset were from both Western and non-Western first writing languages. Out of 150 donors, 15 had a non-Western first writing language, and 135 a Western first writing language. The first writing languages of the subjects in the datasets were: English (122 participants), Russian (6 participants), Chinese, German, French and Greek (2 participants each), and Kurdish, Italian, Polish, Basque, Spanish, Thai, Hebrew, Arabic, Hindi, Albanian, Dutch, Welsh, Portuguese and Romanian (1 participant each).

As an initial investigation, the physical height and width of all 600 (4 signatures x 150 signers) unconstrained signatures was measured by assessing the ink pixel extents in the x and y axes and converting into mm. In this way it was possible to analyse the average and range of signatures across a representative population. Furthermore, by separating the 150 signers according to whether their first writing language was Western and non-Western it is possible to investigate the broad effects on ethnicity, which can be important meta-information within signature assessment.

2.2 Stage 2 – Form Signing Areas

Having established typical ranges of unconstrained signature sizes, the second stage of experimentation assessed a variety of public service application forms to note the box/area sizes provided for signature donation. Whilst it is acknowledged that the signatures donated in these areas are purely for legal completion of the application, in the context of this work by reviewing the sizes for signature donation it will be possible to ascertain whether boxes are constraining typical signature sizes (through a comparison with the result from Stage 1).

In this experiment a total of 98 signature donation boxes/spaces from 56 public service application forms were measured. These forms include UK, EU and US application forms for services such as entry visa application, naturalisation, passport and driving license applications. The forms were chosen as they are in the public domain and are for a range of secure applications that could benefit from the use of biometric signature recognition.

Signing box areas were obtained by physically measuring the areas on each form. If no physical bounding box was present, the extents were defined by text or other bounding objects on the form.

2.3 Stage 3 – Constrained Static Signature Verification

To assess the effects of form constraints on static signature verification, signers donating to the dataset outlined in Stage 1 (Section 2.1) also signed eight sheets (with a single signature per sheet) with a signature donation box with dimensions 80mm by 30mm. This box size, when compared with the average box sizes on public service forms, is rather large, suggesting that any effects of constraining the signature would be amplified when using some of the forms measured in Stage 2 (Section 2.2). The constrained signatures were gathered using an identical method to the unconstrained signatures and were scanned using the same device and resolution. They were also taken in the same session as the unconstrained images and then stored in jpeg format.

The constrained signatures were measured in the x and y direction, as the unconstrained signatures had been, to assess how much constraining the signature affected the size of the static signature sample. The results of this can be found later in the paper.

2.4 Stage 4 – Four Way Matching Experiments

Having both constrained and unconstrained signatures from 150 subjects enabled all four possible real-life combinations of static assessment:

- Scenario 1: Unconstrained enrolment vs. unconstrained verification
- Scenario 2: Unconstrained enrolment vs. constrained verification
- Scenario 3: Constrained enrolment vs. unconstrained verification
- Scenario 4: Constrained enrolment vs. constrained verification

Four separate experiments were conducted representing the above scenarios. The experiments followed the same methodology: Four signatures were used to form an enrolment template against which a series of four genuine signatures per scenario were verified. This was followed by four false signatures verified against the enrolment template. The false signatures were unskilled forgeries taken from other users' signatures so as to maintain the scenarios of constrained or unconstrained images. The verification algorithm used outputted a distance metric, which was used to create a ROC curve and identify the error rates for each scenario. The static ASV system used for these experiments was an algorithm which calculates the signature bounding envelope and interior strokes using a range of geometric polar and Cartesian features as inputs to a Euclidean distance measure [7]. This method was used to assess the signatures because of the proven high performing nature of the algorithm. For these experiments it was treated as a 'black-box' in that the algorithm was not optimised for performance.

3 Results

3.1 Stage 1 – Unconstrained Signature Size Analysis

In the first set of experiments the sizes of four constrained signatures from 150 subjects were determined. Table 1 and Figure 1 show the statistics for unconstrained images, divided into all signatures, those submitted by people whose native writing language was of a western style, and those whose native writing language was of a non-western style.

Table 1. Mean, minimum and maximum values for unconstrained signatures

Writing Language	Axis	Mean (mm)	Min (mm)	Max (mm)
All	x	45.47	11.47	104.70
	y	14.84	5.03	34.45
Western	x	45.80	14.64	104.70
	y	14.37	5.03	33.82
Non-Western	x	42.48	11.47	78.78
	y	18.97	5.88	34.45

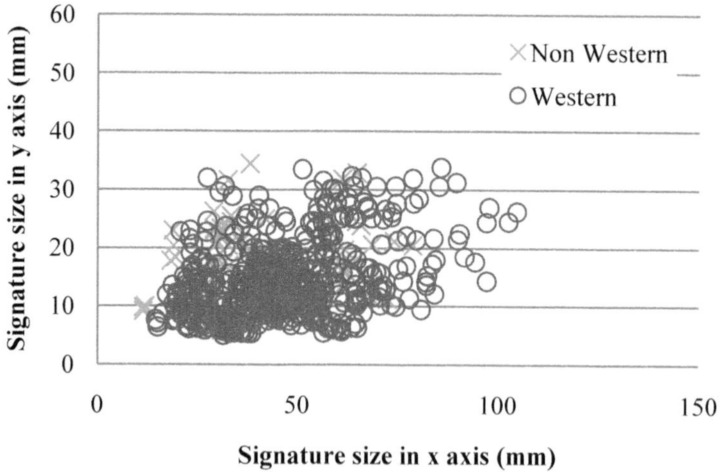

Fig. 1. x and y size values of unconstrained signatures

As can be seen, there is considerable variation between signature sizes, which may make optimum form design difficult. However, if the most important issue is that the signatures do not get deformed when scaled down, an average ratio between the sizes of the signature could be useful so as to design a box of the appropriate proportions. In assessing the signatures of Western participants in the dataset the ratio would be approximately 1:3 (height to width across all signatures). If this ratio is adhered to, deformation of constrained signatures could possibility be minimized.

3.2 Stage 2 – Form Signing Areas

With reference to above unconstrained signature sizes, the box/signing area sizes found on 98 signature donation boxes/spaces from 56 public standard public service forms were analysed to see how they compared. The statistics for the forms examined are shown in Table 2 and Figure 2.

Table 2. Signing area sizes found on standard public service forms

Axis	Mean (mm)	Min (mm)	Max (mm)
x	80.59	23.00	158.00
y	8.33	3.00	18.00

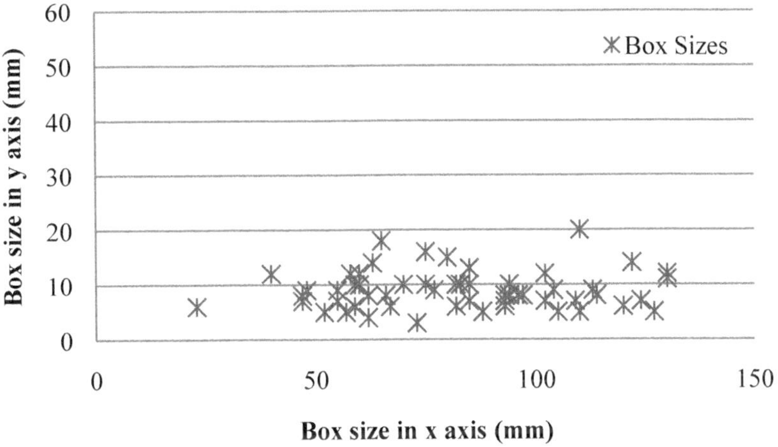

Fig. 2. x and y size values of constraining boxes on public service forms

As can be seen, the smallest size of a box in the y direction was a mere 3mm, which is smaller than even the minimum constrained signature height. The boxes exhibited a range of proportionality, some were very long and narrow, (Figure 3, IAP-66), while others were short and wide (Figure 4, I-17). More examples of boxes found on standard forms are shown in Figures 5, 6 and 7, which all come from the same form, (N644) showing that, not only are these forms not standardised across an agency or country, but in some cases, they are not even standardised on the same form, leading to an inability for these boxes to reliably produce proportional signature data if used as multiple static signature enrolment data within the same enrolment session.

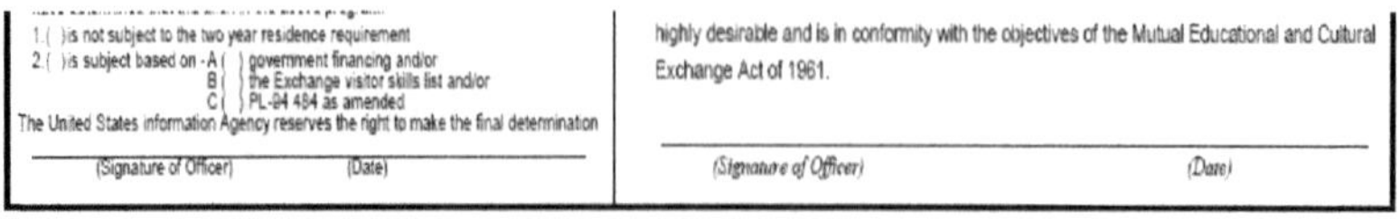

1.( ) is not subject to the two year residence requirement
2.( ) is subject based on - A ( ) government financing and/or
B ( ) the Exchange visitor skills list and/or
C ( ) PL-94 484 as amended
The United States information Agency reserves the right to make the final determination

(Signature of Officer) (Date)

highly desirable and is in conformity with the objectives of the Mutual Educational and Cultural Exchange Act of 1961.

(Signature of Officer) *(Date)*

Fig. 3. Signature box from US form IAP-66 –Exchange Visitor Visa Application

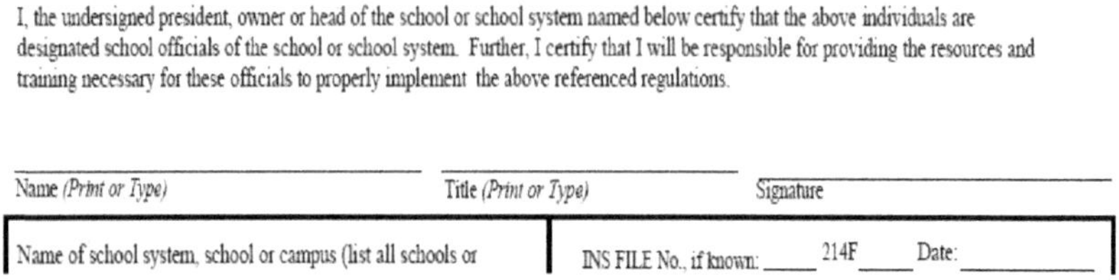

I, the undersigned president, owner or head of the school or school system named below certify that the above individuals are designated school officials of the school or school system. Further, I certify that I will be responsible for providing the resources and training necessary for these officials to properly implement the above referenced regulations.

Name *(Print or Type)* Title *(Print or Type)* Signature

Name of school system, school or campus (list all schools or

INS FILE No., if known: ____ 214F ____ Date: ________

Fig. 4. Signature box from US form I-17- Petition for Approval of School for Attendance by Non-Immigrant Student

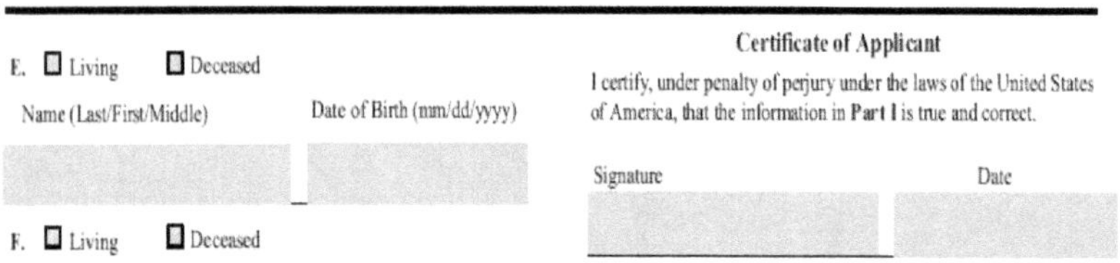

E. ☐ Living ☐ Deceased

Name (Last/First/Middle) Date of Birth (mm/dd/yyyy)

F. ☐ Living ☐ Deceased

Certificate of Applicant

I certify, under penalty of perjury under the laws of the United States of America, that the information in **Part I** is true and correct.

Signature Date

Fig. 5. Signature box from US form N644 – Application for Posthumous Citizenship

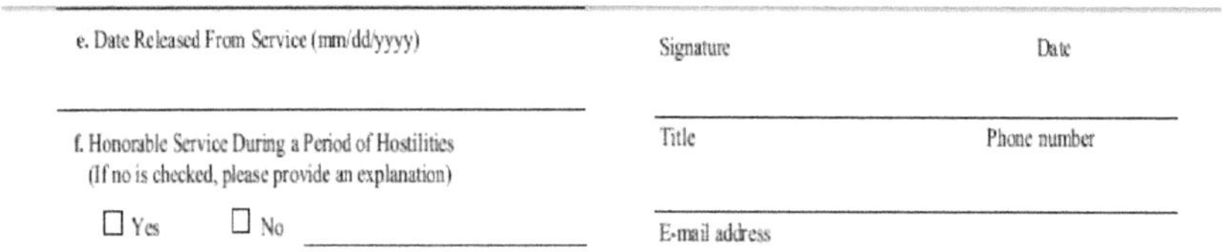

e. Date Released From Service (mm/dd/yyyy)

f. Honorable Service During a Period of Hostilities
(If no is checked, please provide an explanation)

☐ Yes ☐ No

Signature Date

Title Phone number

E-mail address

Fig. 6. Signature box from US form N644 – Application for Posthumous Citizenship

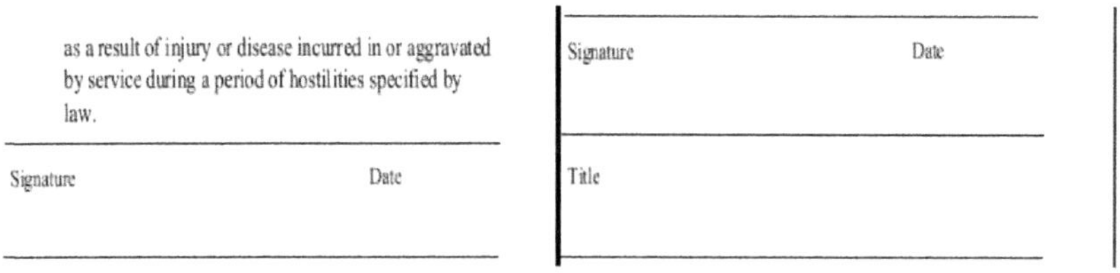

as a result of injury or disease incurred in or aggravated by service during a period of hostilities specified by law.

Signature Date

Signature Date

Title

Fig. 7. Signature box from US form N644 – Application for Posthumous Citizenship

3.3 Stage 3 – Constrained Static Signature Verification

Having established that constraining boxes are often smaller or differently proportioned to an unconstrained signature, it was necessary to identify if constraining the signature significantly distorted the signature to the point of affecting the accuracy of automatic signature verification. The size statistics of signatures in constraining boxes are shown in Table 3 and Figure 8, divided into sub-categories of all signatures, those submitted by people whose native writing language was of a Western style, and those whose native writing language was of a non-Western style.

As can be seen from these data, the unconstrained signatures were generally of a larger size than the constrained. An ANOVA analysis determined that in the *x* direction, the differences were not statistically different, but in the *y* direction, there was a significant variation. This shows that not only does the *y* direction vary in size depending on whether the signature is constrained or unconstrained, but that it varies more than in the *x* direction, meaning that the signature itself is being deformed to different proportions when restricted to a box. This data is from signatures constrained in boxes that were fairly large (80mm x 30mm) compared to the majority of the boxes found in standard forms that are publically used, so this effect would be even higher for many of the boxes currently used.

Table 3. Mean, minimum and maximum values for constrained signatures

Nationality	Axis	Mean (mm)	Min (mm)	Max (mm)
All	x	44.5	10.77	133.86
	y	13.96	4.9	52.76
Western	x	44.62	14.52	89.26
	y	13.61	4.9	46.87
Non-Western	x	43.33	10.77	133.86
	y	17.08	5.31	52.76

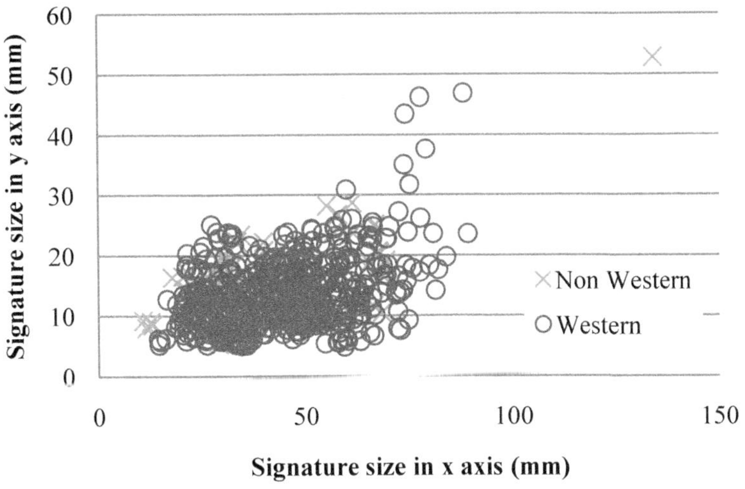

Fig. 8. *x* and *y* size values of constrained signatures

It should also be noted that there are some outlying values within this data – on examining these outlying images it was discovered that some participants had attempted to fill the box with their signature, introducing a further donation method of distorting the signature.

As constraining a signature will deform the static image, a performance assessment was undertaken to examine whether this distortion would affect the accuracy of a static signature verification system. Four-way matching was applied – examining the results of unconstrained enrolment images with unconstrained verification images (Scenario 1), unconstrained enrolment images with constrained verification images (Scenario 2), constrained enrolment images with unconstrained verification images (Scenario 3) and constrained enrolment images with constrained verification images (Scenario 4). The results of these experiments can be found in Table 4 and Figure 9.

Table 4. Performance Evaluation of Constrained vs. Unconstrained Static Signature Verification Using a Four-Way Match

Error Rate	Scenario 1	Scenario 2	Scenario 3	Scenario 4
EER	5.9	7.9	12.5	6.9
FAR	5.9	5.3	11.8	8.6
FRR	5.9	10.5	13.2	5.3

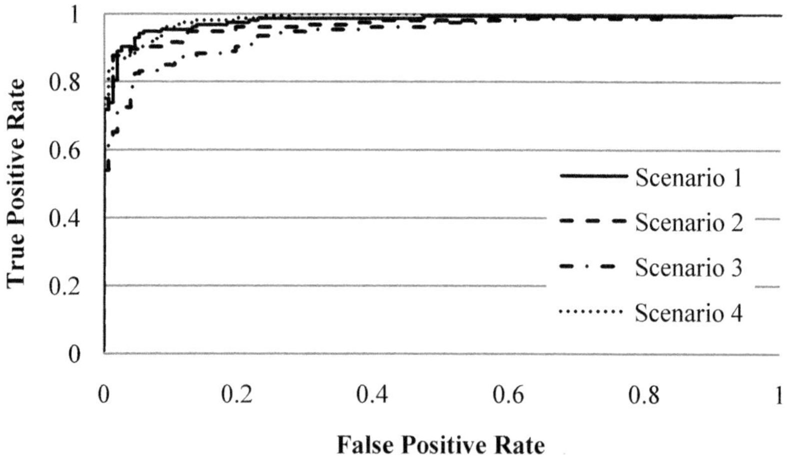

Fig. 9. ROC Curves to Show Performance Evaluation of Constrained vs. Unconstrained Static Signature Verification Using a Four-Way Match

From these results, we can see that the constraining of a signature had a fairly minor effect on system accuracy, when both the enrolment and verification images are both constrained to the same level. However, as soon as one image was constrained and the other unconstrained, particularly if enrolment was constrained but verification unconstrained, as in Scenario 3, the accuracy was severely affected.

4 Conclusions

In this study it has been determined that when people are constrained as to the amount of space they have to sign, their signature will deform, particularly in the *y* axis. This occurs even when the constraining box is larger than the person's unconstrained signature. It is also possible to ascertain that when signature images are constrained, static verification system accuracy is adversely affected. While, in our experimental system both enrolment and verification images are constrained in the same size box, the equal error rate is 6.9%, the accuracy of the system is improved to an equal error rate of 5.9% when neither image is constrained. When either the enrolment or verification samples are constrained, and the other samples unconstrained, accuracy ratings drop considerably (especially when the enrolment template is constrained and the comparison unconstrained, where the error rate rises to 12.5%).

The constrained sample results in this work were obtained using a constraining box of the size 80mm x 30mm. The size of this box in the *x* axis approximates to the mean of the boxes found on public forms in common usage, however, the size of the box in the *y* axis is significantly larger than even the largest box found on a public form. This form constraint is likely to cause even more reduction in accuracy for a biometric system as the *y* axis was the dimension varying the most between constrained and unconstrained signatures. While constraining signatures on boxes will allow for more space on a form, and, if the signature is being stored in a raw image format will lead to a smaller template size, careful thought should be given to the use of constraints on any signature that is to be used for biometric authentication as the accuracy of the system will be adversely affected by constraining the user's signature.

In terms of the practical application of signature systems utilising static signature data to supplement primary authentication data (biometric or otherwise), this work has identified a number of key findings: Firstly, we have identified average signature size (and ranges) from a large population and surveyed how these compare with signing areas on a cross-section of common public service application forms. By noting the relative performance of constrained and unconstrained signatures we can identify that accuracy is maintained if constrained signatures are used for both enrolment and verification. Using form constrained signatures for enrolment and unconstrained for verification (Scenario 3 – a typical implementation using forms at enrol time) produces sub-optimal results. Importantly the results show the possibility of form-based signatures either as a primary or supplementary biometric modality.

References

1. Impedovo, D., Pirlo, G.: Automatic Signature Verification: The State of the Art. IEEE Trans. SMC-C 38(5), 609–635 (2008)
2. Plamondon, R., Lorette, G.: Automatic signature verification and writer identification - the state of the art. Pattern Recognition 22(2), 107–131 (1989)

3. Leclerc, F., Plamondon, R.: Automatic signature verification: the state of the art - 1989-1993. Intl J. Pattern Recognition and Artificial Intelligence 8(3), 643–660 (1994)
4. Jain, A.K., Ross, A., Prabhakar, S.: An Introduction to Biometric Recognition. IEEE Trans. Circuits and Systems for Video Technology, Special Issue on Image- and Video-Based Biometrics 14(1), 4–20 (2004)
5. Kwon, T., Moon, H.: Multi-modal Biometrics with PKI Technologies for Border Control Applications. In: Kantor, P., Muresan, G., Roberts, F., Zeng, D.D., Wang, F.-Y., Chen, H., Merkle, R.C. (eds.) ISI 2005. LNCS, vol. 3495, pp. 99–114. Springer, Heidelberg (2005)
6. Vielhauer, C., Scheidat, T.: Multimodal Biometrics for Voice and Handwriting. In: Dittmann, J., Katzenbeisser, S., Uhl, A. (eds.) CMS 2005. LNCS, vol. 3677, pp. 191–199. Springer, Heidelberg (2005)
7. Ferrer, M.A., Alonso, J.B., Travieso, C.M.: Offline Geometric Parameters for Automatic Signature Verification Using Fixed-Point Arithmetic. IEEE Trans. PAMI 27(6), 993–997 (2005)

Hill-Climbing Attack Based on the Uphill Simplex Algorithm and Its Application to Signature Verification

Marta Gomez-Barrero, Javier Galbally, Julian Fierrez, and Javier Ortega-Garcia

Biometric Recognition Group–ATVS, EPS, Universidad Autonoma de Madrid, C/ Francisco Tomas y Valiente 11, 28049 Madrid, Spain
{marta.barrero,javier.galbally,julian.fierrez,javier.ortega}@uam.es

Abstract. A general hill-climbing attack to biometric systems based on a modification of the downhill simplex algorithm is presented. The scores provided by the matcher are used in this approach to adapt iteratively an initial estimate of the attacked template to the specificities of the client being attacked. The proposed attack is evaluated on a competitive feature-based signature verification system over both the MCYT and the BiosecurID databases (comprising 330 and 400 users, respectively). The results show a very high efficiency of the hill-climbing algorithm, which successfully bypassed the system for over 90% of the attacks with a remarkably low number of scores needed.

1 Introduction

Biometric security systems are nowadays being introduced in many applications, such as access control, sensitive data protection, on-line tracking systems, etc., due to their advantages over traditional security approaches [1]. Nevertheless, they are also susceptible to external attacks that can decrease their security level. Therefore, it is of the utmost importance to analyse the vulnerabilities of biometric systems so that their weaknesses can be found and useful countermeasures against foreseeable attacks can be developed.

There are two main types of attacks that may put at risk the security offered by a biometric system: (*i*) *direct attacks*, carried out against the sensor using synthetic traits, such as printed iris images or gummy fingers [2]; and (*ii*) *indirect attacks*, carried out against some of the inner modules of the system [3,4], and thus requiring for the attacker to have some knowledge about the system (e.g., storage format or matcher used). A more detailed analysis of the vulnerable points of biometric systems is made by Ratha *et al.* in [5]. In this work 8 possible points of attack are identified, the first corresponding to direct ones and the remaining seven to indirect attacks.

Several works have already studied the robustness of biometric systems against direct attacks, specially fingerprint- and iris-based, including [2,3,6]. In the case of indirect attacks, most of the studies use some kind of variant of the hill-climbing algorithm [4]. Some examples include an indirect attack to a face-based

C. Vielhauer et al. (Eds.): BioID 2011, LNCS 6583, pp. 83–94, 2011.

system in [7], and to a PC and Match-on-Card minutiae-based fingerprint verification systems in [8] and [9], respectively. These attacks iteratively change a synthetic template, according to the scores given by the matcher, until the similarity score exceeds a fixed decision threshold. This way, the access to the system is granted. These hill-climbing approaches, except for the one proposed in [10], are all highly dependent of the technology used, only being usable for very specific types of matchers.

In the present paper, a hill-climbing algorithm based on an adaptation of the downhill simplex algorithm [11], is presented. The main contribution of the work lies in the fact that this general approach can be applied to any system working with fixed length feature vectors, regardless of the biometric trait being used. The proposed method uses the scores provided by the matcher to adapt an initial simplex, computed from a development set of users, to the local specificities of the client being attacked. The performance of the attack is evaluated on a feature-based signature verification system using the MCYT [12] and the BiosecurID [13] databases (comprising 330 and 400 users, respectively). In the experiments, the attack showed a remarkable performance, similar with both databases, being able to bypass over 90% of the accounts attacked for the best configuration of the algorithm found.

The paper is structured as follows. The general hill-climbing algorithm is described in Sect. 2, while the case study in signature verification is reported in Sect. 3. In Sect. 3.1 we present the attacked system, and the database and experimental protocol followed are described in Sect 3.2. The results are detailed in Sect. 3.3. Conclusions are finally drawn in Sect. 4.

2 Hill-Climbing Based on the Uphill Simplex Algorithm

Consider the problem of finding a K-dimensional vector $\mathbf{y}$ which, compared to an unknown template $\mathcal{C}$ (in our case related to a specific client), produces a similarity score bigger than a certain threshold δ, according to some matching function J, i.e.: $J(\mathcal{C}, \mathbf{y}) > \delta$. The template can be another K-dimensional vector or a generative model of K-dimensional vectors.

Let us consider a simplex, that is, a polygon defined by $K + 1$ points in the K-dimensional space, obtained randomly from a statistical model G (a K-variate Gaussian with mean $\boldsymbol{\mu}_G$ and diagonal covariance matrix $\boldsymbol{\Sigma}_G$, with $\boldsymbol{\sigma}_G^2 = \text{diag}\boldsymbol{\Sigma}_G$, related to a background set of users, overlapping to some extent with $\mathcal{C}$), and let us assume that we have access to the evaluation of the matching function $J(\mathcal{C}, \mathbf{y})$ for several trials of $\mathbf{y}$. Then, the problem stated above can be solved by adapting the downhill simplex algorithm first presented in [11] to maximize instead of minimize the function J. We iteratively form new simplices by reflecting one point, $\mathbf{y}_l$, in the hyperplane of the remaining points, until we are close enough to the maximum of the function. The point to be reflected will always be the one with the lowest value given by the matching function, since it is in principle the one furthest from our objective. Thus, the different steps followed by the attacking hill climbing algorithm are:

1. Compute the statistical model $G(\boldsymbol{\mu}_G, \boldsymbol{\sigma}_G)$ from a development pool of users.
2. Take $K+1$ samples ($\mathbf{y}_i$) defining the initial simplex from the statistical model $G(\boldsymbol{\mu}_G, \boldsymbol{\sigma}_G)$ and compute the similarity scores $J(\mathcal{C}, \mathbf{y}_i) = s_i$, with $i = 1, \dots, K+1$.
3. Compute the centroid $\bar{\mathbf{y}}$ of the simplex as the average of $\mathbf{y}_i$:

$$\bar{\mathbf{y}} = \frac{1}{K+1} \sum_i \mathbf{y}_i$$

4. Reflect the point $\mathbf{y}_l$ according to the next steps, adapted from the downhill simplex algorithm [11]. In the following, the indices l and h are defined as:

$$h = \arg\max_i (s_i)$$

$$l = \arg\min_i (s_i)$$

4.a. **Reflection**: Given a constant $\alpha > 0$, the *reflection coefficient*, we compute:

$$\mathbf{a} = (1+\alpha)\bar{\mathbf{y}} - \alpha \mathbf{y}_l.$$

Thus, $\mathbf{a}$ is on the line between $\mathbf{y}_l$ and $\bar{\mathbf{y}}$ being α the ratio between the distances $[\mathbf{a}\bar{\mathbf{y}}]$ and $[\mathbf{y}_l\bar{\mathbf{y}}]$. If $s_l < s_a < s_h$ we replace $\mathbf{y}_l$ by $\mathbf{a}$. Otherwise, we go on to step 4b.

4.b. **Expansion or contraction**

4.b.1 **Expansion:** If $s_a > s_h$ (i.e., we have a new maximum) we expand $\mathbf{a}$ to $\mathbf{b}$ as follows:

$$\mathbf{b} = \gamma \mathbf{a} + (1-\gamma)\bar{\mathbf{y}},$$

where $\gamma > 1$ is another constant called *expansion coefficient*, which represents the ratio between the distances $[\mathbf{b}\bar{\mathbf{y}}]$ and $[\mathbf{a}\bar{\mathbf{y}}]$. If $s_b > s_h$, we replace $\mathbf{y}_l$ by $\mathbf{b}$. Otherwise, we have a failed expansion and replace $\mathbf{y}_l$ by $\mathbf{a}$.

4.b.2 **Contraction:** If we have reached this step, then $s_a \le s_l$ (i.e. replacing $\mathbf{y}_l$ by $\mathbf{a}$ would leave s_a as the new minimum). Afterwards we compute

$$\mathbf{b} = \beta \mathbf{y}_l + (1-\beta)\bar{\mathbf{y}},$$

where $0 < \beta < 1$ is the *contraction coefficient*, defined as the ratio between the distances $[\mathbf{b}\bar{\mathbf{y}}]$ and $[\mathbf{y}_l\bar{\mathbf{y}}]$. If $s_b > \max(s_l, s_a)$, then we replace $\mathbf{y}_l$ by $\mathbf{b}$; otherwise, the contracted point is worse than $\mathbf{y}_l$, and for such a failed contraction we replace all the $\mathbf{y}_i$'s by $(\mathbf{y}_i + \mathbf{y}_h)/2$.

5. With the new $\mathbf{y}_l$ value, update the simplex and return to step 3.

The hill climbing algorithm stops when $s_h \ge \delta$ or when the maximum number of iterations M is reached.

The iterative optimization algorithm used here as core of the proposed hill-climbing attack is an adaptation of the downhill simplex first presented in [11], which has been modified in order to maximize a given function and where several redundant conditions have been discarded. From now on, this modified version of the original algorithm will be referred to as *uphill simplex*.

3 Case Study: Attacking a Feature-Based On-Line Signature Verification System

3.1 Signature Verification System

The proposed hill-climbing method attack based on the uphill simplex algorithm is used to attack the feature-based on-line signature verification system considered in [10] so that the results on the performance of the two hill-climbing attacks (i.e., that proposed in [10], and the one presented here) may be compared. The signatures are parametrized using the set of features described in [14]. In that work, a set of 100 global features was proposed, and the individual features were ranked according to their individual discriminant power. A good operating point for the systems tested was found when using the first 40 parameters. In the present contribution we use this 40-feature representation of the signatures, normalizing each of them to the range [0,1] using the tanh-estimators described in [15]:

$$p_k' = \frac{1}{2}\left\{\tanh\left(0.01\left(\frac{p_k - \mu_{p_k}}{\sigma_{p_k}}\right)\right) + 1\right\}, \tag{1}$$

where p_k is the kth parameter, p_k' denotes the normalized parameter, and μ_{p_k} and σ_{p_k} are respectively the estimated mean and standard deviation of the parameter under consideration.

The similarity scores are computed using the Mahalanobis distance between the input vector and a statistical model $\mathcal{C}$ of the attacked client, using a number of training signatures (4 or 5 in our experiments). Thus,

$$J(\mathcal{C}, \mathbf{y}) = \frac{1}{\left((\mathbf{y} - \boldsymbol{\mu}^{\mathcal{C}})^T (\boldsymbol{\Sigma}^{\mathcal{C}})^{-1} (\mathbf{y} - \boldsymbol{\mu}^{\mathcal{C}})\right)^{1/2}}, \tag{2}$$

where $\boldsymbol{\mu}^{\mathcal{C}}$ and $\boldsymbol{\Sigma}^{\mathcal{C}}$ are respectively the mean vector and covariance matrix obtained from the training signatures (i.e., the statistical model of the client) and $\mathbf{y}$ is the 40-feature vector used to attack the system.

3.2 Databases and Experimental Protocol

In order to avoid biased results, two different databases were used in the experiments: the MCYT database [12] and the BiosecurID database [13].

The first of them, MCYT, is used as development set in order to compute the best parameter values of the attack and to obtain a first estimation of its performance, which may be compared to that of the hill climbing attack proposed in [10]. The findings obtained on the MCYT database are then used to analyse the algorithm performance on a totally different database (BiosecurID), in order to get to a realistic overall evaluation of the attacking capabilities and efficiency of the proposed hill climbing technique. Next, the experimental protocol followed with each of the databases is presented.

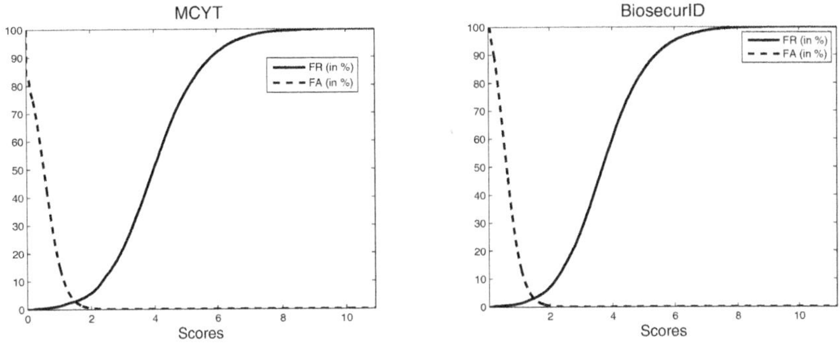

Fig. 1. FA and FR curves the MCYT (left) and BiosecurID (right) databases

MCYT experimental protocol. The initial evaluation experiments are carried out on the MCYT signature database [12], comprising 330 users. The database was acquired in 4 different sites with 5 time-spaced capture sets. Every client was asked to sign 5 times in each set, thus capturing 25 genuine signatures per user.

The experimental protocol is the same followed in [10], so that the final results are fully comparable. Thus, the database is divided into a training set (used to estimate the distribution G from which the initial simplex is taken) and a test set (containing the user's accounts being attacked), which are afterwards swapped (two-fold cross-validation). The training set initially comprises one signature from the genuine ones of the odd users in the database, and the test set the genuine samples of the even users. This way, the donors captured in the 4 sites are homogeneously distributed over the two sets.

For each user, five different genuine models are computed using one training signature from each acquisition set, so that the temporal variability of the signing process is taken into account. With this approach, a total $330 \times 5 = 1,650$ accounts are attacked (825 in each of the two-fold cross-validation process).

In order to set the threshold δ, where we consider that the attack has been successful, the False Acceptance (FA) and False Rejection (FR) curves of the system are computed. Each of the 5 estimated models of every user is matched with the remaining 20 genuine signatures ($5 \times 20 \times 330 = 33,000$ genuine scores), while the impostor scores are generated comparing the 5 statistical models with one signature of the remaining donors, making a total of $5 \times 330 \times 329 = 542,850$ random impostor scores. The FA and FR curves are depicted in Fig. 1 (left), together with three different realistic operating points used in the attack experiments (FA = 0.05%, FA = 0.01%, and FA = 0.0025%).

BiosecurID Experimental Protocol. In order to check whether the algorithm is equally effective with different databases, we established an analogous experimental protocol to the one defined for MCYT using the BiosecurID database [13]. This database comprises 400 users and was acquired in 4 different sessions in a 6 month time-span. Every client was asked to sign 4 times in each set, leading to 16 genuine signatures per user.

Analogously to the MCYT database, 4 different models are computed for each client using one signature from each acquisition set (i.e., 4 different signatures) so that the temporal variability is taken into account.

As before, the threshold δ is fixed after computing the FA and FR curves. The set of genuine and impostor scores are generated respectively matching each of the 4 estimated models of every user against the remaining 12 genuine samples of each subject ($4 \times 12 \times 400 = 19,200$ genuine scores), and against one signature of the other donors (leading to $4 \times 399 \times 400 = 638,400$ impostor scores). The FA and FR curves forgeries are depicted in Fig. 1 (right), together with three different realistic operating points used in the attack experiments (FA = 0.05%, FA = 0.01%, and FA = 0.0025%).

In order to assure that the hill-climbing performance results obtained on the BiosecurID database are in no way data-adapted, the initial G distribution in this experimental protocol is estimated on the MCYT database (i.e., part of the users in MCYT are used as training set), while BiosecurID is used only as test set.

3.3 Results

The goal of the experiments is to analyse in an objective and replicable manner the attacking skills of the proposed hill-climbing algorithm. With this objective, the performance of the attack will be evaluated in terms of the success rate and efficiency, defined as [16]:

- **Success Rate (SR)**: it is the expected probability that the attack breaks a given account. It is computed as the ratio between the number of broken accounts (A_B) and the total number of accounts attacked (A_T):

$$\mathrm{SR} = \frac{A_B}{A_T}$$

  This parameter indicates how dangerous the attack is: the higher the SR, the bigger the threat.
- **Efficiency** (Eff): it indicates the average number of matchings needed by the attack to break an account. It is defined as

$$Eff = \sum_{i=1}^{A_B} \frac{n_i}{A_B},$$

  where n_i is the number of matchings computed to bypass each of the broken accounts. This parameter gives an estimation of how easy it is for the attack to break into the system in terms of speed: the lower the Eff, the faster the attack.

A direct comparison between the attack performance results obtained on the MCYT database and those presented in [10] will also be given in this section.

Analysis of α, γ and β. The goal of the initial experiments carried out on the MCYT database is to study the effect of varying the three parameters of the algorithm (α, γ and β) on the performance of the attack. As described in Sect. 2, these parameters affect how the new point of the simplex is computed at each iteration and denote: α the reflection coefficient, γ the expansion coefficient, and β the contraction coefficient.

The main objective of this experiment is not to search for the optimal values of $[\alpha, \gamma, \beta]$, but rather to understand their effect on the attack behaviour and to find a general suboptimal set of values for which the algorithm may present a good performance under different attacking scenarios. To do so, we will perform three successive steps fixing in each of them two of the parameters and sweeping the other in a given range. According to the original downhill simplex algorithm [11], the best values for the parameters are $\alpha = 1$, $\gamma = 2$ and $\beta = 0.5$. Thus, we run the experiments in ranges centred on those values, taking always into account the constraints explained in Sect. 2, namely: $\alpha > 0$, $\gamma > 1$ and $0 < \beta < 1$. The operating point chosen was FA = 0.05% and FR = 11.80%, for a maximum number of iterations $M = 5,000$.

- **Step 1:** α. First we vary α with $\gamma = 2$ and $\beta = 0.5$. As can be seen in Fig. 2,a good performance point is reached for $\alpha = 1.1$.
- **Step 2:** γ. Then, with $\alpha = 1.1$ and $\beta = 0.5$ fixed, we sweep γ from 1 to 2.5. This second plot reaches a maximum at 1.1.
- **Step 3:** β. Finally, with those two fixed values ($\alpha = 1.1$ and $\gamma = 1.1$), we find a maximum for β at 0.8.

This will be the set of parameter values that will be used in the rest of the experiments, $[\alpha, \gamma, \beta] = [1.1, 1.1, 0.8]$.

Analysis of different operating points. In this experiment, the suboptimal set of parameter values found in the previous section $[\alpha, \gamma, \beta] = [1.1, 1.1, 0.8]$ is used here to analyse the performance of the attack for different operating points of the automatic signature verification system, namely: FA = [0.05%, 0.01%, 0.0025%], which correspond to those considered by Galbally et al. [10]. Therefore, results of both works (shown in Table 1) may be directly compared. The SR difference between both attacks is less than 8%, while the efficiency improved about 75% with our proposed method. This way, the hill-climbing based on the uphill simplex proves to be highly competitive, breaking the accounts remarkably faster than the Bayesian hill-climbing, at the cost of a small loss of accuracy.

Analysis of the initial G distribution. In this last development experiment, also carried out on the MCYT database, the number of users employed for the estimation of the initial distribution G is varied from 5 to 165 in order to study its impact on the attack performance. The SR improvement was lower than 3% in terms of SR and Eff for all operating points, as can be observed in Fig. 3. Thus, the attack proves to be highly competitive with as few as 5 different training signatures compared to over 150 needed by the algorithm proposed in [10].

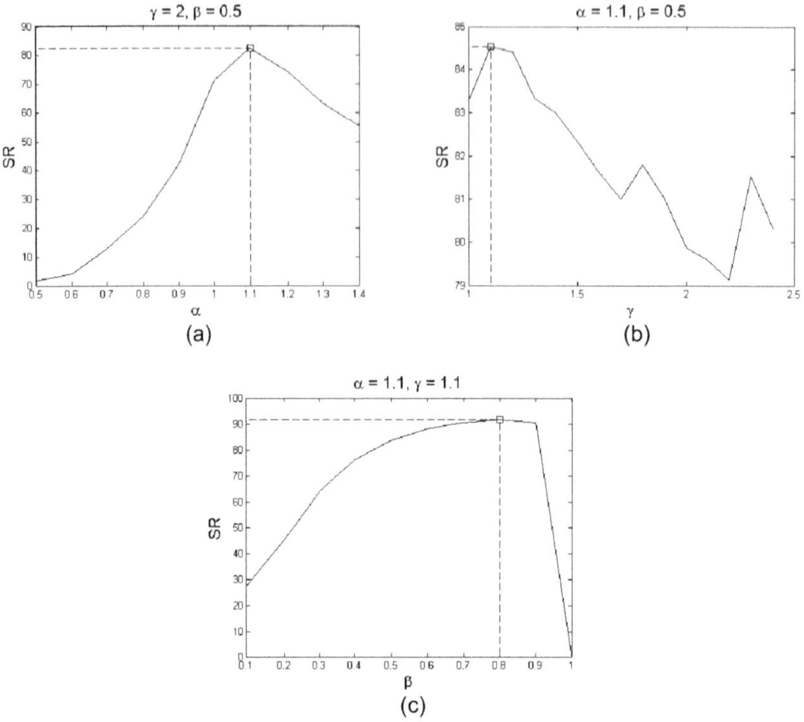

Fig. 2. (a) Success rates for $\alpha \in [0.5, 1.4], \gamma = 2, \beta = 0.5$. Maximum at $\alpha = 1.1$. (b) Success rates for $\gamma \in [1, 2.4], \alpha = 1.1, \beta = 0.5$. Maximum at $\gamma = 1.1$. (c) Success rates for $\beta \in [0.1, 1], \alpha = 1.1, \gamma = 1.1$. Maximum at $\beta = 0.8$.

Analysis of the performance on the BiosecurID database. Finally, the knowledge acquired in the previous experiments was applied to study the dependency of the attack performance on the data being used. Thus, the parameter values fixed in the MCYT database (i.e., $[\alpha, \gamma, \beta] = [1.1, 1.1, 0.8]$) are deployed to attack the accounts of the subjects comprised in the BiosecurID database. As mentioned in Sect. 3.2, the initial distribution G is computed using one signature from each of the initial 5 users in MCYT. This way, the training set (MCYT) and test set (BiosecurID) are totally independent, leading to fully unbiased results.

As shown in Table 2, the performance of the attack is very similar, both in terms of the efficiency and the success rates for both datasets. Even though Eff is a little higher for all the three different operating points, it must be taken into account that in the case of MCYT, the parameters of the algorithm were specifically adjusted for the dataset, while they remained the same for this second database. On the other hand, the SR is about 2% higher in the case of BiosecurID, proving that the algorithm has a high adaptation capability, performing well under different operating conditions.

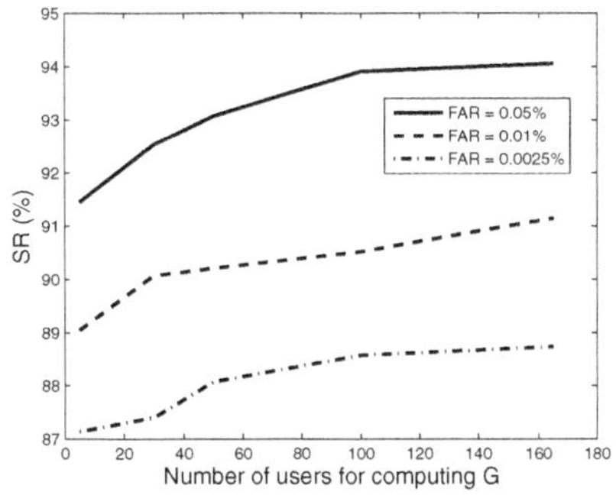

Fig. 3. Success rates for the three operating points tested (FA = 0.05%, FA = 0.01%, FA = 0.0025%), for an increasing number of subjects used to compute the distribution G from which the initial simplex is taken.

Table 1. Efficiency and SR (in %) for each operating point, compared to the performance results given in Galbally et al. [10]

FA	Uphill simplex		Gal. et al. [10]	
	SR	Eff	SR	Eff
0.05%	91.76%	1,556	98.12%	5,712
0.01%	89.58%	1,678	96.60%	6,076
0.0025%	87.82%	1,805	94.90%	6,475

Graphical example. An execution of the attack at the FA = 0.05% operating point and using the best algorithm configuration for the database MCYT is shown in Fig. 4. The signature was successfully attacked in less than 500 iterations. At the top of the figure, we can see a signature of the client being attacked as well as the successive best similarity scores in each iteration until the threshold δ is reached. At the bottom, the evolution of the simplices corresponding to the scores marked with a vertical line are shown for two pairs of parameters (1 and 2 on the left, 3 and 4 on the right). A darker colour denotes a previous iteration and the cross is the target being attacked. It can be observed that the simplices quickly approach the target, diminishing their area at the same time.

Table 2. Success rate (in %) and Efficiency for each operating point tested, using 5 subjects from MCYT for the training of the initial simplex, for both the MCYT and the BiosecurID databases

FA	BiosecurID		MCYT	
	SR	Eff	SR	Eff
0.05%	92.69%	2,051	91.32%	1,178
0.01%	87.94%	2,440	88.43%	1,353
0.0025%	83.44%	2,611	86.77%	1,661

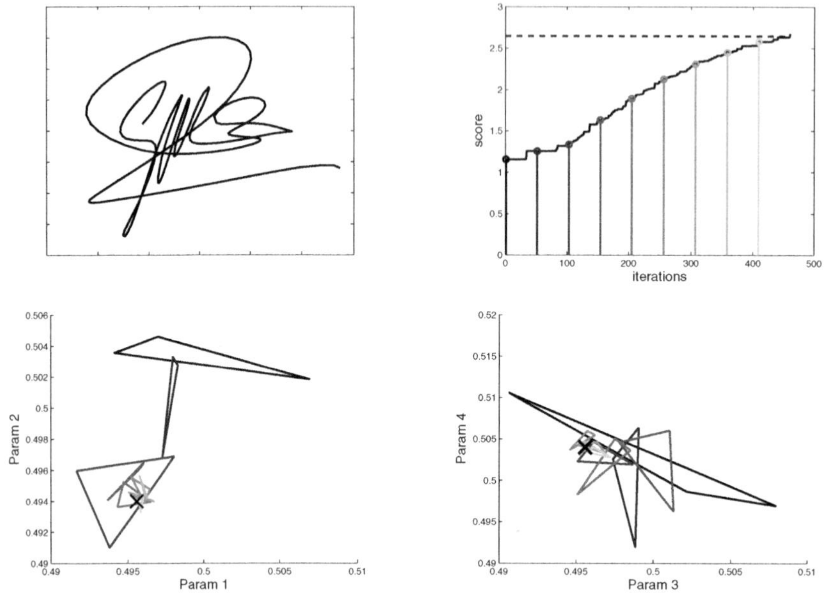

Fig. 4. Evolution of the algorithm in a successful attack. On the top we show one signature of the client attacked (left) and the scores reached for every iteration of the hill-climbing algorithm (right). On the bottom appear the simplices corresponding to the scores marked with a vertical line for parameters one and two (left) and three and four (right). A darker colour denotes a previous iteration while the cross shows the target being attacked.

4 Conclusions

In the present work, a hill-climbing attack based on the uphill simplex algorithm, an adaptation of downhill simplex, was presented and evaluated on a feature-based signature verification system using two different databases comprising 330 and 400 users, respectively. Several experiments proved its high efficiency, reaching success rates over 90% for the best configuration found.

The algorithm performance was also compared to that of the Bayesian hill-climbing attack [10], resulting in very similar success rates but with a convergence speed which is around four times faster (it needs a quarter of the number of matchings to break the same amount of accounts). Furthermore, the proposed algorithm only requires 5 different real signatures to be initialized, in opposition to the Bayesian-based attack, where over 150 samples were used.

The experiments have also shown that the performance of the proposed attack is independent of the data being used, as the results obtained in both databases (MCYT and BiosecurID) were almost identical although the attack parameters had been specifically fixed for the MCYT database.

It should finally be emphasized that the proposed attack can be applied to the evaluation of the vulnerabilities of any biometric system based on fixed length templates of real numbers, regardless of the matcher or biometric trait being used.

Acknowledgements

This work has been partially supported by projects Contexts (S2009/TIC-1485) from CAM, Bio-Challenge (TEC2009-11186) from Spanish MICINN, TABULA RASA (FP7-ICT-257289) from EU, and *Cátedra UAM-Telefónica.*

References

1. Jain, A.K., Ross, A., Pankanti, S.: Biometrics: a tool for information security. IEEE Trans. on Information Forensics and Security 1, 125–143 (2006)
2. Van der Putte, T., Keuning, J.: Biometrical fingerprint recognition: don't get your fingers burned. In: Proc. Conference on Smart Card Research and Advanced Applications (CARDIS), pp. 289–303 (2000)
3. Pacut, A., Czajka, A.: Aliveness detection for iris biometrics. In: Proc. IEEE Int. Carnahan Conf. on Security Technology (ICCST), vol. 1, pp. 122–129 (2006)
4. Soutar, C., Gilroy, R., Stoianov, A.: Biometric system performance and security. In: Proc. IEEE Automatic Identification Advanced Technologies, AIAT (1999)
5. Ratha, N.K., Connell, J.H., Bolle, R.M.: An analysis of minutiae matching strength. In: Bigun, J., Smeraldi, F. (eds.) AVBPA 2001. LNCS, vol. 2091, pp. 223–228. Springer, Heidelberg (2001)
6. Galbally, J., Fierrez, J., Rodriguez-Gonzalez, J., Alonso-Fernandez, F., Ortega-Garcia, J., Tapiador, M.: On the vulnerability of fingerprint verification systems to fake fingerprint attacks. In: Proc. IEEE Int. Carnahan Conf. on Security Technology (ICCST), pp. 130–136 (2006)
7. Adler, A.: Sample images can be independently restored from face recognition templates. In: Proc. Canadian Conference on Electrical and Computer Engineering (CCECE), vol. 2, pp. 1163–1166 (2003)
8. Uludag, U., Jain, A.: Attacks on biometric systems: a case study in fingerprints. In: Proc. SPIE Seganography and Watermarking of Multimedia Contents VI, vol. 5306, pp. 622–633 (2004)
9. Martinez-Diaz, M., Fierrez, J., Alonso-Fernandez, F., Ortega-Garcia, J., Siguenza, J.A.: Hill-climbing and brute force attacks on biometric systems: a case study in match-on-card fingerprint verification. In: Proc. IEEE Int. Carnahan Conf. on Security Technology (ICCST), vol. 1, pp. 151–159 (2006)
10. Galbally, J., Fierrez, J., Ortega-Garcia, J.: Bayesian hill-climbing attack and its application to signature verification. In: Lee, S.-W., Li, S.Z. (eds.) ICB 2007. LNCS, vol. 4642, pp. 386–395. Springer, Heidelberg (2007)
11. Nelder, J.A., Mead, R.: A simplex method for function minimization. Computer Journal 7, 313–368 (1965)
12. Ortega-Garcia, J., Fierrez-Aguilar, J., et al.: MCYT baseline corpus: a bimodal biometric database. IEE Proc. Vis. Image Signal Process. 150, 395–401 (2003)

13. Fierrez, J., Galbally, J., Ortega-Garcia, J., Freire, M.R., Alonso-Fernandez, F., Ramos, D., Toledano, D.T., Gonzalez-Rodriguez, J., Siguenza, J.A., Garrido-Salas, J., Anguiano, E., de Rivera, G.G., Ribalda, R., Faundez-Zanuy, M., Ortega, J.A., Cardeoso-Payo, V., Viloria, A., Vivaracho, C.E., Moro, Q.I., Igarza, J.J., Sanchez, J., Hernaez, I., Orrite-Uruuela, C., Martinez-Contreras, F., Gracia-Roche, J.J.: BiosecurID: a multimodal biometric database. Pattern Analysis and Applications 13, 235–246 (2009)
14. Fierrez-Aguilar, J., Nanni, L., et al.: An On-Line Signature Verification System Based on Fusion of Local and Global Information. In: Kanade, T., Jain, A., Ratha, N.K. (eds.) AVBPA 2005. LNCS, vol. 3546, pp. 523–532. Springer, Heidelberg (2005)
15. Jain, A.K., Nandakumar, K., Ross, A.: Score normalization in multimodal biometric systems. Pattern Recognition 38, 2270–2285 (2005)
16. Galbally, J.: Vulnerabilities and Attack Protection in Security Systems Based on Biometric Recognition. PhD thesis (2009)

Combining Multiagent Negotiation and an Interacting Verification Process to Enhance Biometric-Based Identification

Márjory Abreu and Michael Fairhurst

School of Engineering and Digital Arts, University of Kent, Canterbury, Kent CT2 7NT, UK
{mcda2,M.C.Fairhurst}@kent.ac.uk

Abstract. Designing a biometrics-based system poses many challenges, such as how many and which modalities to use (multimodal configurations being widely adopted), which classification methods are appropriate, user acceptability issues, and so on. Machine learning techniques need as much information as possible to maximise accuracy, but biometric samples are not necessarily straightforward to acquire and usability factors can be very influential. This paper presents a new recognition structure for biometric systems design, using an agent-based approach which maximises the value of the available information. Using handwritten signature as an illustrative modality, we present results which show that carefully structured unimodal systems can deliver excellent performance.

1 Introduction

The emergence of new market sectors, such as electronic commerce and on-line healthcare systems, critically relies on robust security and authentication technologies to achieve reliability and cost effectiveness. Biometric technologies are emerging as increasingly important components in regulating on-line information access, and significant application areas exist and will continue to grow in banking, security monitoring and identity management, database access, document control, forensic investigations and telemedicine, to name just some examples.

The demands of a computational system which deals with biometric recognition efficiently and which offers high performance has especially motivated the study of machine learning techniques in recent years ([18], [5] and [7]). Despite the fact that many classification algorithms appear to produce satisfactory performance, they are nevertheless often found not to generate reliable results in real world tasks (with very complex databases, for instance) [13]. Thus, while optimising the performance attainable with any single particular classifier remains an important consideration, in order to make significant progress towards improving performance levels, the idea of using the different (often complementary) characteristics of different classifiers within a single task domain is often considered as a more effective strategy, and the concept of multiclassifier systems (MCS) has become paramount in recent years ([19] and [20]).

C. Vielhauer et al. (Eds.): BioID 2011, LNCS 6583, pp. 95–105, 2011.

Despite the widespread use and development of multiclassifier techniques (often focusing on the fusion techniques adopted), the choice of the base classifier components of these systems and, especially, determining the optimal choice of a combination method which is most suitable for a specific application, is often a difficult process. Indeed, optimisation often requires the execution of exhaustive testing to choose the best implementation [8]. The main reason for this is that although a multiclassifier approach can be effective, the final decision-making process will always be based on a limited input from the base classifiers (they do not have the opportunity of changing their output once the process has started) sent to a unique method (which is normally one single fusion classification algorithm).

One alternative way to make the decision-making process of a multiclassifier system more dynamic, interactive and flexible is to include the base classifiers within an agent-based architecture, where an agent is able to carry out the classification task and make its decision in a more autonomous, distributed and flexible way ([8] and [2]). In principle, multiagent systems applied in classification scenarios offer a powerful alternative paradigm, allowing the possibility of overcoming the difficulties involved in efficiently handling the combination problem, since they are structured to make their own decisions about the classification output of the system as well as to change opinions (change the first predicted identity) and persuade the other agents to do the same ([3] and [1]).

Nevertheless, the issues which must be addressed in designing a biometrics-based system are not only related to the combination/fusion technique but also relate to the modality(ies) used. Many different technologies are available for person recognition and identity authentication, examples including measures based on information from the face [12], fingerprint [24] and so on. Research interest in such biometric modalities (the chosen measurement domains based on physiological or behavioural characteristics of interest) has never been greater but, while ideas for new and varied modalities continue to emerge, it is increasingly apparent that some currently available modalities offer significant advantages in specific security and identity applications such as those noted above. Moreover, some modalities which have real potential for maximising effective deployment continue to be hampered by technical limitations or, sometimes, by incorrect perceptions of what can be achieved [11].

A case in point is the handwritten signature, a very natural and popular means of establishing and conveying identity information. Yet automatic signature verification, notwithstanding the many advantages it offers over some other options, does not always enjoy the same level of support as some other modalities which may, in fact, prove less appropriate in particular practical scenarios. This is partly because, being a behavioural biometric (it relies on repeatable behavioural actions rather than inherent physiological characteristics), the sample variability often encountered can be troublesome, but against this must be set many other clear advantages such as:

- It is already in everyday use for paper-based authentication purposes, and therefore it has an established legal status [9];

- It is relatively cheap and easy to adopt [9];
- It can have high uptake when (optimally) deployed [4];
- It can be readily integrated into an existing application scenario with little or no disruption to current practice [11];
- Signature data are already collected as part of many current or envisaged enrolment scenarios but not always included in practical identity verification processes [23];
- It can offer supplementary identity information even where it is not adopted as the principal source of identification data [10].

In this paper we propose an approach to enhanced individual identification which exploits both verification and identification agents to improve the accuracy with which practical biometric identification systems can be designed effectively. Although, for the reasons noted above, we will present our proposed method using the signature modality as an interesting and relevant example for illustrative purposes, it is completely general and can be applied to any biometric modality.

2 Developing a Multiagent Approach to Biometrics-Based Identification

The method we propose is an adaptation of an agent-based negotiation method first proposed in [8] for general pattern recognition scenarios. Originally, the method was based only on agents which perform the same classification task and until now it has not been used in a biometric identification task. A key development here is that we propose an automated definition of the level of "punishment" given to each agent taking into account the output of identity verification classifiers.

An intelligent agent is a software-based computer system that has autonomy, social ability, reactivity and pro-activeness [25]. Agents are entities which can communicate, cooperate and work together to reach a common goal. They interact using negotiation protocols. Figure 1 shows the architecture of an agent. As the main goal of all agents is the same, the general structure for all agents is the same. This agent has four main modules, which are:

- *Controller module*: This receives the user queries and defines the activation order of its internal processes. For instance, this module decides, based on the negotiation result, if it is important for the agent to change its existing result in order to reach a common result.
- *Decision-making module*: This is responsible for reasoning about its knowledge in order to define the best output for a classifier. The main idea of this module is to search for a result, eliminating those which do not fit the existing conditions. Then, it ranks the results in decreasing order, according to a set of evaluation criteria. Finally, it picks the first (best) ranked entry and defines this as the correct result.

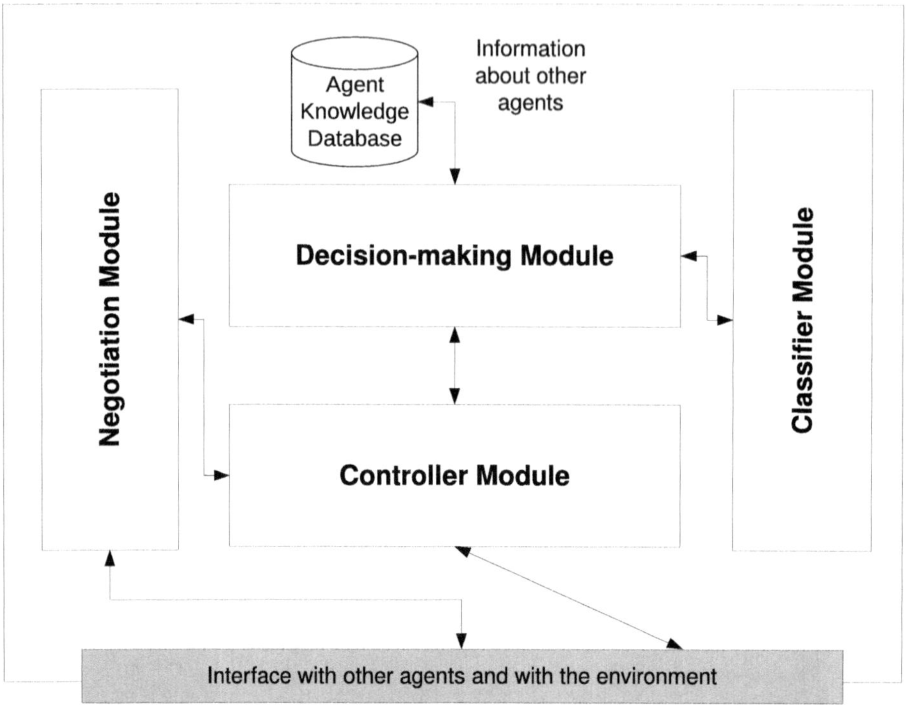

Fig. 1. Architecture of the agent

- *Negotiation module*: This is responsible for the communication with other agents in order to reach an agreed result. It builds an action plan for negotiation or uses a previously determined action plan. During the negotiation process, it can be suggested that an agent should change its result. However, the agent has autonomy to decide whether to change or to confirm its current result.
- *Classifier module*: This is responsible for executing the classifier algorithm of the agent. It is beneficial that each agent should have a different classifier structure, thereby providing different analyses for an input pattern.

A piece of information used as an essential component for the fusion/negotiation methods is called *confidence degree* and we will designate this as *Conf.* All the classifiers used in the work reported here will produce outputs for all the possible classes and the winner class (the one with the highest output value) is assigned the overall output (decision) of this classifier. In the negotiation technique which will be presented here we will use all the outputs or confidence degrees for all the classes of the problem.

The basic idea underpinning our proposed method is that a decrease in the confidence degree of the agents is considered through the use of a sensitivity analysis during the testing phase. This analysis can be achieved by excluding and/or varying the values of an input attribute and analysing the variation in the performance at the classifier level. The main aim of this analysis is to investigate the sensitivity of a classifier to a certain attribute and to use this information in the agent negotiation process. This analysis is performed with respect to all attributes of the input patterns in an identity prediction classifier in the agents as well as in the verification classifier.

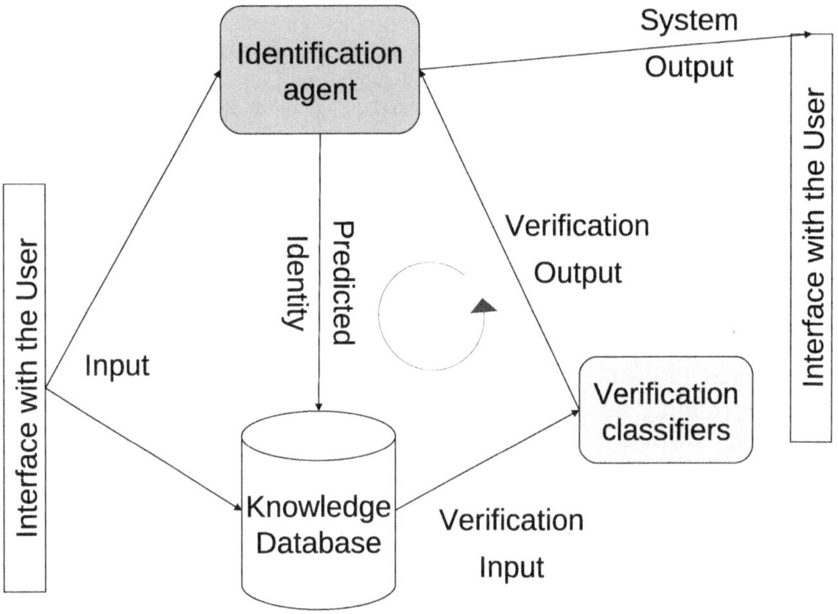

Fig. 2. Multiagent-based system workflow

A schematic view of this multiagent-based system can be seen in Figure 2. All agents should allow their classifier module to be trained and to negotiate an agreed result for a test (input) pattern. Our proposed method for the production of an action plan is described as follows:

1. Allow all the classifiers in the system to be trained. During the training phase we carry out a sensitivity analysis as well as determining the training mean for all features in each classifier.
2. Start the negotiation process by trying to show the other agents that their results are not good ones, using a punishment measure (which suggests a decrease in their confidence level):
   (a) Rank in decreasing order the calculated difference between the input feature (test pattern) and the training mean of that feature for all classes;
   (b) For the first N attributes, do the following:
      i. Choose an agent and let it choose another agent to attack.
      ii. Check the class assigned by the attacked agent and the sensitivity of the corresponding classifier to this attribute.

   iii. Check the output of the verification classifier related to the predicted identity. In this phase, the test sample will be tested against a template stored in the *Knowledge Database* correspondent to the predicted identity of the *classifier module* in the agent. The verification classifiers will produce either "yes" (if the test sample is correctly verified against the template of the predicted identity) or "no" (otherwise) as results.
   iv. Send a message to the other agent suggesting a punishment by reducing the confidence level of that agent;
3. After the negotiation process, the classifier agent with the highest confidence degree is assumed to be the most suitable one to classify the test pattern and its output is considered as the overall identity output.

It is important to emphasise that once one agent sends a suggestion to decrease the confidence degree of the other agent, the second agent will also send a suggestion to punish the first agent. Each cycle within which all agents suggest punishment constitutes a "round". This process proceeds until all N features are seen or when only one of the agents has non-negative confidence.

The principal idea behind this process is that the more distant an attribute is from the training mean, the higher is the probability that a sensitive classifier is wrong. Also, if there is evidence that the sample is not a match to its corresponding template (checking the verification classifiers), this information is used to suggest a decrease in the confidence degree of an agent. The punishment value is calculated as follows (Equation 1):

$$Pun_i = \frac{D_i * S_i}{R_i * Ln(n_{verified-as-no})} \tag{1}$$

where:

- D: is the difference between the current i attribute of the test pattern and its training mean;
- S: is the sensitivity of the classifier to the corresponding i attribute of the chosen class;
- R: is the ranking of the i attribute in its difference from the training mean;
- $Ln(n_{verified-as-no})$: is the natural logarithm of $n_{verified-as-no}$ (the number of verification classifiers which have as output "no").

The natural logarithm is used in Equation 1 in order to give differentiated weighting depending on the verification classifiers with negative outcome. The sensitivity analysis and the training mean, along with the analysis of whether the sample is a match or not (as undertaken by the verification classifiers), are transformed into rules and constitute the overall domain knowledge base of the classifier agent.

An agent can be asked to change its result. This occurs when the punishment parameter is higher than a threshold during a set of rounds (features). Then an agent can choose an alternative class (usually a classifier provides a decreasing list of possible classes to which a pattern belongs) or undertake a new decision-making process.

3 Methodology

In order to investigate and evaluate performance in our experimental study, a range of different individual classifiers were selected and used for identity and verification prediction. The base classifiers used are Multi-Layer Perceptron (MLP) [16], Optimised IREP (Incremental Reduced Error Pruning) (JRip) [14], Support Vector Machines (SVM) [22] and K-Nearest Neighbours (KNN) [6].

In the investigation reported here we chose a ten-fold-cross-validation approach because of its relative simplicity, and because it has been shown to be statistically sound in evaluating the performance of classification tasks [21]. The comparison of two classification methods is accomplished by analysing the statistical significance of the difference between the error mean of the classification rate on independent test sets from the methods evaluated. In order to evaluate this the p-value provided by the t-test [21] measures the degree of confidence in the result. In our case, we use a confidence level of 95%, where one sample is deemed to be statistically different from another only when the p-value is lower than 0.05.

In order to ensure a valid statistical evaluation, we also implemented simple Majority Voting [19] and Sum-based fusion [17] using the same base classifiers as we adopted in the agent-based system. Each system has used three identity prediction classifiers in the case of the centralised fusion techniques and three identity prediction classifiers and three verification classifiers for the agent-based system.

The advantages and disadvantages of new techniques can often be best seen when tested using challenging datasets. Therefore, in the experimental work to be reported here we have used two rather different handwritten signature databases, which we will refer to in our discussion as Database A and Database B.

The first handwritten signature database adopted, Database A was generated as part of a more general multimodal database, the data being collected in the Department of Electronics at the University of Kent in the UK, in a controlled environment, as part of a Europe-wide project undertaken by the EU BioSecure Network of Excellence [23]. For the compilation of the database, each of 79 users provided their information in two sessions. Specifically, the database contains 50 signature samples for each subject, where 30 are samples of the subject's true signature and 20 are attempts to imitate another user's signature (skilled forgeries). In this investigation we have used all 50 samples of each subject. The data were collected using an A4-sized graphics tablet with a density of 500 lines per inch. There are 16 representative biometric features extracted from each signature sample (a mix of dynamic and static features). These features are chosen to be representative of those known to be commonly adopted in signature processing applications. All the available biometric features are used in the classification process as input to the system.

The second handwritten signature database, Database B, contains signature samples collected as part of an earlier BTG/University of Kent study [15] from 359 volunteers (129 male, 230 female) representing a cross-section of the general public. The capture environment was a typical retail outlet, providing a real-world scenario in which to acquire credible data. There are 7428 signature samples in total, where the number of samples from each individual varies between 2 and 79. There are no attempts of forgeries (no skilled forgeries). The data was collected using an A4-sized graphics tablet with a density of 500 lines per inch. Because of the nature of the data collection exercise itself, the number of samples collected differs considerably across participants. We impose a lower limit of 10 samples per person for inclusion in our experimentation, this constraint resulting in a population of 273 signers and 6956 signatures for experimentation.

These two fundamentally different databases as well as the different base classifiers forming the fusion/agent negotiation structures will provide interesting insights about how beneficial the proposed new multiagent-based technique can be when used in this type of application.

4 Analysis of the Results

In order to understand the results generated by the fusion and negotiation methods, it is important first to analyse the base classifiers adopted for the experiments. Table 1 shows the error rate and the standard deviation for these classifiers both for the identification classifiers and for the verification classifiers for each of the handwritten signature databases.

Table 1. Results for the individual classifiers

	Database A		**Database B**	
Classifiers	**Identification**	**Verification**	**Identification**	**Verification**
MLP	12.81%±3.21	8.79%±2.10	9.88%±2.92	9.32%±2.98
Jrip	14.47%±3.94	9.03%±1.84	15.72%±3.12	10.21%±2.67
SVM	13.59%±3.71	9.09%±2.77	10.78%±4.21	10.35%±2.79
KNN	16.05%±3.44	9.98%±2.37	17.71%±3.18	11.96%±2.37

As expected, the verification classifiers generated a better result than the identification classifiers, largely because the verification task is, of course, less complex and challenging than the identification task. Also, it is possible to see that different algorithms perform differently according to the target task. Some very important facts must be taken into account when analysing these results:

- Database A contains skilled forgeries and was collected in a controlled environment and
- Database B contains different numbers of samples per user and was collected in a non-controlled environment.

Even though these characteristics make the databases very different, they still produce similar error rates. Using different classifiers shows us the possibilities of dealing with different problems reflected in the data sources used. These results indicate that the MLP and SVM classifiers are statistically better suited to deal with the more unbalanced (i.e. different number of samplers per user creating a more complex learning class) and noisier data when performing identification than are the Jrip and KNN classifiers.

These differences are not to be found when the verification classifiers are considered, but when the error rates are subdivided into skilled forgeries and non-skilled forgeries for the Database A, it can be observed that around 60% of the overall error rate is attributable to the skilled forgeries.

The most interesting results are obtained when the fusion/negotiation methods are applied, as can be seen in Table 2. Clearly, the agent-based result is considerably better than the sum-based and the vote-based results, as is confirmed by the application of the t-test.

Table 2. Results for the fusion techniques

Fusion Techniques	**Database A**	**Database B**
Multiagent system	3.14%±1.39	2.98%±1.36
Majority Vote	8.69%±2.44	7.51%±2.56
Sum	7,21%±1.75	7.26%±1.48

These results are very positive, and illustrate a very significant point about our proposed structure. Specifically, our model requires no information beyond that which is normally adopted in biometric processing, but our structure makes better use of the information available as an inherent consequence of the paradigm employed, increasing the reliability of the overall result compared with what can be achieved when more traditional processing structures are adopted.

It is noteworthy that using a verification module in the system also helps to identify instances of incorrect classification or, more particularly, the occurrence of skilled forgeries more efficiently, this being clearly reflected in the intensity of the applied punishment.

5 Conclusions

This paper has introduced a novel approach to developing a processing structure well suited to applications in biometrics, and which uses intelligent agent-based negotiation to improve the quality of decision-making. Although some work has been reported using game theory and auction paradigms [11], here we have adopted a structure based on a sensitivity-related negotiation paradigm, with very encouraging results. The interaction between identification and verification processing as part of the overall decision-making is also a new concept which has been shown to offer benefits.

The independence and individuality of each agent taking part in the identification process offer an important new dimension to the principles of biometric identification processing. The results presented also point to the potential benefits, especially using the negotiation strategy, of allowing the agents to carry the configuration process further.

We have shown that modalities which may on first examination, with respect to a specific application scenario, be considered too unstable or insufficiently powerful for adoption, but which would offer other positive advantages might, within our proposed processing framework, now offer a more suitable option. What is most important here is that the empirical study reported increases an awareness of the importance of adopting a flexible and task-related strategy for developing an optimal solution in specific circumstances. For example, the handwritten signature (our illustrative case of a modality which may not always be considered to offer sufficiently robust performance in some applications) can be seen to generate greatly improved performance when implemented in an effective way, even when skilled forgeries are used to attack the system.

The results presented have supported the view that, at least in terms of error-rate indicators, it is possible to develop powerful systems based on a single modality which offers scenario-oriented operational advantages, rather than necessarily resorting to more complex (and perhaps less user-friendly) multimodal strategies.

References

1. Abreu, M.C.D.C., Fairhurst, M.: Enhancing identity prediction using a novel approach to combining hard- and soft-biometric information. IEEE Transactions on Systems, Man, and Cybernetics, Part C: Applications and Reviews (99), 1–9 (2010)
2. Abreu, M.C.C., Canuto, A.M.P.: Analysing the benefits of using a fuzzy-neuro model in the accuracy of the neurage system: an agent-based system for classification tasks. In: International Joint Conference on Neural Networks (IJCNN 2006), Vancouver, BC, pp. 2959–2966 (2006)
3. Abreu, M.C.C., Fairhurst, M.: Analysing the benefits of a novel multiagent approach in a multimodal biometrics identification task. IEEE Systems Journal 3(4), 410–417 (2009)
4. Abreu, M.C.C., Fairhurst, M.C.: Improving forgery detection in off-line forensic signature processing. In: The 3rd International Conference on Imaging for Crime Detection and Prevention, ICDP 2009 (2009)
5. Alkoot, F.M., Kittler, J.: Experimental evaluation of expert fusion strategies. Pattern Recognition Letter 20(11-13), 1361–1369 (1999)
6. Arya, A.: An optimal algorithm for approximate nearest neighbors searching fixed dimensions. Journal of ACM 45(6), 891–923 (1998)
7. Bittencourt, V.G., Abreu, M.C.C., de Souto, M.C.P., Canuto, A.M.P.: An empirical comparison of individual machine learning techniques and ensemble approaches in protein structural class prediction. In: IEEE International Joint Conference on Neural Networks (IJCNN 2005), vol. 1, pp. 527–531 (2005)
8. Canuto, A.M.P., Abreu, M.C.C., Medeiros, A., Souza, F., Gomes Junior, M.F., Bezerra, V.S.: Investigating the use of an agent-based multi-classifier system for classification tasks. In: Pal, N.R., Kasabov, N., Mudi, R.K., Pal, S., Parui, S.K. (eds.) ICONIP 2004. LNCS, vol. 3316, pp. 854–859. Springer, Heidelberg (2004)
9. Dyer, A.G., Found, B., Rogers, D.: Visual attention and expertise for forensic signature analysis. Journal of Forensic Science 51(6), 1397–1404 (2006)

10. Fairhurst, M.C., Abreu, M.C.C.: An investigation of predictive profiling from handwritten signature data. In: 10th International Conference on Document Analysis and Recognition (ICDAR 2009), Barcelona, Spain, pp. 1305–1309. IEEE Computer Society, Los Alamitos (2009)
11. Fairhurst, M.C., Abreu, M.C.C.: Balancing performance factors in multisource biometric processing platforms. IET Signal Processing 3(4), 342–351 (2009)
12. Franco, A., Maio, D., Maltoni, D.: 2d face recognition based on supervised subspace learning from 3d models. Pattern Recognition Letter 41(12), 3822–3833 (2008)
13. Fumera, G., Roli, F.: A theoretical and experimental analysis of linear combiners for multiple classifier systems. IEEE Transactions on Pattern Analysis and Machine Intelligence 27(6), 942–956 (2005)
14. Furnkranz, J., Widmer, G.: Incremental reduced error pruning. In: Proceedings the Eleventh International Conference on Machine Learning (ICML 1994), New Brunswick, NJ, pp. 70–77 (1994)
15. Guest, R.M.: The repeatability of signatures. In: The 9th International Workshop on Frontiers in Handwriting Recognition (IWFHR 2004), Washington, DC, USA, pp. 492–497. IEEE Computer Society, Los Alamitos (2004)
16. Haykin, S.: Neural networks: a comprehensive foundation. The Knowledge Engineering Review 13(4), 409–412 (1999)
17. Kittler, J., Alkoot, F.M.: Sum versus vote fusion in multiple classifier systems. IEEE Transactions on Pattern Analysis and Machine Intelligence 25(1), 110–115 (2003)
18. Kittler, J., Hatef, M., Duin, R.P.W., Matas, J.: On combining classifiers. IEEE Transactions on Pattern Analysis and Machine Intelligence 20(3), 226–239 (1998)
19. Kuncheva, L.I.: Combining Pattern Classifiers: Methods and Algorithms. Wiley-Interscience, Hoboken (2004)
20. Kuncheva, L.I., Rodriguez, J.J.: Classifier ensembles with a random linear oracle. IEEE Transactions on Knowledge and Data Engineering 19(4), 500–508 (2007)
21. Mitchell, T.M.: Machine Learning. McGraw-Hill, New York (1997)
22. Nello, C., John, S.T.: An introduction to support vector machines and other kernel-based learning methods. Robotics 18(6), 687–689 (2000)
23. Ortega-Garcia, J., Alonso-Fernandez, F., Fierrez-Aguilar, J., Garcia-Mateo, C., Salicetti, S., Allano, L., Ly-Van, B., Dorizzi, B.: Software tool and acquisition equipment recommendations for the three scenarios considered. Technical Report Report No.: D6.2.1. Contract No.: IST-2002-507634, Universidad Politechnica de Madrid (June 2006)
24. Ross, A., Shah, J., Jain, A.K.: From template to image: Reconstructing fingerprints from minutiae points. IEEE Transactions on Pattern Analysis and Machine Intelligence 29, 544–560 (2007)
25. Wooldridge, M.: An introduction to multi-agent systems. John Wiley & Sons, Chichester (2002)

Performance Evaluation in Open-Set Speaker Identification

Amit Malegaonkar[1,*] and Aladdin Ariyaeeinia[2]

[1] Auraya Systems Pty. Ltd. Sydney, Australia
[2] University of Hertfordshire, College Lane, Hatfield, Hertfordshire, UK
amit.malegaonkar@auraya.net, a.m.ariyaeeinia@herts.ac.uk

Abstract. The concern in this study is the approach to evaluating the performance of the open-set speaker identification process. In essence, such a process involves first identifying the speaker model in the database that best matches the given test utterance, and then determining if the test utterance has actually been produced by the speaker associated with the best-matched model. Whilst, conventionally, the performance of each of these two sub-processes is evaluated independently, it is argued that the use of a measure of performance for the complete process can provide a more useful basis for comparing the effectiveness of different systems. Based on this argument, an approach to assessing the performance of open-set speaker identification is considered in this paper, which is in principle similar to the method used for computing the diarisation error rate. The paper details the above approach for assessing the performance of open-set speaker identification and presents an analysis of its characteristics.

1 Introduction

In general, speaker identification is defined as the process of determining the correct speaker of a given test utterance from a population of registered speakers [1-2]. If this process includes the option of declaring that the test utterance does not belong to any of the registered speakers, then it is specifically referred to as open-set speaker identification. An inherent feature of this process is that it provides the possibility of establishing individuals' identities without the need for any identity claims. This in turn offers the capability for enhancing the security aspect of speaker verification through the screening process. Such screening may be required at the enrolment phase to minimise the possibility of multiple identity acquisition, or deployed at the verification stage to increase the capability to detect access attempts by impostors.

Given a set of registered speakers and a sample test utterance, this task is defined as a twofold problem [3]. Firstly, it is required to identify the speaker model in the registered set that best matches the given test utterance. This is the process of identification. Next, it is required to determine if the test utterance is actually produced by the best matched speaker or it is originated by a speaker from outside the registered set. This is the process of verification. When the speaker is not required to provide an utterance of a specific text, the task is called Open-Set, Text-Independent Speaker Identification (OSTI-SI).

[*] During the course of this work, Malegaonkar was with the University of Hertfordshire.

C. Vielhauer et al. (Eds.): BioID 2011, LNCS 6583, pp. 106–112, 2011.

In the literature, it is acknowledged that OSTI-SI is the most challenging class of speaker recognition [3-4]. A factor influencing the complexity of OSTI-SI is the size of the population of registered speakers. In theory, as this population grows, the confusion in discriminating amongst the registered speakers is likely to increase and therefore the number of incorrect identifications is likely to increase as well. The growth in the said population also increases the difficulty in confidently declaring a test utterance as not belonging to any of the registered speakers, when this is indeed the case. The reason is that, as the population size grows, the possibility of a voice originating from an unknown speaker being very close to one of the registered speaker models increases. The problem of OSTI-SI is further complicated by undesired variation in speech characteristics due to anomalous events. These anomalies can have different forms ranging from the communication channel and environmental noise to uncharacteristic sounds generated by the speakers. The resultant variation in speech causes a mismatch between the corresponding test and pre-stored voice patterns. This can in turn lead to degradation of the OSTI-SI performance.

Conventionally, the evaluation of OSTI-SI performance has been based on separate representations of the identification and verification effectiveness. However, for the purpose of comparing the performance of different systems, it is thought to be beneficial to consider a measure of performance for the complete process.

2 Evaluation Methodology

Figure 1 summarises the process of open-set, text-independent speaker identification (OSTI-SI). As shown in this figure, the given test utterance is assigned to the speaker model that yields the maximum similarity over all speaker models in the system, if this maximum likelihood score itself is greater than the threshold. Otherwise, it is declared as originated from a non-registered speaker. It is evident from the above description and Figure 1 that three types of error are possible in this process. These, which collectively define the conventional approach to evaluating the performance of OSTI-SI, are described as follows.

- A test utterance from a specific registered speaker, showing its highest similarity to the reference model for another registered speaker.
- Assigning the test utterance to one of the speaker models in the registered set when it does not belong to any of them.
- Declaring the test utterance, which belongs to one of the registered speakers, as originated from a non-registered speaker.

For the purpose of this paper, these types of error are referred to as OSIE, OSI-FA and OSI-FR respectively (where OSI, E, FA, and FR stand for open-set identification, error, false acceptance, and false rejection respectively).

It is clear that the identification process is responsible for generating OSIE whereas, both OSI-FA and OSI-FR are the consequences of the decisions made in the verification process. It should be noted that an OSIE in the first stage would always lead to an error regardless of the decision in the second stage. Therefore, in evaluating the performance in the verification stage, it is important to discard the false speaker nominations received from the first stage (when the actual speakers are within the registered set).

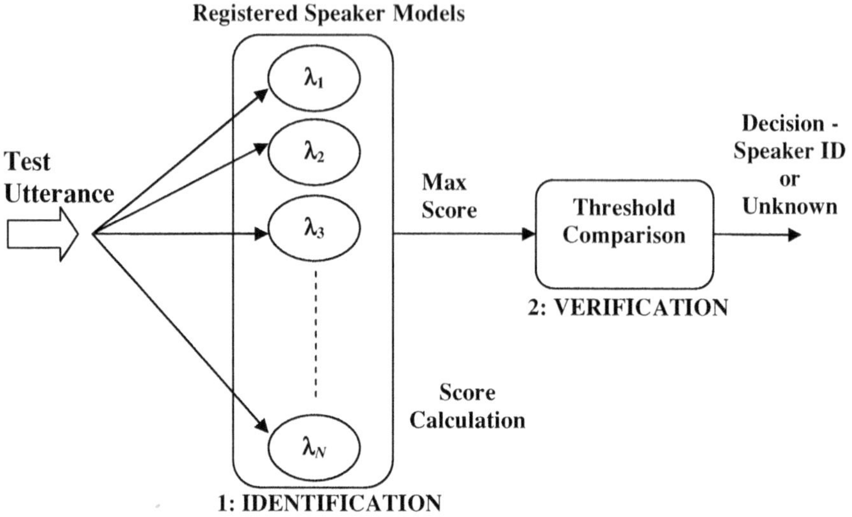

Fig. 1. Overview of the open-set, text-independent speaker identification process

As indicated earlier, an alternative approach to evaluating OSTI-SI is that based on observing the complete performance of the system. For this purpose, the operations involved in OSTI-SI are considered hidden in a box as shown in Figure 2. The system input is a test utterance and the output can either be a decision giving the identity of a speaker or a decision declaring that the test utterance does not belong to any of the registered speakers (shown as Unknown).

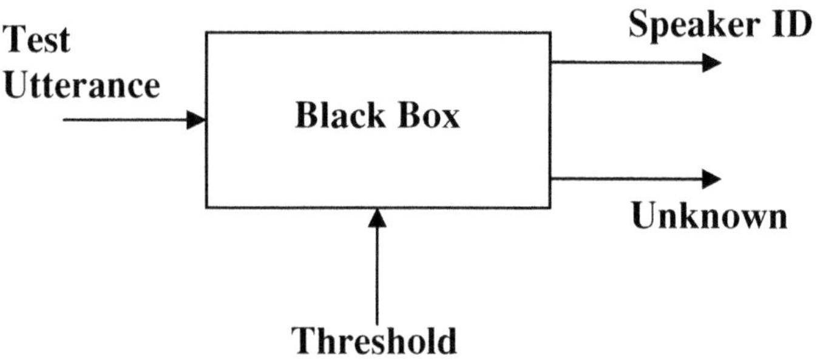

Fig. 2. Proposed basis for the evaluation of OSTI-SI

With such a configuration, three types of error can be recorded for a given threshold as follows.

- A test utterance from a registered speaker is associated with an incorrect speaker identity.
- A test utterance from a registered speaker is declared to have been produced by an unknown speaker.

- A test utterance from an unknown speaker is associated with a registered speaker identity.

In this study, the above errors are referred to as Mislabelling (ML), False Rejection (FR) and False Acceptance (FA) respectively.

In order to obtain the overall performance of OSTI-SI, a measure for combining all the possible types of errors is required. Motivated by the method used for calculating the diarisation error rate [5], an appropriate measure that can be proposed for this purpose is that of Accumulative Error Rate (AER). This is expressed as

$$\text{AER}(\varsigma) = 100 \times \frac{\text{ML}(\varsigma) + \text{FR}(\varsigma) + \text{FA}(\varsigma)}{T}, \qquad (1)$$

where ς is the adopted threshold, T is the total number of tests, and X(ς) is the number of decision errors of type X for the adopted threshold ς. It should be noted that all three error types identified in this methodology, and hence AER are dependent on the decision threshold. Therefore, if required, equation (1) provides a means for setting the threshold such that the total error in OSTI-SI is minimised.

3 Experimental Investigations

This section details the experimental work conducted in order to further analyse the characteristics of the proposed evaluation methodology for OSTI-SI.

3.1 Speech Data

The speech data adopted for this investigation is based on the dataset used for the 1-speaker detection task of NIST SRE 2003 database. The protocol used in this work is based on that devised in [3]. The overall configuration of this dataset is given in Table 1.

3.2 Speech Features and Speaker Representation

Each speech frame of 20ms duration is subjected to pre-emphasis and then analysed to extract a 12th order linear predictive coding-derived cepstral (LPCC) feature vector at a rate of 10ms. The static features are mean normalised. The first derivative parameters are also adopted and are based on the polynomial fit over 15 frames. These parameters are appended to the static features.

In this work, each registered speaker is represented by an adapted Gaussian Mixture Model (GMM) with 1024 components. For this purpose, a gender independent universal background model (UBM) is first obtained by pooling two gender dependant UBMs. The models for the registered speakers are then obtained using a single step adaptation of the gender-independent universal background model [6-7].

3.3 Results and Discussions

The results of this study in terms of ML, FR, FA, and AER as a function of the threshold are presented in Figure 3. In this figure, MLR, FAR and FRR are the rates

Table 1. Configuration of the dataset

	Female	Male
Registered Speakers	80	62
Registered Tests	767	526
Non-registered Speakers	93	48
Non-registered Tests	893	515
Speakers for Universal Background Model (UBM)	58	42
UBM Data Length	4.8 hrs	3.3 hrs

of ML, FA and FR errors respectively. As observed in this figure, ML and FA errors decrease by increasing the threshold whereas FR error shows an increasing trend with an increase in the threshold. Variation in AER shows an interesting trend. This curve shows a distinct point of minima which is referred to as the point of Minimum-AER (M-AER). This point represents minimal total incorrect decisions in OSTI-SI. Hence this point can be an appropriate basis for setting the system threshold for OSTI-SI. Moreover, this measure is useful in comparing the performance of alternative OSTI-SI systems. It can also be observed that the largest component of errors at M-AER point is FR and the increase in FR is associated with reduction in ML decisions.

As discussed earlier, the individual processes of identification and verification in OSTI-SI are responsible for generating the overall decision errors in OSTI-SI. In addition to observing the overall performance of these processes, the analysis of the individual processes is certainly useful for understanding the limitations of the techniques used in implementing these processes. This is further useful for developing suitable techniques in order to improve the performance of either of the two specific processes, and hence OSTI-SI.

The variation in OSIE, OSI-FA and OSI-FR with the threshold is shown in Figure 4. The results in this figure are based on the same speech material as that used for the plots in Figure 3. It is observed that, in this analysis method, OSIE is independent of the threshold. The performance of the verification stage is then evaluated at the point of equal OSI-FA and OSI-FR. This is the point of Equal Error Rate (EER) for the verification stage and is referred to as OSI-EER.

Comparing figures 3 and 4, it is observed that FAR and OSI-FAR curves are exactly the same. The reason for this is that the tests originating from non-registered speakers are handled in a similar manner, regardless of whether the internal processes are considered independently or jointly.

It can also be noted that OSI-FRR curve is different from FRR. The reason for this difference is that (as indicated earlier) in evaluating OSI-FRR, the tests resulting in OSIE are discarded. It is also observed that MLR curve has a characteristic similar to FAR curve. The reason for this is that, like FA decisions, ML decisions are generated due to acceptance decisions in the verification stage. Lastly, it should be noted that M-AER point is different from OSI-EER point and these are associated with different thresholds.

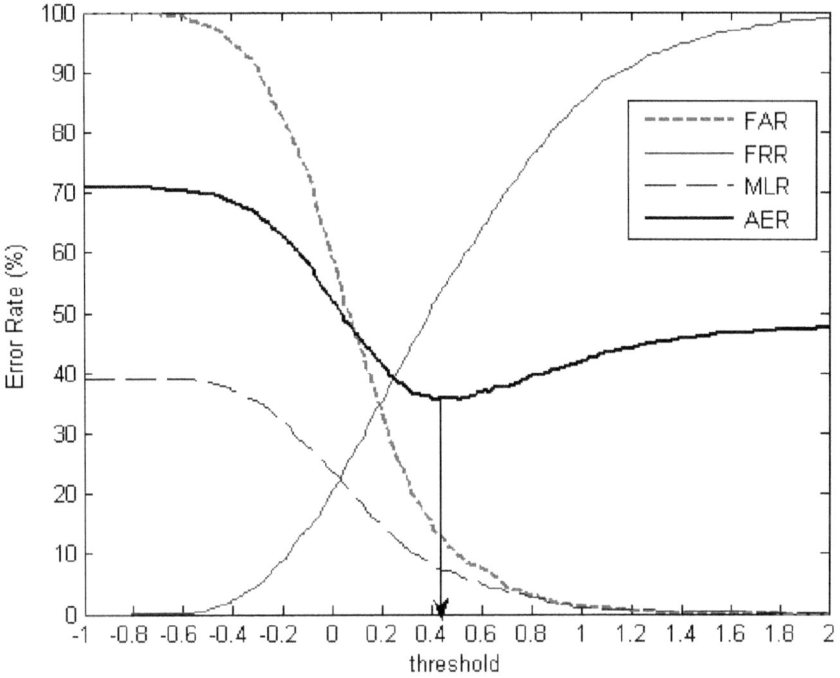

Fig. 3. Variation of error rates in OSTI-SI with the threshold

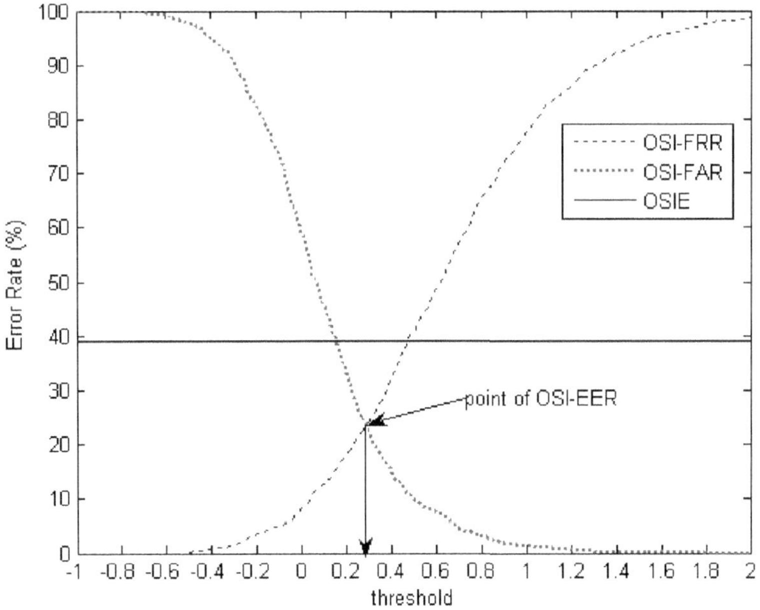

Fig. 4. Variation in OSIE, OSI-FA and OSI-FR with the threshold

4 Conclusion

An alternative methodology for evaluating the performance of open-set, text-independent speaker identification (OSTI-SI) has been investigated. The introduction of this methodology is motivated by the approach commonly used in computing DER (diarisation error rate). It involves a holistic approach to the analysis of the performance in OSTI-SI rather than the independent consideration of the effectiveness in each of the two stages of the process (i.e. identification and verification). For this purpose, the use of three measures of the overall performance in OSTI-SI, i.e. mislabelling (ML), false acceptance (FA) and false rejection (FR) are considered. The integration of these measures has been achieved through the introduction of a metric termed Minimum-Accumulative Error Rate (M-AER). It has been shown that ML, FA and FR are all influenced by the threshold level adopted in open-set identification, and that it may not be possible to achieve equal rates of these errors using a single threshold level. However, it has been demonstrated that the threshold can be set such as to minimise the Accumulative Error Rate. The Minimum-Accumulative Error Rate provides a valuable basis for comparing the overall effectiveness of different open-set speaker identification systems. It has also been argued that, along with such a combined evaluation approach, the independent analysis of the individual processes involved in OSTI-SI can also be beneficial.

References

1. Pillay, S., Ariyaeeinia, A., Sivakumaran, P., Pawlewski, M.: Open-Set Speaker Identification under Mismatch Conditions. In: Proc. 10th Annual Conference of the International Speech Communication Association (Interspeech 2009), pp. 2347–2350 (2009)
2. Ariyaeeinia, A., Fortuna, J., Sivakumaran, P., Malegaonkar, A.: Verification Effectiveness in Open-Set Speaker Identification. IEE Proceedings Vision, Image and Signal Processing 153(5), 618–624 (2006)
3. Fortuna, J., et al.: Relative effectiveness of score normalisation methods in open-set speaker identification. In: Proc. the Speaker and Language Recognition Workshop (Odyssey), pp. 369–376 (2004)
4. Singer, E., Reynolds, D.: Analysis of multi-target detection for speaker and language recognition. In: Proc. the Speaker and Language Recognition Workshop (Odyssey), pp. 301–308 (2004)
5. Anguera Miró, X.: PhD Thesis, Speech Processing Group, Department of Signal Theory and Communications, Universitat Politècnica de Catalunya (2006), `http://www.xavieranguera.com/phdthesis/node108.html`
6. Reynolds, D., et al.: Speaker verification using adapted Gaussian mixture models. Digital Signal Processing 10(1-3), 19–41 (2000)
7. Fortuna, J., et al.: Open set speaker identification using adapted Gaussian mixture models. In: Proc. Interspeech, pp. 1997–2000 (2005)

Effects of Long-Term Ageing on Speaker Verification

Finnian Kelly and Naomi Harte*

Department of Electronic and Electrical Engineering,
Trinity College Dublin, Ireland
{kellyfp,nharte}@tcd.ie

Abstract. The changes that occur in the human voice due to ageing have been well documented. The impact of these changes on speaker verification is less clear. In this work, we examine the effect of long-term vocal ageing on a speaker verification system. On a cohort of 13 adult speakers, using a conventional GMM-UBM system, we carry out longitudinal testing of each speaker across a time span of 30-40 years. We uncover a progressive degradation in verification score as the time span between the training and test material increases. The addition of temporal information to the features causes the rate of degradation to increase. No significant difference was found between MFCC and PLP features. Subsequent experiments show that the effect of short-term ageing (<5 years) is not significant compared with normal inter-session variability. Above this time span however, ageing has a detrimental effect on verification. Finally, we show that the age of the speaker at the time of training influences the rate at which the verification scores degrade. Our results suggest that the verification score drop-off accelerates for speakers over the age of 60. The results presented are the first of their kind to quantify the effect of long-term vocal ageing on speaker verification.

1 Introduction

With ageing, the subsystems which make up the human speech production system undergo progressive physiological change, bringing about significant changes in the voice. The respiratory system is affected by the decreasing rate and strength of muscle contraction. In the larynx, ossification of cartilages and atrophy of muscle tissue are the primary anatomic changes. Changes to the supralaryngeal system include loss of functionality of the tongue and facial muscles. These changes have been documented in numerous studies [1,2,3,4]. These anatomical changes affect the acoustic properties of the voice in a number of ways. Pitch, the rate and intensity of speech, and the 'quality' of the voice are the properties of the voice most affected [3,5]. In general, elderly speakers' voices experience more variability than younger speakers' [1,2].

Much research attention has been payed to the characteristics of the ageing voice. Very little attention however has been devoted to the effect of vocal ageing

* This research has been funded by the Irish Research Council for Science, Engineering and Technology.

C. Vielhauer et al. (Eds.): BioID 2011, LNCS 6583, pp. 113–124, 2011.

on the accuracy of speaker verification. With the increased use of biometric technology for security and forensic applications, understanding the impact ageing has on speaker verification is important. The primary difficulty in assessing this effect experimentally is a lack of longitudinal data. The effect of the ageing voice on the accuracy of speech recognition has been studied using two different sets of speakers from 'adult' and 'older' populations [6] . For speaker verification, a database of the same speakers over an extended time period is required. Some available databases [7,8] contain 'long-term' data covering a time span of 2-3 years. In [9], an attempt is made to observe vocal ageing effects on speaker verification over a 3 year period. However, in the context of vocal ageing, where the onset of change as well as the rate at which it progresses is speaker specific [1], a significantly longer time span would be required to uncover any definite trend. In this work, we examine the effect of a 30-40 year time span on the speaker verification accuracy of a number of subjects. We experimentally uncover a long term degradation in performance which is outside the bounds of expected session variability. We also present results which show that the rate of verification drop-off is not constant across all ages, with the rate of degradation appearing to increase above the age of 60. These results correlate well with expectations in terms of ageing [1,3], but to our knowledge this is the first work to quantify long-term ageing effects in terms of their impact on speaker verification.

These are early stage findings and are investigative in nature. The emphasis is not on system performance but rather uncovering previously unquantified effects of age on a speaker verification system. Finally, we recognise that although our database is limited in terms of the number of speakers, there is a sufficient quantity and variation of speech to reach some important conclusions.

2 Speech Data

To carry out the longitudinal analysis in this paper, an ageing database of 13 speakers was compiled. The database contains 15 hours of speech from 7 males and 6 females and was obtained from the archive material of the national broadcasters of the U.K. and Ireland: the BBC (British Broadcasting Corporation) and RTÉ (Raidió Teilifís Éireann). It contains audio recordings of interviews and speeches from a variety of radio broadcasts. The earliest recording is from 1953 and the most recent from 2010. The age profile of the speakers ranges from 19 at the time of the first recording to 96 at the time of the last recording.

The amount of material available for each speaker is varied. For two speakers (one male and one female) from the BBC archives, there are recordings for every 2-3 years over the entire time span. For the remainder of the speakers in the database we have compiled recordings approximately 10 years apart. To minimise any large noise and channel variations, the spectral content of the recordings was examined, and a number of early recordings, deemed to vary too greatly from the later recordings in terms of frequency content, were discarded. In addition to our ageing database, for background modelling two other data sources were used; the TIMIT corpus [10] and the 'University of Florida Vocal Aging Database 2 - Extemporaneous' (UFvadEX) [11].

3 The Speaker Verification System

A Gaussian Mixture Model and Universal Background Model (GMM-UBM) system, as introduced by Reynolds [12] was used in this work. A gender-independent UBM is first created. This is a GMM trained using the Expectation-Maximisation (EM) algorithm using data from a large population of speakers. The individual speaker models are then generated by Bayesian adaption of the UBM. In this work, a 1024 mixture UBM (as in [12]) was generated from 1 hour of speech taken in equal amounts from TIMIT and UFvadEX. The UBM data was carefully composed to avoid biasing it towards any of the speakers or recording channels. Rosenberg [13] notes that a UBM composed with gender-balanced speech with recording conditions matching the test conditions achieves good performance. We applied this finding to our database by ensuring our UBM contained age-balanced as well as gender-balanced data. Age balanced data was retrieved by taking equal amounts of speech from the following age profiles: under 35, 36-55, over 55 (the ages of speakers are given in the documentation of both databases). As our database covers a range of 40 years, it inherently contains a variety of recording conditions. To reflect this variation in our UBM, we used data from both TIMIT and UFvadEX, where TIMIT data consists of clean recordings of scripted speech and UFvadEX contains conversational speech over a wide variety of channels and speaking styles. Composing the UBM content in this way was an effort to ensure that it contained a balanced variety of recording conditions, phonetic content, accents, ages and genders.

Front end processing of the speech consisted of downsampling to 16kHz, energy-based silence removal, and pre-emphasis. 12-dimensional Mel-Frequency Cepstral Coefficients (MFCCs) were extracted over a 20ms windows with 50% overlap. Mean and variance normalisation was applied after RASTA filtering [15]. GMMs for each speaker were trained by adaption [12] of the UBM using 30 second segments of data. During testing, the likelihood of the test data given both a speaker's GMM and the UBM were calculated. Scoring was then done using the standard likelihood ratio framework [14], by subtracting the log likelihood score of the UBM from the log likelihood score of the speaker model.

4 Experimental Study

To uncover any effects of vocal ageing on the speaker verification system described in Section 3, several experiments were conducted on our ageing database. Our aim was to address several questions of interest:

1. How does a speaker's verification score change as the test data moves further away in time from the data on which the model was trained?
2. Is this trend consistent across different feature sets?
3. Accounting for inter and intra-session variability, is any trend in Question 1 significant?
4. Does the age of the speaker at time of model generation influence a long-term trend?

4.1 Long-Term Speaker Verification

The first experiment was designed to answer Question 1 above. Two models were trained for each speaker, one using 30 seconds of data from their first year of available speech and the other using 30 seconds of data from their last year of speech. 'Forward' testing was done by testing each speaker's first model with data from all subsequent years of their speech material. 'Reverse' testing was done by testing each speaker's last model with data from all previous years of their material. Each test score was generated by computing the log likelihood ratio for three separate 30 second segments and taking the average. An initial assumption is made that performance degrades linearly with time and thus a linear least squares fit was computed for each speaker's scores. The test scores along with their line fits for each of the 13 speakers (from 'QUEEN' to 'PLOMLEY', as indicated by the legend) are given for the forward direction in Fig 1 and the reverse direction in Fig 2. The average of the speaker line slopes in the forward and reverse directions are -0.011 and 0.015 respectively. It is evident that there is a significant degradation of verification score that is reasonably consistent across speakers in both forward and reverse testing.

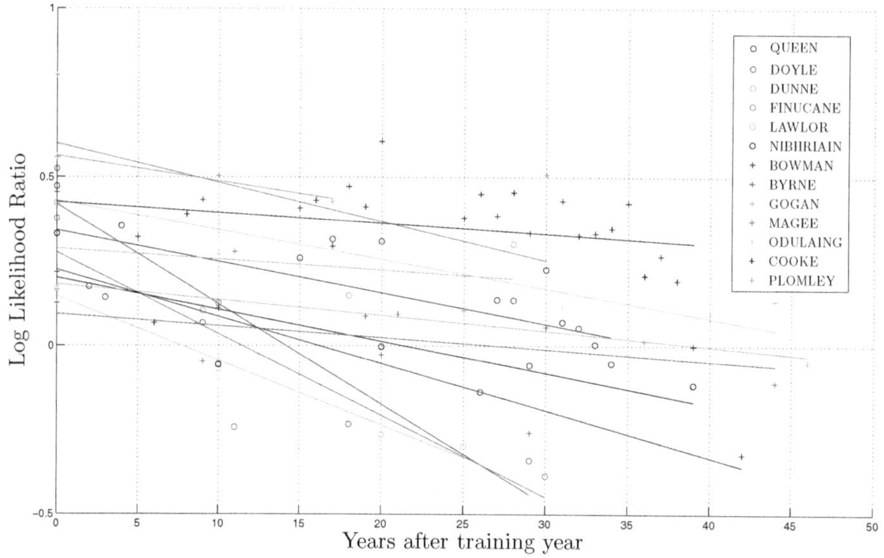

Fig. 1. Long-term verification, testing forward in time, with MFCC features

Speaker verification systems typically incorporate temporal information by taking first and second order time derivatives of the feature vector (referred to as delta and double-delta coefficients) and appending them to the original feature vector. Including dynamic information in this way has been shown to improve verification accuracy [16]. Our experiment above was repeated using MFCCs with both delta and double-delta coefficients appended. Deltas and double-deltas were extracted as time differences over a window of length ± 2 samples. Results

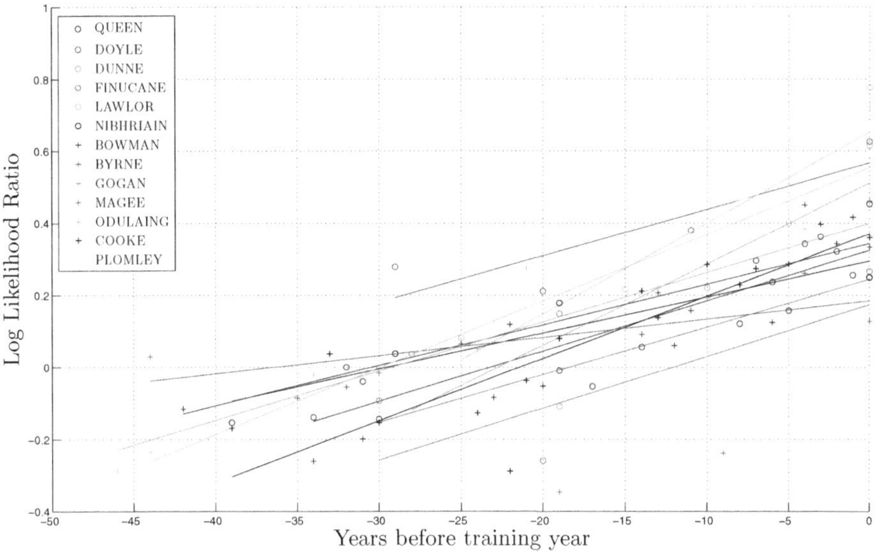

Fig. 2. Long-term verification, testing backwards in time, with MFCC features

of the log likelihood score versus age are plotted for the forward direction for MFCCs with delta coefficients in Fig 3 and delta & delta-delta coefficients in Fig 4. A trend consistent with 1 is seen in these results. The average of the speaker slopes in Fig 3 and 4 are -0.026 and -0.030 respectively. Testing in the reverse direction yields average slopes of 0.027 and 0.036. Thus the rate of decrease of verification score increases progressively with the addition of temporal information.

For comparison to MFCCs, an alternative feature set, Perceptual Linear Predictive (PLP) [17] coefficients were extracted. In [18], it is suggested that there is no clear advantage to using PLPs over MFCCs. However, it has been observed that MFCCs can outperform PLPs in clean conditions, while PLPs offer better performance in noise [21]. The long-term verification experiment was rerun using 12-dimensional PLPs extracted over 20ms windows with 50% overlap. The resulting scores are very similar to those using MFCC results, with forward and reverse slopes of -0.016 and 0.021 respectively. Based on these initial results, MFCCs (without dynamic coefficients) were used exclusively for subsequent experiments.

4.2 Comparison with Inter and Intra-session Variability

The results presented in Section 4.1 demonstrate a consistent decrease in verification score as the time span between training and testing grows. Caution must be observed before attributing this effect solely to ageing however. In [9], Lawson concluded that the influence of 'long-term' ageing of 3 years on speaker verification scores was consistent with simple inter-session variability. Degradation due

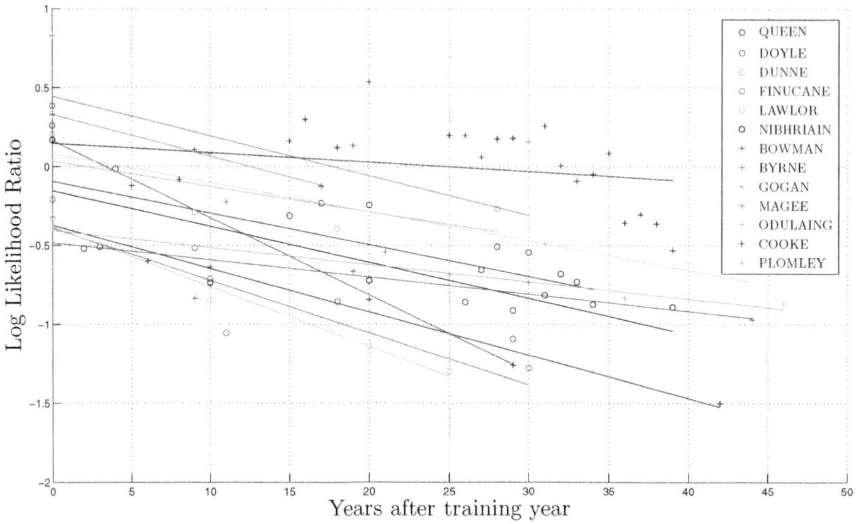

Fig. 3. Long-term verification, testing forward in time, with MFCC features + first order dynamic coefficients

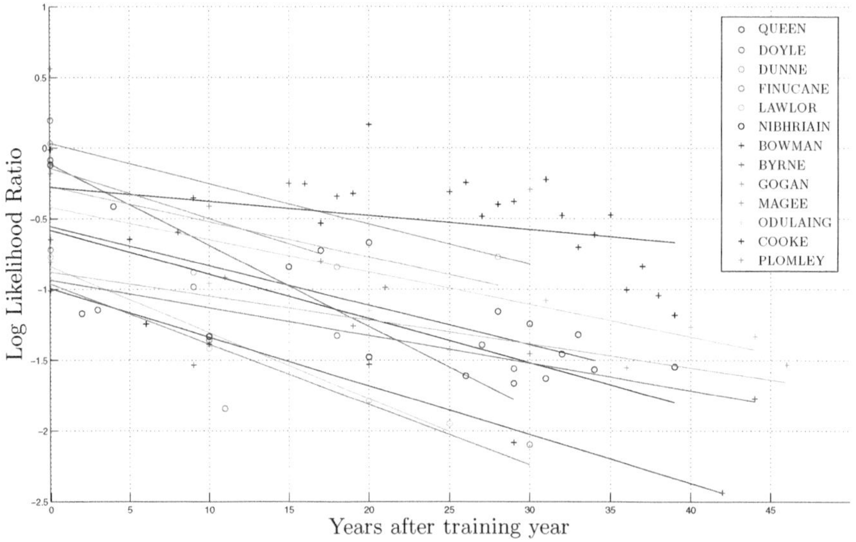

Fig. 4. Long-term verification, testing forward in time, with MFCC features + first and second order dynamic coefficients

to inter-session variability was demonstrated on the MARP corpus by [19]. Similarly, in [20], it is mentioned that results presented on NIST-SRE '05 showing a fall in verification accuracy over a period of one month is more attributable to variabilities other than ageing.

Our second experiment was designed to compare intra and inter-session variability with the potential ageing effect uncovered in Section 4.1 and answer Question 3 above. As short-term inter-session data (recordings from different sessions within a given year) was available for one speaker only, Alistair Cooke, we based our analysis on his speech only.

Short-term inter-session scores were obtained by training a model for each session with 30 seconds of data and testing it against 30 second segments from all other sessions in that year. Intra-session scores were found by training a model with the first 30 seconds of a session and testing it with all subsequent 30 second segments from that session. This was done for all sessions. Long-term inter-session scores were generated by training a model for each session with 30 seconds of data and testing it with 30 second segments from all other sessions across all years. The score distributions of these three sets of results are given in Fig 5. As expected, intra-session scores and long-term inter-session scores at a time span of 0 years are closely aligned. Short-term inter-session scores lie below this range. Interestingly, long-term inter-session scores at a time span of 5 years occupy a similar range to short-term inter-session results. This agrees with previous findings that ageing effects of ≈ 3 years are insignificant compared to normal inter-session variability.

At time spans of 10, 20 and 30 years however, the verification score distribution shifts progressively downwards, beyond the range of the short-term inter-session score distribution. This supports the existence of a negative long-term (> 5 years) effect of vocal ageing on speaker verification.

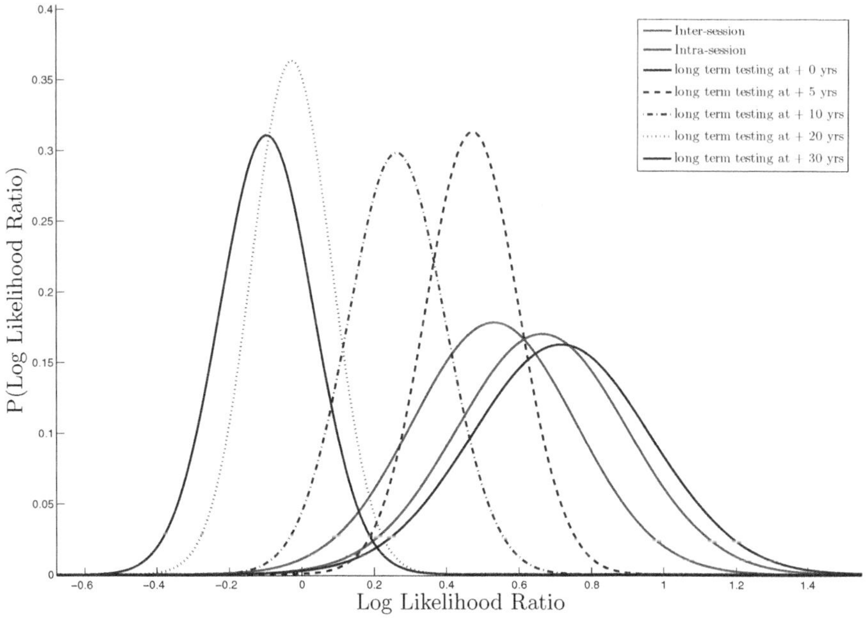

Fig. 5. Distributions of inter/intra-session and long-term verification scores for Alistair Cooke

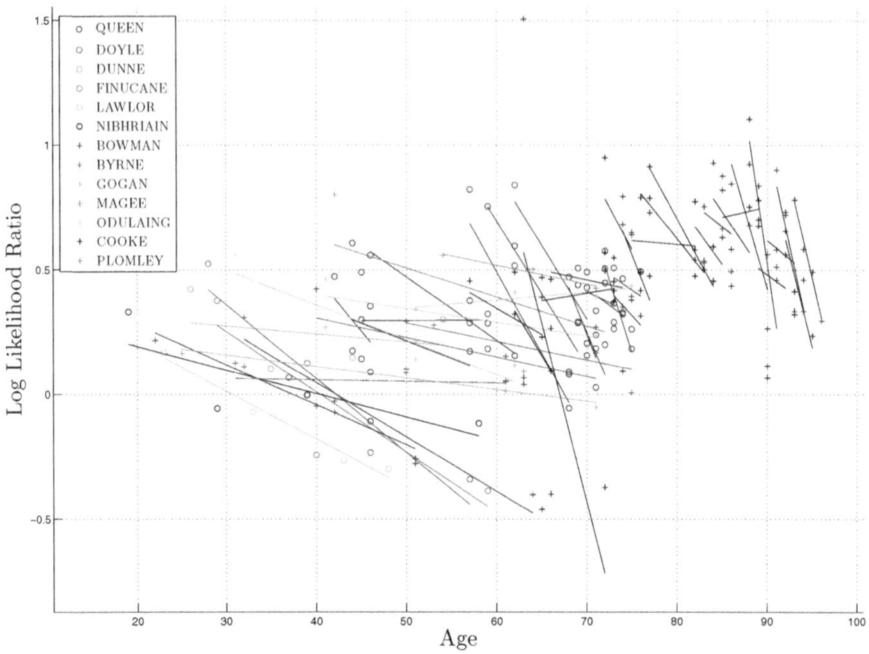

Fig. 6. Long-term verification results, testing forward in time, for individual speakers over multiple age ranges. Taking the speaker 'BYRNE' (symbol +) as an example: three lines are plotted for this speaker, each representing the score trend over different intervals. The first line is fitted to the scores of this speaker's model trained at age 31 and tested with data from age 31, 40, 50 and 61. The second is fitted to the scores of the model trained at age 40 and tested with data from age 40, 50, 61 and 71. Finally, the third is fitted to the model trained at age 50 and tested with data from age 50, 61, 71 and 75.

4.3 Age Dependent Long-Term Speaker Verification

In Section 4.1 we had modelled the drop in verification score between a speaker's first and last recordings as a linear relationship. In reality however, vocal ageing is not constant over time. One of the indicators of an 'elderly' voice is its variability (in pitch, intensity etc) relative to a young speaker [2]. It would be expected then, that the drop in verification scores would be somewhat dependent on the age of the speaker. Furthermore, the onset of vocal changes and the degree of change varies between individuals [1]. We would expect to see evidence of this in verification scores.

To investigate these issues, and address Question 4, the experiment in Section 4.1 was repeated over multiple time spans. A model was trained using data from year 1 and tested with data from year 1 to year $1 + N$. A new model was created with data from year 2 and tested with data from year 2 to $2 + N$ and so on. N was taken as 3. Note that N was not the span in years, but rather the span

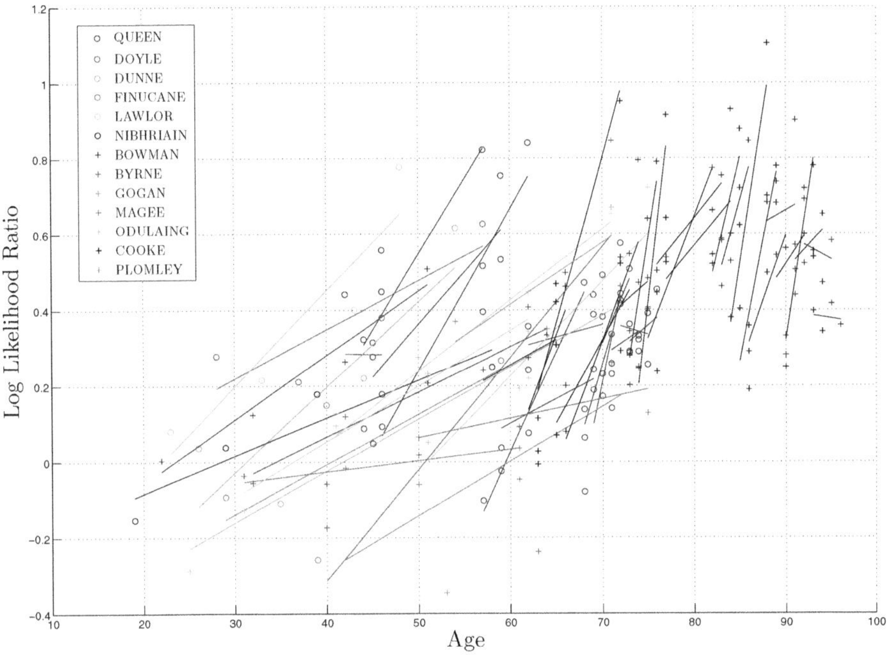

Fig. 7. Long-term verification results, testing backwards in time, for individual speakers over multiple age ranges

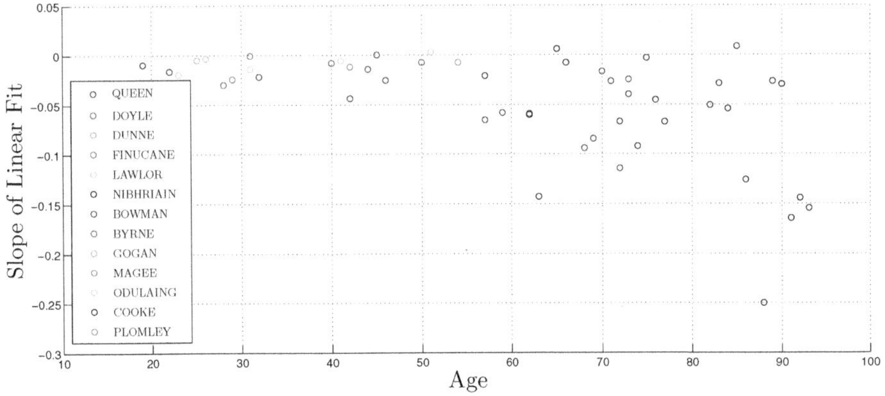

Fig. 8. Slopes of line fits over age ranges in Fig 6

in *available* years of data for a speaker. This was also done in reverse, testing a model from the most recent year Y with data from year Y to $Y - N$, and so on. This was done for all 13 speakers. Results for each of the speakers are presented in Fig 6 and 7. Again, the assumption is made that the score degradation across $N + 1$ points can be approximated linearly.

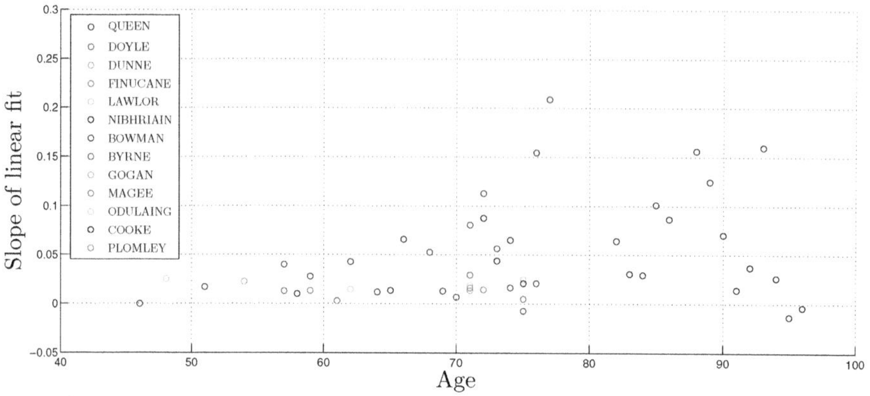

Fig. 9. Slopes of line fits over age ranges in Fig 7

While there are some outliers, a trend emerges in which speaker's models experience a sharper drop off in verification score as their age increases. This change is non-linear, with age of 60 appearing to be a turning point after which the rate of decrease of verification score increases. For clarity, the slopes of each line plot in Fig 6 and 7 are plotted against age in Fig 8 and 9.

5 Conclusions

In this work, we have presented some early-stage results on the effect of ageing on speaker verification.

We have shown that there is a degradation in verification score as the time span between model training and testing increases. This trend is consistent in forward and reverse directions. This behaviour agrees with expectations based on physiological research around vocal ageing. We found little difference in using either MFCC or PLP features.

Including temporal information in the extracted features increases the rate of verification score degradation. As noted in the introduction, a major change in the voice with age is a change in the rate of speech production. Therefore incorporating temporal coefficients, which capture rate information, leads to a fall in accuracy. This introduces an interesting dilemma for building a speaker verification system. In the short-term, temporal information has been shown to increase accuracy, as it captures person-specific information. However, this trait is far less robust to ageing. It is conceivable that other features, such as those derived from pitch and energy, which are advantageous in the short-term, will be similarly detrimental in the long-term.

A major issue in speaker verification is session variability. As discussed, previous studies have considered speaker ageing as insignificant compared with normal inter-session variabilities. We have attempted to separate the effects of session variability from a longer term ageing effect. Our experiment shows how score variation over a time span of up to 5 years lies within the range of short-term inter-session variability. At greater time spans, of 10, 20 and 30 years, this score distribution shifts outside the expected inter-session variation. This demonstrates a clear effect of vocal ageing outside the realm of normal inter-session variability. This has obvious implications for the life cycle management of biometric templates.

Our final experiment showed the effect of ageing is not constant across all ages. A greater rate of score degradation is seen in older speakers. Based on our limited database, an acceleration in score drop-off is seen above the age of 60. While the degree of vocal change and the time of onset differs between individuals, changes in the voice become generally more marked in older speakers. This is reflected in the increased score variability of older speakers in our examination.

Future work will incorporate a larger cohort of speakers and consider feature sets which are more robust to the changing voice. Different modelling approaches, particularly concerning the UBM composition and training strategy should also be considered.

Acknowledgements

The authors would like to thank James Harnsberger and Rahul Shrivastav, University of Florida, for providing the UFvadEX database.

References

1. Mueller, P.B.: The Aging Voice. Seminars in speech and language 18(2), 159–168 (1997)
2. Linville, S.E.: Vocal aging. Current Opinion in Otolaryngology & Head and Neck Surgery 3, 183–187 (1995)
3. Linville, S.E.: The Sound of Senescence. Journal of Voice 10(2), 190–200 (1996)
4. Sataloff, R.T.: Vocal aging. Current Opinion in Otolaryngology & Head and Neck Surgery 6, 421–428 (1998)
5. Reubold, U., et al.: Vocal aging effects on F0 and the first formant: A longitudinal analysis in adult speakers. Speech Communication 52, 638–651 (2010)
6. Vipperla, R., et al.: Ageing Voices: The Effect of Changes in Voice Parameters on ASR Performance. EURASIP Journal on Audio, Speech, and Music Processing (2010)
7. Cole, R., et al.: The CSLU speaker recognition corpus. In: Proceedings of the International Conference on Spoken Language Processing, pp. 3167–3170 (1998)
8. Lawson, A.D., et al.: The Multi-Session Audio Research Project (MARP) Corpus: Goals, Design and Initial Findings. In: INTERSPEECH 2009, Brighton (2009)
9. Lawson, A.D., et al.: Long term examination of intra-session and inter-session speaker variability. In: INTERSPEECH 2009, Brighton, United Kingdom (2009)
10. Garofolo, J.S.: TIMIT Acoustic-Phonetic Continuous Speech Corpus. Linguistic Data Consortium, Philadelphia (1993)
11. Harnsberger, J.D., et al.: Modeling perceived vocal age in American English. To be presented at Interspeech 2010 (2010)

12. Reynolds, D.A., et al.: Speaker Verification Using Adapted Gaussian Mixture Models. Digital Signal Processing 10, 19–41 (2000)
13. Rosenberg, A.E., et al.: Speaker background models for connected digit password speaker verification. In: ICASSP 1996 (1996)
14. Bimbot, F., et al.: A Tutorial on Text-Independent Speaker Verification. EURASIP Journal on Applied Signal Processing 4, 430–451 (2004)
15. Hermansky, H., et al.: RASTA processing of speech. IEEE Transactions on Speech and Audio Processing 2, 578–589 (1994)
16. Furui, S.: Comparison of speaker recognition methods using statistical features and dynamic features. IEEE Transactions on Acoustics, Speech and Signal Processing 29(3), 342–350 (1981)
17. Hermansky, H., et al.: Perceptual Linear Predictive (PLP) Analysis-Resynthesis Technique. In: IEEE ASSP Workshop on Applications of Signal Processing to Audio and Acoustics, Final Program and Paper Summaries, pp. 37–38 (1991)
18. Kinnunen, T., et al.: An overview of text-independent speaker recognition: From features to supervectors. Speech Communication 52, 12–40 (2010)
19. Lawson, A.D., et al.: External factors influencing the performance of speaker identification of the multisession audio research project (MARP) corpus, 153rd Meeting of the Acoustical Society of America (June 2007)
20. Campbell, J.P., et al.: Forensic speaker recognition. IEEE Signal Processing Magazine 26(2), 95–103 (2009)
21. Kinnunen, T.: Optimizing Spectral Feature Based Text-Independent Speaker Recognition, PhD thesis, Department of Computer Science, University of Joensuu (2005)

Features Extracted Using Frequency-Time Analysis Approach from Nyquist Filter Bank and Gaussian Filter Bank for Text-Independent Speaker Identification

Nirmalya Sen[1] and T.K. Basu[2]

[1] Signal Processing Research Group, C.E.T, IIT Kharagpur, India
[2] Electrical Engineering Department, IIT Kharagpur, India
nirmalya75@rediffmail.com, basutk02@yahoo.co.in

Abstract. This paper compares the feature sets extracted using frequency-time analysis approach and time-frequency analysis approach for text-independent speaker identification. The impetus for the frequency-time analysis approach comes from the band pass filtering view of STFT. Nyquist filter bank and Gaussian filter bank both have been used for extracting features using frequency-time analysis approach. Experimental evaluation was conducted on the POLYCOST database with 130 speakers using Gaussian mixture speaker model. Results reveal that, the feature sets extracted using frequency-time analysis approach performs significantly better compared to the feature set extracted using time-frequency analysis approach.

Keywords: Speaker identification, Feature extraction, Frequency-time analysis.

1 Introduction

The Mel-frequency cepstral coefficients (MFCC) feature was first proposed for speech recognition [1]. This is a filter bank based approach but implemented using time-frequency analysis technique. Here, first time analysis is done through framing operation and then frequency analysis is done by passing that frame through filter bank. As the time analysis is done first, MFCC needs overlapping frames. Filters are designed in such a way that they resemble the human auditory frequency perception. Later people used MFCC satisfactorily for speaker recognition also [2]. Presently MFCC is the most widely used feature set for speaker recognition. In the MFCC filter bank, the low frequencies are given more importance compared to the high frequencies. This structure is very much suitable for speech recognition. But for speaker recognition point of view, researchers performed various experiments through which it is evident that high frequency zone should also be given similar importance as the low frequency zone.

S. Hayakawa and F. Itakura found that, the speaker recognition rate of the frequency band from 0 to 4 kHz was roughly the same as that of the frequency band from 4 to 10 kHz [3]. They observed that a relatively small amount of speaker specific information is available in the frequency region between 500 Hz to 2 kHz. They concluded that a rich amount of speaker specific information is contained in the

C. Vielhauer et al. (Eds.): BioID 2011, LNCS 6583, pp. 125–136, 2011.

higher frequency band, and it is useful for speaker recognition. Similarly L. Besacier and J.F. Bonastre from their detailed investigation using subband architecture concluded that, the low-frequency (under 600 Hz) and the high-frequency (over 3 kHz) contain more speaker specific information than the middle-frequency subbands [4]. Recently X. Lu and J. Dang demonstrated that the speaker specific information is concentrated mainly in three regions in the frequency domain [5]. Glottal information is in the region from 50Hz to 300 Hz. Piriform fossa information is in the region from 4kH to 5.5kH. Third region is from 6.5 kHz to 7.8 kHz which may be related to the consonants. They observed that comparatively less information was available from 500Hz to 3.5 kHz.

S. Chakroborty et al. proposed a flipped MFCC filter bank using the inverted Mel scale [6]. After that they calculated a new feature set named Inverted Mel Frequency Cepstral Coefficients (IMFCC), following the same procedure as normal MFCC but using the reversed filter bank structure. Identification accuracy of features calculated using flipped MFCC filter bank was comparable with conventional MFCC features. They also used the fusion of IMFCC features with MFCC features. Identification accuracy, after fusion, was higher compared to MFCC features.

But all the above works were based on the time-frequency analysis approach. N. Sen et al. defined a new Nyquist window [7]-[9] and using the cosine modulation of the proposed window they constructed a filter bank [10]. They used that filter bank for text-independent speaker identification in a frequency-time analysis approach. Here first frequency analysis is done through filter bank and then time analysis is done through framing the output signal of each filter. It is easy to visualize that, due to the inner product operation of the speech signal and impulse responses of the filters; there is no need to take overlapping frames in case of frequency-time analysis approach.

In this paper we have used the standard database POLYCOST for closed set Text-Independent speaker identification experiments. We compared the features extracted using frequency-time analysis approach using the Nyquist filter bank and the Gaussian filter bank. Comparison with MFCC is also given.

2 Proposed Modification in the STFT

The expression for the discrete-time STFT of a sequence $x[n]$ at time n is given by the following equation [10],

$$X(n,\omega) = \sum_{m=-\infty}^{\infty} x[m]w[n-m]\exp(-j\omega m) \qquad (1)$$

Here $w[n]$ is referred to as the analysis window function.

The discrete STFT is obtained from the discrete time STFT using the sampling of the frequency axis $\omega = (2\pi / N)k = (\omega_c)k$ for $k = 0,1,...,N-1$. The mathematical formulation for the discrete STFT of a sequence $x[n]$ is given below,

$$X(n,k) = \sum_{m=-\infty}^{\infty} x[m]w[n-m]\exp(-j(2\pi / N)km) \qquad (2)$$

After manipulation of equation (2) we get the following alternative form

$$X(n,k) = (\exp(-j(2\pi / N)kn))(x[n] * w[n]\exp(j(2\pi / N)kn)) \quad (3)$$

Here the sequence $x[n]$ is first passed through the modulated window which acts as a band pass filter bank where each filter is centered on its selected frequency. The output of each filter is then demodulated by $\exp(-j(2\pi / N)kn)$. Thus the discrete STFT can be viewed as a collection of sequences, each corresponding to the frequency components of $x[n]$ falling within a particular frequency band.

Filter Bank Summation (FBS) method is a well known synthesis technique to get back the original signal from the discrete STFT sequences [10]. Here the each sequence $X(n,k)$ is modulated with a complex exponential, $\exp(j(2\pi / N)kn)$ and these modulated outputs are summed at each instant of time to retrieve the corresponding time sample of the original sequence as given below,

$$y[n] = \frac{1}{Nw[0]} \sum_{k=0}^{N-1} X(n,k)\exp(j(2\pi / N)nk) \quad (4)$$

Using equation (3) in equation (4) we have the following alternative representation

$$y[n] = (1/Nw[0])(x[n] * (w[n]\sum_{k=0}^{N-1} \exp(j(2\pi / N)nk))) = (1/w[0])(x[n] * (w[n]\sum_{r=-\infty}^{\infty} \delta[n-rN])) \quad (5)$$

$$\Rightarrow y[n] = x[n] \text{ iff } w[n]\sum_{r=-\infty}^{\infty} \delta[n-rN] = w[0]\delta[n] \quad (6)$$

Hence perfect reconstruction is possible, provided the analysis window $w[n]$ is chosen in such a way, that every N th sample is zero as shown in equation(7). This type of window is called the Nyquist window.

$$w[rN] = 0 \quad \text{for } r = \pm 1, \pm 2, \pm 3, \cdots \quad (7)$$

Fourier transform of both sides of equation (6) yields the following result,

$$\sum_{k=0}^{N-1} W(\omega - (2\pi / N)k) = Nw[0] \quad (8)$$

From equation (8) we conclude that, for perfect reconstruction, the analysis filter bank must be an allpass complementary filter bank.

Fig.1 shows the analysis and synthesis section of the STFT. It is evident from the block diagram that, the demodulation operations in the analysis sections and the modulation operations in the synthesis section together form an identity transformation block. Therefore it is possible to omit the modulations and demodulations operations.

In the band pass filtering view of the STFT analysis section as shown in Fig.1 the impulse response of each filter is generated from the prototype filter (i.e. window) through exponential modulation. Hence the impulse response of each filter is complex.

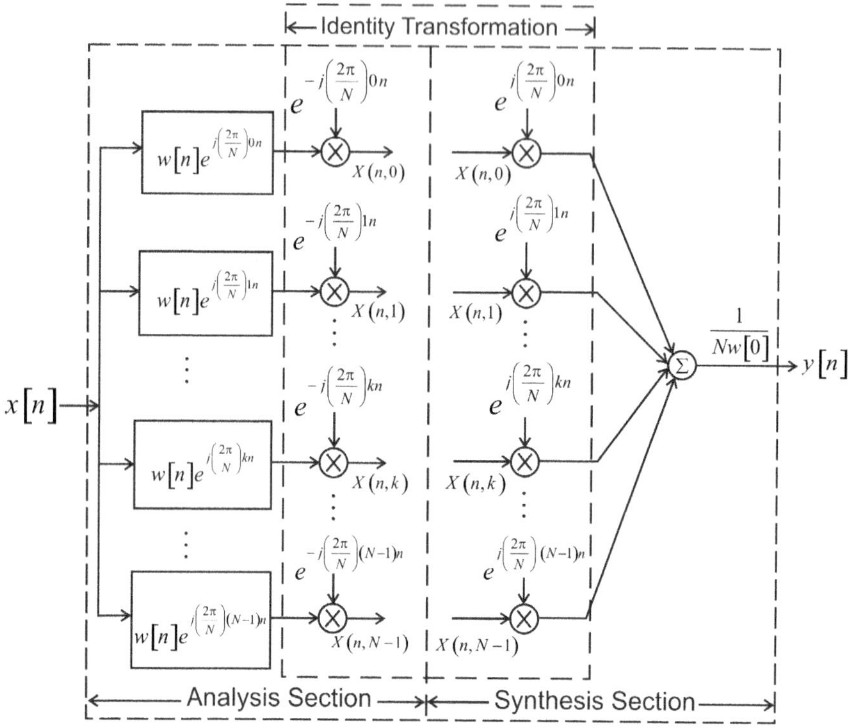

Fig. 1. Analysis section and synthesis section of the STFT

Therefore it requires high computation time. To overcome the problem of complex modulation, we have used the fact that the filters are in parallel.

From equation (5) it is evident that, except the constant factor, the impulse response of the overall system is given by the following equation,

$$h[n] = w[n]\sum_{k=0}^{N-1} \exp(j(2\pi/N)nk) = w[n]\{1+\exp(j\pi n)+\sum_{k}\exp(j(2\pi/N)nk)\} \tag{9}$$

here $k = 1, 2, .., ((N/2)-1), ((N/2)+1), .., (N-1)$

For any general term when $k = p$ and $k = N - p$ we have,

$$h_{p,N-p}[n] = \exp(j(2\pi/N)pn) + \exp(j(2\pi/N)(N-p)n) = 2\cos((2\pi/N)pn) \tag{10}$$

Hence the overall impulse response of the system can be expressed by the following equation,

$$h[n] = w[n]\{1+2\cos((2\pi/N)n)+...+2\cos((2\pi/N)((N/2)-1)n)+\cos(\pi n)\} \tag{11}$$

From the equation (11) it is very clear that, if the window is a real valued function, then the impulse response of all the filters in the filter bank will also be real valued.

3 Design of the Analysis Window

3.1 Filtering Using the Nyquist Filter Bank

From the above discussions it is evident that, for perfect reconstruction of original signal using the filter bank summation method, we need to use Nyquist filter as the analysis window. From frequency domain point of view, allpass complementary filter bank is required.

We have used the analysis window which is cosine-square in the frequency domain. The frequency domain equation of the window function is given below [7],

$$\begin{aligned} H(\omega) &= \cos^2(\gamma\omega) \quad -\omega_c \le \omega \le \omega_c \qquad \text{Here } \omega_c = (2\pi / N) \\ &= 0 \quad -\omega_c \ge \omega \ge \omega_c \end{aligned} \tag{12}$$

Here γ is a parameter which is used for scaling the filters in the frequency domain. The relation between the parameter γ and the unit frequency ω_c is given by

$$\gamma = (\pi / 2\omega_c) = (N/4) \tag{13}$$

The corresponding time domain relation of the window function is given below;

$$\begin{aligned} w[n] &= \frac{2\gamma^2 \sin(\omega_c n)}{\pi(4\gamma^2 n - n^3)} \qquad \text{for} \quad n \ne 0 \\ &= (\omega_c / 2\pi) \qquad \text{for} \quad n = 0 \\ &= (\omega_c / 4\pi) \qquad \text{for} \quad n = \pm(\pi / \omega_c) \end{aligned} \tag{14}$$

Equation (14) shows that, the window function is a Nyquist filter. Fig.2 and Fig.3 show an example of the above window function, in time domain and frequency domain respectively. Fig. 4 shows the overall filter bank using the above window.

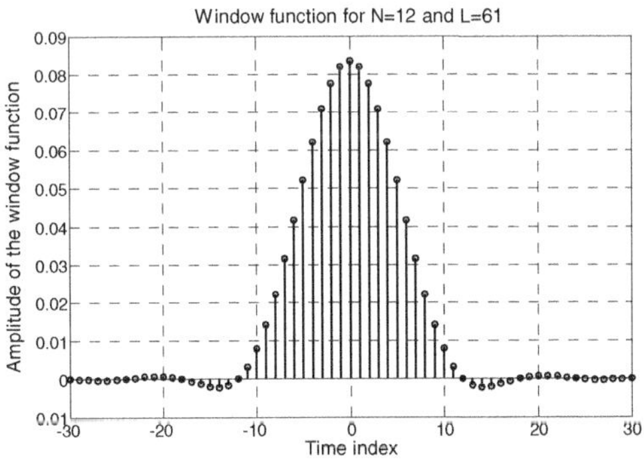

Fig. 2. Proposed Window function for *N*=12 and length *L*=61

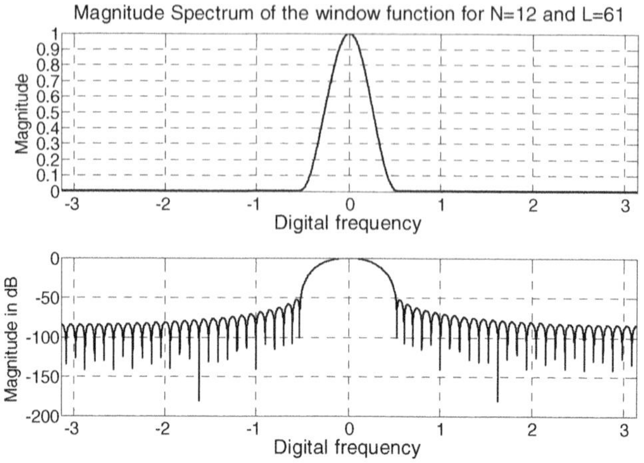

Fig. 3. Magnitude Spectrum of the proposed window function for N=12 and length L=61

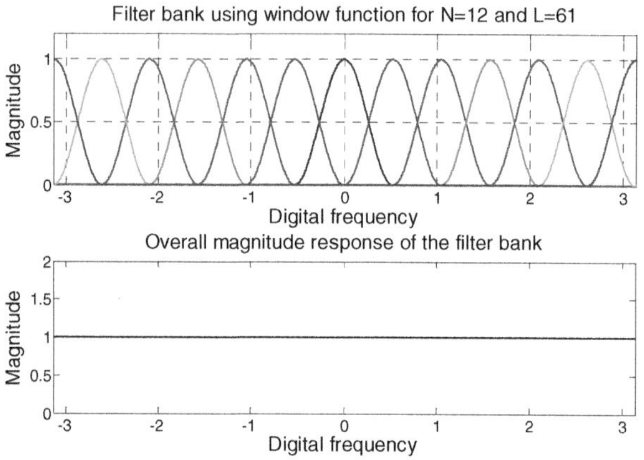

Fig. 4. Filter bank using proposed window function for N=12 and L=61 and the overall allpass magnitude response of the filter bank

It is evident from Fig.2 that, the centre lobe of the window extends from $-(N-1)$ to $(N-1)$ and contains more than 99.948% of total energy. Fig.3 shows the magnitude spectrum of the window function for $N=12$ and $L=61$. The minimum sidelobe attenuation is -52 dB. Fig. 4 shows the filter bank generated using the above window function. There are total seven filters in the filter bank. This is due to the fact that, as $N=12$ hence the total number of sequences will be $(1+(N/2))=7$. The all pass property of the overall magnitude response of the filter bank does not depend on the window length, because our window function is a Nyquist filter [10].

3.2 Filtering Using the Gaussian Filter Bank

It is known that the Gaussian window is not a Nyquist filter. Hence it cannot produce the allpass complementary filter bank. But the Gaussian window has the lowest time-bandwidth product [11]. Therefore it has been used extensively for time-frequency analysis. Fig.5 shows an example of the overall magnitude response of the filter bank generated using eight Gaussian filters. If the frequency domain variance of the Gaussian window increases then the ripple in the overall magnitude response decreases. But this will decrease the frequency selectivity of the filter bank. Hence for the filter bank generated using the Gaussian window function, there is a tradeoff between the allpass complementary nature and frequency selectivity of the filter bank.

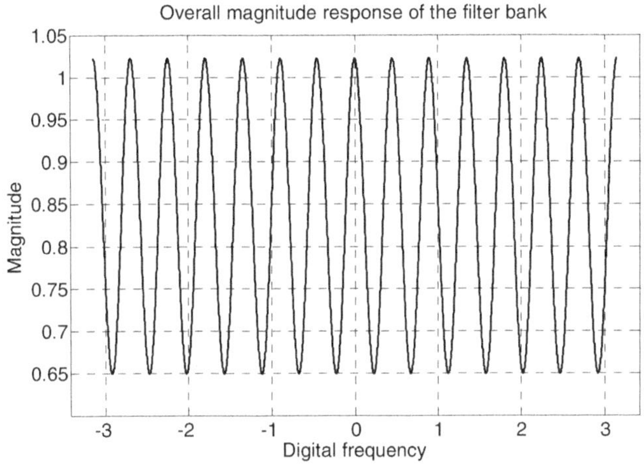

Fig. 5. Overall magnitude response of the filter bank generated using eight Gaussian filters for an example Gaussian window function with $\omega_c = (\pi / 7)$ and $\sigma_\omega = (\omega_c / 3)$

Fig.5 shows an overall magnitude response of the Gaussian filter bank generated using eight filters. Hence N=14. This is due to the fact that, (1+ (14/2)) =8. Hence the unit frequency is given by, $\omega_c = (2\pi / 14) = (\pi / 7)$.

4 Time-Bandwidth Product Comparison

It is known that for a given function the time-bandwidth product is unique. We have considered the discrete formulation of root mean square duration $Td_{r.m.s}$ of signal and root mean square frequency duration $Bw_{r.m.s}$ of its spectrum as given below [11],

$$Td_{r.m.s} = \left[\frac{\sum_{n=-(L-1)/2}^{(L-1)/2} n^2 |w[n]|^2}{\sum_{n=-(L-1)/2}^{(L-1)/2} |w[n]|^2} \right]^{\frac{1}{2}} \quad \text{and} \quad Bw_{r.m.s} = \left[\frac{\sum_{l=-(L-1)/2}^{(L-1)/2} (\frac{2\pi}{L} l)^2 |W[l]|^2}{\sum_{l=-(L-1)/2}^{(L-1)/2} |W[l]|^2} \right]^{\frac{1}{2}} \tag{15}$$

Here L is the length of the window function after truncation.

For L=9025 the Gaussian window function has time-bandwidth product $Td_{r.m.s} \times Bw_{r.m.s} = 0.5$ which is lowest. For L=9025 our proposed Nyquist window function has time-bandwidth product $Td_{r.m.s} \times Bw_{r.m.s} = 0.513$ which is very near to the optimal value.

The Mel frequency filter bank also provides the flat frequency response from the centre frequency of first filter to the centre frequency of the last filter. Fig. 6 shows a single prototype filter which is used to create the MFCC filter bank. The corresponding time domain relation of Mel frequency filter whose frequency response is shown in Fig. 6 is given below [9],

$$\begin{aligned} mfcc[n] &= \frac{e^{jc_\omega n} - e^{js_\omega n}}{2\pi(c_\omega - s_\omega)n^2} + \frac{e^{je_\omega n} - e^{jc_\omega n}}{2\pi(c_\omega - e_\omega)n^2} \qquad \text{for } n \neq 0 \\ &= (e_\omega - s_\omega)/4\pi \qquad \text{for } n = 0 \end{aligned} \tag{16}$$

For L=9025 the Mel frequency filter $mfcc[n]$ has time-bandwidth product $Td_{r.m.s} \times Bw_{r.m.s} = 0.55968$.

Therefore the proposed Nyquist window function provides 9.34% improved time-bandwidth product compared to MFCC function. At the time of calculation of improvement, the Gaussian window has been considered as the reference [7, 9].

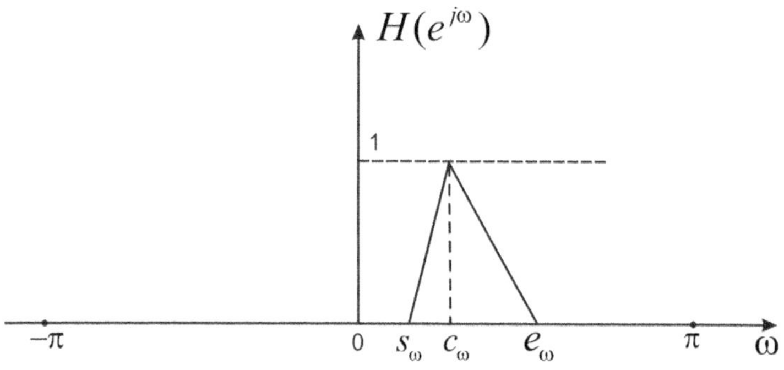

Fig. 6. Frequency response of a single MFCC filter

5 Proposed Feature Extraction Technique Using Frequency-Time Analysis Approach

Fig.7 shows the block diagram of the proposed feature extraction technique using frequency-time analysis approach with the help of Nyquist filter bank or Gaussian filter bank.

Here the speech signal is passed through a bank of parallel FIR filters. The output of each filter is passed through a framing operation, to create a temporal time zone. The length of each frame is 20 milliseconds. As our proposed technique is based on the frequency-time analysis approach, we do not need any overlapping frame. In the next paragraph we elaborate this concept.

The conventional feature extraction technique for speaker identification such as the MFCC is based on time-frequency analysis approach. Here at first, time analysis is

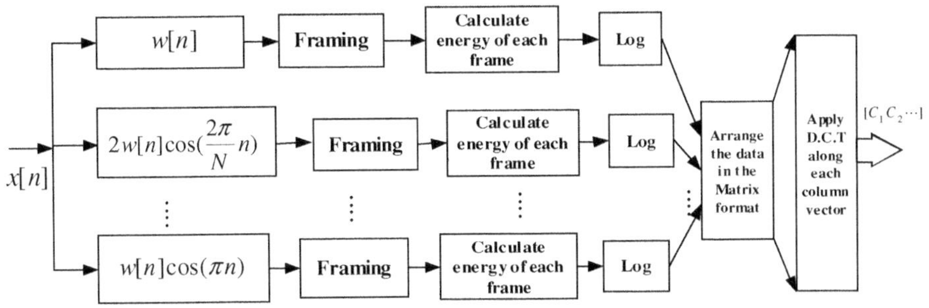

Fig. 7. Block diagram of the proposed Temporal Energy Subband Cepstral Coefficients (TESBCC) feature extraction technique using frequency-time analysis approach

done through the framing operation and then frequency analysis is done through Fourier transform. Since speech signals are quasi periodic, ideally we need to take variable length window to get a stationary portion of speech. This is however, too complicated for automatic implementation. A much easier approach to get a stationary portion of speech is overlapping frames. Generally overlap varies from 25% to 75% of the length of window. But the techniques which are based on frequency-time analysis approach, the frequency analysis is done first by taking the inner product of the original speech signal with the impulse responses of FIR filters that are connected in parallel. Each impulse response represents a specific frequency band. The filters are FIR; hence from the position of impulse response, we know which time zone of speech signal is under consideration for analysis. The position of impulse response can be found out from the output coefficients of inner product as follows,

Let the impulse response of an FIR filter be h[n] of duration L. Hence the output of the filter y[n] for an input signal x[n] is given by

$$y[n] = \sum_{r=0}^{L-1} h[r]x[n-r] = h[0]x[n] + h[1]x[n-1] + \ldots + h[L-1]x[n-L+1] \tag{17}$$

$$y[n+1] = \sum_{r=0}^{L-1} h[r]x[n+1-r] = h[0]x[n+1] + h[1]x[n] + \ldots + h[L-1]x[n-L+2] \tag{18}$$

From equation (17) and (18) it is clear that for output $y[n]$ and $y[n+1]$ for each value of n, the analysis zone of the speech signal is from $x[n]$ to $x[n-L+1]$ and from $x[n+1]$ to $x[n-L+2]$ respectively. Hence the impulse response of FIR filter is acting as a fixed length overlapping window with overlap $L-1$ which is the maximum possible overlap. Hence this procedure is very efficient to manage the quasi periodic nature of the speech signal. When we do framing at the output sequence of filter, then the last point of a frame and the first point of the next frame represent two positions of filter impulse response which are shifted by one point. Due to this maximum possible inherent overlap of input speech signal, we do not need any more overlap at output stage during framing operation.

To get the cepstral vector, we need to calculate the energies from various frequency bands of speech signal in a limited time zone. In a frequency-time analysis approach, the output of each filter is in a specific frequency band. By doing framing of the output sequence of filter, we have created various limited time zones.

We calculate the energy of each frame. These energies are called the temporal energy of subband. Arrange all the energy values in a matrix format. The number of rows of the matrix represents the number of filters in the filter bank and number of columns represents the number of time frames.

Log compression and DCT is applied along each column vector to get the cepstral coefficients. Now each column vector of the matrix $[C_1\ C_2\ C_3 \cdots]$ is a feature vector called Temporal Energy Subband Cepstral Coefficients (TESBCC).

6 Experimental Evaluations

We have used the POLYCOST database [12] for our experimental evaluation of the performances of the two newly proposed feature sets (i.e. TESBCC using Nyquist filter bank and TESBCC using Gaussian filter bank) and compared these with MFCC feature set. We have used 20 filters. After DCT the first coefficient (i.e. DC value) is discarded since it contains only the energy of the spectrum and the resulting 19 dimensional vector is used. We have kept the overall operating frequency zone same for proposed technique with the MFCC. To achieve this, we first divide the complete spectrum using 22 filters. Then we discard the first and last filter. The rest of the 20 filters are used for proposed TESBCC feature extraction.

6.1 Database Description

The POLYCOST database [12] was recorded as a common initiative within the COST 250 action during January-March 1996. It contains around 10 sessions recorded by 134 subjects from 14 countries. Each session consists of 14 items. The database was collected through the European telephone network. The recording has been performed with ISDN cards on two XTL SUN platforms with an 8 kHz sampling rate. Four speakers (M042, M045, M058 and F035) are not included in our experiments as they provide sessions which are lower than 6. All speakers (130 after deletion of four speakers) in the database were registered as clients.

For training the speaker model, we have concatenated the speech form first five sessions and used to train GMM model. All the data for each speaker from session six to last available session for an individual speaker were used for testing. A total eleven hours of data were put under test.

6.2 Comparison through GMM Classifier

In the present work, Gaussian mixture model (GMM) has been used as classifier [2]. The initialization of seed vectors for Gaussian centers was done by split vector quantization algorithm. This was followed by the Expectation and Maximization (E&M)

algorithm with 40 iterations. We took three types of model orders (8, 16 and 32 components GMM). For all cases, diagonal covariance matrices were chosen. Training speech length was 90 seconds. The identification accuracy using GMM classifier for MFCC, TESBCC using Nyquist filter bank and TESBCC using Gaussian filter bank are given in Table 1, Table 2 and Table 3 respectively.

Table 1. Identification Performance for MFCC Feature Set

Model Order	Test Speech Lengths			
	20 seconds	15 seconds	10 seconds	5 seconds
8	80.45	79.97	79.43	76.91
16	82.38	81.96	81.38	79.58
32	83.50	83.23	82.96	81.06

Table 2. Identification Performance for TESBCC Feature Set using Nyquist Window

Model Order	Test Speech Lengths			
	20 seconds	15 seconds	10 seconds	5 seconds
8	90.69	90.18	89.36	87.05
16	91.92	91.33	90.99	89.35
32	92.46	91.81	91.49	90.26

Table 3. Identification Performance for TESBCC Feature Set using Gaussian Window

Frequency Domain Variance	Model Order	Test Speech Lengths			
		20 seconds	15 seconds	10 seconds	5 seconds
$\omega_c = (\pi/21)$ $\sigma_\omega = 0.6(\omega_c/3)$	8	88.71	88.42	87.51	84.87
	16	90.16	89.73	89.25	87.02
	32	90.74	90.45	89.96	88.18
$\omega_c = (\pi/21)$ $\sigma_\omega = 0.8(\omega_c/3)$	8	89.73	89.45	88.51	86.14
	16	90.85	90.53	89.78	88.08
	32	91.87	91.25	91.07	89.22
$\omega_c = (\pi/21)$ $\sigma_\omega = 1(\omega_c/3)$	8	88.98	88.94	87.93	85.95
	16	90.37	90.25	89.81	88.28
	32	90.96	90.73	90.38	89.20
$\omega_c = (\pi/21)$ $\sigma_\omega = 1.8(\omega_c/3)$	8	89.41	89.70	88.88	87.02
	16	90.64	90.33	89.99	88.80
	32	91.06	91.29	90.89	89.78
$\omega_c = (\pi/21)$ $\sigma_\omega = 2(\omega_c/3)$	8	88.98	89.26	88.57	86.39
	16	90.42	90.45	90.02	88.77
	32	90.90	90.97	90.65	89.59
$\omega_c = (\pi/21)$ $\sigma_\omega = 2.8(\omega_c/3)$	8	86.84	87.39	86.96	84.85
	16	88.98	88.94	88.38	87.23
	32	89.62	89.50	88.91	88.18
$\omega_c = (\pi/21)$ $\sigma_\omega = 3(\omega_c/3)$	8	86.30	86.51	85.72	84.13
	16	88.50	88.26	87.83	86.46
	32	88.87	89.06	88.57	87.65

7 Conclusions

From the above results of the MFCC feature set, TESBCC feature set using Nyquist window and TESBCC feature set using Gaussian window it is evident that the TESBCC feature sets are performing far better compared to the MFCC feature set. Therefore the feature sets extracted using frequency-time analysis approach capture better speaker specific spectral information compared to the feature sets extracted using time-frequency analysis approach.

For TESBCC feature set using Gaussian window, initially the accuracy increases when the frequency domain variance σ_ω increases but later accuracy decreases. Because when σ_ω increases, the ripple in the overall magnitude response of the filter bank decreases. Hence accuracy increases. But when σ_ω increases, the frequency selectivity of the filter decreases. Hence after a certain point the overall accuracy decreases.

The TESBCC features extracted using Nyquist filter bank performs 9.51% better compared to the MFCC features. Similarly the TESBCC features extracted using the Gaussian filter bank performs 7.86% better compared to the MFCC features. Therefore the TESBCC feature set extracted using Nyquist window performs little better compared to the TESBCC feature set extracted using the Gaussian window.

References

1. Davis, S.B., Mermelsteine, P.: Comparison of parametric representation for monosyllabic word recognition in continuously spoken sentences. IEEE Trans. Acoust., Speech, Signal Processing ASSP-28(4), 357–365 (1980)
2. Reynolds, D.A., Rose, R.C.: Robust Text-Independent speaker identification using Gaussian mixture speaker models. IEEE Trans. Speech and Audio Processing 3(1), 72–83 (1995)
3. Hayakawa, S., Itakura, F.: Text-dependent speaker recognition using the information in the higher frequency band. In: ICASSP 1994, pp. 137–140 (1994)
4. Besacier, L., Bonastre, J.-F.: Subband architecture for automatic speaker recognition. Signal Processing 80(7), 1245–1259 (2000)
5. Lu, X., Dang, J.: An investigation of dependencies between frequency components and speaker characteristics for text-independent speaker identification. Speech Communication 50, 312–322 (2008)
6. Chakroborty, S., Roy, A., Saha, G.: Improved closed set text-independent speaker identification by combining MFCC with evidence from flipped filter banks. International Journal of Signal Processing 4(2), 1304–4478 (2007) ISSN 1304-4478
7. Sen, N., Basu, T.K.: A New Nyquist window with near optimal time-bandwidth product. In: IEEE Conference INDICON (2009)
8. Sen, N., Patil, H.A., Basu, T.K.: A New transform for robust Text-Independent speaker identification. In: IEEE Conference INDICON (2009)
9. Sen, N., Basu, T.K., Patil, H.A.: Significant improvement in the closed set text-independent speaker identification using features extracted from Nyquist filterbank. In: 5th International Conference on Industrial and Information Systems, ICIIS 2010, pp. 61–66 (2010)
10. Quatieri, T.F.: Discrete-Time Speech Signal Processing Principles and Practice. Pearson Education, London
11. Haykin, S., Veen, B.V.: Signals and Systems. John Wiley & Sons, Inc., Chichester (2001)
12. Petrovska, D., et al.: POLYCOST: A Telephonic speech database for speaker recognition. In: RLA2C, Avignon, France, April 20-23, pp. 211–214 (1998)

Entropy-Based Iterative Face Classification

Marios Kyperountas[1], Anastasios Tefas[1], and Ioannis Pitas[1,2]

[1] Department of Informatics, Aristotle University of Thessaloniki, Greece
[2] Informatics and Telematics Institute, Centre for Research and Technology Hellas, Greece
{mkyper,tefas,pitas}@aiia.csd.auth.gr

Abstract. This paper presents a novel methodology whose task is to deal with the face classification problem. This algorithm uses discriminant analysis to project the face classes and a clustering algorithm to partition the projected face data, thus forming a set of discriminant clusters. Then, an iterative process creates subsets, whose cardinality is defined by an entropy-based measure, that contain the most useful clusters. The best match to the test face is found when one final face class is retained. The standard UMIST and XM2VTS databases have been utilized to evaluate the performance of the proposed algorithm. Results show that it provides a good solution to the face classification problem.

Keywords: face classification, entropy, discriminant analysis.

1 Introduction

In the past several years, great attention has been given to the active research field of face classification. For the Face Recognition (FR) problem, the true match to a test face, out of a number of N different training faces stored in a database, is sought. The performance of many state-of-the-art FR methods deteriorates rapidly when large, in terms of the number of faces, databases are considered [1, 2]. Specifically, the facial feature representation obtained by methods that use linear criteria, which normally require images to follow a convex distribution, is not capable of generalizing all the introduced variations due e.g. to large differences in viewpoint, illumination and facial expression, when large data sets are used. When nonlinear face representation methods are employed, problems such as over-fitting, computational complexity and difficulties in optimizing the involved parameters often appear [1]. Recently, various methods have attempted to solve the aforementioned problems. A widely used principle that has been used is the 'divide and conquer', which decomposes a database into smaller sets in order to piecewise learn the complex distribution by a mixture of local linear models. In [1], a separability criterion is employed to partition a training set from a large database into a set of smaller maximal separability clusters (MSCs) by utilizing a variant of linear discriminant analysis (LDA). Based on these MSCs, a hierarchical classification framework that consists of two levels of nearest neighbour classifiers is employed and the match is found. The work in [3] concentrates on the hierarchical partitioning of the feature spaces using hierarchical discriminant analysis (HDA). A space-tessellation tree is generated using the most expressive features (MEF), by employing Principal Component Analysis (PCA), and the most

C. Vielhauer et al. (Eds.): BioID 2011, LNCS 6583, pp. 137–143, 2011.

discriminating features (MDF), by employing LDA, at each tree level. This is done to avoid the limitations linked to global features, by deriving a recursively better-fitted set of features for each of the recursively subdivided sets of training samples. In general, hierarchical trees have been extensively used for pattern recognition purposes. In [4], an owner-specific LDA-subspace is developed in order to create a personalized face verification system. The training set is partitioned into a number of clusters and only a single cluster, which contains face data that is most similar to the owner face, is retained. The system assigns the owner training images to this particular cluster and this new data set is used to determine an LDA subspace that is used to compute the verification thresholds and matching score when a test face claims the identify of the owner. Rather than using the LDA space created by processing the full training set, the authors show that verification performance is enhanced when an owner-specific subspace is utilized.

This paper presents a novel framework, onwards referred to as EbIC (Entropy-based Iterative Classification), which applies a person-specific iterative classification that is based on an entropy measure. The clustering and discriminant analysis parameters of EbIC are heavily affected by the characteristics of the test face. This methodology is not restricted to face classification, but is able to deal with any problem that fits into the same formalism. At this point, it is imperative that two terms that are frequently used in this paper are defined: 'class' refers to a set of face images from the same person, whereas 'cluster' refers to a set of classes. The ith face class is denoted by $\mathcal{Y}_i$ whereas the ith cluster by C_i. It should be mentioned that face images of one person may even be partitioned into multiple clusters; thus, each of these clusters will contain a class from that particular person.

Initially, the training and test face vectors are projected onto a LDA-space by employing Fisher's criterion [5, 6], thus producing the most discriminant features (MDF). Subsequently, k-means is used to partition the training data into a set of K discriminant clusters C_i and the distance of the test face from the cluster centroids is used to collect a subset of K' clusters that are closest to the test face. The cardinality of this subset is set through an entropy-based measure that is calculated by making use of the discrete probability histogram. The training data that reside in these K' clusters are merged and a new MDF-space of the merged face classes is found by applying LDA and k-means is once again used to partition the data into a set of clusters in a discriminant space. This process is repeated in as many iterations as necessary, until a single cluster is selected. Then, discriminant analysis is performed on this cluster, by using the data that reside in this cluster to produce the MDF-space, and the face class that is most similar to the test face is set as its identity match.

2 Adaptive Discriminant Clustering

The EbIC algorithm is an iterative process which, during each iteration, uses an adaptive MDF space that is closely related to the characteristics of the test face. More specifically, the set of clusters to be included in the training process that will define the future MDF space are selected based on how close they are to the test face in the current MDF space. Let us assume that an image $\mathbf{X}$ of a test face is to be assigned to one of the Y distinct classes $\mathcal{Y}_i$ that lie in the training set space $\mathcal{T}$. In addition, assume that each ith class in $\mathcal{T}$ is represented by $N_{\mathcal{Y}_i}$ images and the total number of training images is $N_{\mathcal{Y}}$. Thus, the face images that comprise the training set $\mathcal{T}$ can be represented by $\mathbf{Y}_n$, $n=1,\ldots,N_{\mathcal{Y}}$.

2.1 Linear Discriminant Analysis

In order to linearly transform the face vectors such that they become separable, they are projected onto an MDF space. Let S_W and S_B be within-class and between-class scatter matrices [7, 8] of the training set $\mathbf{Y}$. A well known and plausible criterion is to find a projection that maximizes the ratio of the between-class scatter vs. the within-class scatter (Fisher's criterion):

$$J(\mathbf{W}) = \frac{\mathbf{W}^{\mathrm{T}} S_B \mathbf{W}}{\mathbf{W}^{\mathrm{T}} S_W \mathbf{W}}. \tag{1}$$

Therefore, LDA is applied on $\mathbf{Y}$ and the discriminant matrix $\mathbf{W}$ of (1) is found. The training and test feature vectors are then projected to the MDF-space by

$$\mathbf{y}'_n = \mathbf{W}^{\mathrm{T}}\mathbf{y}_n, \quad n = 1,\ldots,N_{\mathcal{Y}}, \text{ and} \tag{2}$$

$$\mathbf{x}' = \mathbf{W}^{\mathrm{T}}\mathbf{x}. \tag{3}$$

where $\mathbf{y}_n$ and $\mathbf{x}$ are the training and test images in the form of vectors. Each training feature vector $\mathbf{y}'_n$ is stored in a column of $\mathbf{Y}'$.

2.2 Clustering Using k-Means

The k-means algorithm is then employed in an effort to partition the training data into the Y distinct face classes. Given a set of N data vectors, realized by $\mathbf{y}_n$, $n=1,\ldots,N$, in the *d*-dimensional space, *k*-means is used to determine a set of K vectors in $\Re^d$, called cluster centroids, so as to minimize the sum of vector-to-centroid distances, summed over all K clusters. The objective function of *k*-means that is used in this paper employs the squared Euclidean distance and is presented in [9]. After the K cluster centroids are found, e.g. $K=Y$, a single vector $\mathbf{y}'_n$ can be assigned to the cluster with the minimum vector-to-cluster-centroid distance, among the Y distances that are calculated. The distance between each training feature vector and the Y centroids, $\boldsymbol{\mu}_i$, can be calculated by the Euclidean distance measure:

$$D_i^n\left(\mathbf{y}'_n, \boldsymbol{\mu}_i\right) = \left\|\mathbf{y}'_n - \boldsymbol{\mu}_i\right\|, \quad i = 1,\ldots,Y. \tag{4}$$

2.3 Entropy-Based Generation of MDF-Spaces

Let us consider a set of K clusters, or partitions, in the data space $\mathcal{T}$. The surrounding *Voronoi region* of the *i*-th cluster is denoted as V_i. Theoretically, the a-priori probability for each cluster to be the best matching one to any sample vector $\mathbf{x}$ of the feature space is calculated as such, if the probability density function $p(\mathbf{x})$ is known:

$$P_i = P(\mathbf{x} \in V_i) = \int_{V_i} p(\mathbf{x}) d\mathbf{x} . \tag{5}$$

For discrete data, the discrete probability histogram can replace the continuous probability density function:

$$P_i = P(\mathbf{x} \in V_i) = \frac{\#\{j \mid \mathbf{x}_j \in V_i\}}{N}, \tag{6}$$

where $\#\{\cdot\}$ represents the cardinality of a set and N the size of the training data set whose members are $\mathbf{x}_j$, $j = 0,1,\ldots,N-1$. Let us consider a set of K partitions in the training data space $\mathcal{T}$ and their distribution $P = (P_1, P_2, \ldots, P_K)$. The entropy, a commonly used measure that indicates the randomness of the distribution of a variable, can be defined as [10]:

$$H = H(P) = -\sum_{i=1}^{K} P_i \log_2 P_i \tag{7}$$

An 'ideal' data partitioning separates the data such that overlap between partitions, e.g. the class overlap, is minimal, which is equivalent to minimizing the expected entropy of the partitions over all observed data.

In this paper, the entropy-based measure is calculated in a new data space $\mathcal{T}' \subset \mathcal{T}$, which consists of a subset that retains K' of the total K clusters that are generated by the *k*-means algorithm. Let us assume that the K' clusters contain Y' face classes. A needed assumption used to calculate the entropy is that a true match to the test face class $\mathcal{X}$ exists within the $\mathcal{T}'$ space. Let the probability for the i-th face class $\mathcal{Y}_i'$, that is now contained in $\mathcal{T}'$, to represent a true match for $\mathcal{X}$ be $P_i = p(\mathcal{Y}_i' \mid \mathcal{X})$. Since the prior probabilities $p(\mathcal{Y}_i' \mid \mathcal{X})$ are unknown, they can be defined using the discrete probability histogram, as in (6), as:

$$P_i = p(\mathcal{Y}_i' \mid \mathcal{X}) = \frac{N_{\mathcal{Y}_i'}}{N_{\mathcal{Y}'}}, \tag{8}$$

where $N_{\mathcal{Y}'}$ is the total number of face images contained in $\mathcal{T}'$, and $N_{\mathcal{Y}_i'}$ is the number of times that class i is represented in $\mathcal{T}'$, e.g. $N_{\mathcal{Y}_i'}$ different images of the person associated with class i are contained in $\mathcal{T}'$. The value of K' is limited by the threshold T_H applied on the entropy value, which, in order to guarantee a low computational cost is approximated by substituting (8) into (7), so that the following is satisfied:

$$-\sum_{i=1}^{K'} \frac{N_{\mathcal{Y}_i'}}{N_{\mathcal{Y}'}} \log_2\left(\frac{N_{\mathcal{Y}_i'}}{N_{\mathcal{Y}'}}\right) \le T_H \,. \tag{9}$$

The approximated entropy values are used to guarantee that at each step of the EbIC algorithm an easier, in terms of the ability to achieve better separation among the classes, classification problem is defined. Threshold T_H is applied on the entropy value H to limit the number of different classes that $\mathcal{T}'$ will contain. Essentially, this is done by limiting the number of clusters K' that comprise $\mathcal{T}'$.

In the new MDF-space, created using the face data from the K' clusters, LDA will attempt to discriminate the different classes found in each of the K' clusters. This enables the algorithm to formulate a clustering process that considers possible large variations in the set of images that represent each face class. For example, a portion of the set of images that corresponds to the ith training person may present this person having facial hair, whereas others as not having facial hair. If these variations are larger than identity-related variations, then they are clustered into disjoint clusters. Thus, the match with the subset of the training images of class i whose appearance is most similar to the test face is considered, so the best match can be found.

3 Experimental Results

In this section, the classification ability of EbIC is investigated by observing FR experiments using data from the XM2VTS and UMIST databases. Essentially, as in most FR applications, the classification experiments that are carried out fall under the small sample size (SSS) problem where the dimensionality of the samples is larger than the number of available training samples per subject [11, 12]. The performance of EbIC is presented for various degrees of how severe the SSS problem is. This is done by providing recognition rates for experiments where each face class $\mathcal{Y}_i$ is represented by the smallest to the largest possible number of training samples, N_{T}. Since EbIC employs discriminant analysis, the smallest possible value is 2. The largest possible value of training samples for each face class $\mathcal{Y}_i$ is determined by the number of available images in this class, $N_{\mathcal{Y}_i}$, and by considering that at least one of these samples needs to be excluded in order to be able to evaluate the recognition performance for that particular class. The remaining images that do not comprise the training set are used to test the performance of EbIC, thus, they constitute the test set. The training and test sets are created by random selection on each set of the $N_{\mathcal{Y}_i}$ images of each face class. To give statistical significance to our experiments, this random selection is repeated N_{R} times, thus, N_{R} recognition rates are averaged in order to obtain the final recognition rate R_{rec}.

The UMIST database consists of $K = 20$ different face classes, each of which is represented by at least $N_{\mathcal{Y}_i} = 19$ images. Consequently, 17 recognition rates were derived for training sets that contained $N_{\mathrm{T}} = 2,\ldots,18$ images from each of the 20 face

Table 1. Mean recognition rates for various numbers of training samples per subject

UMIST				XM2VTS	
Training Samples N_T	R_{rec} (%)	Training Samples N_T	R_{rec} (%)	Training Samples N_T	R_{rec} (%)
2	58.9	11	96.6	2	31.8
3	81.1	12	96.9	3	92.1
4	89.8	13	97.0	4	95.9
5	91.2	14	97.2	5	96.7
6	91.8	15	97.7	6	97.2
7	94.1	16	97.9	7	**98.6**
8	94.5	17	98.3		
9	94.6	18	**99.1**		
10	95.4				

classes. Each corresponding rate was the average out of $N_R = 10$ repetitions. The XM2VTS database consists of $K = 200$ different face classes, each of which is represented by $N_{\mathcal{Y}_i} = 8$ images. The number of clusters K' that are retained at each clustering level is selected by using (9). The face classes residing in the final cluster are projected to the MDF-space that is created by processing only this specific set of data. The face class that is closest to the test face in this MDF-space is selected as the true match in identity. Table 1 reports the mean recognition rates, R_{rec}, obtained for FR experiments carried out on both face databases, for $N_R = 10$ independent runs. The entropy-based measure, which is utilized to determine the number of clusters that should be retained, leads to more accurate results than the ones in [13], where a power function that converges to unity was used instead.

4 Conclusion

A novel face classification methodology that employs person-specific adaptive discriminant clustering is proposed and its performance is evaluated. By making use of an entropy-based measure, the EbIC algorithm adapts the coordinates of the MDF-space with respect to the characteristics of the test face and the training faces that are more similar to the test face. Thus, the FR problem is broken down to multiple easier classification tasks, in terms of achieving linear separability. The performance of this method was evaluated on standard face databases and results show that the proposed framework provides a good solution for face classification.

Acknowledgments

This work has been performed within the COST Action 2101 on Biometrics for Identity Documents and Smart Cards, and partly funded by the European Community's Seventh Framework Programme (FP7/2007-2013) under grant agreement n° 211471 (i3DPost).

References

1. Lu, J., Plataniotis, K.N.: Boosting face recognition on a large-scale database. In: Proc. IEEE Int. Conf. on Image Processing (ICIP 2002), Rochester, New York, USA, September 22-25 (2002)
2. Guo, G.D., Zhang, H.J., Li, S.Z.: Pairwise face recognition. In: Proc. 8th IEEE Int. Conf. on Computer Vision, Vancouver, Canada, vol. 2, pp. 282–287 (2001)
3. Swets, D.L., Weng, J.: Hierarchical discriminant analysis for image retrieval. IEEE Trans. on Pattern Analysis and Machine Intelligence 21(5), 386–401 (1999)
4. Liu, H.-C., Su, C.-H., Chiang, Y.-H., Hung, Y.-P.: Personalized face verification system using owner-specific cluster-dependent LDA-subspace. In: Proc. of the 17th Int. Conf. on Pattern Recognition (ICPR 2004), August 23-26, vol. 4, pp. 344–347 (2004)
5. Lu, J., Plataniotis, K.N., Venetsanopoulos, A.N.: Face recognition using LDA based algorithms. IEEE Trans. on Neural Networks 14(1), 195–200 (2003)
6. Kyperountas, M., Tefas, A., Pitas, I.: Methods for improving discriminant analysis for face authentication. In: Proc. IEEE Int. Conf. on Acoustics, Speech, and Signal Processing, Philadelphia (March 2005)
7. Fukunaga, K.: Introduction to Statistical Pattern Recognition. Academic Press, New York (1990)
8. Kyperountas, M., Tefas, A., Pitas, I.: Face verification using locally linear discriminant models. In: Proc. IEEE Int. Conf. on Image Processing, San Antonio, September 16-19, vol. 4, pp. 469–472 (2007)
9. Camastra, F., Verri, A.: A novel kernel method for clustering. IEEE Trans. on Pattern Analysis and Machine Intelligence 27(5), 801–805 (2005)
10. Koskela, M., Laaksonen, J., Oja, E.: Entropy-based measures for clustering and SOM topology preservation applied to content-based image indexing and retrieval. In: Proc. 17th Int. Conf. on Pattern Recognition, vol. 2, pp. 1005–1009 (2004)
11. Lu, J., Plataniotis, K.N., Venetsanopoulos, A.N.: Selecting kernel eigenfaces for face recognition with one training sample per subject. In: Proc. IEEE Int. Conf. on Multimedia and Expo, pp. 1637–1640 (July 2006)
12. Kyperountas, M., Tefas, A., Pitas, I.: Weighted piecewise LDA for solving the small sample size problem in face verification. IEEE Trans. on Neural Networks 18(2), 506–519 (2007)
13. Kyperountas, M., Tefas, A., Pitas, I.: Face recognition via adaptive discrimi-nant clustering. In: Proc. IEEE Int. Conf. on Image Processing, San Diego, pp. 2744–2747 (October 2008)

Local Binary LDA for Face Recognition

Ivan Fratric and Slobodan Ribaric

Faculty of Electrical Engineering and Computing, University of Zagreb, Unska 3, 10000 Zagreb, Croatia
{ivan.fratric,slobodan.ribaric}@fer.hr

Abstract. Extracting discriminatory features from images is a crucial task for biometric recognition. For this reason, we have developed a new method for the extraction of features from images that we have called local binary linear discriminant analysis (LBLDA), which combines the good characteristics of both LDA and local feature extraction methods. We demonstrated that binarizing the feature vector obtained by LBLDA significantly improves the recognition accuracy. The experimental results demonstrate the feasibility of the method for face recognition as follows: on XM2VTS face image database, a recognition accuracy of 96.44% is obtained using LBLDA, which is an improvement over LDA (94.41%). LBLDA can also outperform LDA in terms of computation speed.

Keywords: Biometrics, Face recognition, Linear discriminant analysis, Local features.

1 Introduction

Biometrics is an emerging technology [1, 2] that is used to identify people by their physical and/or behavioral characteristics. The face is a biometric characteristic that contains a variety of features that are suitable for biometric recognition. However, extracting these discriminatory features from face images is a difficult task. The extracted features must provide good recognition accuracy and be robust to intra-class variations, which is a major problem due to variations in the position of the face, facial expressions, lighting, appearance caused by aging, etc.

The most popular group of feature extraction methods for face recognition are the appearance-based methods, such as PCA [3] and LDA [4]. These methods observe entire images as a feature vector and then apply transformations that optimize some criterion function. Principal component analysis (PCA) finds the optimal transformation for the image representation; however, this transformation is not necessarily optimal for recognition, which is why linear discriminant analysis (LDA) usually gives better recognition accuracy. LDA finds a linear transformation that, when applied to a set of images, maximizes the between-class variance, while at the same time minimizing the within-class variance. Various modifications to the basic LDA approach have been proposed [5, 6, 7, 8].

Pentland et al. [9] used PCA to extract local features from rectangular patches placed on salient facial features: eyes, nose and mouth. Recently, even more attention has been given to local features, most notably the features extracted using a Gabor

C. Vielhauer et al. (Eds.): BioID 2011, LNCS 6583, pp. 144–155, 2011.

filter [10] and local binary patterns [11]. Local features are lighting-invariant and can give a better recognition accuracy than global features, such as those extracted using appearance-based approaches.

Several approaches combine different local features or both local and global features for face recognition. Méndez-Vázquez et al. [12] combine local binary patterns and local discrete cosine transform (DCT) for face recognition. They first discard low-frequency DCT coefficients as a preprocessing step, and than apply local binary patterns to represent the facial features. Pan and Cao [13] combine local features obtained by applying 2D non-negative matrix factorization (NMF) in 2D DCT domain with the global features obtained by 2D PCA.

We propose a new feature extraction method called local binary linear discriminant analysis (LBLDA) that combines the good characteristics of both appearance-based methods and methods based on local features. The general idea is to use LDA to locate and extract the discriminant local features. The images are divided into a set of possibly overlapping regions and then LDA is performed using the data for each region separately. In this way, we can extract the optimal local features in terms of the LDA criterion function. Based on this criterion function, we can also extract more features from the regions in the image that contain more discriminatory information. We take only the sign of the features and discard the magnitude in order to obtain a binary feature vector. Although it may appear that we are losing important discriminatory information by doing this, we demonstrate experimentally that using binary features significantly increases the recognition accuracy.

There are several benefits of using binary features. In a recent paper, Sun and Tan [14] present several of the benefits of using ordinal measures for feature representation, but these benefits hold for binary features as well:

(i) High-level measurements (i.e., measurements expressed as exact values) are sensitive to illumination changes, blur, noise, deformation, and other image degradations. Fine models of visual objects based on high-level measurements are useful for image detail preservation and image reconstruction, but are unnecessary for object recognition.
(ii) Binary features are more compact and faster to process due to the simpler computations.
(iii) Binary features are biologically plausible. For example, DeAngelis et al. [15] found that many striate cortical neurons' visual responses saturate rapidly with the magnitude of the contrast as the input. This indicates that the determining factor of visual perception is not the absolute value of the contrast, but its polarity.

The rest of the paper is organized as follows. In Section 2 we give a detailed description of the proposed method. In Section 3 we describe experiments that demonstrate the feasibility of the method for face recognition. The conclusions and suggestions for future work are given in Section 4.

2 LDA and LBLDA

LDA, as commonly used in image-based biometrics [4, 16], involves using the information from the entire image. All the images in the training set are treated as

n-dimensional vectors $\mathbf{x}_i$, $i = 1, 2, \ldots, N$, where N is the number of training images and n is the number of pixels in an image. LDA finds a transformation W_{LDA} that transforms the original image vectors into a new space in which the between-class variance is maximized, while the within-class variance is minimized.

LDA maximizes the criterion function

$$J(\mathbf{W}) = \frac{\left|\mathbf{W}^T \mathbf{S}_B \mathbf{W}\right|}{\left|\mathbf{W}^T \mathbf{S}_W \mathbf{W}\right|} \tag{1}$$

where $\mathbf{S}_B$ is the between-class variance matrix and $\mathbf{S}_W$ is the within-class variance matrix:

$$\begin{aligned} \mathbf{S}_B &= \sum_{i=1}^{N_C} N_i (\mathbf{m}_i - \mathbf{m})(\mathbf{m}_i - \mathbf{m})^T \\ \mathbf{S}_W &= \sum_{i=1}^{N_C} \sum_{\mathbf{x} \in \omega_i} (\mathbf{x} - \mathbf{m}_i)(\mathbf{x} - \mathbf{m}_i)^T \end{aligned} \tag{2}$$

where N_i is the number of samples in class ω_i, $\mathbf{m}_i$ is the mean sample of class ω_i and $\mathbf{m}$ is the mean of all the samples.

The solutions of the optimization problem (eq. 1) are the vectors $\mathbf{w}_j$, obtained as a solution of the generalized eigenvector problem $\lambda_j \mathbf{S}_W \mathbf{w}_j = \mathbf{S}_B \mathbf{w}_j$, that correspond to the largest generalized eigenvalues λ_j. The maximum dimensionality of the LDA space is $C - 1$, where C is the number of classes.

One problem that often arises with LDA in biometrics is that of the small sample size: if $N < n - C$, the within-class scatter matrix $\mathbf{S}_W$ is singular, and the computation of the LDA subspace becomes impossible by traditional means. The usual way of solving this problem is to first reduce the dimensionality of the training samples by means of PCA [4]. However, other solutions have also been proposed, such as direct LDA [5], regularized LDA [6] or discriminative common vectors [7].

In our approach, we use LDA to extract the local features. First, the image is divided into a set of N_R possibly overlapping regions. In our implementation, we use square regions obtained by using a sliding-window approach. A window of size p x p pixels is positioned in the upper-left corner of the image. The first region is composed of all the pixels that fall inside the window. The window is then translated by $t \leq p$ pixels to the right and, when the window falls outside of the image, it is moved t pixels down and all the way to the left of the image. The process is concluded when the bottom-right corner of the window reaches the bottom-right corner of the image. Each window position defines one of the N_R regions R_r, $r = 1, 2, ..., N_R$, where each region consists of p x p pixels.

For each region R_r and for each training image, we form a vector $\mathbf{x}_i^r$, $i = 1, 2, \ldots, N$; $r = 1, 2, \ldots, N_R$ by arranging into a vector all the pixels from the image i that fall into the region R_r. The size of each vector $\mathbf{x}_i^r$ is p x p. For each region R_r:

(i) We perform local PCA on the vectors $\mathbf{x}_i^r$, $i = 1, 2, \ldots, N$ and obtain a subspace $\mathbf{W}^r_{PCA}$. We project each of the vectors $\mathbf{x}_i^r$ into this subspace and obtain the vectors $\mathbf{z}_i^r$. The size of the vectors $\mathbf{z}_i^r$ is N_{PCA}, $N_{PCA} \leq \min(N\text{-}1, p \text{ x } p)$.

(ii) We perform LDA on the vectors $\mathbf{z}_i^r$, $i = 1, 2, \ldots, N$. In this process we obtain a subspace $\mathbf{W}^r_{\mathrm{LDA}}$.
(iii) We obtain a final subspace for the region R_r, $\mathbf{W}^r_{\mathrm{PCA+LDA}}$ by multiplying the transformation matrices of $\mathbf{W}^r_{\mathrm{PCA}}$ and $\mathbf{W}^r_{\mathrm{LDA}}$. This subspace is spanned by the local LDA basis vectors $\mathbf{w}_j^r$, $j = 1, 2, \ldots, N_{\mathrm{LDA}}$. N_{LDA} is the subspace dimensionality, $N_{\mathrm{LDA}} = \min(C\text{-}1, N_{\mathrm{PCA}})$. The size of each vector $\mathbf{w}_j^r$ is p x p. For each vector $\mathbf{w}_j^r$, we also note the corresponding LDA eigenvalues λ_j^r, which give information about the goodness of the vector $\mathbf{w}_j^r$ in terms of the LDA criterion function (eq. 1).

We now have a set of N_{LDA} x N_{R} vectors $\mathbf{w}_j^r$ and the corresponding eigenvalues λ_j^r. N_{LDA} x N_{R} can be quite large, for example, for 64x64 images with $p = 16$ and $t = 8$ we could obtain up to 12544 vectors $\mathbf{w}_j^r$. In order to select the most discriminatory features, we sort the vectors $\mathbf{w}_j^r$ by the falling values of the LDA eigenvalues λ_j^r. By taking the first $N_{\mathrm{LBLDA}} \leq N_{\mathrm{R}}$ x N_{LDA} vectors $\mathbf{w}_j^r$ we form the local feature space. In this way we can take more features from the image locations that are more discriminatory and fewer, or even no features, from the locations that do not contain significant discriminatory information.

Finally, we organize the obtained optimal basis into a data structure that we call the local subspace. This local subspace consists of N_{LBLDA} records, where each record contains a region index r and the basis vector $\mathbf{w}_k$, where $\mathbf{w}_k$ is the k-th vector in the sorted sequence of vectors $\mathbf{w}_j^r$.

In the recognition phase, for an unknown image I, we can use this local subspace to extract a N_{LBLDA}-dimensional feature vector $\mathbf{y}$ as follows. The image I is divided into N_{R} regions in the same manner as used to obtain the local subspace. The k-th component of this feature vector y_k is obtained by computing the scalar product of $\mathbf{w}_k$ and a (p x p)-dimensional vector obtained by arranging the pixels of region R_r of the image I into a vector, where $\mathbf{w}_k$ and r are components of the k-th record of the local subspace.

To obtain a binary feature vector **b,** we simply take only the signs of the components of $\mathbf{y}$ ($b_k = 1$ for $y_k > 0$ and $b_k = 0$ otherwise). This binary feature vector is called a binary live template.

The use of binary feature vectors has been shown to significantly increase the recognition accuracy in our experiments. By taking only the signs of the components of the feature vector $\mathbf{y}$ we in fact use only information about whether the correlation between the pixels of the region R_r and the local LDA basis $\mathbf{w}_k$ is positive or negative, while disregarding the exact extent of the correlation.

An alternate way to view the obtained local features is to observe them as filter responses. Instead of using predefined filters, such as the Gabor filter, these filters are learned on the training data, separate for each image location, so that they emphasize the differences between the classes, while suppressing the within-class variances. We extract the features from each image region using the appropriate filter and take only the binary response, in a similar manner the responses of the Gabor filters are encoded to form the iris code [17] and the palm code [18].

The classification is based on the Hamming distance between the binary live template and the binary templates stored in the database.

3 Experimental Evaluation

The proposed method was tested on the XM2VTS face image database [19]. The database consists of 2360 images of 295 individuals (8 images per person). The images were taken in four sessions with two images taken per session. Prior to the experiments on this database, all the images were normalized in such a way that the images contain only the face; the person's eyes were always in the same position, all the images were 64x64 pixels in size and a lighting normalization by histogram fitting [20] was performed. Four images of each person (images from the first two sessions) were used for the training, and the remaining four were used for the experiments. Fig. 1 shows several normalized images from the XM2VTS face image database.

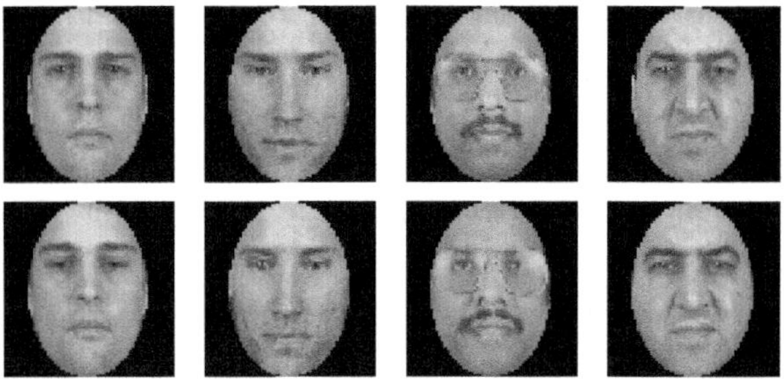

Fig. 1. Several normalized images from the XM2VTS face image database. Images in the same column belong to the same person.

The following experiments were performed. Firstly, we show the recognition results of our method on the described datasets for different parameter combinations (Experiment 1). Secondly, we examine the image regions from which the most features are taken by the method and compare the results to the results obtained when the regions of interest are manually placed on the visually salient facial features (Experiment 2). Thirdly, we compare the results of our method to the results obtained by "classic" LDA on the same databases (Experiment 3) and examine the effect of binarization on the performance of our method (Experiment 4). Finally, we evaluate and compare the computation time requirements of the methods.

Experiment 1: Recognition results of our method for different parameter combinations
There are four main parameters in our method:

(i) p – determines the local window width and height in pixels.
(ii) t – determines how many pixels the local window is translated to define the next region. If $t = p$ the regions do not overlap.
(iii) N_{PCA} – determines the dimensionality to which local samples are reduced prior to performing LDA. If $N_{PCA} = p \times p$, the reduction of the dimensionality is not necessary.
(iv) N_{LDA} – determines the feature vector length.

A series of recognition experiments was performed with different values of these parameters on our test dataset. For each combination of window size p and translation

Table 1. Face recognition results for different parameter combinations

Window size p	Window translation step t	N_{PCA} for best recognition accuracy	N_{LBLDA} for best recognition accuracy	Best recognition accuracy
8	8	64	400	91.44%
8	4	64	1500	94.32%
8	2	64	4000	95.17%
16	16	100	300	91.53%
16	8	100	1000	95.25%
16	4	150	1500	**96.19%**
16	2	100	7300	**96.44%**
32	32	100	200	88.56%
32	16	200	400	93.98%
32	8	200	800	95.34%

step t we marked the best score together with the corresponding N_{PCA} and feature vector length N_{LDA}. The experiments were performed using the 1-NN classifier with the Hamming distance. The results of the experiment are shown in Table 1.

Several conclusions can be made based on these experiments. Firstly, the recognition results are better for the overlapping than for the non-overlapping regions. When t is decreased to p/2 or p/4 the recognition accuracy is improved as more discriminant features are added. However, in this case the feature vector length increases. In some cases, even better recognition results can be achieved with $t = p/8$, for example, when $p = 16$, but this leads to a dramatic increase in the binary feature vector length (for example, from 1500 to 7300; see Table 1).

In most cases the best recognition results were achieved with input parameter $N_{PCA} = 100$ or 150. An increase in N_{PCA} beyond 150 usually results in a decrease of the recognition accuracy. The interpretation of these results is as follows. LDA, like all supervised learning methods, tends to give good results on the training set, but poor results on the unseen data, when given too many degrees of freedom. Often, it is better to limit the size of the vectors that are input into the LDA in order to achieve a better generalization.

The optimal window size and the translation step for the database used in the experiments were $p = 16$ and $t = 4$. Although we cannot claim that these parameters would also perform best on different databases, they pose a good estimate for the optimal values of the parameters.

3.1 Regions of Interest

LBLDA takes more features from the image regions that carry more discriminatory information. In this subsection we will show such regions for our database and compare the recognition accuracy to the one obtained using local binary features extracted from patches manually placed on the visually salient facial features.

In Fig. 2 we visualize the number of features taken from each image region when LBLDA is learned on the face database. Several images are given, corresponding to the different total number of features (N_{LBLDA}). The lighter areas correspond to the image regions from which the larger number of features are taken and the black areas correspond to the image regions from which no features are taken.

From Fig. 2 it is obvious that the most features are taken from the areas of the eyes, nose, mouth and eyebrows, which is consistent with the human perception of the distinctive features on faces.

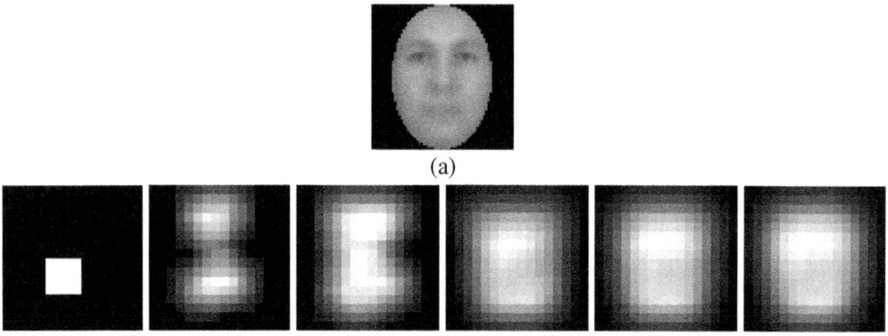

(a)

$N_{LBLDA} = 1$ $N_{LBLDA} = 50$ $N_{LBLDA} = 100$ $N_{LBLDA} = 500$ $N_{LBLDA} = 1000$ $N_{LBLDA} = 1500$

(b)

Fig. 2. (a) Mean face image from the database, (b) visualization of the number of features taken from different face image regions. The lighter areas correspond to image regions from which the larger number of features are taken and the black areas to the image regions from which no features are taken.

Experiment 2: Comparison of the recognition results based on features extracted from regions that are located by our method and local binary features extracted from manually marked regions.

We compared the results of our method to the results obtained when local binary features are extracted from patches manually placed on the visually salient facial features. Fig. 3 shows a mean face image from the face database with manually marked overlapping regions of interest.

Fig. 4. presents the recognition results of the experiment. The input parameters p = 16, t = 8 and N_{PCA} = 100 are used in LBLDA.

It is clear from Fig. 4 that the selection of image regions by our method gives a better recognition accuracy. This suggests that, although the majority of discriminant features are located in the manually marked regions (these regions correspond to the lightest areas in Fig. 2), other areas of the image still contain discriminant features that may significantly improve the recognition accuracy.

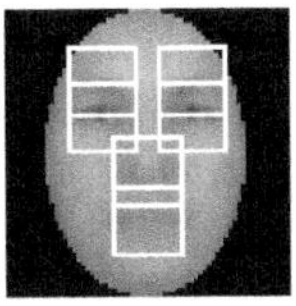

Fig. 3. Mean face image with overlapping regions of interest marked manually

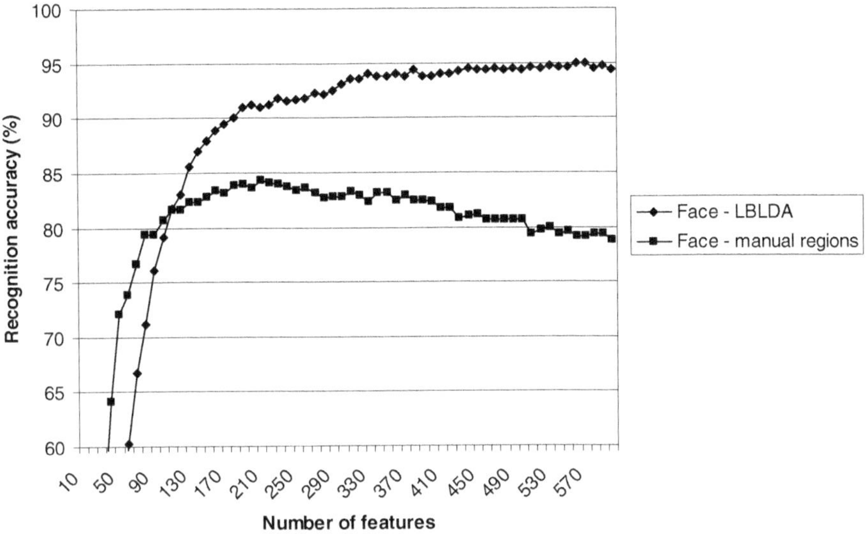

Fig. 4. Comparison of recognition results with regions located by our method and manually marked regions

3.2 Comparison of Recognition Results of LBLDA and LDA

Experiment 3: Comparison of LBLDA and "classic" LDA.

In order to demonstrate the feasibility of our method, the recognition results obtained using LBLDA were compared to the results obtained using features extracted by "classic" LDA on the same database.

We also wanted to test how global features extracted by the LDA perform if they are binarized in a similar way to the local features and the Hamming distance is used to compare them. We will call this method global binary LDA (GBLDA) in the remainder of the text.

Recognition experiments with all the feature extraction methods were performed using the 1-NN classifier. A normalized correlation was used as a matching measure for the LDA feature vectors, as it was demonstrated [21] that this performs better than the Euclidean distance.

The results are shown in Fig. 5. The figure shows the recognition accuracy depending on the length of the feature vectors. For all the methods the parameters giving the highest recognition accuracy were used. The results show that LBLDA outperforms LDA and GBLDA in terms of recognition accuracy. LBLDA achieves better recognition accuracy with a larger number of features (above 1300), but it is important to note that LBLDA uses binary feature vectors, which are simple to store and process.

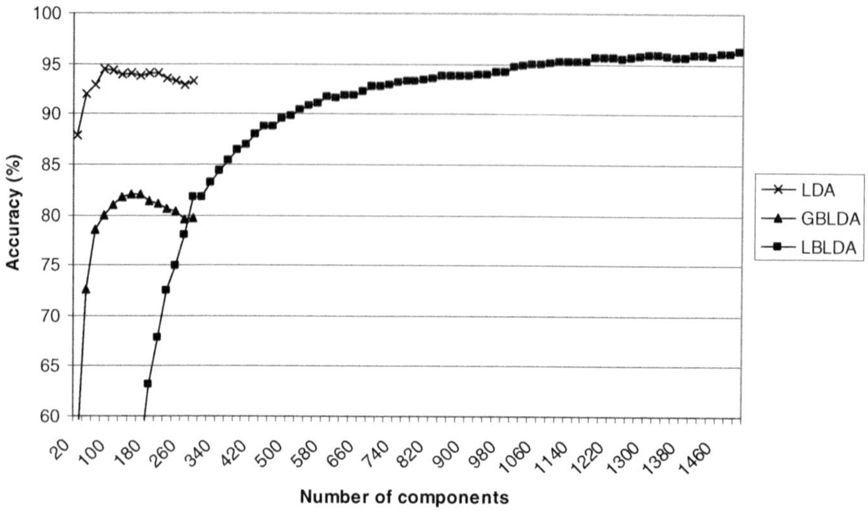

Fig. 5. Recognition accuracy of PCA, LDA, GBLDA and LBLDA on the face database depending on the number of features

Experiment 4: Effect of binarization on local LDA and using different distance measures.

We made an experiment showing the effect of binarization and different distance measures on the recognition accuracy, with local features extracted using local LDA. Fig. 6 shows the recognition accuracy for our method (LBLDA), and our method without binarization with the Euclidean distance and the normalized correlation for face recognition.

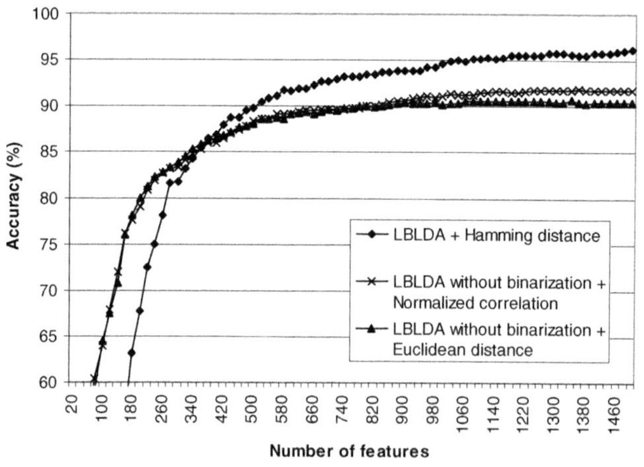

Fig. 6. Comparison of recognition accuracy obtained using the Hamming distance, the normalized correlation (without feature vector binarization) and the Euclidean distance (without feature vector binarization) on the face database, depending on the number of features

From Fig. 6 we can see that using binary features gives the best recognition accuracy, while the normalized correlation gives slightly better results than the Euclidean distance, as is the case with "classic" LDA.

Table 2 gives a summary of the best recognition accuracies for the different feature extraction methods and the distance measures.

Table 2. The best recognition accuracies for the different feature extraction methods and the distance measures

Features	**Recognition accuracy**
LDA + Euclidean distance	90.00%
LDA + Normalized correlation	94.41%
Global binary LDA (GBLDA) + Hamming distance	82.03%
LBLDA + Hamming distance	**96.18%**
LBLDA without binarization + Euclidean distance	90.67%
LBLDA without binarization + Normalized correlation	91.86%

3.3 Computation Speed

There are several steps that need to be performed in a biometric recognition system using LBLDA features. Here, we examine the time cost of each of them separately and compare them to the time cost of the same steps in LDA.

Firstly, the transformations need to be learned, which is the most time-consuming task, but this task needs to be performed only once, during the training stage. Secondly, features have to be extracted from the images. This task needs to be performed once per image. Thirdly, there is the time cost of computing the distance between two feature vectors. The number of comparisons depends on the number of feature vectors stored in the database during the enrollment.

Table 3 shows the processing time for each of these steps for LDA and LBLDA on the face database. Both LDA and LBLDA were implemented in C++. The experiments were run on an Intel Core 2 Quad processor running at 2.4 GHz, using only a single core.

LBLDA not only gives a better recognition accuracy, but, as shown in Table 3, it can also perform faster when compared to LDA. The speed increase in learning and feature extraction is obtained with LBLDA because it does not require computations

Table 3. Processing time for LDA and LBLDA on the face database

	LDA $N_{LDA} = 100$	LBLDA $p = 16, t = 8,$ $N_{PCA} - 100,$ $N_{LBLDA} = 1000$	LBLDA $p = 16, t = 4,$ $N_{PCA} = 150,$ $N_{LBLDA} = 1500$
Learning time	233s	34s	139s
Feature extraction time	0.67ms	0.59ms	1.40ms
Distance computation time	0.43ns	0.16ns	0.22ns

on as large matrices as LDA does. The speed increase in the distance computation is obtained because the Hamming distance is much simpler to compute using binary operations and lookup tables than the normalized correlation used in the LDA.

4 Conclusion

Extracting discriminatory features from images is a crucial task for biometric recognition based on the face features. We propose a new method of feature extraction from images, called local binary linear discriminant analysis (LBLDA), which combines the good characteristics of both LDA and local feature extraction methods. LBLDA uses LDA to extract a set of local features that carry the most discriminatory information. A feature vector is formed by projecting the corresponding image regions onto a subspace defined by the combination of basis vectors, which are obtained from different image regions and sorted by the descending order of their corresponding LDA eigenvalues. We demonstrated that binarizing the components of this feature vector significantly improves the recognition accuracy. Experiments performed on the face image databases suggest that the LBLDA outperforms "classic" LDA both in terms of recognition accuracy and speed.

In the future we plan to apply LBLDA on different datasets to test the robustness of the method to lighting and facial expression.

References

1. Jain, A.K., Bolle, R., Pankanti, S.: Biometrics: Personal Identification in Networked Society. Kluwer Academic Publishers, Dordrecht (1999)
2. Zhang, D.: Automated Biometrics: Technologies & Systems. Kluwer Academic Publishers, Dordrecht (2000)
3. Turk, M., Pentland, A.: Eigenfaces for Recognition. J. Cognitive Neurosicence 3(1), 71–86 (1991)
4. Belhumeur, P.N., Hespanha, J.P., Kriegman, D.J.: Eigenfaces vs. Fisherfaces: Recognition Using Class Specific Linear Projection. IEEE Trans. Pattern Analysis and Machine Intelligence 19(7), 711–720 (1997)
5. Yu, H., Yang, J.: A Direct LDA Algorithm for High-Dimensional Data with Application to Face Recognition. Pattern Recognition 34(10), 2067–2070 (2001)
6. Dai, D.Q., Yuen, P.C.: Regularized discriminant analysis and its application to face recognition. Pattern Recognition 36(3), 845–847 (2003)
7. Cevikalp, H., Neamtu, M., Wilkes, M., Barkana, A.: Discriminativen common vectors for face recognition. IEEE Trans. Pattern Analysis and Machine Intelligence 27(1), 4–13 (2005)
8. Kim, T.K., Kittler, J.: Locally linear discriminant analysis for multimodally distributed classes for face recognition with a single model image. IEEE Trans. Pattern Analysis and Machine Intelligence 27(3), 318–327 (2005)
9. Pentland, A., Moghaddam, B., Starner, T.: View-based and modular eigenspaces for face recognition. In: Proc. CVPR 1994, pp. 84–91 (1994)
10. Serrano, A., de Diego, I.M., Conde, C., Cabello, E.: Recent advances in face biometrics with Gabor wavelets: A review. Pattern Recognition Lett. 31(5), 372–381 (2010)

11. Marcel, S., Rodriguez, Y., Heusch, G.: On the Recent Use of Local Binary Patterns for Face Authentication. Int'l J. on Image and Video Processing, Special Issue on Facial Image Processing, 1–9 (2007)
12. Méndez-Vázquez, H., García-Reyes, E., Condes-Molleda, Y.: A New Combination of Local Appearance Based Methods for Face Recognition under Varying Lighting Conditions. In: Ruiz-Shulcloper, J., Kropatsch, W.G. (eds.) CIARP 2008. LNCS, vol. 5197, pp. 535–542. Springer, Heidelberg (2008)
13. Pan, C., Cao, F.: Face Image recognition Combining Holistic and Local Features. In: Yu, W., He, H., Zhang, N. (eds.) ISNN 2009. LNCS, vol. 5553, pp. 407–415. Springer, Heidelberg (2009)
14. Sun, Z., Tan, T.: Ordinal Measures for Iris Recognition. IEEE Trans. Pattern Analysis and Machine Intelligence 31(12), 2211–2226 (2009)
15. DeAngelis, G.C., Ohzawa, I., Freeman, R.D.: Spatiotemporal Organization of Simple-Cell Receptive Fields in the Cat's Striate Cortex, I. General Characteristics and Postnatal Development. J. Neurophysiology 69(4), 1091–1117 (1993)
16. Wu, X., Zhang, D., Wang, K.: Fisherpalms Based Palmprint Recognition. Pattern Recognition Lett. 24(15), 2829–2838 (2003)
17. Daugman, J.: High confidence visual recognition of persons by a test of statistical independence. IEEE Trans. Pattern Analysis and Machine Intelligence 15(11), 1148–1161 (1993)
18. Zhang, D., Kong, W.K., You, J., Wong, M.: Online Palm Print Identification. IEEE Trans. Pattern Analysis and Machine Intelligence 25(2), 1041–1050 (2003)
19. Messer, K., Matas, J., Kittler, J., Luettin, J., Maitre, G.: XM2VTSDB: The extended M2VTS database. In: Proc. AVBP 1999, pp. 72–77 (1999)
20. Gonzales, R.C., Woods, R.E.: Digital Image Processing. Addison Wesley, Reading (1993)
21. Kittler, J., Li, Y.P., Matas, J.: On Matching Scores for LDA-based Face Verification. In: Proc. British Machine Vision Conference 2000, pp. 42–51 (2000)

From 3D Faces to Biometric Identities

Marinella Cadoni, Enrico Grosso, Andrea Lagorio, and Massimo Tistarelli

University of Sassari
Computer Vision Laboratory
Porto Conte Ricerche, Tramariglio, Alghero, Italy
{maricadoni,grosso,lagorio,tista}@uniss.it

Abstract. The recognition of human faces, in presence of pose and illumination variations, is intrinsically an ill-posed problem. The direct measurement of the shape for the face surface is now a feasible solution to overcome this problem and make it well-posed. This paper proposes a completely automatic algorithm for face registration and matching. The algorithm is based on the extraction of stable 3D facial features characterizing the face and the subsequent construction of a signature manifold. The facial features are extracted by performing a continuous-to-discrete scale-space analysis. Registration is driven from the matching of triplets of feature points and the registration error is computed as shape matching score. A major advantage of the proposed method is that no data pre-processing is required. Therefore all presented results have been obtained exclusively from the raw data available from the 3D acquisition device.

Despite of the high dimensionality of the data (sets of 3D points, possibly with the associate texture), the signature and hence the template generated is very small. Therefore, the management of the biometric data associated to the user data, not only is very robust to environmental changes, but it is also very compact. This reduces the required storage and processing resources required to perform the identification.

The method has been tested against the Bosphorus 3D face database and the performances compared to the ICP baseline algorithm. Even in presence of noise in the data, the algorithm proved to be very robust and reported identification performances in line with the current state of the art.

Keywords: Face authentication, 3D, geometric invariants.

1 Introduction

The acquisition and processing of 3D data, allows to overcome the limitations due to the 2D to 3D projection ambiguities generated when analyzing 2D face images. The information in the 3D face shape can be exploited to devise a robust and accurate identification system. Performing recognition on 3D data, involves the alignment of the shapes and the computation of their similarity. Particularly with deformable objects, such as human faces, shape registration either based

C. Vielhauer et al. (Eds.): BioID 2011, LNCS 6583, pp. 156–167, 2011.

on 3D or texture data can be very difficult due to ambiguities in the characterization of anchor points. Therefore, a good registration of the face shapes from two individuals, already provides a measure of their similarity. In fact, the registration error can be used a matching score between the two individuals. The Iterative Closest Point (ICP) algorithm [1] is often used as a reference to compare the performances of face recognition algorithms. It proved to be very effective to accurately register (or match) 3D face scans, but an approximate initial alignment of the two point sets is required to bootstrap the algorithm. For this reason, an accurate and efficient face registration is always mandatory to perform face recognition. Therefore, in this paper 3D face recognition is tackled as a by product of the registration of 3D point sets.

More and more 3D databases are available to the scientific community, many of them consisting of high resolution scans of many individuals acquired with different poses and expressions [2]. The management of identities requires the construction of compact biometric templates, which require a limited storage and minimal computational resources. This may seem unfeasible when dealing with high dimensional data, such as dense 3D face shape representations. The geometric approach proposed in this paper is aimed at minimizing the required storage for the face template by extracting and processing a limited number of characteristic 3D points. The resulting template requires only a few KBytes of data. The algorithm is based on the extraction of facial features characterizing the face and the subsequent construction of a signature manifold. Registration is driven from the matching of triplets of feature points. After registration two different processes are performed: the registration error is computed first as shape matching score, secondly the coarse registration is refined by using the Iterative Closest Point (ICP) technique [1]. The final match score is determined by the registration error computed after the last iteration.

The proposed algorithm was tested on the Bosphorus database [3], particularly with faces under different poses. Previous works on this database have concentrated on landmarks detection robust to occlusions and noise ([4,5]). In [6], benchmark algorithms have been tested on selected subsets of the database. The algorithm proposed in this paper significantly outperform the benchmarks algorithms based on automatic features extraction. Several experimental tests are performed on the Bosphorus database and the produced results demonstrate the efficiency of the algorithm in real application scenarios.

2 Features Extraction

2.1 Scale-Space Theory for 3D Face Analysis

Recognition of faces from 3D information only can be achieved by registering the data from two individuals and measuring the goodness of fit. This process requires to identify anchor points on the faces which are similar for all faces but also to locate 3D features which may be highly distinguishing. Starting from the observation "all faces are similar and different at the same time" the aim is to localize points in areas that almost every face share, "common" points such as eyes corners, nose tip etc, and, at the same time, points that are peculiar to a face such as a chin dimple or a prominent cheekbone. The first kind of points present a certain degree of variability amongst faces which is useful to distinguish faces from different individuals. These points should be localized with the highest possible accuracy. Moreover, in order to compute the signature of an individual's face also the 3D surface normals at those points are required. Considering a 3D face scan as a smooth surface, both kind of points are either local maxima or minima of the Gaussian curvature. Our aim is then to find an algorithm to extract local maxima and minima of curvature, with a given approximation.

The scale-space theory [7], originally proposed to describe the gray level variations in 2D intensity images, can be applied to 3D face scan to optimally select all "common" points, namely 3D features, to be extracted from a set of 3D faces. According to this theory, a signal $f : \mathbb{R}^n \rightarrow \mathbb{R}$ (the face surface in our case) can be modeled by a scale-space representation: $L : \mathbb{R}^n \times \mathbb{R} \rightarrow \mathbb{R}$ where $L(x,t) = G(x,t) \otimes f(x)$, $G(\,, t)$ is a Gaussian kernel of width t and $\otimes$ is the convolution operation [9]. Given a scale-space representation of the face, we can characterize the face at each scale by means of the Gaussian curvature at each point. Following this finding, we conjecture that the scale at which the scale space curvature reaches its maximum is likely to be a relevant scale to represent that patch of the face. This would imply that, by varying the scale, it is possible to localize all required points (common and peculiar) on a face. Furthermore, the surface normal computed at the same relevant scale is expected to be more robust to noise.

In order to adapt the scale-space theory to a face scan represented by a discrete set of points, a similar scheme as in [8] is adopted. Due to computational time and memory limits, the scale can not be varied continuously, nor can the cloud of points be model with a parametrized surface. This problem can be overcome by extracting, for each 3D scanned point p_i, an approximation of the Gaussian curvature computed on the set of spherical neighbors $N_{p_i}(r_j)$, centered at the point p_i and of increasing radius r_j. The scale step, i.e. the difference between the radii of two consecutive neighbors can be chosen on the basis of the sampling density of the scan. In the performed experiments the scale step was determined by constraining, on average, the difference between two neighbors to be equal to 10 points. Given a 3D point p_i and the 3D neighbors $N_{p_i}(r_j)$, an approximation of the Gaussian curvature can be obtained by computing the Principal Components of $N_{p_i}(r_j)$. The eigenvalues $\lambda_0 \leq \lambda_1 \leq \lambda_2$ and the respective eigevectors v_0, v_1, v_2 corresponding to the principal directions, are computed. The absolute value of the curvature is then defined as $\mathcal{C}(p_i, r_j) = \dfrac{2|(p_i - p_g) \cdot v_0|}{d_m^2}$, where p_g is the center of gravity of the neighbor $N_{p_i}(r_j)$ and d_m^2 is the mean of distances $|p_i - p_j|$, $p_j \in N_{p_i}(r_j)$. The surface normal $\nu(p_i, r_j)$ at the point p_i at scale r_j is computed as the principal direction corresponding to the smallest eigenvalue λ_0.

2.2 Multi-scale Feature Extraction

The scale-space analysis of the 3D face scans can be summarized as follows:

- Two extreme values for the search radius are set, i.e. a starting radius r_s and an end radius r_e. It is worth noting that these two values are metric parameters which are fixed on the basis of anthropometric facial measures. Therefore they do not depend on the training data nor on the acquisition device. For example, the smallest radius r_s should be small enough to detect the nose of a child, while the largest radius r_e should be large enough to detect an adult nose. In the experimental tests the two radii were set empirically to 6mm and 22mm.
- The scale step σ_s is defined to partition the interval (r_s, r_e) into a set of $n_\sigma = \dfrac{r_s - r_e}{\sigma_s} + 1$ intervals of equal length.
- For each point p_i of a face scan, the curvature $\mathcal{C}(p_i, r_j)$ is computed for $j = s, s + \sigma_s, s + 2\sigma_s, \ldots, e$. The curvature values are then interpolated to produce a function $\mathcal{C}(p_i) : [s, e] \to \mathbb{R}$. A median filter is applied to smooth the curve, and the scale $\sigma_m(p_i)$ for which the curvature $\mathcal{C}(i) = \mathcal{C}(p_i, \sigma_m(p_i))$ reaches a maximum is computed. Should the maximum correspond to the first scale (r_s), $\sigma_m(p_i)$ is set to be the scale at which the curvature is equal to the median value of all curvatures. This is necessary because often the maximum is a consequence of noise which can highly affect the processing at small radius scales. The normal ν_i at point p_i is determined as $\nu(p_i, \sigma_m(p_i))$.

As a result, for each point p_i of the face scan an optimal curvature value $\mathcal{C}_i$ and an optimal normal vector $\nu(i)$ are obtained. In order to avoid detecting the face edges as local maxima, all points belonging to the border of the face scan are first detected and marked to be excluded from the successive processing. Given $r = (r_e - r_s)/2$, and for each p_i in the face scan, p_i is defined to be a local maxima or minima of the curvature if $|\mathcal{C}_i|$ is the largest of all $|\mathcal{C}_k|$ for $p_k \neq p_i \in N_{p_i}(r)$. The extracted extrema curvature points are retained as 3D face feature points.

While the number of features is naturally bounded by the radius r, up to 12 points of highest curvature are selected amongst them. This value was experimentally proved to be sufficient to include a sufficient number of common and distinguishing points to characterize and match a 3D face. In figure 1 (a), the projected surface of a sample 3D face scan is shown. The surface color encodes the curvature values computed at the fixed scale $(r_e - r_s)/2$. The marked points on the surface represent the extracted 3D features. As it can be noticed, the extracted features include stable points such as the nose tip, the eye corners as well as distinguishing points for this face such as the chin dimples and the little bump on the nose.

In figure 1 (a) the point sampling appears to be quite uniform, but this is due to the coincidence of the direction of view with the direction of the original scanning. In most 3D acquisition devices, due to small distance between the (or small number of) cameras employed, the sampling density of the face scan is lower exactly in those areas where curvature variation occurs. This non-uniform

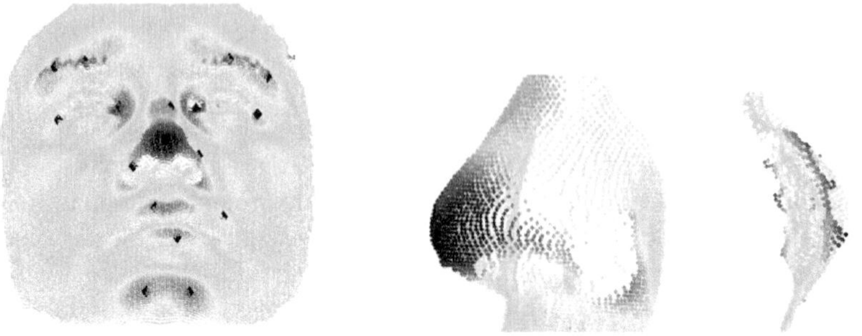

(a) (b) (c)

Fig. 1. (a) Feature points extracted from a sample face scan from the Bosphorus database, (b) Subsampled nose area, (c) Noisy eye area

sampling may lead to occlusions and thus impair the extraction of feature points. For example, the nostril on the right hand side of the surface in figure 1 is located slightly upwards with respect to the left one. This is not due to an anatomical asymmetry or to an error in the curvature computation, but rather to a missing patch in the nostril area (see figure 1(b)). Another example of errors in the sampled points is shown in figure 1(c). In this case the eye area contains spurious points which are detected as spikes on the surface. Probably due to the specular reflectance of the cornea all facial scans of the Bosphorus database contain noise peaks within the areas including the eyes. Despite the occlusions and noise in the data, preprocessing of the data has been carefully avoided. It is worth stressing that all results presented in the experimental section were obtained without applying any kind of data preprocessing. This allows to better evaluate the performance on face registration and matching as related to the raw data only and not to the quality of any pre-processing step.

3 3D Face Registration

The registration algorithm is based on the Moving Frame Theory [10]. The procedure that leads to the generation of the invariants and the signature are discussed in full detail in [11]. Only the fundamental issues are discussed here.

Given a surface F, the Moving Frame Theory defines a framework (and an algorithm) to calculate a set of invariants, say $\{I_1, \dots I_n\}$, where each I_i is a real valued function that depends on one or more points of the surface. By construction, this set contains the minimum number of invariants that are necessary and sufficient to parametrize a "signature" $S(I_1, \dots, I_n)$ that characterizes the surface up to Euclidean motion. The framework offers the possibility of choosing the number of points the invariants depend on, and this determines both the number n of invariants we get and their differential order. The more the points the invariants depend on the lower the differential order. For instance, invariants that are functions of only one point varying on the surface ($I = I(p)$, $p \in F$)

have differential order equal to 2. These are the classical Gaussian and Mean curvatures. In order to trade the computational time with robustness to noise the invariants are built depending on three points at one time. The result is a set of nine invariants, three of differential order zero, and six of order one.

3.1 3-Points Invariants

Let p_1, p_2, $p_3 \in F$ and ν_i be the normal vector at p_i. The directional vector v of the line between p_1 and p_2 and the normal vector ν_t to the plane through p_1, p_2, p_3, are defined as:

$$v = \frac{p_2 - p_1}{\|p_2 - p_1\|} \qquad \text{and} \qquad \nu_t = \frac{(p_2 - p_1) \wedge (p_3 - p_1)}{\|(p_2 - p_1) \wedge (p_3 - p_1)\|}.$$

The zero order invariants are the inter-point distances $I_1 = \|p_2 - p_1\|$, $I_2 = \|p_3 - p_2\|$ and $I_3 = \|p_3 - p_1\|$ whereas the first order invariants are

$$J_k(p_1, p_2, p_3) = \frac{(\nu_t \wedge v) \cdot \nu_k}{\nu_t \cdot \nu_k} \quad \text{and} \quad \tilde{J}_k(p_1, p_2, p_3) = \frac{v \cdot \nu_k}{\nu_t \cdot \nu_k} \quad \text{for } k = 1, 2, 3.$$

Each triplet (p_1, p_2, p_3) on the surface can now be linked with a point of the signature in 9-dimensional space whose coordinates are given by

$$(I_1, I_2, I_3, J_1, J_2, J_3, \tilde{J}_1, \tilde{J}_2, \tilde{J}_3).$$

3.2 Registration of Two Face Scans

For each triplet of feature points extracted from a sample face scan F the invariants are computed and stored into a signature S that characterizes F. Given a test scan F', the same procedure is applied to obtain another signature S'. The two face scans can be compared by computing the intersection between the two signatures S and S'. If the intersection between S and S' is not null, then exists a subset of feature points belonging to the two scans holding the same properties, i.e. the same inter-point distances and normal vectors (up to Euclidean motion). The signature points are compared by computing the Euclidean distance: given a threshold ϵ, if $s \in S$, $s' \in S'$ and $|s - s'| \leq \epsilon$, then the triplets that generated the signature points are matched. From the triplets the roto-translation $(\mathbf{R}, \mathbf{t})$ that takes the second into the first can be computed. Given $\{t_1, \ldots, t_m\}$ the set of triplets of the face scan F that are matched to the triplets in S', each matched triplet generates a roto-translation $(\mathbf{R}_i, \mathbf{t}_i)$. To select the best registration parameters among those computed, each $(\mathbf{R}_i, \mathbf{t}_i)$ is applied to F', so that $F'' = \mathbf{R}F' + \mathbf{t}$ and the registration error is computed according to the following procedure.

For each point $q_i \in F'$ the closest point p_i in F is computed together with the corresponding Euclidean distance $d_i = \|q_i - p_i\|$. A set of distances $D = \{d_i\}_{i \in I}$ is obtained where I is the cardinality of F'. The registration error is defined to be the median of $D = \{d_i\}_{i \in I}$. The pair $(\mathbf{R}_m, \mathbf{t}_m)$ corresponding to the minimum registration error d_m is chosen as the best registration between the two faces. It might happen that the scans are so different that the registration step fails (there are no matching points in the signature space and so triplets). In this case the result is accounted as a negative match.

3.3 Identification

The registration error defined above can be used as matching score between two faces F and F'. However, we should keep into consideration that the input data might not be reliable enough for the feature points to be calculated accurately, simply because often the same point is not present in two scans of the same subject due to occlusions (see figure 1 (b)). Also, big variations in sampling density might lead to a slight displacement of a feature point. This will lead to a coarse registration that, if refined, would lead to a smaller registration error. In light of this, the feature extraction and subsequent registration through invariants can be thought of an automatic coarse registration of faces, to be followed by a refinement. We chose to use ICP to refine the registration. In the first iteration ICP will take as input the two scans aligned through invariants. The registration error after the last iteration will be the matching score. After registration, two scans will be considered a match, i.e. belonging to the same individual, id the matching score is below a fixed threshold σ. After a successful registration of two fairly neutral scans of the same subject, the median distance d_m can be assumed to be $\delta/2 < d_m < \delta$ where δ is the average resolution of the scans, therefore σ can be fixed easily by knowing the resolution of the acquisition device.

4 Experimental Results

The proposed algorithm was tested on the Bosphorus database [3]. The database contains scans of 105 individuals, of which 61 male and 44 female subjects. From the total male subjects, 31 male subjects have a beard and mustaches. For each subject there are about 50 scans. Each scan either presents a different facial expression (anger, happiness, disgust), corresponding to a "Face Action Unit", or a head rotation along different axes. Since the subjects to be identified can be assumed to be cooperative, we will simulate an authentication scenario using the sets of faces that are fairly neutral and only slightly rotated sideways, upwards and downwards. Examples of the scans for two subjects are shown in figure 2. The picture shows (in a clockwise direction): a neutral pose, a slight downwards rotation, a slight upwards rotation, a 10° head rotation on the right.

For each pose, the data points are stored in a file containing the coordinates of about 30,000 3D points, a color 2D image of the face texture and a set of landmark points. The landmarks were manually selected on the 2D images and mapped on the corresponding 3D points. This database has been chosen because it contains a large number of subjects and an excellent variety of poses. Furthermore, despite only geometric information (3D points) is used for the authentication, the availability of landmark points constitutes a ground truth which makes it possible to compare the methodology with a baseline algorithm.

The database was divided into a gallery set G and two probe sets P_1, P_2. The gallery G consists of one neutral face scan for each individual (named N-N in the database). The neutral scan could be stored in a smart card or ID card of an individual in the form of text file, whereas the poses in P_i, $i = 1, 2$ can

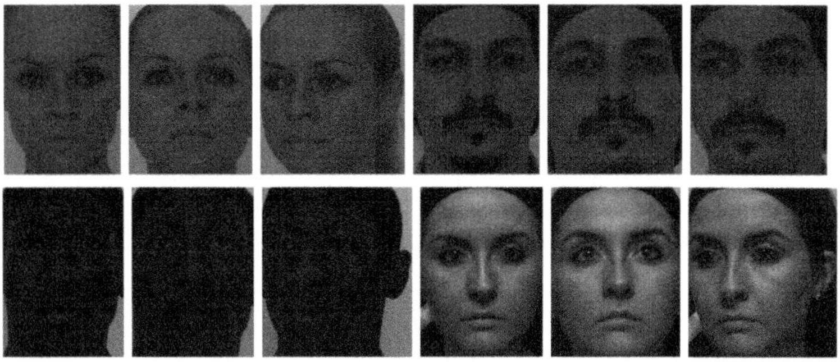

Fig. 2. Sample 3D scans of four subjects in the Bosphorus database

be assumed to be the scans taken from the acquisition device when the subject undergoes authentication.

Three authentication tests were run. In all of them, the gallery consisted of the neutral poses (the first image in figure 2).

1. **P_1 v G.** The probe set P_1 consists of the scans labeled PR-SU in the database (105 scans in total, one for each subject). The pose is a slight rotation of the face upwards as shown in the second image of each subject in figure 2. Each scan of P_1 was compared to all scans of the neutral gallery G using the methodology described in section 3.3.
2. **P_2 v G.** The probe set P_2 consists of the scans labeled YR-R10 in the database (105 scans in total, one for each subject). The pose is a rotation of the face of about 10 deg on one side, as shown in the third image of each subject in 2. Again, each scan of P_2 was compared to all scans of the neutral gallery G as in 3.3.
3. **Manual P_1 v G.** This is the baseline algorithm. Each scan in P_1 was roughly aligned with each scan of G using three of the manually selected landmarks provided by the database (the two inner eye corners and nose tip) and the alignment refined with ICP.

All algorithms were implemented in MatLab. On a consumer PC, the computational time to extract the features from a face scan of 30.000 points was on average $2m$. The signature generation took about $3s$. For the registration of two scans, times varied from $2s$ for scans of different subjects to $20s$ for those of the same subject. By optimizing the algorithms, the total time to compare two scans could be reduced to a few seconds. The results of the tests are summarized in table 1.$F.R.$, standing for failed registrations, is the number of subjects for which the registration failed (after features extraction no triples were matched in the signature space). These numbers are indicative of the robustness of the method, since if a registration fails there is no later chance of refinement. As it can be seen from table 1, no registration failures occurred in tests 1 and 2.

In the third column of table 1, $A.R.$ indicates the authentication rate (number of correctly identified subjects over the total of 105) obtained using as matching

Table 1. Matching scores

Experiment	F.R.	A.R.	T.P.	F.P.	F.N.	T.N.	Acc
1	0	0.981	103	0	2	10920	0.9998
2	0	0.924	97	0	8	10920	0.9992
3	0	0.99	104	0	1	10920	0.9999

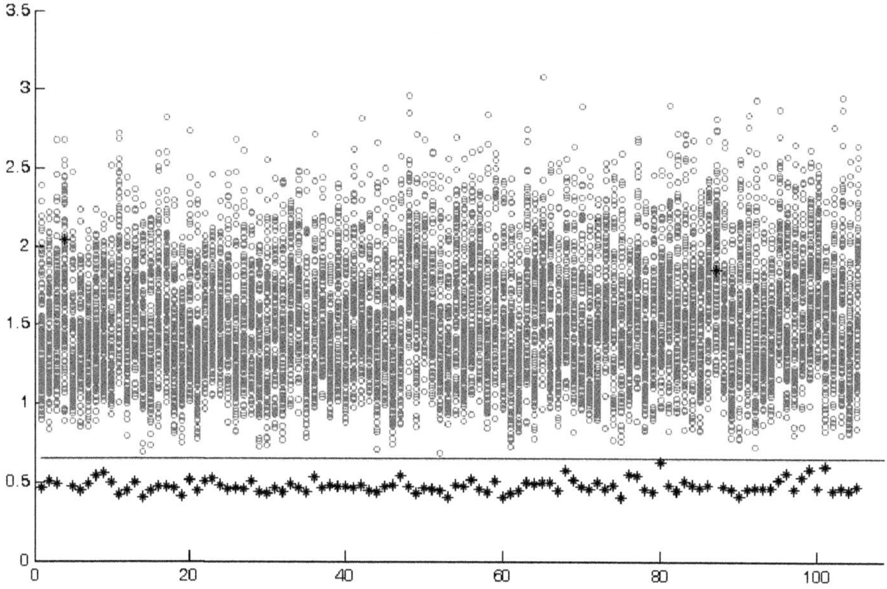

Fig. 3. Distribution of scores from experiment 1

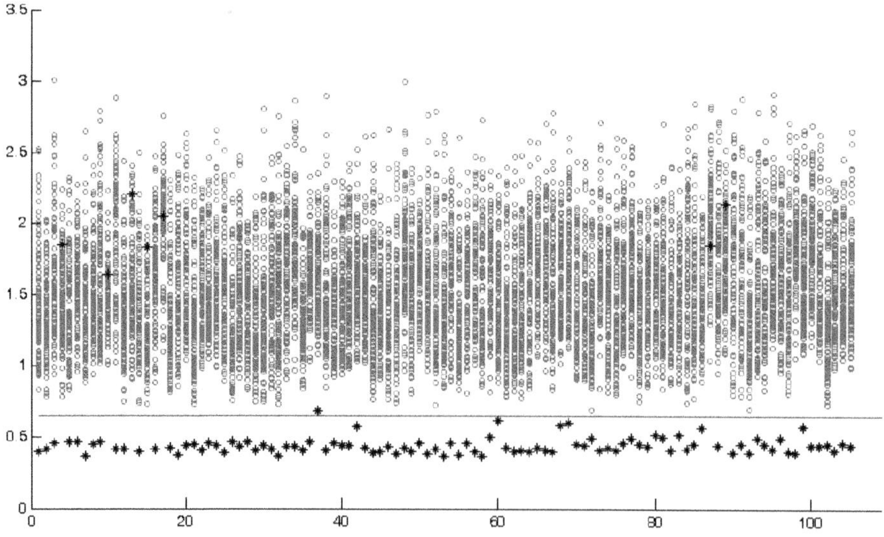

Fig. 4. Distribution of scores from experiment 2

score the registration error that follows from the automatic feature extraction and the registration through invariants refined by ICP. *T.P.* is the number of true positives, *F.P.* the number of false positives, *F.N.* that of false negatives, and *T.N.* that of true negatives. In the last column, *Acc* stands for accuracy and it is defined by $Acc = \frac{TP+TN}{P+N}$, where $P = 105$ is the number of positives and $N = 10920$ is the number of negatives. The noise associated to some of the scans accounts for the false negative, therefore preprocessing the data or acquiring them with a lower noise system would reduce the number significatively. In figures 3, 4 and 5, the matching scores after regisgtration of the probe scans to the gallery scans are shown, while the cases of registration failure between different subjects are omitted. For each of the figures, in the x-axis each number from 1 to 105 refers to the gallery scan of a subject. For such a subject i, in the column (i, y) the matching scores of after registration of the gallery scan with all probe scans are represented by gray circles if the probe subject is different from the i subject and with a black star if the probe scan is of subject i. As we can see from figures 3 and 4, the threshold (horizontal line, set to be equal to 0.65 for this database), separates the two classes client and impostor very well. The performance as the threshold varies is shown by the two ROC curves in figure 6. The images in figure 7 show the separation of the client and impostor classes in experiment 1 and 3. On the x-axis a similarity measure of two faces is given as the inverse of the registration error. It can be seen that the baseline algorithm does not significantly improve the separation of classes obtained with the automatic one, although it manages to identify one of the two subjects on which the proposed method fails.

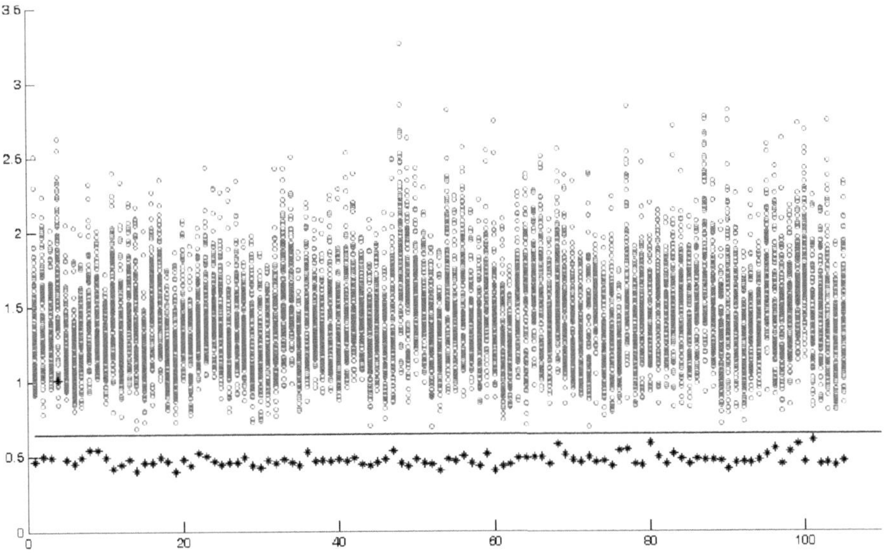

Fig. 5. Distribution of scores from the baseline experiment 3

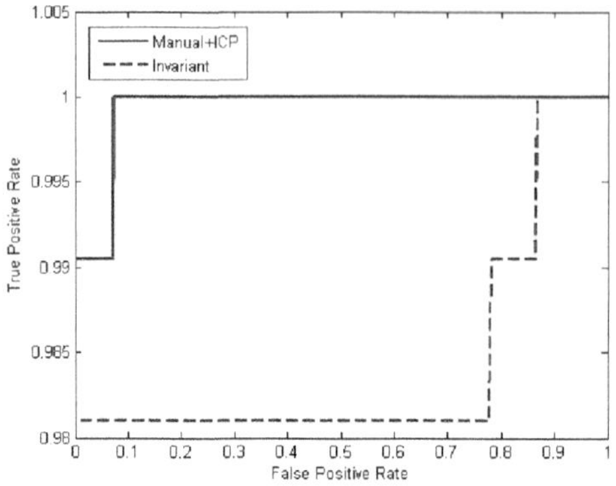

Fig. 6. ROC curves for experiments 1 (red) and 3 (blue)

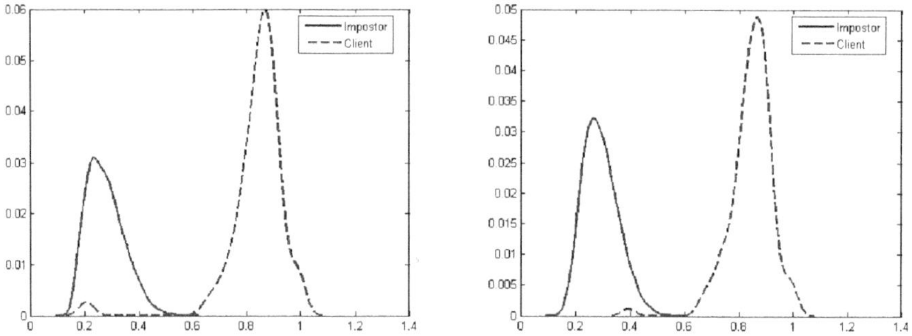

Fig. 7. Impostor and client distribution for experiment 1 (left), and 3 (right)

5 Conclusions

The identification of individuals on the basis of 3D shape information only has been addressed. This is a very promising and challenging biometric technology at the same time, because of the difficulties in processing three-dimensional data and of the advantages such as the relative insensitivity to illumination changes. The proposed method, based on the scale-space theory for the extraction of stable 3D feature points and on the generation of an invariant signature to characterize the face shape, proved to be very robust at identifying subjects, providing very good performances in terms of matching accuracy avoiding any data pre-processing to either fill-in holes or smooth the face surface to remove spikes within the points cloud. Moreover, the procedure is highly flexible regarding the storage and on-line processing: by storing the 3D points only more on-line processing is required, whereas by storing the feature points or the signature of the face shape, on-line processing is increasingly reduced. Experimental evaluations performed on the 3D Bosphorus database showed that the proposed method performance is in line with the well known baseline manual+ICP matching. Also, a slight rotation of the head (experiment 2) does not massively impair the identification, which is desirable in the authentication phase when the acquisition is not supervised. Further performance improvements are expected with a light data pre-processing, e.g. cropping the central part of the face to remove spikes due to hair or acquisition artifacts, or by consolidating the extraction the feature points of the gallery image with the aid of texture information.

References

1. Besl, P.J., McKay, N.D.: A Method for Registration of 3-D Shapes. IEEE Trans. on Pattern Analysis and Machine Intelligence 14, 239–256 (1992)
2. http://www.face-rec.org/databases/
3. Savran, A., Alyüz, N., Dibeklioğlu, H., Çeliktutan, O., Gökberk, B., Sankur, B., Akarun, L.: Bosphorus Database for 3D Face Analysis. In: Schouten, B., Juul, N.C., Drygajlo, A., Tistarelli, M. (eds.) BIOID 2008. LNCS, vol. 5372, pp. 47–56. Springer, Heidelberg (2008)
4. Çeliktutan, O., Çinar, H., Sankur, B.: Automatic Facial Feature Extraction Robust Against Facial Expressions and Pose Variations. In: IEEE Int. Conf. on Automatic Face and Gesture Recognition, Amsterdam, Holland (September 2008)
5. Dibekliolu, H., Salah, A., Akarun, L.: 3D Facial Landmarking Under Expression, Pose, and Occlusion Variations. In: IEEE 2nd International Conferance on Biometrics: Theory, Applications, and Systems (IEEE BTAS), Washington, DC, USA (September 2008)
6. Gorkberk, B., Savran, A., Ali, A., Akarun, L., Sankur, B.: 3D Face Recognition Benchmarks on the Bosphorus Database with Focus on Facial Expressions. In: Schouten, B., Juul, N.C., Drygajlo, A., Tistarelli, M. (eds.) BIOID 2008. LNCS, vol. 5372, pp. 57–66. Springer, Heidelberg (2008)
7. Lindeberg, T.: Feature Detection with Automatic Scale Selection. International Journal of Computer Vision 30(2), 77–116 (1998)
8. Pauly, M., Keiser, R., Gross, M.: Multi-scale Feature Extraction on Point-sampled Surfaces. In: Proceedings of Eurographics 2003, vol. 22(3) (2003)
9. Witkin, A.: A Scale Space Filtering. In: Proc. 8th Int. Joint Conference on Artificial Intelligence (1983)
10. Olver, P.J.: Joint Invariants Signatures. Found. Comput. Math. 1, 3–67 (2001)
11. Cadoni, M., Bicego, M., Grosso, E.: 3D Face Recognition Using Joint Differential Invariants. In: Tistarelli, M., Nixon, M.S. (eds.) ICB 2009. LNCS, vol. 5558, pp. 11–25. Springer, Heidelberg (2009)

Face Classification via Sparse Approximation

Elena Battini Sőnmez[1], Bülent Sankur[2], and Songul Albayrak[3]

[1] Computer Science Department, Bilgi University, Dolapdere, Istanbul, TR
[2] Electric and Electronic Engineering Department, Boğazici University, Istanbul, TR
[3] Computer Engineering Department, Yıldız Teknik University, Istanbul, TR

Abstract. We address the problem of 2D face classification under adverse conditions. Faces are difficult to recognize since they are highly variable due to such factors as illumination, expression, pose, occlusion and resolution. We investigate the potential of a method where the face recognition problem is cast as a sparse approximation. The sparse approximation provides a significant amount of robustness beneficial in mitigating various adverse effects. The study is conducted experimentally using the Extended Yale Face B database and the results are compared against the Fisher classifier benchmark.

Keywords: Face classification, sparse approximation, Fisher classifier.

1 Introduction

Automatic identification and verification of humans using facial information has been one of the most active research areas in computer vision. The interest on face recognition is fueled by the identification requirements for access control and for surveillance tasks, whether as a means to increase work efficiency and/or for security reasons. Face recognition is also seen as an important part of next-generation smart environments, [1], [2].

Face recognition algorithms under controlled conditions have achieved reasonably high levels of accuracy. However, under non-ideal, uncontrolled conditions, as often occur in real life, their performance becomes poor. Their main handicaps are the changes in face appearances caused by such factors as occlusion, illumination, expression, pose, make-ups and aging. In fact the intra-individual face differences due to some of these factors can easily be larger than the inter-individual variability [3], [6].

We briefly point out below some of the main roadblocks to wide scale deployment of reliable face biometry technology.

Effects of Illumination: Illumination changes can vary the overall magnitude of light intensity reflected back from an object and modify the pattern of shading and shadows visible in an image, [6]. It was shown that varying illumination is most detrimental to both human and machine accuracies in recognizing faces. It suffices to quote simply the fact in FRGC face recognition, the 17 algorithms competing in the controlled illumination track have achieved a median verification rate of 0.91 while in contrast, the seven algorithms competing in the

C. Vielhauer et al. (Eds.): BioID 2011, LNCS 6583, pp. 168–179, 2011.

uncontrolled illumination experiment have achieved a median verification rate of only 0.42 (both figures at a false acceptance rate of .001). The difficulties posed by variable illumination conditions, therefore, remain still one of the main roadblocks to reliable face recognition systems.

Effects of Expression: Facial expression is known to affect the face recognition accuracy though in the current literature, a full-fledged analysis of the deterioration caused by expressions has not been documented. Instead, most studies either focus on expression recognition alone or on face identification alone. It is quite interesting that this dichotomy is also encountered in biological vision. There is strong evidence that facial identity and expression might be processed by separate systems in the brain, or at best they are loosely linked, [7].

Effects of Pose: Facial pose or viewing angle is a major impediment to machine-based face recognition. As the camera pose changes, the appearance of the face changes due to projective deformation (causing stretching and foreshortening of different part of face); also self-occlusions and/or uncovering of face parts can arise. The resulting effect is that image-level differences between two views of the same face are much larger than those between two different faces viewed at the same angle. While machines fail badly in face recognition under viewing angle changes, that is, when trained on a gallery of a given pose and tested with a probe of set of a different viewing angle, [8], humans have no difficulty in recognizing faces at arbitrary poses. It has been reported in [8] that the performance of PCA-based method decreases dramatically beyond 32 degree yaw and those for LDA beyond 17 degree rotation.

Effects of Occlusion: The face may be occluded by facial accessories such as sunglasses, a snow cap, a scarf, by facial hair or other paraphernalia. Furthermore the subjects in an effort to eschew being identified can purposefully cover parts of their face. Although it is very difficult to systematically experiment with all sorts of natural or intentional occlusions, results reported in [8] shows that methods like PCA and LDA fail quite badly (e.g., sunglasses and scarf scenes in AR database). Recent work on recognition by parts shows that methods that rely on local information, can perform fairly well under occlusion, [4], [5], [9].

Effects of Low Resolution: The performance loss of face recognition with decreasing resolution is well known and documented, [10]. For example, 30 percentage point drops are reported in [10] as the resolution changes from 65×65 to 32×32 faces. The robustness to varying resolution becomes relevant especially in uncontrolled environments where the face may be captured by a security camera at various distances within its field of view.

In this paper we consider the effects of the resolution, the ones of degree of over-completeness, as well as the illumination compensation capability, the robustness to noise and to planar rotation of a recently introduced sparse approximation based classification algorithm. That is, we investigate the robustness of a non-linear face recognition method, called Sparse Representation-based Classifier (SRC), [9], $vis - \grave{a} - vis$ the well-known Fisher linear discriminant (FLDA) Classifier. The rationale of this approach is to use an over-complete dictionary whose base elements consist of training samples themselves, and to search for a parsimonious representation of the target object in terms of these samples. The discrimination between faces is enabled by the sparse nature of the solution. This is in contrast to parametric classifiers where all training samples are used to estimate the parameters. This approach is data driven, non parametric, hence it does not make any assumptions on the distribution of the data, and being a generalization of the nearest neighbor (NN) approach, it does not require any training.

The main contribution of our work is to demonstrate experimentally the superior recognition performance of the SRC classifier under adverse conditions. We want to prove the conjecture that a sparse representation enables the creation of templates robust against various factors that otherwise impede accurate face recognition.

In section 2, we review briefly face recognition paradigms, and describe the Sparse Representation-based Classifier: SRC. In section 3, we run a number of experiments to test the robustness of SRC method to adverse conditions comparatively against FDA. Conclusions are drawn in Section 4.

2 Face Recognition Methods

The plethora of face recognition methods can be categorized under template-based and geometry-based paradigms. In the template-based paradigm one computes the correlation between a face and one or more model templates for face identity. Methods such as Principal Component Analysis (PCA), Linear Discriminant Analysis, Kernel Methods, and Neural Networks as well as statistical tools such as Support Vector Machines (SVM) can be put under this category, [11], [8]. In the geometry-based paradigm one analyses explicit local facial features and their configurational relationships. Since the SRC method can be interpreted a non-linear template matching method, in this work we study comparatively two algorithms in the template-based paradigm, namely SRC versus FDA.

2.1 Linear Discriminant Analysis Based Classifier

Fisher Discriminant Analysis (FDA), [12], builds a discriminative subspace by searching for projection lines that maximize the between-class variance, while minimizing the within-class variance.

FDA is a parametric model, which assumes that the classes are completely described by their means and covariances. The linear classifier is optimal only in the case when the template and/or the object have not suffered any geometric distortion such as due to mis-registration, perspective distortion, 3D rotation, expression deformation etc. In other words, under pattern variability the matched filter resulting from the log-likelihood ratio, is optimal if there is no geometric distortion, and additive Gaussian noise is the only source of contamination.

However, geometric distortions causes the differences between the observed object and the template to follow instead a non-Gaussian distribution, for example a broad-tailed distribution like Cauchy, [11]. This is typical of the situations where template-object distances are mostly small, but also a few outliers samples dominate the distribution of errors, [12], [16], [17], [15].

Non-linear methods are usually much more effective in the case of errors having broad-tailed distributions. In this context, we view the SRC as a non-linear similarity measure and a template building approach.

2.2 Sparse Representation Based Classifier

The idea underlying this technique is that a face can be represented as a sparse linear combination of training samples, which are alternate images of the same subject, and that the resulting combiner coefficients contain discriminative information. SRC can also be interpreted as a synthesis algorithm based on the solution of an overdetermined system of equations:

$$y = \Phi \cdot x \; . \tag{1}$$

where y is the test face to be identified/verified, x is the sparse solution vector, and Φ is an over-complete dictionary of faces, in $\mathbf{R}^{N \times M}$. Every column of Φ is an atom $\in \mathbf{R}^N$, it is a face. Every subject is represented in the dictionary by at least one, typically several, face images.

Theoretically, the sparsest solution can be obtained by solving (1) as a non-convex constrained optimization method:

$$||y - \Phi \cdot x||_2 + \tau ||x||_0 \; . \tag{2}$$

where, $||x||_0$ is simply the count of non-zero elements. Practically, this solution is infeasible, because the problem is NP-hard.

Compressive sensing theory showed that, under certain sparsity conditions, [13], the convex version of this optimization criterion yields exactly the same solution. That is, instead of solving (2) we obtain the same results by solving a much easier convex version (3):

$$||y - \Phi \cdot x||_2 + \tau ||x||_1 \; . \tag{3}$$

Many interesting phenomena in nature lie in a smaller, often much smaller dimensional subspace as compared to the observed signal dimensionality. The intrinsic dimensionality of a signal subspace encompasses all the variations that the signal incurs. Sparse approximation methods attempt to discover this subspace, and to represent events and objects in that subspace. Face recognition is a good case in point.

To implement a face classifier from SRC, one can use two approaches. The first one is the idea of Distance from Face Space (DFS) [9] defined as follows:

$$argmin||y - \Phi \cdot (0 \ldots 0, x_1^i, \ldots, x_{k_i}^i, 0 \ldots 0)||_2 \; . \tag{4}$$

where $x_{|c_i} = (0 \ldots 0, x_1^i, \ldots, x_{k_i}^i, 0 \ldots 0)$ denotes the limitation of the M-long coefficient vector to the dictionary columns pertaining to the i-th individual,

$class_i$. DFS in (4) corresponds to the residual error when the face is reconstructed from the class coefficients found by the solution in Eq.3.

In the second approach, the decision variable, called Mean of the Class Coefficients (MCC) is defined simply as:

$$argmax(mean(x_1^i, \ldots, x_{k_i}^i)) \ . \tag{5}$$

where k_i is the cardinality of $class_i$. Notice that MCC simply calculates the average of the class coefficients.

3 Experimental Results

We used the cropped face sub-directory [16] of the Extended Yale Face B database, [15] to test the robustness of SRC-based face recognition in adverse conditions. The database consists of aligned and cropped face images of 192*168=32,256 pixels. For each of the 38 subjects, there is a subdirectory consisting of between 59 to 64 images of that person under various illumination changes. These images differ in azimuthal and elevation directions of illumination, and these angles are spaced by a few tens of degrees. In total we worked with 2432 face images.

Figure 1 shows samples of faces used in our experiments.

Unless otherwise stated, in all experiments we select 30 training and 29 test images per class, and we work with reduced images of size 504 (corresponding

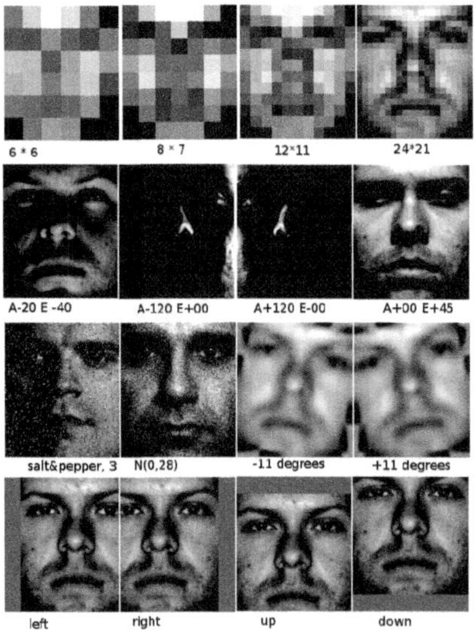

Fig. 1. Samples of faces under adverse conditions: In the 1st row, there are images at different resolution, the 2nd row stores faces under various illumination effects, the 3th row shows a 3% salt&pepper noisy image, a Gaussian noisy face, N(0,28), and two rotated pictures, and the 4th row stores 3 pixels shifted faces in all directions.

to images of size 24×21 after down-sampling by a factor of 8 in each direction). Thus the resulting dictionary Φ has size 504×1140, since there are 30 images for each of the 38 subjects (classes). It follows that the Fisher classifier, which is our benchmark, has 37 discriminant planes.

3.1 Experiment 1: Best Classifier Using Sparse Approximation

In section 2.2 we discussed two methods of building a classifier using sparse approximation coefficients, namely, DFS and MCC as in eqs. 4 and 5. Actually several other variations on this theme, like L2 norm or the p-quantile of the class coefficients, were considered, but they did not prove to be any better.

Table 1. Performance of Face Classification: SRC-DFS vs SRC-MCC.

Testing Conditions	DFS	MCC	Fisher
24x21 faces	98.28	98.09	95.28
6x6 faces	94.52	94.61	45.28
24x21 faces under Gaussian noise PSNR=38.91 dB	97.91	98	92.47
24x21 faces under 7% salt&pepper noise	93.92	93.74	11.80

Table 1 shows the results of the experiments under various testing conditions. We compared performances of MCC and DFS varieties of SRC-based classification at two resolution levels and under two types of noise contamination. Though not exhaustive, these preliminary experiments show us that both variants perform in a similar way, with MCC being slightly better. For this reason in the sequel, we will use only MCC, which has also the advantage of being computationally simpler than DFS. That is, in the rest of the paper, the MCC variety of SRC method is used; however we will refer to it in the tables simply as SRC.

3.2 Experiment 2: Effects of the Resolution

While the original YaleB face images are 32.256-dimensional, we investigated the extent the dimensionality could be lowered without compromising any performance. Among dimensionality reduction methods, we considered decimation, random projections and PCA subspace representations.

Decimation is simply the operation of low-pass filtering and sub-sampling. PCA subspace representation is obtained by projecting the faces onto PCA basis vectors and reconstructing them with the fewer most energetic ones. Thus columns 36, 56 .. 504 in Table 2 indicate that faces were classified with 36, 56 .. 504 PCA bases. Random projections uses random, unit-norm, zero-mean Gaussian vectors, and the given performance is averaged over 5 trials. The rationale of representing faces by their random projection is Compressed Sensing theory. Accordingly it was shown that signals that are intrinsically low-dimensional can be reconstructed using constrained sparse optimization from far fewer random projections as compared to their Nyquist rate [14]. In this experiment we simulated the work of Wright et al., [9], that is, out of every directory we selected in

Table 2. Effect of Image Resolution on Classifier Performance

Image Dimension	SRC(36)	SRC(56)	SRC(132)	SRC(504)	Fisher (37)
Decimation	94.61	97.10	98.92	99.50	95.28
Random Projection	82	87	92	94	94
PCA	95.64	97.37	97.82	97.82	95.58

a random way half of the images for training and the other half for testing. As a result, every class has a different number of training samples, varying from 30 to 32.

The results in Table 2 need some interpretation. First, reducing the signal dimensionality by random projections is not propitious, perhaps because the dictionary and the test samples both look like random vectors and smooth waveform structure is absent. Second, it is surprising to see that by keeping all training samples in the dictionary and doing classification by their linear combiner coefficients is much better as compared to amassing all the training data information in a statistical model, that is, class means and variances. In fact, with faces decimated to size 24×21 the SRC method achieves 99.50% recognition rate, 4 percentage points above that of FDA. The price to pay for this higher performance is the need to store and operate on all the sample feature vectors. These results should be interpreted with some precaution though: the Extended Yale Face B database provides a dense sampling of the face manifold under illumination directions so that any test face can find a close companion image, in other words, for each test image, there are training faces that differ slightly in azimuth or elevation angle of the illumination direction.

3.3 Experiment 3: Effect of the Degree of Over-Completeness

In this set of experiments we consider the effect of the dictionary size on the performance of the SRC classifier and concomitantly of the training data size for the Fisher classifier. As we increase the number of sample images per subject we have a richer training set. To this effect, we change the enrollment size in steps of 5, from 10 to 50, using each time random selections of subsets of the gallery. Thus for example, at one extreme we select 50 faces for training and 10 for testing; at the other extreme 10 faces for training and 50 for testing. In this experiment, we used only 24×21 face images (504 pixels). The training, hence testing subsets are randomly selected from the given Extended Yale Face B subdirectory. That is, every trial is based on a random permutation, which partition the images of every subject into training and test sets. In order to limit the effect of the random choice, the given performance is the median value over 5 trials.

These results show that both algorithms, SRC and Fisher, do increase their recognition rates as the enrollment size increases. It is surprising to notice the superior performance of a data driven method: much more robust for low size

Table 3. Effect of Enrolment Size on Classifier Performance

Enrolment Size	5	10	15	20	25	30	35	40	45	50
SRC	78.7	86.3	94.62	96.36	98.37	99.18	99.12	99.48	99.44	99.71
Fisher	69.88	75.51	81.88	90.62	95.28	95.46	97.7	97.81	98.87	99.42

enrollment and still better than Fisher also in case of large degree of over-completeness. That is, the recognition rate of SRC is 9 percentage points above Fisher in case of enrollment size 5, and still slightly better than LDA with 50 training pictures per subject.

3.4 Experiment 4: Illumination Compensation Capability

We investigated the robustness of the classifiers against illumination effects and whether it was possible for the detector to operate with faces which are subjected to unseen illumination effects. In order not to bias the results we did not apply any illumination normalization algorithm.

For this purpose we carried out two experiments:

1. Azimuth Angle Segmentation: The classifiers were trained with left-sided illumination and tested with right-sided illumination faces. We grouped the Extended Yale Face B database images into two sets, which consisted respectively of all images with negative azimuth, and all images with positive azimuth, independent of their tilt (elevation) angles.
2. Elevation Angle Segmentation: The classifiers were trained with from-above-illuminated faces and test with from-below-illuminated faces. We grouped the Extended Yale Face B database images into two sets, which consisted respectively of all images with positive elevation angles and all images with negative elevation angles, independent to their azimuth. In both experiments, we select 30 images for training and 19 for testing, (because this is the maximum number of available pictures for some subjects).

The following table shows the resulting performance:

Table 4. Illumination Compensation Capability

Illumination Direction	SRC	Fisher
Azimuthal Segmentation	90.72	90.44
Elevation Segmentation	97.37	96.26

The results of Table 4 show that SRC classifier is more robust than Fisher classifier to changes in both azimuth and elevation angles. Interesting to notice that both methods are not very sensitive to the elevation angle segmentation experiment. The reason for that is probably due to the particular structure of the database which varies the azimuth angle in a wide range, from [-130, + 130], while keeps most of the picture into the elevation angle's range [-45, +45]. That is, the first experiment is more challenging than the second one.

3.5 Experiment 5: Robustness to Noise

We evaluated the robustness of the SRC algorithm to both additive and multiplicative noise that simulate impairments due sensor noise. We run an uninformed experiment, that is we added Gaussian noise and salt&pepper noise to the test images, already down-sampled by a factor of 8. Gaussian noise is gauged according to PSNR (Peak Signal to Noise Ratio) and salt&pepper noise is characterized by the percentage of pixels contaminated.

Table 5. Recognition Performance under Gaussian (left) and Salt&Pepper Noise (right)

PSNR	SRC(504)	Fisher (37)	Percentage	SRC (504)	Fisher (37)
inf	98.28	95.92	0	98.28	95.92
47.81	98.28	95.46	1	97.19	54.36
38.91	98	92.47	3	96.19	24.89
31.58	97.55	82.30	7	93.74	11.80
25.67	97.37	51.18	10	91.65	10.07
19.39	96.1	20.15	20	80.40	5.54

The results stored in table 5 show the superior performance of SRC Classifier also in case of noise. As expected, Fisher, which is a discriminative method is not robust to noise. The impressive result is that SRC performs always better than Fisher and it is also robust to noise. That is, with a PSNR of 20 the performance of SRC is only 2 points less than the original recognition rate. Moreover, the initial gap with Fisher increases from 3 percentage points up to 76.

3.6 Experiment 6: Robustness to Planar Geometric Distortions

In real applications images rarely are in perfect registration, that is, presented fully frontally and in the correct scale and position. In order to test the robustness of the classifiers against mis-registration effects, we perturbed the faces with shifts, in-plane rotations and zoom. To preclude the confounding effects of illumination, we previously selected faces with nearly frontal illumination, that is, those having azimuth in the range of [-25,+25]. This results in 23 pictures per class, which are then randomly divided into training (20 images) and test (3 pictures) sets. All experiments are repeated 5 times and the given recognition rate is the median value.

In the zoom experiment, down-sampled test images were zoomed by a scale factor in the range [0.5:0.1:1.5]. In the shift experiment we worked with original sized test images so as to consider also fractional shifts. The 192×168 test samples were shifted from 2 to 16 pixels in all directions (up, down, left, right); as usual classification was then performed in the low dimensional space, 504. In the rotation experiment down-sampled test faces were rotated in-plane by ± 1, ± 3, ± 5, ± 7, ± 9, and ± 11 degrees. To avoid imaging artifacts, image parts overflowing the 24×21 were cropped; conversely, if background was disclosed it was padded with average image gray level.

Table 6. Recognition Performance under Geometric Distortions

Zoom Scale	SRC	Fisher	Shift pixels	SRC	Fisher	Rotation degrees	SRC	Fisher
0.5	2.63	2.63	2	100	100	+/-1	100	100
0.6	3.51	3.51	4	100	99.56	+/-3	100	100
0.7	3.51	4.39	6	96.93	78.51	+/-5	99.12	73.25
0.8	14.91	6.23	8	75.66	35.31	+/-7	85.09	34.21
0.9	72.81	7.89	10	50.66	13.82	+/-9	64.91	15.35
1	100	100	12	29.39	6.8	+/-11	45.18	7.46
1.1	47.37	13.16	14	18.86	3.95			
1.2	26.32	6.14	16	13.16	3.73			
1.3	5.26	4.39						
1.4	3.51	3.51						
1.5	1.75	1.75						

The performance of zoomed, shifted, and rotated images is stored into table 6. These results show that both algorithms are heavily affected by geometric distortions. The problem is solved in [18] were Wagner et al. present a "deformable SRC" algorithm, a variation of SRC robust also to deformed faces.

3.7 Conclusions

We have investigated the robustness of SRC, [9], a new non linear face classifier based on sparse approximation. Experimental results show that the SRC algorithm is uniformly superior to Fisher Linear Discriminant, [12], under all the adverse conditions tested. This implies that a classifier method based on sparse representation, in fact a generalization of the nearest neighbor method, is better than the well-known parametric method, like Fisher Discriminant Analysis. Our experiments show that:

- Resolution: The performance of SRC for decimated images with factor 24 is still 2 points better that the one of Fisher.
- Enrollment size: For enrollment size above 30, SRC reaches almost perfect recognition for the Extended Yale Face B database. For enrollment sizes at and below 15, SRC outperforms Fisher by at least 10 points.
- Illumination: Both methods suffer when training and test images are severely different.
- Additive and multiplicative noise: SRC outperforms Fisher in case of both additive and multiplicative noise, and it proves to be robust to noise.
- Geometric distortions: SRC outperforms Fisher also here, even if such a low performance is not acceptable in both cases. Interesting to notice that both algorithms are more affected by shift and zoom perturbations, rather than rotation.

One advantages of the SRC method is that it does not need any training, similar to the nearest neighbor method, which makes it computationally simple.

The price to pay for this simplicity is a little increase in the testing time; in fact for the Extended Yale Face B database with the enrollment size of 35, SRC runs in 292 seconds while Fisher needs 74 seconds.

There are several avenues of research as a follow-up. Obviously the performance of the system is affected by the type of database. Hence first we are going to consider the reproducibility of these results over alternate databases, like Texas 3D, Cohn Kanade, Bogazici, AR, CMU PIE, FRGC, MMI, ...

Among the possible issues to be addressed there is: i) Testing the robustness to expression changes, face landmark detection, age progression; ii) Implementing the face recognition with 3D images; iii) Testing the robustness against out-of-plane rotations.

References

1. Pentland, A., Choudhury, T.: Face recognition for smart environments. IEEE Computer 33(2), 50–55 (2000)
2. Jain, A., Kumar, A.: Biometrics of Next Generation: an Overview, Second Generation Biometrics. Springer, Heidelberg (2010)
3. Adini, Y., Moses, Y., Ullman, S.: Face recognition: the problem of compensating for changes in illumination direction. IEEE Transactions on Pattern Analysis and Machine Learning 19, 721–732 (1997)
4. Tarrés, F., Rama, A.: A Novel Method for Face Recognition under partial occlusion or facial expression variations. In: 47th International Symposium ELMAR 2005, Multimedia Systems and Applications, Zadar, Croatia, June 8-10 (2005)
5. Kim, J., Choi, J., Yi, J., Turk, M.: Effective Representation Using ICA for Face Recognition Robust to Local Distortion and Partial Occlusion. IEEE Transactions on Pattern Analysis and Machine Intelligence 27(12), 1977–1981 (2005)
6. OToole, A.J., Jiang, F., Roark, D., Abdi, H.: Predicting human performance for face recognition. In: Zhao, W.-Y., Chellappa, R. (eds.) Face Processing: Advanced Methods and Models. Elsevier, Amsterdam (2006)
7. Calder, A.J., Young, A.W.: Understanding the recognition of facial identity and facial expression. Nature Review Neuroscience 6(8), 641–651 (2005)
8. Gross, J., Shi, J., Cohn, J.: Quo vadis Face Recognition? Robotics Institute Carnegie Mellon University, Pittsburg, Pennsylvania 15213 (June 2001)
9. Wright, J., Yang, A.Y., Ganesh, A., Sastry, S.S., Ma, Y.: Robust Face Recognition via Sparse Representation. IEEE Transactions on Pattern Analysis and Machine Intelligence 31(2), 210–227 (2009)
10. Arandjelovic, O., Cipolla, R.: A Manifold Approach to Face Recognition from Low Quality Video Across Illumination and Pose using Implicit Super-Resolution. In: IEEE International Conference on Computer Vision, Rio de Janeiro, Brazil (October 2007)
11. Brunelli, R.: Template matching techniques in computer vision. Wiley, Chichester (2010)
12. Belhumeur, P.N., Hespanha, J.P., Kriegman, D.J.: Eigenfaces vs Fisherfaces: recognition using class specific linear projection. IEEE Trans. on Pattern analysis and Machine Intelligence 19(7) (July 1997)
13. Bruckstein, A., Donoho, D.L., Elad, M.: From Sparse Solutions of Systems of Equations to Sparse Modelling of Signals and Images. SIAM Review 51(1), 34–81 (2009)

14. Elad, M.: Optimized Projections for Compressive Sensing. IEEE Trans. on Signal Processing 55(12), 5695–5702 (2007)
15. Georghiades, A., Belhumeur, P., Kriegman, D.: From Few to Many: Illumination Cone Models for Face Recognition under Variable Lighting and Pose. IEEE Trans. Pattern Anal. Mach. Intelligence (PAMI) 23(6), 643–660 (2001)
16. Lee, K.C., Ho, J., Kriegman, D.: Acquiring Linear Subspaces for Face Recognition under Variable Lighting. IEEE Trans. Pattern Anal. Mach. Intelligence (PAMI) 27(5), 684–698 (2005)
17. Fidler, S., Skocaj, D., Leonardis, A.: Combining Reconstructive and discriminative subspace methods for robust classification and regression by subsampling. IEEE Transactions on Pattern Analysis and Machine Intelligence 28(3), 337–350 (2006)
18. Wagner, A., Wright, J., Ganesh, A., Zhou, Z., Ma, Y.: Towards a Practical Face Recognition System: Robust Registration and Illumination by Sparse Representation, pp. 597–604. IEEE, Los Alamitos (2009)

Principal Directions of Synthetic Exact Filters for Robust Real-Time Eye Localization

Vitomir Štruc[1,2], Jerneja Žganec Gros[1], and Nikola Pavešić[2]

[1] Alpineon Ltd, Ulica Iga Grudna 15, SI-1000 Ljubljana, Slovenia
{vitomir.struc,jerneja.gros}@alpineon.com
[2] Faculty of Electrical Engineering, University of Ljubljana, Tržaška cesta 25, SI-1000 Ljubljana, Slovenia
{vitomir.struc,nikola.pavesic}@fe.uni-lj.si

Abstract. The alignment of the facial region with a predefined canonical form is one of the most crucial steps in a face recognition system. Most of the existing alignment techniques rely on the position of the eyes and, hence, require an efficient and reliable eye localization procedure. In this paper we propose a novel technique for this purpose, which exploits a new class of correlation filters called Prinicpal directions of Synthetic Exact Filters (PSEFs). The proposed filters represent a generalization of the recently proposed Average of Synthetic Exact Filters (ASEFs) and exhibit desirable properties, such as relatively short training times, computational simplicity, high localization rates and real time capabilities. We present the theory of PSEF filter construction, elaborate on their characteristics and finally develop an efficient procedure for eye localization using several PSEF filters. We demonstrate the effectiveness of the proposed class of correlation filters for the task of eye localization on facial images from the FERET database and show that for the tested task they outperform the established Haar cascade object detector as well as the ASEF correlation filters.

Keywords: Biometrics, eye localization, advanced correlation filters.

1 Introduction

Advanced correlation filters have been receiving increasing attention in recent years because of their desirable properties such as mathematical simplicity, computational efficiency and robustness to distortions [8]. They have successfully been applied to various problems ranging from pattern recognition tasks such as face and palmprint recognition to basic computer vision problems related to object detection and tracking.

Correlation filters exhibit a high degree of similarity with templates and correlation-based template matching techniques, where patterns of interest in images are searched for by cross-correlating the input image with one or more example templates and examining the resulting correlation plane for large values - also known as correlation peaks. With properly designed templates, these correlation peaks can be exploited to determine the presence and/or location

C. Vielhauer et al. (Eds.): BioID 2011, LNCS 6583, pp. 180–192, 2011.

of patterns of interest in the given input image [8]. Early template matching techniques relied on rather primitive templates, computed, for example, through simple averaging of the available training images. Contemporary methods, on the other hand, use correlation templates (also referred to as *correlation filters*) that are constructed by optimizing specific performance criteria [7], [8], [1]. Popular examples of these advanced correlation filters include Synthetic Discriminant Function (SDF) filters [4], Minimum Average Correlation Energy (MACE) filters [9], Distance Classifier Correlation Filters (DCCF) [10], Maximum Average Correlation Height (MACH) filters [11], Optimal Tradeoff Filters (OTF) [13], Unconstrained Minimum Average Correlation Energy (UMACE) filters [14], and Average of Synthetic Exact Filters (ASEF) [1].

In this paper we introduce a new class of correlation filters named Principal directions of Synthetic Exact Filters (PSEFs). These filters extend the recently proposed class of advanced correlation filters called Average of Synthetic Exact Filters (ASEF) [1]. Instead of only relying on the average of a set of Synthetic Exact Filters (SEFs), as it is the case with the ASEF filters, we employ the eigenvectors of the correlation matrix of the SEFs as correlation templates (or filters). Hence, the name PSEFs. We apply the proposed filters to the task of eye localization and demonstrate their effectiveness in comparison with ASEF filters as well as the established Haar cascade classifier proposed in [17].

2 Principal Directions of Synthetic Exact Filters

2.1 Review of ASEF Filters

ASEF filters represent a class of recently proposed correlation filters that have already been successfully applied to the tasks of eye localization and pedestrian detection [1], [2]. As with all correlation filters, a pattern of interest in an image is detected with an ASEF filter by cross-correlating the input image with the computed filter and examining the correlation plane for possible correlation peaks. While ASEF filters are deployed much in the same way as other existing correlation filters, they differ from most other filters in the way they are constructed.

Unlike the majority of existing correlation filters, which specify only a single correlation value per training image, ASEF filters define the entire correlation plane for each available training image. As stated by Bolme et al. [1], this correlation plane commonly features only a high peak centered at the pattern of interest and (near) zeros at all other image locations (Fig. 1 - middle image). Such a synthetic correlation output results in so-called synthetic exact filters (SEFs) (Fig. 1 - right image) that can be used to locate the pattern of interest in the training image, from which they were constructed.

Unfortunately, these SEF filters do not pride themselves with broad generalization capabilities, instead they produce distinct peaks only for the images that were used for their construction. To overcome this shortcoming Bolme et al. [1] proposed to compute a new filter by averaging all of the synthetic exact filters corresponding to a specific pattern of interest. By doing so, the authors ensured greater generalization capabilities of the computed ASEF filters and elegantly avoided an important problem of many existing correlation filters, namely, overfitting.

Formally, the presented procedure of ASEF filter construction can be described as follows. Consider a set of n training images $\mathbf{x}_1, \mathbf{x}_2, ..., \mathbf{x}_n$ and n corresponding image locations of our pattern of interest[1] $(x_1, y_1), (x_2, y_2), ..., (x_n, y_n)$. The first step towards computing an ASEF filter for our pattern of interest is the construction of the desired correlation outputs $\mathbf{y}_1, \mathbf{y}_2, ..., \mathbf{y}_n$ for all n training images, i.e.,

$$\mathbf{y}_i(x, y) = e^{-\frac{(x-x_i)^2+(y-y_i)^2}{\sigma^2}}, \quad \text{for} \quad i = 1, 2, ..., n, \tag{1}$$

where σ denotes the standard deviation of the Gaussian-shaped correlation output, which controls the balance of the robustness of the filters against noise and the sharpness of the correlation peaks, and (x_i, y_i) represents the coordinates pair corresponding to the location of the pattern of interest in the i-th training image.

Once the correlation outputs have been determined, a SEF is calculated for each of the n pairs $(\mathbf{x}_i, \mathbf{y}_i)$ as follows:

$$H_i^* = \frac{Y_i \odot X_i^*}{X_i \odot X_i^* + \epsilon}, \quad \text{for} \quad i = 1, 2, ..., n, \tag{2}$$

where, $X_i = \mathcal{F}(\mathbf{x}_i)$ and $Y_i = \mathcal{F}(\mathbf{y}_i)$ denote the Fourier transforms of the i-th training image and its corresponding synthetic correlation output, $H_i = \mathcal{F}(\mathbf{h}_i)$ stands for the Fourier transform of the i-th SEF filter $\mathbf{h}_i$, ϵ denotes a small constant that prevents divisions by zero, $\odot$ stands for the Schur product and " $*$ " represents the conjugate operator. It has to be noted that the division in Eq. (2) must be performed element-wise.

In the final step, all n SEFs are simply averaged to produce an ASEF filter (see left image of Fig. 4 for a visual example) that can be used to locate the pattern of interest in a given input image. Here, the ASEF filter in the frequency domain is defined as [1]:

$$H^* = \frac{1}{n}\sum_{i=1}^{n} H_i^*, \tag{3}$$

or equivalently in the spatial domain

$$\mathbf{h} = \frac{1}{n}\sum_{i=1}^{n} \mathbf{h}_i, \quad \text{where} \quad \mathbf{h}_i = \mathcal{F}^{-1}(H_i). \tag{4}$$

An example of the filter construction procedure up to the averaging step is also visualized in Fig. 1. Here, the left image depicts an sample face image, which has been transformed into the log domain, normalized to zero mean and unit variance and finally weighted with a cosine window. The second image shows

[1] In our case the image locations correspond to the location of the left eye in all n training images.

Fig. 1. Construction of a synthetic exact filter (SEF): normalized input image multiplied with a cosine window (left), the synthetic correlation output plane (middle), the synthetic exact filter corresponding to the training image on the left (right)

the visual appearance of a synthetic correlation output with the desired peak response centered at the location of the left eye. Finally, the last image in Fig. 1 represents the SEF filter computed based on the first two images.

Before we turn our attention to the proposed extension of the ASEF filters, let us say a few more words on their characteristics. To ensure adequate generalization capabilities of the ASEF filters, a large number of training images must be used in their construction. Alternatively, a moderate number of training images may be used, however, in this case the SEF filter must be constructed using only the largest Fourier coefficients that contain 95% of the total energy [2]. This alternative approach is also used in our experiments.

2.2 ASEF Filters for Localization

As we have already indicated several times in the paper, ASEF filters can among others also be used for facial landmark localization. In this setting the input image in simply cross-correlated with the ASEF filter corresponding to the desired pattern of interest and the correlation output is then examined for its maximum. The location of the maximum is then declared the location of the pattern of interest. For efficiency reasons all computations are performed in the frequency domain using simple element-wise multiplications:

$$Y = X_t \odot H^*, \tag{5}$$

where Y denotes the correlation output in the frequency domain, $X_t = \mathcal{F}(\mathbf{x}_t)$ denotes the Fourier transform of a test image $\mathbf{x}_t$, H stands for the ASEF filter in the frequency domain and $\odot$ again represents the Schur (i.e., element-wise) product. The procedure is also shown in Fig. 2.

2.3 Beyond Averaging

The filter construction procedure presented in Section 2.1 ensures high generalization capabilities of the ASEF filters by averaging the individual synthetic exact filters. However, this procedure implicitly assumes that the SEF filters represent a random variable drawn from a uni-modal symmetric distribution and, thus, that their distribution is adequately described by their sample mean.

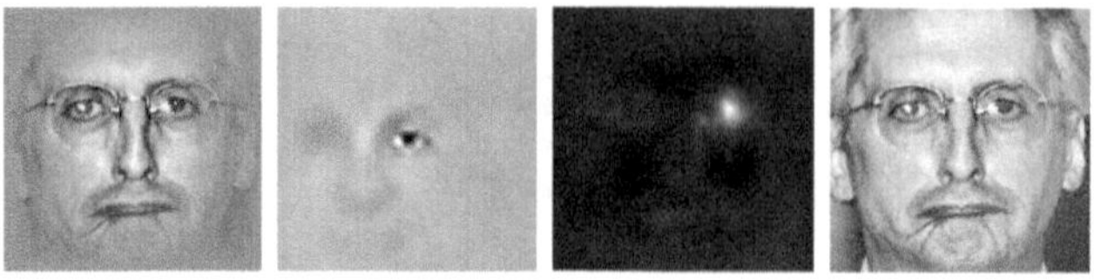

Fig. 2. Visualization of the facial landmark localization procedure using ASEF filters (from left to right): the modified input image, the ASEF filter for the right eye (with shifted quadrants), the correlation output, the input image with the detected correlation maximum

For our derivation, presented in the remainder of this section, we will make a similar assumption and presume that the SEF filters are drawn from a multivariate Gaussian distribution. Under this assumption, we are able to extend the concept of ASEF filters to a more general form, namely, to Principal directions of Synthetic Exact Filters (PSEFs). The basic reasoning for our generalization stems from the fact that the first eigenvector of the correlation matrix of some sample data corresponds to the data's mean (or average), while the remaining eigenvectors encode the variance of the sample data in directions orthogonal to the data's average. By using more than only the first eigenvector (note that the first eigenvector is actually the ASEF filter) of the SEF correlation matrix for the localization procedure, we should be able to further improve upon the localization performance of the original ASEF filters. Similarly as we have done for the ASEF filters, let us now formalize the procedure for PSEF filter construction. Again consider a set of n training images $\mathbf{x}_1, \mathbf{x}_2, ..., \mathbf{x}_n$, for which we have already computed n corresponding SEFs for some pattern of interest, i.e., $\mathbf{h}_1, \mathbf{h}_2, ..., \mathbf{h}_n$, in accordance with the procedure presented in Section 2.1. Furthermore, assume that the SEFs reside in a d-dimensional space and that they are arranged into the columns of some matrix $\boldsymbol{\zeta} \in \mathbb{R}^{d \times n}$. Instead of simply averaging the SEFs to produce an ASEF filter with high generalization capabilities, we compute the sample correlation matrix $\boldsymbol{\Sigma}$ of the SEFs:

$$\boldsymbol{\Sigma} = \boldsymbol{\zeta}\boldsymbol{\zeta}^T \in \mathbb{R}^{d \times d}, \tag{6}$$

where ^{T} denotes the transpose operator, and use its leading eigenvectors as our PSEF filters, i.e.:

$$\boldsymbol{\Sigma}\mathbf{f}_j = \lambda_j \mathbf{f}_j, \quad \text{where} \quad j = 1, 2, ..., \min(d, n) \quad \text{and} \quad \lambda_1 \geq \lambda_2 \geq \cdots \geq \lambda_{\min(d,n)}. \tag{7}$$

The presented procedure very much resembles the commonly used principal component analysis [16], [15] with the only difference that the SEF filters are not centered around their global mean.

One problem arising from the presented derivation of the PSEF filters $\mathbf{f}_j$ is the sign ambiguity of the eigenvectors. Since the computed PSEF filters can be multiplied by -1 and still represent valid eigenvectors of $\boldsymbol{\Sigma}$, we have to alleviate this sign ambiguity to be able to use our PSEF filters for localization purposes.

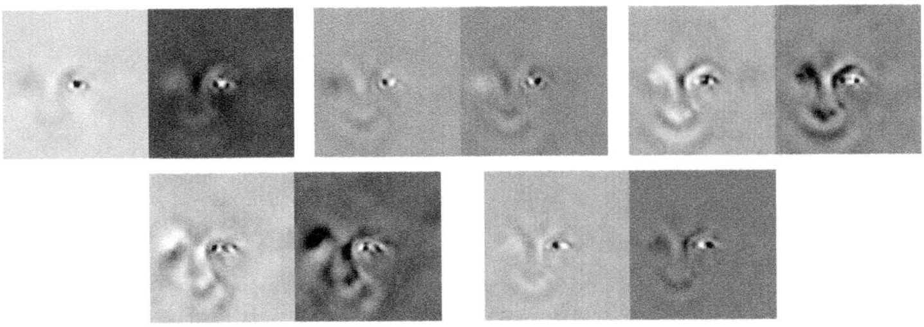

Fig. 3. Visual appearance of the first five PSEFs. The upper row depicts (from left to right) the PSEFs corresponding the largest three eigenvalues of the SEF correlation matrix and the lower row depicts the PSEFs corresponding to the next two eigenvalues, i.e., the fourth and fifth largest eigenvalues. In each image pair the left image represents the computed PSEF multiplied with +1 and the right image represents the computed PSEF multiplied with -1.

In the experimental section we will try to solve the sign ambiguity of our filters through some preliminary experiments. For the moment let us just take a look at the visual appearance of the first five PSEF filters (corresponding to the five largest eigenvalues of $\boldsymbol{\Sigma}$) shown in Fig. 3. Note that the visual appearance of the first PSEF filter (first image in the upper row of Fig. 3) is identical to the appearance of the ASEF filter (Fig. 2 - second image from the left).

2.4 Exploiting Linearity

Similarly to the ASEF filters, PSEF filters can also be exploited for the localization of facial landmarks. The procedure is identical the one presented in Section 2.2, except for the fact that we have more than a single filter at our disposal and, hence, obtain more than one correlation output:

$$Y_j = X_t \odot F_j^*, \quad \text{for } j \in \{1, 2, ..., \min(d, n)\}, \tag{8}$$

where $X_t = \mathcal{F}(\mathbf{x}_t)$ again denotes the Fourier transform of the given test image $\mathbf{x}_t$, F_j denotes the Fourier transform of the j-th PSEF filter $\mathbf{f}_j$ and Y_j refers to the j-th correlation output in the Fourier domain.

To determine the location of our pattern of interest in the given input image, we obviously have to examine all correlation outputs Y_j for maxima and somehow combine all of the obtained information. A straight forward way of doing this is to examine only the linear combination of all correlation outputs for its maximum and use the location of the detected maximum as the location of our pattern of interest. Thus, we have to examine the following combined correlation output:

$$\mathbf{y}_c = \sum_{i=1}^{k} w_i \mathbf{y}_i, \tag{9}$$

where $\mathbf{y}_i$ denotes the correlation output (int the spatial domain) of the i-th PSEF filter, w_i denotes the weighting coefficient of the i-th correlation output,

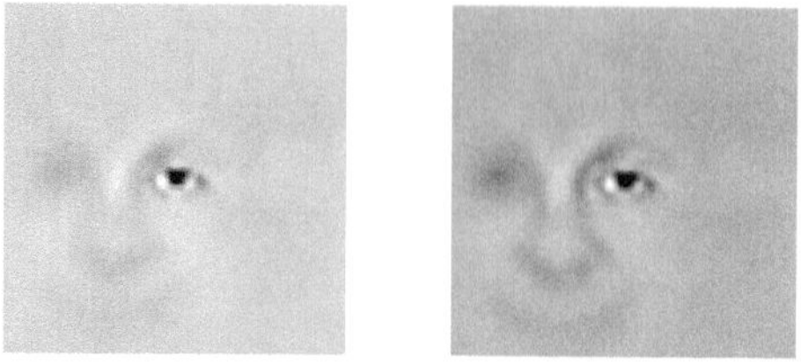

Fig. 4. Comparison of the visual appearance of an ASEF filter (left) and the combined PSEF filter (right). Both images show "right eye" filters with shifted quadrants.

$\mathbf{y}_c$ denotes the combined correlation output, and k stands for the number of PSEF filters used ($1 \leq k \leq \min(d, n)$). From the above equation we can see that if $k = 1$ the combined correlation output is identical to the correlation output of the ASEF filter. On the other hand if $k > 1$ we add additional information to the combined correlation output by including additional PSEF filters into the localization procedure. The presented procedure requires one filtering operation for each PSEF filter used. However, the computation can be speeded up by exploiting the linearity of Eq. 9. Instead of combining the correlation outputs, we simply combine all employed PSEF filters into one single filter with hopefully enhanced localization capabilities, i.e.:

$$\mathbf{y}_c = \sum_{i=1}^{k} w_i \mathbf{y}_i = \sum_{i=1}^{k} w_i (\mathbf{f}_i \otimes \mathbf{x}_t) = (\sum_{i=1}^{k} w_i \mathbf{f}_i) \otimes \mathbf{x}_t = \mathbf{f}_c \otimes \mathbf{x}_t, \tag{10}$$

where $\mathbf{f}_c = \sum_{i=1}^{k} w_i \mathbf{f}_i$, and $\sum_{i=1}^{k} w_i = 1$. In the presented equations $\mathbf{f}_c$ stands for the combined PSEF filter and $\otimes$ denotes the convolution operator. We can see that instead of using k PSEF filters and produce k correlation outputs that are linearly combined, we simply combine the k employed filters into a single filter and, hence, perform only a single filtering operation. The localization procedure has, therefore, exactly, the same computational complexity as the procedure relying on ASEF filters regardless of the number of PSEF filters selected for the localization of our pattern of interest.

The last issue to be solved before we turn our attention to the experimental section is the choice of the weighting coefficients w_i, for $i = 1, 2, ..., k$. While an optimization procedure could be exploited to determine the best possible combination of the k filters, we choose in this paper to select the coefficients in accordance with the following expression:

$$w_i = \frac{\lambda_i}{\sum_{i=1}^{k} \lambda_i}, \tag{11}$$

where λ_i represents the eigenvalue corresponding to the i-th PSEF filter $\mathbf{f}_i$ (see Eq. 7). This procedure is clearly sub-optimal, but it is, nevertheless, enough to demonstrate the usefulness of the proposed filter combination. An example of the visual appearance of the combined PSEF filter obtained with the presented weighting procedure (after the sign ambiguity has been eliminated - see

Section 3) is shown on the right hand side of Fig. 4. For comparison purposes the left hand side image of Fig. 4 also shows the original ASEF filter.

3 Experiments

To assess the effectiveness of the proposed localization procedure relying on PSEF filters we adopt two popular face databases, namely, the grey FERET database [12] and the Labeled Faces in the Wild (LFW) database [5]. We extract the facial regions from all images of the two databases using the Haar cascade classifier proposed by Viola and Jones [17]. Here, we rely on the freely available implementation of the Haar face detector that ships with the OpenCV library [3]. After determining the location of the facial regions in all images, we select 640 images from the LFW database and manually label the locations of the left and right eye. Next, we produce 40 variations of the facial region of each of the 640 LFW images by randomly shifting the location of the facial regions by up to ± 5 pixels, rotating them by up to ± 15, scaling them by up to 1.0 ± 0.15 and mirroring them around the y axes. Through these transformations, we augment the initial set of 640 images to a set of 25600 images (of size 128×128 pixels) that we employ for training of the ASEF and PSEF filters.

For testing purposes we apply the same random transforms to 3815 images from the FERET database. Here, we produce only 12 modifications of each facial region, which results in 45780 facial images being available for our assessment. Some examples of the 12 modifications of a face image from the FERET database are also shown in Fig. 5.

Prior to subjecting the face images to the proposed localization procedure, all face images are transformed into the log-domain and normalized using zero mean and unit variance normalization. In the last step the images are weighted with a cosine window to reduce the frequency effects of the edges commonly encountered when applying the Fourier transform [1]. Once the localization procedure has been performed, we employ the following criteria to measure the effectiveness of our approach [6]:

$$\eta_{se} = \frac{\|l_{se} - r_{se}\|}{\|r_{le} - r_{re}\|} \quad \text{and} \quad \eta_{te} = \frac{\max\left(\|l_{le} - r_{le}\|, \|l_{re} - r_{re}\|\right)}{\|r_{le} - r_{re}\|}, \tag{12}$$

where η_{se} and η_{te} stand for the "single eye" and "two eye" criterion, respectively; l_{se} denotes the location of the single eye of interest found by the assessed

Fig. 5. Visual examples of a sample face region from the FERET database detected with the Viola-Jones face detector and its eleven modifications

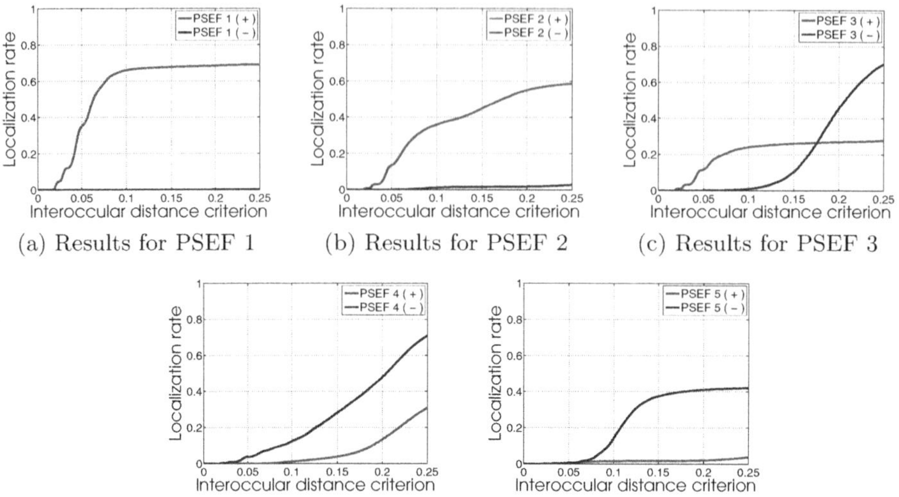

(a) Results for PSEF 1 (b) Results for PSEF 2 (c) Results for PSEF 3

(d) Results for PSEF 4 (e) Results for PSEF 5

Fig. 6. Results of preliminary experiments aimed at alleviating the sign ambiguity of the computed PSEFs (using the "two-eye" criterion)

procedure, r_{se} denotes the reference location of the single eye of interest, the expression $\|r_{le} - r_{re}\|$ represents the interoccular L_2 distance, and the subscripts le and re stand for the left and right eye, respectively. We can see that the "two eye" criterion is more restrictive, as it requires both eyes to be near their reference locations for the criterion to have a small value. The "single eye" criterion, on the other hand, requires only the eye of interest to be near the reference location. For our assessment we observe the correct localization rate for different operating points, i.e., $\eta_{se}, \eta_{te} < \Delta \in \{0.05, 0.10, 0.15, 0.20, 0.25\}$.

Our first series of experiments aims at alleviating the sing ambiguity of the computed PSEF filters. To this end, we compute 5 PSEF filters (corresponding to the 5 largest, non-zero eigenvalues of Eq. 7), derive two filters from each of the 5 PSEF filters by multiplying them with $+1$ and -1, and normalizing the result to zero mean and unit variance. With the 5 computed filter pairs, we conduct localization experiments with the 45780 face images of the FERET database and plot the results in form of graphs as shown in Fig. 6. We select the "two eye" criterion with $\Delta = 0.25$ as the relevant operating point and based on this value determine the appropriate sign of each of the five PSEF filters. Note here that more (or less) filters than 5 could be used for our experiments, the presented results, however, are enough to show the feasibility of our approach.

If we take a look at the presented results in Fig. 6, we can see that in our case the best localization results are obtained with the first two filters being multiplied with $+1$ and the remaining filters being multiplied with -1. Furthermore, we can notice, that the best localization performance is obtained with the first PSEF filter, which in fact corresponds to an ASEF filter, while the remaining filters perform worse. Nevertheless, they hopefully contain complementary information

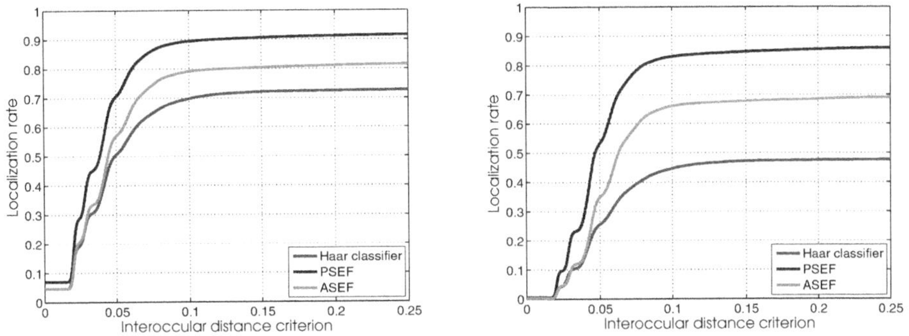

(a) Localization results for the left eye (b) Localization results for both eyes

Fig. 7. Comparison of the eye localization performance of different localization techniques using the: (a) "single eye" and (b) "two eye" criterion. In the experiments the entire 128 × 128 face region of the test images was searched for the eyes.

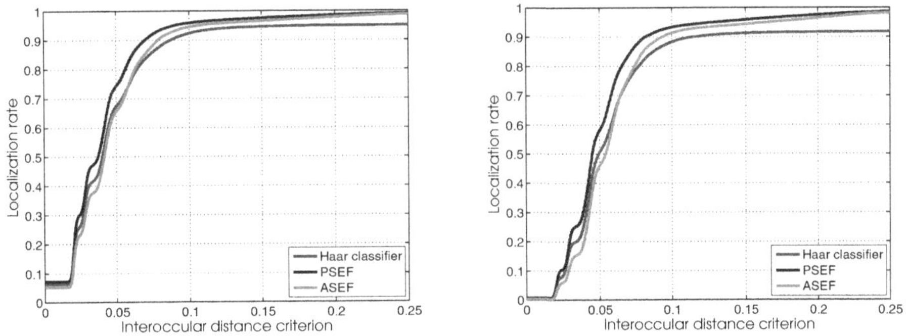

(a) Localization results for the left eye (b) Localization results for both eyes

Fig. 8. Comparison of the eye localization performance of different localization techniques using the: (a) "single eye" and (b) "two eye" criterion. In the experiments only the upper left quadrants of the 128 × 128 face regions were searched for the left eye and the upper right quadrants for the right eye.

to the first PSEF filter. Our second series of experiments comprises two types of tests. The first type uses no a priori knowledge about the locations of the left and right eye, while the second type relies on a priori knowledge about the eye locations and, hence, looks for the left eye only in the upper left quadrant of the test images and for the right eye only in the upper right quadrant of the test images. This setup is identical to the experimental setup adopted in [1] and is used here to allow for a comparison of the localization performance with previously published results.

The results for the first type of experiments are shown in Fig. 7, while the results of the second type of experiments are shown in Fig. 8. Some numerical results for different values of Δ are also summarized in Table 1. Note that the proposed PSEF filters outperform both tested alternatives to eye localization,

Table 1. Localization rates (in %) at different criterion thresholds. Note that for the localization rates corresponding to the "Left eye" columns the "single eye" criterion was used, while for the localization rates corresponding to the "Both eyes" columns the "two eye" criterion was adopted

Criterion	Unconstrained search space						Constrained search space					
	Left eye			Both eyes			Left eye			Both eyes		
	Haar	ASEF	PSEF	Haar	ASEF	PSEF	Haar	ASEF	PSEF	Haar	ASEF	PSEF
0.05	50.5	56.9	70.5	25.6	35.0	53.0	67.5	65.6	74.3	50.6	46.1	58.2
0.10	69.8	79.2	89.5	44.7	66.1	83.0	92.4	94.6	95.9	88.3	91.4	93.3
0.15	71.1	80.5	90.7	47.2	67.8	84.7	94.6	96.5	97.6	91.3	94.4	95.8
0.20	72.5	81.2	91.2	47.5	68.6	85.5	95.0	97.8	98.5	91.7	96.5	97.5
0.25	72.7	81.5	91.5	47.7	69.1	86.0	95.0	98.7	99.1	91.8	98.1	98.6

Table 2. Best average time needed for the localization procedure

Face part	Unconstrained search space		Constrained search space	
	Haar classifier	Correlation filter	Haar classifier	Correlation filter
Left eye	21.6 ms	0.65 ms	11.5 ms	0.66 ms
Right eye	24.8 ms	0.35 ms	13.6 ms	0.35 ms
Both eyes	46.4 ms	1.00 ms	25.1 ms	1.01 ms

namely, ASEF filters as well as the Haar cascade classifier. The proposed filters perform best for both criteria, i.e., the "single eye" and the "two eye" criterion, and both types of conducted experiments.

If we look at the execution times in Table 2 needed for the localization procedure, we can see that the correlation filters require significantly less time for the localization of both eyes than the Haar cascade classifier. Moreover, we can see that the localization time with the Haar classifier for each of the two eyes is more or less identical, while the correlation filters require approximately half the time for the second eye due to the fact that the test image only needs to be transformed into the Fourier domain once. Thus, when looking for the right eye, we already have the frequency representation of the test image at our disposal. It should be noted here that all durations presented in Table 2 represent the best average duration of the localization procedure we have measured in our experiments.

The final comment we need to make before concluding the experimental section refers to the time needed to train the eye locators. The ASEF filters typically require only a few minutes to be trained, since the rely only on a simple average of the exact synthetic filters. The PSEF filters require a few hours for their training, as this involves the computation of a large correlation matrix and its decomposition. Finally, the Haar cascade classifier is known to have training times in the order of days or even weeks. While the training is commonly performed off-line, it is nevertheless important that it is as rapid as possible, as small changes (such as changes in the photometric normalization procedure used) in the systems relying on eye localization procedures often induce the need for retraining of the eye locator.

4 Conclusion

We have presented a new class of correlation filters called Principal directions of Synthetic Exact Filters and applied them to the task of eye localization. We have shown that the filters outperform the recently proposed ASEF filters and the established Haar cascade classifier at this task, and that they exhibit some desirable properties such as extremely low execution times.

Acknowledgements

The presented work has been performed in scope of the BioID project and has been partly financed by the European Union from the European Social Fund, contract No. PP11/2010-(1/2009).

References

1. Bolme, D.S., Draper, B.A., Beveridge, J.R.: Average of synthetic exact filters. In: Proc. of CVPR 2009, pp. 2105–2112 (2009)
2. Bolme, D.S., Liu, Y.M., Draper, B.A., Beveridge, J.R.: Simple real-time human detection using a single correlation filter. In: Proc. of the 12th Workshop on Performance Evaluation of Tracking and Surveillance, pp. 1–8 (2009)
3. Bradski, G., Kaehler, A.: Learning OpenCV: computer vision with the OpenCV library. O'Reilly Media, Sebastopol (2008)
4. Hester, C.F., Casasent, D.: Mulitvariant technique for multiclass pattern recognition. Applied Optics 19(11), 1758–1761 (1980)
5. Huang, G.B., Ramesh, M., Berg, T., Learned-Miller, E.: Labeled Faces in the Wild: a database for studying face recognition in unconstrained environments. University of Massachusetts, Amherst, Technical Report 07-49 (October 2007)
6. Jesorsky, O., Kirchberg, K.J., Frischholz, R.W.: Robust face detection using the hausdorff distance. In: Bigun, J., Smeraldi, F. (eds.) AVBPA 2001. LNCS, vol. 2091, pp. 90–95. Springer, Heidelberg (2001)
7. Kerekes, R.A., Kumar, B.V.K.V.: Correlation filters with controlled scale response. IEEE Transactions on Image Processing 15(7), 1794–1802 (2006)
8. Kumar, B.V.K.V., Mahalanobis, A., Takessian, A.: Optimal tradeoff circular harmonic function correlation filter methods providing controlled in-plane rotation response. IEEE Transactions on Image Processing 9(6), 1025–1034 (2000)
9. Mahalanobis, A., Kumar, B.V.K.V., Casasent, D.: Minimum average correlation energy filters. Applied Optics 26(17), 3633–3640 (1987)
10. Mahalanobis, A., Kumar, B.V.K.V., Sims, S.R.F.: Distance-classifier correlation filters for multiclass target recognition. Applied Optics 35(17), 3127–3133 (1996)
11. Mahalanobis, A., Kumar, B.V.K.V., Song, S., Sims, S.R.F., Epperson, J.: Unconstrained correlation filters. Applied Optics 33(17), 3751–3759 (1994)

12. Phillips, P.J., Moon, H., Rizvi, S.A., Rauss, P.J.: The FERET evaluation methodology for face-recognition algorithms. IEEE Transactions on Pattern Analysis and Machine Intelligence 22(10), 1090–1104 (2000)
13. Refregier, P.: Optimal trade-off filters for noise robustness, sharpness of the correlation peak, and Horner efficiency. Optics Letters 16(11), 829–831 (1991)
14. Savvides, M., Kumar, B.V.K.V.: Efficient design of advanced correlation filters for robust distortion-tolerant face recognition. In: Proc. of the IEEE Conference on Advanced Video and Signal Based Surveillance, pp. 45–52 (2003)
15. Štruc, V., Gajšek, R., Pavešić, N.: Principal Gabor filters for face recognition. In: Proc. of BTAS 2009, pp. 1–6 (2009)
16. Turk, M., Pentland, A.: Eigenfaces for recognition. Journal of Cognitive Neuroscience 3(1), 71–86 (1991)
17. Viola, P., Jones, M.J.: Robust real-time face detection. International Journal of Computer Vision 57, 137–154 (2004)

On Using High-Definition Body Worn Cameras for Face Recognition from a Distance

Wasseem Al-Obaydy and Harin Sellahewa

Department of Applied Computing, University of Buckingham,
Buckingham, MK18 1EG, UK
{wasseem.alobaydy,harin.sellahewa}@buckingham.ac.uk
http://www.buckingham.ac.uk

Abstract. Recognition of human faces from a distance is highly desirable for law-enforcement. This paper evaluates the use of low-cost, high-definition (HD) body worn video cameras for face recognition from a distance. A comparison of HD vs. Standard-definition (SD) video for face recognition from a distance is presented. HD and SD videos of 20 subjects were acquired in different conditions and at varying distances. The evaluation uses three benchmark algorithms: Eigenfaces, Fisherfaces and Wavelet Transforms. The study indicates when gallery and probe images consist of faces captured from a distance, HD video result in better recognition accuracy, compared to SD video. This scenario resembles real-life conditions of video surveillance and law-enforcement activities. However, at a close range, face data obtained from SD video result in similar, if not better recognition accuracy than using HD face data of the same range.

Keywords: HD video, Face Recognition, Face Database, Surveillance, Eigenfaces, Fisherfaces, Wavelet Transforms.

1 Introduction

Automatic recognition of human faces from video sequences has many applications. Most notable among them include law-enforcement, surveillance, forensics and content-based video retrieval. Much progress has been made in developing systems to recognise faces in controlled, indoor environments. However, accurate recognition of human faces in unrestricted environments still remains a challenge [10]. This is due to significant intra-class variations caused by changes in illumination, head pose and orientation, occlusion, sensor quality and video resolution [8,9].

Normally, video signals captured by digital imaging devices are digitised at resolution levels lower than that of still images; hence the quality of a frame extracted from a video sequence is lower than that obtained from a still imaging device. Developing a robust video-based face recognition system that operates in unrestricted environments is a difficult task. This is due to the poor quality of face images in terms of image degradation, motion blur and low resolution. Therefore, the resolution of video frames could play a vital role in face

C. Vielhauer et al. (Eds.): BioID 2011, LNCS 6583, pp. 193–204, 2011.

recognition from a distance. The understanding of the gains and losses of using high-resolution video in face recognition is an important factor when designing a biometric system to recognise faces in unrestricted conditions.

Recently, high definition (HD) video has been introduced as a new video standard that provides high quality video with high resolution as opposed to low-resolution standard definition video (SD). The availability of low-cost, miniature, high-definition video capture devices, combined with advanced wireless communication technologies, provide a platform on which real-time biometric systems that could recognise faces in unrestricted environments can be realised. The expectation is that, the recognition accuracy can be improved by increasing the video resolution. Recent studies have shown that using high quality/resolution video result in better face recognition accuracy [1,14,10]. Law-enforcement, forensics, video surveillance and counter-terrorism are areas that can benefit from such biometric systems. An example scenario is the real-time analysis a of video stream, captured by a camera worn on the uniform of a police officer to identify if a missing (or wanted) person is in the area that the police officer is patrolling.

This paper contributes to the current research in face recognition by investigating the use of HD body worn cameras to recognise faces from a distance and in outdoor conditions. The study looks at recognising faces captured at four different distance ranges in indoor and outdoor recording conditions. We evaluate the effects of using HD and SD video images for three benchmark face recognition algorithms: 1) Eigenfaces [15] 2) Fisherfaces [2] and 3) Wavelets [11]. A new face video database has been recorded at the University of Buckingham[1]. Videos of 20 subjects were acquired in HD and SD formats using a low-cost HD body worn digital video camera. An evaluation protocol is defined for the experiments conducted in this phase of the study.

The rest of the paper is organised as follows: Sec. 2 introduces the features of the newly acquired HD/SD video database. Section 3 describes the three baseline face recognition algorithms used in this evaluation. Experiments and results are discussed in Sec. 4. Our concluding remarks and future works are presented in Sec. 5.

2 High and Standard Definition (HSD) Video Database

2.1 High Definition vs. Standard Definition Video

The formats of NTSC, PAL and any video with vertical resolution less than 720 pixels are classified as standard definition (SD) video formats. Originally, NTSC and PAL are analogue standards, the digital representations of which can be obtained by digitising (sampling) the video frames. The NTSC video frame is digitised to 640×480 pixels, while a PAL video frame is sampled to 768×576 pixels [4]. Both NTSC and PAL systems have a 4:3 aspect ratio, and follow the

[1] The UBHSD database can be obtained for research purposes by contacting the second author of this paper.

interlaced scanning system. The actual frame rate of NTSC video is 29.97 fps but it is often quoted as 30 fps, whereas the frame rate of PAL video is 25 fps [4].

In recent years, an increasing demand for high quality video has resulted in rapid adoption of HD digital video, particularly for home entertainment and digital TV broadcast. HD video is any video that contains 720 or more horizontal lines of the vertical resolution of the video frame. The Advanced Television System Committee (ATSC) states that the frame size of the HD video is either 1280×720 or 1920×1080 pixels [3]. All HD video formats support a widescreen aspect ratio of 16:9. Thus, HD video provides a high quality picture with high spatial resolution compared to the SD video. HD video with 720 pixels supports only progressive scanning, and is denoted by 720p, while HD video with 1080 pixels supports both interlaced and progressive scanning, and is denoted by 1080i and 1080p respectively [4]. Unlike SD video, HD video offers a variety of frame rates: 24, 30 and 60 fps.

2.2 HD Body Worn Camera

The videos in the database were acquired using a iOPTEC-P300; a HD body worn digital video camera, designed for police forces and security agencies for covert/overt surveillance and to collect real-time audio/video evidence. In order to maintain consistency of different physical properties of a camera (e.g. camera optics, lens) that affects its video quality, the same HD camera was used to capture both HD and SD videos. The SD video was recorded at a resolution 848×480 pixels, and at 25fps. The HD video was acquired at a resolution of 1920×1080p pixels, and at 30fps. Both the SD and HD videos were recorded in MOV file format.

2.3 UBHSD Database

Data Collection. The database contains a total of 160 videos of 20 distinct subjects. The videos of each subject were recorded in two sessions; each session includes two conditions: indoor and outdoor. The period between the two recording sessions was at least two days. In each condition, two video recordings (one HD and one SD) of the subject were captured sequentially by the same HD camera. All indoor recordings were captured in the same room under semi-controlled lighting with a uniform background. Outdoor videos were captured in an uncontrolled environment. These recording conditions represent realistic scenarios under which applications of face recognition at a distance can be applied.

During a recording, a subject walk a distance of 4 meters (indoor) and 5 meters (outdoor) toward the camera, from a start-point to a stop-point, providing face data at different distances. The minimum distance betweeen the camera and the subject (stop-point) is a meter. The subjects face the camera while they walk toward it. However, they were free to walk in a natural way which included head movements and facial expressions. A video recording lasted about 5 to 10 seconds depending on the speed at which the subject walks. Figure 1 shows video frames

(a) HD video, Indoor (distance range from left to right: R_1 - R_4)

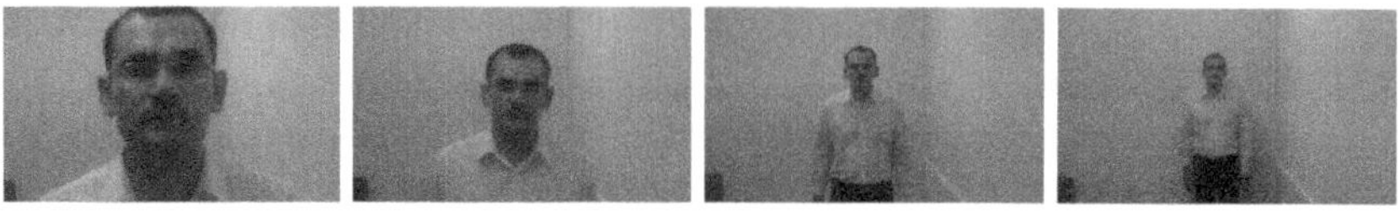

(b) SD video, Indoor (distance range from left to right: R_1 - R_4)

(c) HD video, Outdoor (distance range from left to right: R_1 - R_4)

(d) SD video, Outdoor (distance range from left to right: R_1 - R_4)

Fig. 1. A sample of indoor and outdoor video frames of the High/Standard Definition Video Database

extracted from a typical indoor and outdoor recording conditions for a subject. The frames of HD and SD videos are scaled down at different levels for display purposes.

Data Preparation. Twelve frames of from each video are selected in a systematic way to capture the subject at four distance ranges from the camera position. Each distance range is represented by 3 frames. The frames in the first range, *Range 1* (R_1), are nearest to the camera, while the frames in the fourth range, *Range 4* (R_4), are the farthest away from the camera. Each row in fig. 1 consists of four frames, each representing a distance range.

The total walking distance is sectioned into 4 ranges is by dividing the total number of video frames by 4. Then, the mid, $mid + 5$, and $mid + 10$ frames in each range are selected and extracted from the video. This ensures that the subject, who appears in HD frames at certain distance range, appears also in their corresponding SD frames at the same distance range from the camera. In some cases, the mid+15 frame was chosen instead of one of the three frames when the latter suffers from severe motion blur. Yet, the database consists of blurred face images, faces with eyes closed and slightly varying poses. Each subject has 96 face images, thus the total number of face images in the database is 1920.

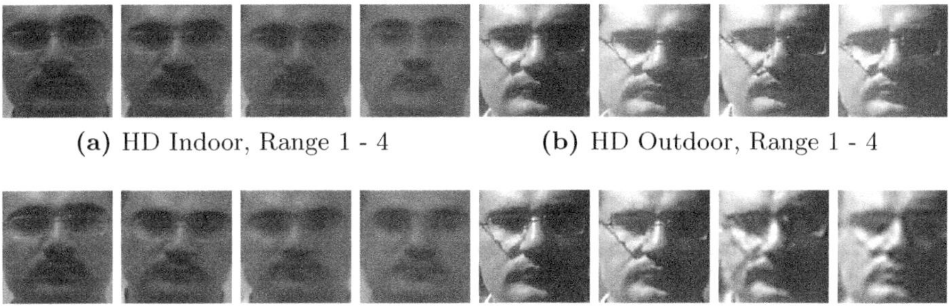

(a) HD Indoor, Range 1 - 4 (b) HD Outdoor, Range 1 - 4

(c) SD Indoor, Range 1 - 4 (d) SD Outdoor, Range 1 - 4

Fig. 2. Examples of cropped and rescaled face images from HD and SD videos captured in indoor and outdoor conditions

The face region in each frame was manually cropped at the top or middle of the forehead, bottom of the chin, and at the base of the ears. Then, all face images were converted to grayscale and rescaled to size of 128×128 pixels. The experiments reported here are based on these images. Figure 2 shows the cropped and rescaled face images extracted from the respective HD and SD videos frames in Fig. 1.

3 Baseline Algorithms

A brief description of each of the three benchmark face recognition algorithms, namely Eigenfaces, Fisherfaces and wavelet-based face recognition is given in this section. As shown in Fig. 1, videos of subjects in UBHSD database are captured under varying lighting conditions. There are many normalisation techniques that can be used to deal with the problem of varying illumination conditions [13,7]. We tested the effect of the commonly used histogram equalisation (HE) and z-score normalisation (ZN) on the recognition rates of the three algorithms. For Eigenfaces and Fisherfaces, ZN was applied on the cropped and rescaled face images while for the wavelet-based scheme, the selected wavelet subband was normalised by ZN.

3.1 Eigenfaces

Turk and Pentland [15] presented the Eigenfaces approach using Principle Component Analysis (PCA) to efficiently represent face images. PCA is a statistical analysis tool used to reduce the large dimensionality of data by exploiting the redundancy in multidimensional data. In this approach, each face image in the high dimensional *image space* can be represented as a linear combination of a set of vectors in the new low dimensional *face space*. These vectors, calculated by PCA, are the eigenvectors of the covariance matrix of the face images in the training set. Each eigenvector can be displayed as a "ghostly" face image, hence eigenvectors are commonly referred to as eigenfaces. When a probe face image is presented for recognition, it is projected into the *face space* and a nearest neighbour classification method is used to assign an identity to the probe image.

3.2 Fisherfaces

Belhumeur et al. [2] presented Fisherfaces, a face recognition scheme claimed to be insensitive to illumination variations and facial expressions. The authors state that since the training images are labeled with classes (i.e. individual identities), it makes sense to exploit class information to build a reliable method to reduce the dimensionality of the feature space. This approach is based on using class specific linear methods for dimensionality reduction and simple classifiers to produce better recognition rates than Eigenfaces method which does not use the class information for dimensionality reduction. Fisher's Linear Discriminant Analysis (FLD or LDA) is used to find a set of projecting vectors (i.e. weights) that best discriminate different classes. FLD achieves that objective by maximising the ratio of the between-class scatter to that of the within-class scatter.

3.3 Wavelet-Based Face Recognition

Discrete wavelet transforms (DWT) can be used as a dimension reduction technique and/or as a tool to extract a multiresolution feature representation of a given face image [5,11,6]. In the enrolment stage, each face image in the gallery set is transformed to the wavelet domain to extract its facial feature vector (i.e. a subband). The choice of an appropriate subband could vary according to the operational circumstances of the recognition application. The decomposition level is predetermined based on the efficiency and accuracy requirements and the size of the face image. In the recognition stage, a nearest neighbour classification method is used to classify the unknown face images.

4 Experiments and Results

In this paper, we report the results of the first phase of our evaluation of HD and SD video in face recognition from a distance. Firstly, we define an evaluation protocol for the HSD video database to ensure repeatability and comparability of the work reported here and for future works using this database. The evaluation protocol is introduced in Sec. 4.1 followed by experimental results in Sec. 4.2.

4.1 Evaluation Protocol

The evaluation protocol involves four configurations for each video resolution: 1) Matched Indoor (MI), 2) Matched Outdoor (MO), 3) Unmatched Indoor (UI) and 4) Unmatched Outdoor (UO). Each configuration has four test cases (e.g. $\text{MI}_1, \ldots, \text{MI}_4$,). The gallery set G of test-case i ($i = 1, \ldots, 4$) consists only range R_i face images in Session 1. For each test case, images from all four ranges, in both indoor and outdoor videos in Session 2 are used as probe images (P). There is no overlap between the gallery and probe sets. In Matched configurations, both the gallery and probe images come from the same video resolution. In Unmatched configurations, gallery and probe images are from different video resolutions. For each test-case, the gallery set consists of 60 images (3 images per subject) and the probe set consists of 480 images (24 images per subject). Table 1 describes the gallery and probe sets for different configurations.

Table 1. The test configurations for the HSD video database

Configuration		Session 1				Session 2			
		HD video		SD video		HD video		SD video	
		Indoor	outdoor	Indoor	outdoor	Indoor	outdoor	Indoor	outdoor
HD	MI_i	G,R_i				P,R_{1-4}	P,R_{1-4}		
	MO_i		G,R_i			P,R_{1-4}	P,R_{1-4}		
	UI_i	G,R_i						P,R_{1-4}	P,R_{1-4}
	UO_i		G,R_i					P,R_{1-4}	P,R_{1-4}
SD	MI_i			G,R_i				P,R_{1-4}	P,R_{1-4}
	MO_i				G,R_i			P,R_{1-4}	P,R_{1-4}
	UI_i			G,R_i		P,R_{1-4}	P,R_{1-4}		
	UO_i				G,R_i	P,R_{1-4}	P,R_{1-4}		

4.2 Recognition Results

A number of experiments have been conducted using the newly created HSD video database to evaluate the use of HD and SD video in face recognition from a distance. All three face recognition algorithms use L1 (CityBlock) distance to calculate a match score between two feature vectors. The Haar wavelet transform is used for the wavelet-based recognition and we report results for LL_3 and LH_3 subbands based on recent work in [12]. Rank one recognition accuracy for MI and MO configurations based on Eigenfaces (PCA), Fisherfaces (LDA) and DWT (LL-subband and LH-subband) are presented in Fig. 3 through Fig. 6. We also report results for UI configuration, based on LH_3 subband features (with z-score normalisation), in Tab. 2.

The overall recognition rates of all test cases indicate that the use of HD video data for face recognition at a distance has a significant advantage over that of SD video data. This observation is in agreement with our expectation that using high-resolution video data would lead to better recognition rates for face recognition at a distance. However, a closer examination of individual tests reveals an interesting pattern. When the gallery set is the collection of face images nearest to the camera (i.e. Test $Case_1$), SD video data result in similar if not significantly higher recognition accuracy compared to that of using HD video data, irrespective of the distance range of the probe images. There could be a number of reasons for this behaviour.

Firstly, a Range 1 face image taken from HD video has to be down sampled by a much larger factor than the one used for a face image taken from SD video (to produce a 128×128 pixel face image). The resulting degradation of quality

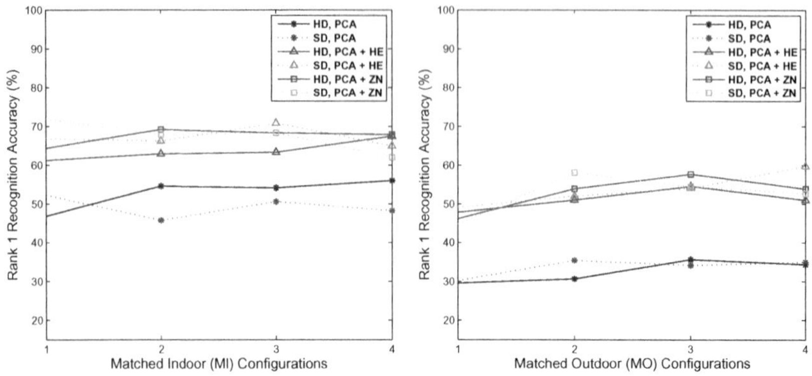

Fig. 3. Rank 1 recognition accuracy of HD & SD video using PCA

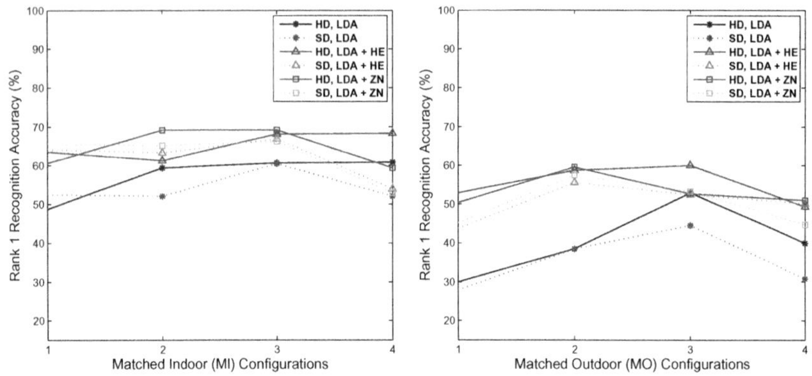

Fig. 4. Rank 1 recognition accuracy of HD & SD video using LDA

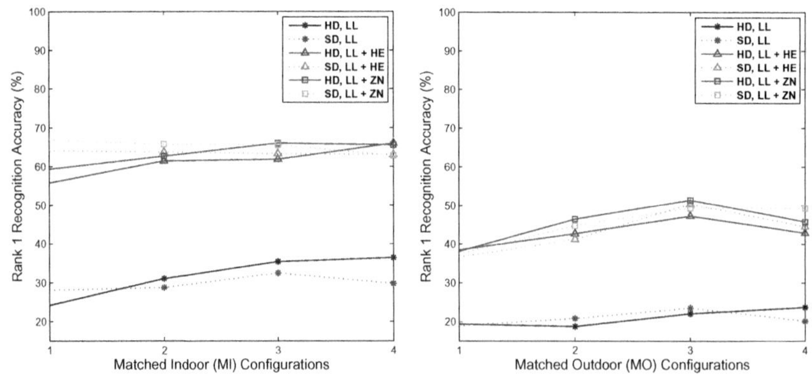

Fig. 5. Rank 1 recognition accuracy of HD & SD video using LL_3

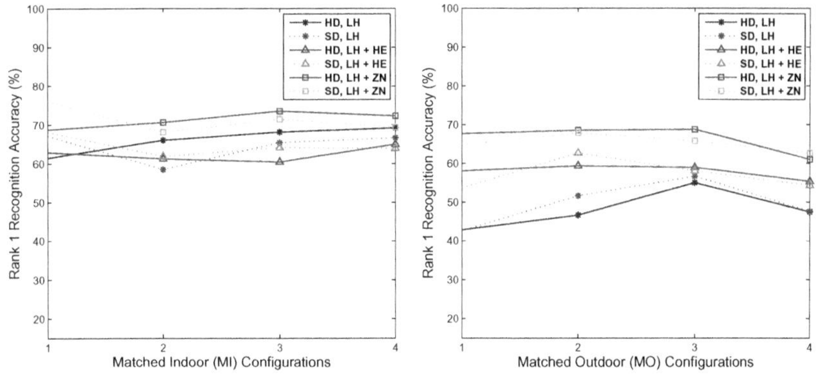

Fig. 6. Rank 1 recognition accuracy of HD & SD video using LH_3

depends on the down sampling technique (in our case, we used MATLAB 'imresize' with the default bicubic interpolation) and it is higher on face images taken from HD videos than it would on face images taken from SD videos. Aliasing, caused by down sampling, could also be a factor. To establish if downsampling has an adverse effect on HD video images at Range−1, we repeated the Matched Indoor tests using Gallery images from $Range_1$ for different face sizes: 1) 64×64, 2) 96×96, 3)160×160 and 4) 200×200. The rank 1 recognition accuracies for HD and SD data are given in Tab. 3. The results give some indication that less downsampling is better for HD (the size of face images captured in HD at close range are much larger than those captured from SD). This requires further investigation to identify why at Range1 SD-SD outperforms HD-HD.

On the other hand, it could be that "more is less", meaning having too much information (e.g. high image resolution) is not necessarily a good thing in face recognition. This could be the reason for lower accuracy of HD video image using Eigenfaces approaches. It is also possible that 60 high resolution training samples (3 per subject) are insufficient to obtain a good discriminative *face space* for recognition because of data redundancy. We noticed a significant increase in recognition accuracy when the number of training samples was increased from 1 to 3. Note that the training images used for each subject are obtained from video frames that are nearer to each other. Hence, there is little variation among them. This is in contrast to the gallery data selection techniques proposed in [14], which aim to use training samples that capture variations. In our test configurations, we try to simulate conditions that may have a limited choice of gallery images for each subject.

We have reproduced in Tab. 4, a selection of experimental results by Thomas et al. in [14] that shows the recognition accuracy of three different cameras. The JVC is a high-definition camera and the Canon is a standard-definition camera. Note that in [14], the number of samples used in the gallery set for the selected results is 12 or 15 as opposed to 3 samples we have used in our evaluation.

Figure 3 through Fig. 6 also present rank one recognition rates for two illumination normalisation techniques. Normalisation has significantly improved the recognition rates of all algorithms. Its effect is prominent in Eigenfaces and LL-subband based recognition; two feature representations that are known to be severely affected by varying lighting conditions. In terms of HD video vs. SD video in face recognition, the HD video is still the better of the two standards, except when gallery images are from Range 1, SD video is the better option. Surprisingly, z-score normalisation resulted in much higher recognition accuracy than the commonly used histogram equalisation for illumination normalisation.

A comparison of the three face recognition algorithms shows that the recognition rates of Fisherfaces approach is similar, if not better than the recognition rates of Eigenfaces approach. However, simply using the LH-subband of wavelet transformed images as face features significantly outperforms both Fisherfaces and Eigenfaces schemes.

It is worth noting the significant decrease in recognition accuracy when outdoor video images are used as a gallery set. These results highlight the challenges of recognising faces from a distance and in unrestricted environments.

Table 2. Rank 1 recognition accuracy of Matched and Unmatched configurations

Gallery	Probe	Gallery Image Range			
Set	Set	$Range_1$	$Range_2$	$Range_3$	$Range_4$
HD	HD	68.75	70.62	73.54	72.29
HD	SD	68.75	65.83	72.08	75.00
SD	SD	76.04	68.12	71.46	69.38
SD	HD	75.83	71.04	71.25	68.33

Table 3. Recognition accuracy vs. face size. Gallery Images from $Range_1$

	Face image size (pixels)				
Gallery/Probe	64×64	96×96	128×128	160×160	200×200
HD/HD	68.12	72.08	68.75	72.92	69.58
SD/SD	75.42	76.46	76.04	74.79	75.00

Table 4. Rank 1 recognition rates by Thomas et al. in [14], Tab. 18.1

Gallery (NEHF)	Probe	Accuracy Rate	Number of Images
JVC	JVC	82.9	12
JVC	Canon	78.1	15
Canon	Canon	79.0	12
Canon	JVC	76.2	12

5 Conclusions and Future Work

In this paper, we presented a performance evaluation of HD and SD video in face recognition from a distance. We created a new face biometric database consisting HD and SD videos of 20 different subjects, captured at different distances using a low-cost HD body worn camera. We used three benchmark algorithms, namely Eigenfaces, Fisherfaces and Wavelets-based approaches for the evaluation of HD and SD video in face recognition from a distance.

The overall recognition rates of all test configurations favour the use of HD video data for face recognition from a distance as opposed to using SD video data. This is in line with the expectation that high-resolution video data would lead to better recognition rates for face recognition from a distance. Previous work also suggests the same. However, for recognition at a close range, HD video might not provide an added benefit in terms of recognition accuracy, when compared with SD video.

This brings us to the important question; should we use HD video or SD video for face recognition from a distance? Based on the evaluation presented here, the choice of HD or SD depends on the quality of the gallery set and the probe images presented for identification. For applications where person identification from a distance is a requirement, HD video offers a clear advantage over SD video. However, SD video has shown to produce higher recognition rates for face recognition at a close range. Therefore, a face recognition system in unrestricted environments (e.g. CCTV with automatic face recognition) should be able to select the appropriate resolution (or zoom in and out) when attempting identify a person.

It must be emphasised that the benefits of HD video comes at the cost of high bandwidth, storage and processing requirements. In situations where the use of HD video is unaffordable, super resolution techniques could be used to improve the accuracy of low-resolution, SD video data. It is also important to understand the effects of various pre-processing techniques (e.g. resizing, illumination normalisation) that are commonly applied on face images prior to using them as gallery or probe images. These are important questions that require further investigation. This brings us to the next phase of the evaluation. Our future works include the use and evaluation of super resolution techniques in face recognition at a distance. We will also evaluate the performance of state-of-the-art face recognition algorithms on the newly acquired HD and SD video database and investigate the performance of HD video data with varying sample sizes in the gallery set.

References

1. Bailly-Baillière, E., Bagnio, S., Bimbot, F., Hamouz, M., Kittler, J., Mariéthoz, J., Matas, J., Messer, K., Popovici, V., Porée, F., Ruiz, B., Thiran, J.: The BANCA Database Evaluation Protocol. In: Kittler, J., Nixon, M.S. (eds.) AVBPA 2003. LNCS, vol. 2688, pp. 625–638. Springer, Heidelberg (2003)
2. Belhumeur, P.N., Hespanha, J.P., Kriegman, D.J.: Eigenfaces vs. Fisherfaces: Recognition Using Class Specific Linear Projection. IEEE Transactions on Pattern Analysis and Machine Intelligence 19(7), 711–720 (1997)
3. Browne, S.E.: High Definition Postproduction: Editing and Delivering HD Video. Focal Press (December 2006)
4. Chapman, N., Chapman, J.: Digital Multimedia, 3rd edn. John Wiley & Sons, Ltd., Chichester (2009)

5. Chien, J.T., Wu, C.C.: Discriminant Waveletfaces and Nearest Feature Classifiers for Face Recognition. IEEE Transactions on Pattern Analysis and Machine Intelligence 24(12), 1644–1649 (2002)
6. Ekenel, H.K., Sankur, B.: Multiresolution face recognition. Image and Vision Computing 23(5), 469–477 (2005)
7. Gross, R., Brajovi, V.: An Image Preprocessing Algorithm for Illumination Invariant Face Recognition. In: Kittler, J., Nixon, M.S. (eds.) AVBPA 2003. LNCS, vol. 2688, pp. 11–18. Springer, Heidelberg (2003)
8. Kung, S.Y., Mak, M.W., Lin, S.H.: Biometric Authentication:A Machine Learning Approach. Prentice Hall, New Jersey (2005)
9. Park, U.: Face Recognition: face in video, age invariance, and facial marks. Ph.D. thesis, Michigan State University, USA (2009)
10. Phillips, P.J., Flynn, P.J., Beveridge, J.R., Scruggs, W.T., O'toole, A.J., Bolme, D.S., Bowyer, K.W., Draper, B.A., Givens, G.H., Lui, Y.M., Sahibzada, H., Scallan, J.A., Weimer, S.: Overview of the multiple biometrics grand challenge. In: Proc. International Conference on Biometrics, pp. 705–714 (June 2009)
11. Sellahewa, H., Jassim, S.: Wavelet-based face verification for constrained platforms. In: Biometric Technology for Human Identification II. Proc. SPIE, vol. 5779, pp. 173–183 (March 2005)
12. Sellahewa, H., Jassim, S.: Image quality-based adaptive face recognition. IEEE Transactions on Intrumentation & Measurements 59, 805–813 (2010)
13. Shan, S., Gao, W., Cao, B., Zhao, D.: Illumination Normalization for Robust Face Recognition Against Varying Lighting Conditions. In: IEEE International Workshop on Analysis and Modeling of Faces and Gestures, pp. 157–164 (2003)
14. Thomas, D., Boyer, K.W., Flynn, P.J.: Strategies for improving face recognition from video. In: Ratha, N.K., Govindaraju, V. (eds.) Advances in Biometrics - Sensors, Algorithms and Systems, ch. 18, pp. 339–361. Springer, Heidelberg (2008)
15. Turk, M., Pentland, A.: Eigenfaces for Recognition. Journal of Cognitive Neuroscience 3(1), 71–86 (1991)

Adult Face Recognition in Score-Age-Quality Classification Space

Andrzej Drygajlo, Weifeng Li, and Hui Qiu

LIDIAP Speech Processing and Biometrics Group
Swiss Federal Institute of Technology Lausanne (EPFL)
CH-1015 Lausanne, Switzerland
andrzej.drygajlo@epfl.ch
http://scgwww.epfl.ch

Abstract. Face verification in the simultaneous presence of age progression and changing face-image quality is an important problem that has not been widely addressed. In this paper, we study the problem by designing and evaluating a generalized Q-stack model, which combines the age and class-independent quality measures together with the scores from a baseline classifier using local ternary patterns, in order to obtain better recognition performance. This allows for improved long-term class separation by introducing a multi-dimensional parameterized decision boundary in the score-age-quality classification space using a short-term enrolment model. This generalized method, based on the concept of classifier stacking with age- and quality (head pose and expression) aware decision boundary compares favorably with the conventional face verification approach, which uses decision threshold calculated only in the score space at the time of enrolment. The proposed approach is evaluated on the MORPH database.

Keywords: face verification, face aging, stacking classifier, quality measures.

1 Introduction

Aging and changing quality of face images degrade the performance of face recognition systems in large-scale, long-term applications, e.g. biometric e-passports and national identity cards. However, combination of age and quality measures to further improve the recognition performance has perhaps been studied the least. Although not so significant shifts of face structure as introduced during growth years, adults undergo gradual variations that occur in the face as their age progresses that will affect outcomes of face-based biometric systems [1], [2], [3], [4], [5]. Periodically updating (e.g., every six months) large-scale-application face databases with more recent images of persons might be necessary for the success of face verification systems. Since periodical updating such large databases would be a tedious and very costly task, a better alternative would be to develop aging and quality aware face verification methods. Only such methods will have the best prospects of success in longer stretches of time [6], [7].

C. Vielhauer et al. (Eds.): BioID 2011, LNCS 6583, pp. 205–216, 2011.

Most of the reported studies in relation to adult face aging have focused on age estimation and modeling of the changes in face appearance as time progresses [1], [8], [9], [10]. Most of these investigations are based on a computational model of facial aging which is subsequently employed for synthesizing virtual views of the test facial images at the target age. When comparing two face images, these methods either transform one face image to have the same age as the other, or transform both to reduce the aging effects [11], [5]. However, since there are many different ways in which a face (shape and texture) can potentially age, developing an effective computational model of facial aging is very difficult and the generated aging images may differ from the actual images [12]. Also, simulating face images at target age assumes that both the base and target age are known or can be estimated which by itself is a difficult problem in real applications.

Instead of explicitly modeling the facial changes with age progression in the feature domain or adapting a static face recognition model by periodically updating the person's data, in [13], [14] Drygajlo et al. have adopted Q-stack classifier [15], [27], the recently developed framework of stacking classification with quality measures, and created a new face verification system robust to aging of biometric templates. The Q-stack solution allows for automatic tracking the changes of the scores of the baseline classifiers of a specific user across aging and find the decision boundary which can be adapted to those changes. The novelty of this approach is that it opens a new way for the combination of age information with multiple baseline classifiers and different quality measures to further improve the verification performance [24]. In this paper we explore the combination of age information with other quality measures, in particular with those corresponding to head pose and expression changes, for improving the class separation of genuine and impostor scores in face verification systems using local ternary patterns (LTPs) [25].

On the other hand, it is evident that the manner in which a face ages is individual-dependent, i.e., the changes of one person are different from those of other person. As a result, the recognition performance of an aging-face biometric system is supposed to be dependent on the user-specific models. Therefore, developing a user-specific biometric system is substantially imperative for aging face verification [7]. In this paper we adopt a user-specific approach to find the age-aware decision boundaries via the Q-stack framework.

The organization of the paper is as follows. Section 2 describes the experimental data, local ternary patterns (LTPs) extraction, and baseline classifier used in the experiments. Section 3 presents aging metadata quality measure as well as head pose and expression based quality measures. Section 4 provides the analysis of the influence of age progression and other quality measures on the baseline classifier. Section 5 presents generalized Q-stack aging model. Section 6 presents comparison and performance evaluation of face verification systems on aging face images and Section 7 gives conclusions and a brief discussion on continued research.

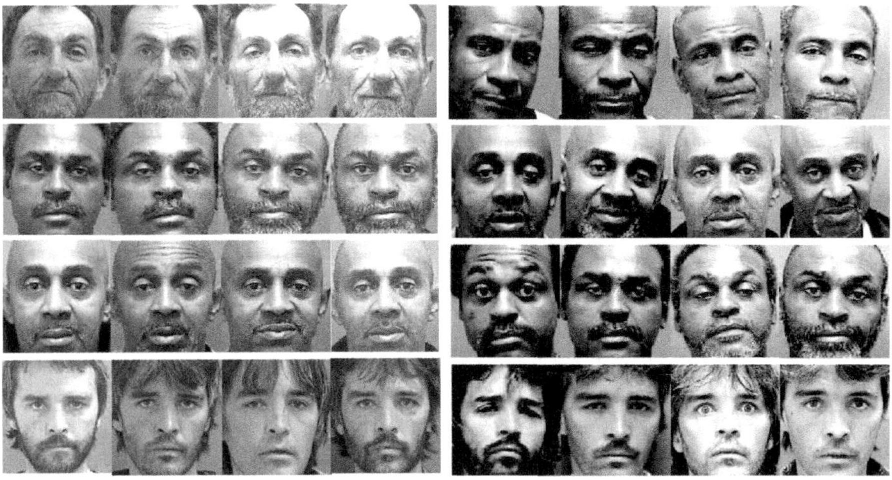

Fig. 1. MORPH Database 1 (left) and Database 2 (right) sample face images as the age increases (from left to right for each person)

2 Databases, Feature Extraction and Baseline Classifier

Our studies utilize the MORPH Database, a publicly available database developed for investigating age progression, in which the images represent a diverse population with respect to age, gender, ethnicity, etc. [16]. The face images are not taken under controlled conditions, they are not distributed uniformly in time and each person is represented by different number of face images. Many of these images are with different variations in head pose, illumination and facial expression.

For these studies, two sub-databases were extracted from the whole MORPH database: Database 1 and Database 2. Database 1 includes 42 persons, each represented by more than 5 images without significant changes in head pose, facial expression and illumination. Database 2 includes 45 persons represented by more than 20 images for each individual with changes in head pose, expression and illumination. For each person the sequence of different number of images is arranged in an age-ascending order. Figure 1 shows the image samples with the age progression after performing face detection using OpenCV [17]. Database 1 allows us to model mainly age progression in human faces and Database 2 to build a face verification system not only robust to age progression but also to changing quality of images including head pose and expression.

In present study Local Ternary Pattern (LTP)based local features are employed for taking into account different variations due to illumination, head pose and facial expression. The Local Ternary Pattern (LTP) [22] is an extension of the Local Binary Pattern (LBP) [20], [21], which is defined as a gray-scale invariant texture measure and derived from a general definition of texture in a local neighborhood. Since the threshold is exactly the value of the central pixel, LBP

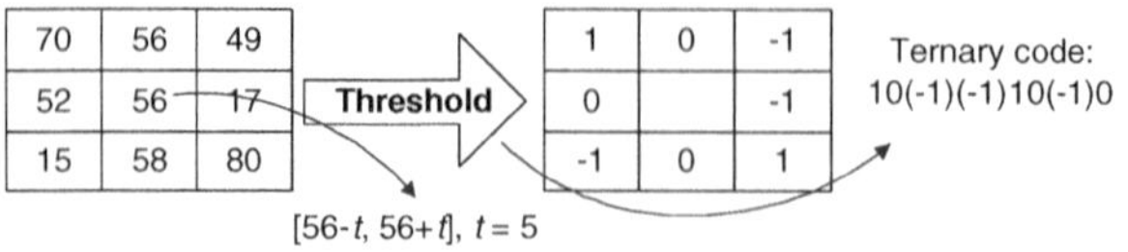

Fig. 2. Linear Ternary Pattern (LTP) encoding process

tends to be sensitive to random and quantization noise. LTP extends LBP from binary (0 and 1) code by providing 3-value code (-1, 0, 1). LTP inherits most of the advantages of LBP such as its invariance against illumination changes and computational efficiency, and adds an improved resistance to noise. Figure 2 shows the LTP encoding process. The measure of the influence of age progression and quality measures on the baseline LTP classifier is based on the 2D Euclidean distance between the template image, created during enrolment, and test image, as used in [14], [25].

3 Aging, Head Pose and Expression Quality Measures

Aging based metadata quality measure of each test image is defined as the time elapsed between enrolment, when a template is created, and use of the test image. The first enrolment image is set to zero in time, and for the other images it is set as the time difference between enrolment and test moments. It should be noted that the absolute age information is not directly used in our experiments [13].

It has been demonstrated in numerous reports that a degradation of biometric data quality is a frequent cause of significant deterioration of classification performance [15]. In this paper, two simple quality measures are used in combination with aging metadata quality measure, one in relation with the head pose (roll angle deviation) and second taking into account other distortions such as expression and general deviation from frontal position.

Head poses are distributed over pitch, yaw, and roll directions [18]. Because it is observed that the variations in the pitch and yaw directions are not obvious, we focus on estimating the roll angle only. The main idea to measure this angle is based on several steps. First, we find the eyes position in the image by using SUSAN-based edge detector [19] and use a subsequent K-means clustering [28], and then calculate the angle between the line connecting two eyes and the horizontal line [23].

In Database 2 images were not collected under controlled recording conditions. Therefore, most of the face images are non-frontal and include variations because of the changing expression. These two types of facial deviations become the main factors that degrade the image quality. In order to measure a quality corresponding to such deviations the Euclidean distance between a test image and the average frontal face (reference image) is defined as the quality measure.

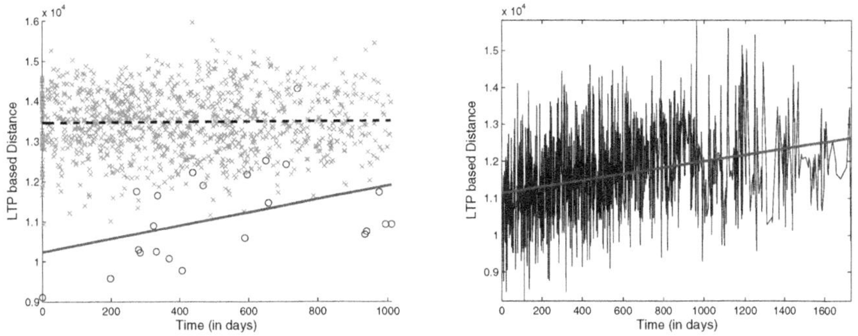

Fig. 3. Tendency of the LTP classifier scores (genuine and impostor distance values) for the first person of Database 2 from Figure 1 (left) and variations of the distance values of the genuine users for all 45 persons of this database (right)

In order to obtain such a reference image, we used one part of Database 1, which contains 14 persons with 10 images for each person. The chosen images are frontal with neutral expression. Then we extracted Principal Component Analysis (PCA) based features from those 140 images and obtained a mean eigenvector. Finally, we reconstructed an average frontal face (reference image) from this mean eigenvector.

4 Influence of Age, Head Pose and Expression on the Baseline Classifier

In order to address the problem of aging influence on the baseline classifier, first we used the face images of 42 persons from Database 1. The first face image of each individual was set as the reference sample and all others were set as test data [26]. The obtained results confirmed that there is evident conditional dependency between age progression and baseline LTP classifier scores given reduced variations due to illumination, pose and expression.

Then we repeated the experiment for Database 2 but we used the first ten images of each person to build the average face reference model. Figure 3 shows the effects of age progression on the LTP classifier scores (genuine and impostor distance values) for the first person of Database 2 from Figure 1 and variations of the distance values of the genuine users for all 45 persons of this database. The obtained tendency for genuine and impostor scores is very similar to that when using Database 1 but including more variations because of less controlled conditions regarding head pose and expression. Generally, as the age increases, the distance values generally increase. However, for the impostors there does not exist such a tendency. In Figure 3 The '○' and '×' marks represent the genuine and impostor scores and the straight lines represent linear fittings for tendencies.

Figure 4 shows the effects of the first quality measure corresponding to head rotation (roll angle) on the LTP distance values (classifier scores) of the genuine

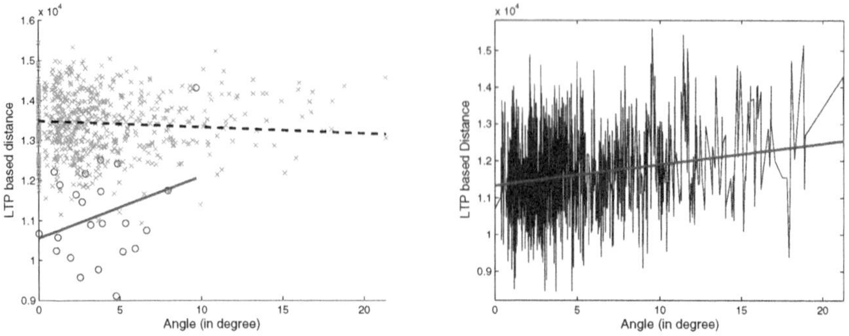

Fig. 4. Tendency of the LTP distance values (classifier scores) of the genuine and the impostor classes for a particular person dependent on head rotation (roll angle) quality measure (left), and the influence of head rotation on the classifier scores of the genuine class over all the 45 persons of Database 2 (right)

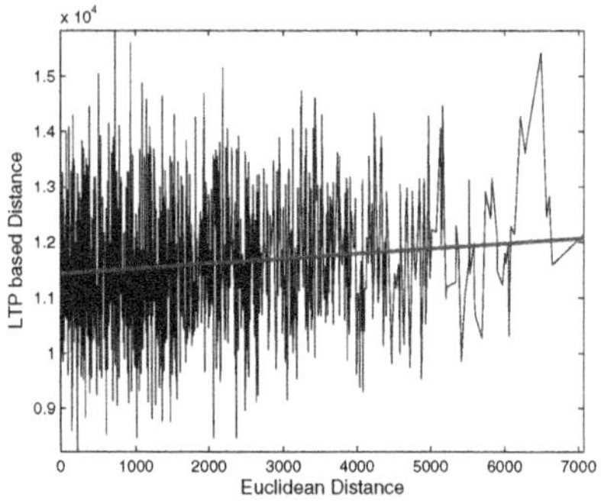

Fig. 5. Tendency of the LTP genuine class scores dependent on the Euclidean distance between a test image and the average frontal face for all 45 persons of Database 2

and the impostor classes for a particular person, as well as the influence of head rotation on the classifier scores of the genuine class over all the 45 persons of Database 2.

From Figure 5, generated for Database 2 as well, we notice that the tendency line of genuine class scores corresponding to the Euclidean distance between a test image and the average frontal face is not flat. This means that if the distance is larger the test face image is of lower quality regarding face expression and its frontal position.

From Figures 3, 4 and 5 we can draw following observations:

- There exists a conditional dependency between the distances calculated by the LTP classifier of the genuine class and the age progression, head rotation and Euclidean distance from the average frontal face. As the age or angle or Euclidean distance increase the LTP classifier distance values (scores)

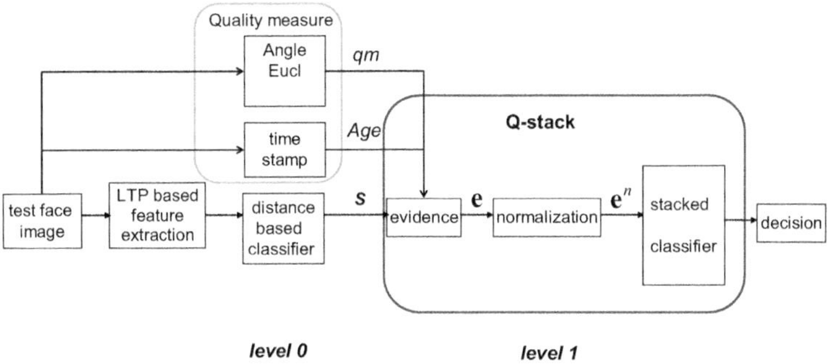

Fig. 6. Diagram of the Q-stack model with distance based baseline classifier

generally increase. For the impostor classes, however, such tendencies do not exist.
- The variances of the genuine and impostor score distributions are different. This, to some degree, reflects the fact that the age progression and quality measures affect differently the genuine and impostor score distributions.
- As shown in Figures 3 and 4, although the genuine and impostor classes are well separated in short term and for higher quality images, there is a clear tendency towards overlapping between these two classes if age progresses and quality of images becomes lower.

5 Q-Stack Aging Model

Q-stack aging model is based on the stacked generalization, in which several *level-0* baseline classifiers are first trained and tested on the original training set. Then the different sets of scores from *level-0* classifiers are combined together with the original class labels to form a training data for the *level-1* classifier. This concept of stacked generalization was employed for the face verification applications [15] by incorporating the quality measures as features into the evidence vector in the *level-1* classifier. In this paper, quality measures (head rotation, angle and Euclidean distance from average frontal face) and age metadata information are used as quality features [13], [14]. Time difference (age progression) has an obvious influence on the face recognition scores as shown in Section 4. This influence translates into a statistical dependence between the baseline classifier scores, quality measures and age information. This dependence is consequently modeled and exploited by the age-dependent decision boundary for improving the performance of a verification system. Similarly head rotation angle also has an influence on the baseline classifier scores. This dependence can be modeled in order to further improve the recognition performance of adult face verification systems.

Figure 6 shows a diagram of the proposed stacking approach for the face verification. Given a test face image, after Local Ternary Pattern (LTP) based feature extraction we obtain a score value S from the LTP classifier. From the

Table 1. Recognition performance in terms of false acceptance rate (FAR), false rejection rate (FRR) and half total error rate (HTER) for MORPH Database 2 using LTP

Evidence **e**	[S]	[S, Age]	[$S, Age, Angle$]	[$S, Age, Angle, Eucl$]
		Baseline		
FAR [%]	2.35			
FRR [%]	34.34			
HTER [%]	18.35			
		SVM-lin		
FAR [%]		1.95	1.59	2.10
FRR [%]		35.99	34.84	32.70
HTER [%]		18.97	18.22	17.41
		SVM-rbf		
FAR [%]		3.59	1.94	2.25
FRR [%]		32.45	34.18	33.60
HTER [%]		18.02	18.06	17.93

estimation of head pose angle ($Angle$) and Euclidean distance from average frontal face ($Eucl$), we have quality measures qm for that image. At the same time, the time stamp (age progression information) of the face is known as Age. The output score values from the distance based classifier is concatenated with the estimated quality measures and aging information to form an evidence vector $\mathbf{e} = [S, Age, qm]$. Then a Z-score normalization [29] is performed on $\mathbf{e}$:

$$\mathbf{e}^n = \frac{\mathbf{e} - \mu_e}{\sigma_e} \tag{1}$$

where μ_e and σ_e are the mean and standard deviation vectors of $\mathbf{e}$ obtained from the training data. Finally the vector $\mathbf{e}^n$ is fed into the stacked classifier (i.e. *level-1* classifier) for the verification.

In this paper, Support Vector Machine (SVM) [30] based classifiers with linear (SVM-lin) and radial basic function (SVM-rbf) kernels are employed as stacked classifiers. SVM belongs to the class of maximum margin based discriminative classifiers. In 3D input space (score, age and quality), it performs pattern recognition between two classes (genuine and impostor) by finding a decision boundary that has maximum distance to the closest points in the training set which are termed as support vectors. In our experiments the optimal parameters of a SVM are found experimentally.

6 Aging Face Verification Experiments

We conducted a series of experiments with various configurations of available evidence. The experiments aimed at showing that Q-stack framework, which combines baseline classifier scores, age information and quality measures simultaneously, gives better classification results than the baseline classifier only or

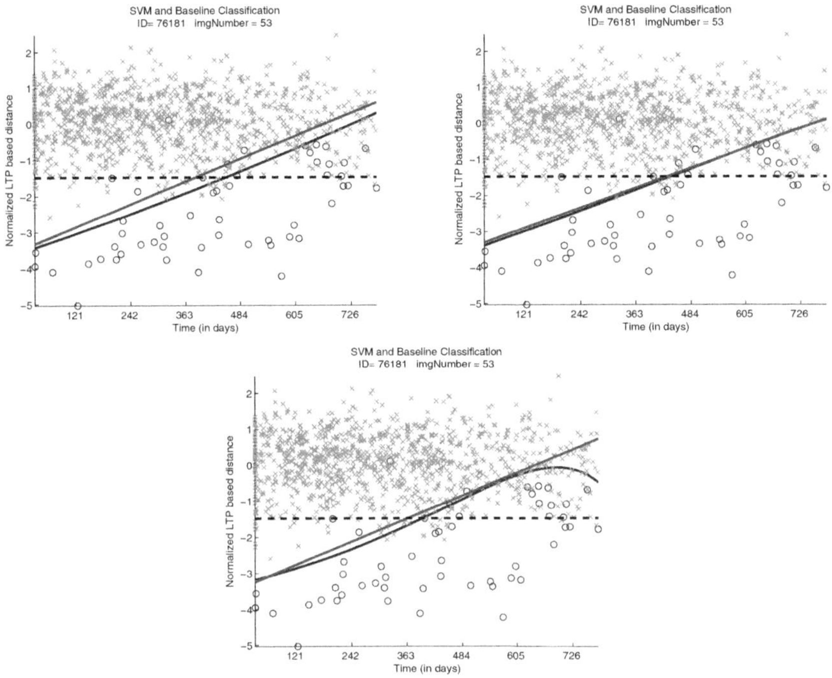

Fig. 7. Class separation in the score-age plane by using user-specific decision boundaries with different combination of quality measures in three classification spaces: 1. $[S, Age]$, 2. $[S, Age, Angle]$, 3. $[S, Age, Angle, Eucl]$, using SVM-lin (red line) and SVM-rbf (blue line)

a combination of baseline classifier scores and age information only. For each person the data from this person are identified as genuine class, and the data from the remaining persons are identified as impostor class. The face verification performance is measured in terms of false acceptance rate (FAR), false rejection rate (FRR) and half total error rate (HTER). We adopt the following user-specific processing for finding the optimal decision boundary. In this approach, the training data are composed of the first 10 images from one particular person. A SVM stacked classifier is trained for each of the persons to yield a decision boundary, which is then applied to the data for that person.

Table 1 summarizes the recognition performance over all the 45 individuals from Database 2. Figure 7 shows an example of class separation in the score-age plane by using user-specific decision boundaries with different combination of quality measures in three classification spaces: 1. $[S, Age]$, 2. $[S, Age, Angle]$, 3. $[S, Age, Angle, Eucl]$. In Figure 7 the baseline classifier decision threshold is represented by a horizontal line (not changing across the age progression), which is user-specific and calculated by minimizing half total error rate (HTER) in the training data.

From Table 1 we can see that SVM-rbf generally performs better than SVM-linear by exploiting the non-linear decision boundaries. Stacking either kind of quality measure (e.g., head pose and distance from average frontal face) into evidence vector yields a decrease of HTER. Combination of age information and quality measures with the baseline classifier scores leads to a further decrease of HTER, which shows the effectiveness of combining quality measures into the Q-stack aging face verification framework.

From Fig. 7 we can see that just after enrollment, the baseline classifier can separate the genuine and impostor scores quite well. However as the time passes the baseline classifier cannot have a good separation performance. This is because the baseline classifier decision threshold is fixed across the time and as the time progresses the baseline classifier decision boundary becomes less effective to separate the genuine and impostor scores, which change their position. By the subsequent training the Q-stack models (SVM-lin and SVM-rbf) using the first 10 images of each person, we incorporate the aging information and other quality measures into the Q-stack model. Since there is a strong conditional dependency between the aging and the baseline classifier scores as shown in Figure 3, the Q-stack decision boundaries (SVM-lin and SVM-rbf) display significant shift-ups as the age increases. Incorporating other quality measures into evidence vector further improves the recognition performance in terms of a decreased HTER. The performance results obtained in this paper for the LTP based classifier, which uses local features, are very similar to the results obtained for the PCA based classifier, using global features, reported in [23].

7 Conclusions

In this paper, we studied the aging influence on the face recognition performance of baseline classifier using Linear Ternary Patterns (LTPs), and then we presented a generalized Q-stack aging model allowing for face verification in the score-age-quality space. Our experiments show that the tendencies of the impostor scores are different from those of genuine ones. As a result, modeling and tracking the genuine scores is of critical importance. The results obtained in this paper show that the proposed user-specific Q-stack aging model is a powerful method of combining the age progression and quality measures with the baseline classifier scores for improved classification. This approach will allow us in the near future for exhaustive experiments on the combination of age with other classifiers and quality measures and their combination to further improve the recognition performance of face verification systems.

References

1. Lanitis, A., Draganova, C., Christodoulou, C.: Comparing Different Classifiers for Automatic Age Estimation. IEEE Trans. Systems, Man, and Cybernetics, Part B 34, 621–628 (2004)

2. Suo, J., Min, F., Zhu, S., Shan, S., Chen, X.: A Multi-Resolution Dynamic Model for Face Aging Simulation. In: IEEE Conference on Computer Vision and Pattern Recognition (CVPR), pp. 1–8. IEEE Computer Society, Minneapolis (2007)
3. Poh, N., Kittler, J., Smith, R., Tena, J.R.: A Method for Estimating Authentication Performance over Time, with Applications to Face Biometrics. In:12th Iberoamerican Congress on Pattern Recognition (CIARP 2007), pp. 360–369. IEEE Press, Valparaiso (2007)
4. Ling, H., Soatto, S., Ramanathan, N., Jacobs, D.: A Study of Face Recognition as People Age. In: IEEE 11th International Conference on Computer Vision (ICCV 2007), pp. 1–8. IEEE Press, Rio de Janeiro (2007)
5. Park, U., Tong, Y., Jain, A.K.: Face Recognition with Temporal Invariance: A 3D Aging Model. In: 8th IEEE International Conference on Automatic Face and Gesture Recognition, pp. 1–7. IEEE Computer Society, Amsterdam (2008)
6. Patterson, E., Sethuram, A., Albert, M., Ricanek, K., King, M.: Aspects of Age Variation in Facial Morphology Affecting Biometrics. In: First IEEE International Conference on Biometrics: Theory, Application and Systems (BTAS 2007), pp. 1–6. IEEE Press, Washington DC (2007)
7. Poh, N., Wong, R., Kittler, J., Roli, F.: Challenges and Research Directions for Adaptive Biometric Recognition Systems. In: Tistarelli, M., Nixon, M.S. (eds.) ICB 2009. LNCS, vol. 5558, pp. 753–764. Springer, Heidelberg (2009)
8. Zhou, Z.-H., Geng, X., Smith-Miles, K.: Automatic Age Estimation Based on Facial Aging Patterns. IEEE Trans. Pattern Analysis and Machine Intelligence 29, 2234–2240 (2007)
9. Ramanathan, N., Chellappa, R.: Modeling Age Progression in Young Faces. In: IEEE Conference on Computer Vision and Pattern Recognition (CVPR), pp. I-387–I-394. IEEE Computer Society, New York (2006)
10. Schroeder, G., Magalhes, L.P., Rodrigues, R.: Facial Aging Using Image Warping. In: 2007 Western New York Image Processing Workshop. IEEE Press, Rochester (2007)
11. Lanitis, A., Taylor, C.J., Cootes, T.F.: Toward Automatic Simulation of Aging Effects on Face Images. IEEE Trans. Pattern Analysis and Machine Intelligence 24, 442–455 (2002)
12. Biswas, S., Aggarwal, G., Chellappa, R.: A Non-generative Approach for Face Recognition Across Aging. In: IEEE Second International Conference on Biometrics: Theory, Application and Systems (BTAS 2008). IEEE Press, Washington DC (2008)
13. Drygajlo, A., Li, W., Zhu, K.: Q-stack Aging Model for Face Verification. In: 17th European Signal Processing Conference (EUSIPCO 2009), pp. 65–69. EURASIP, Glasgow (2009)
14. Drygajlo, A., Li, W., Zhu, K.: Verification of Aging Faces using Local Ternary Patterns and Q-stack Classifier. In: Fierrez, J., Ortega-Garcia, J., Esposito, A., Drygajlo, A., Faundez-Zanuy, M. (eds.) BioID MultiComm2009. LNCS, vol. 5707, pp. 25–32. Springer, Heidelberg (2009)
15. Kryszczuk, K., Drygajlo, A.: Improving Classification with Class-Independent Quality Measures: *Q-stack* in Face Verification. In: Lee, S.-W., Li, S.Z. (eds.) ICB 2007. LNCS, vol. 4642, pp. 1124–1133. Springer, Heidelberg (2007)
16. Ricanek, K., Tesafaye, T.: MORPH: A Longitudinal Image Database of Normal Adult Age-Progression. In: 7th IEEE International Conference on Automatic Face and Gesture Recognition, pp. 341–345. IEEE Computer Society, Southampton (2006)

17. OpenCV, Open source computer vision, `http://opencv.willowgarage.com/`
18. Vatahska, T., Bennewitz, M., Behnke, S.: Feature-Based Head Pose Estimation from Images. In: IEEE-RAS 7th International Conference on Humanoid Robots (Humanoids), pp. 330–335. IEEE Press, Pittsburgh (2007)
19. Tan, X., Chen, S., Zhou, Z.-H., Zhang, F.: SUSAN - A New Approach to Low Level Image Processing. International Journal of Computer Vision 23, 45–78 (1997)
20. Ahonen, T., Hadid, A., Pietikäinen, M.: Face Recognition with Local Binary Patterns. In: Pajdla, T., Matas, J. (eds.) ECCV 2004. LNCS, vol. 3021, pp. 469–481. Springer, Heidelberg (2004)
21. Ojala, T., Pietikainen, M., Harwood, D.: A Comparative Study of Texture Measures with Classification Based on Feature Distributions. Pattern Recognition 29, 51–59 (1996)
22. Tan, X., Triggs, B.: Enhanced Local Texture Feature Sets for Face Recognition under Difficult Lighting Conditions. In: 2007 IEEE International Workshop on Analysis and Modeling of Faces and Gestures (AMFG), pp. 168–182. IEEE Computer Society, Rio de Janeiro (2007)
23. Li, W., Drygajlo, A., Qiu, H.: Combination of Age and Head Pose for Adult Face Verification. In: 9th IEEE Conference on Automatic Face and Gesture Recognition (FG 2011), IEEE Computer Society, Santa Barbara (2011)
24. Li, W., Drygajlo, A.: Multi-Classifier Q-stack Aging Model for Adult Face Verification. In: 20th International Conference on Pattern Recognition (ICPR 2010), pp. 1310–1313. IEEE Computer Society, Istanbul (2010)
25. Li, W., Drygajlo, A.: Global and Local Feature Based Multi-Classifier A-Stack Model for Aging Face Identification. In: IEEE 17th International Conference on Image Processing (ICIP 2010), pp. 3797–3800. IEEE Signal Processing Society, Hong Kong (2010)
26. Li, W., Drygajlo, A., Qiu, H.: Aging Face Verification in Score-Age Space using Single Reference Image Template. In: IEEE Fourth International Conference on Biometrics: Theory, Applications and Systems (BTAS 2010), IEEE Systems, Man and Cybernetics Society, Washington DC (2010)
27. Kryszczuk, K., Drygajlo, A.: Improving Biometric Verification with Class Independent Quality Information. IET Signal Processing 3, 310–321 (2009)
28. Bishop, C.M.: Neural Networks for Pattern Recognition. Oxford University Press, Oxford (1995)
29. Shalabi, A., Shaaban, Z.: Normalization as a Preprocessing Engine for Data Mining and the Approach of Preference Matrix. In: 2006 International Conference on Dependability of Computer Systems, pp. 207–214. IEEE Computer Society, Szklarska Poreba (2006)
30. Cristianini, N., Shawe-Taylor, J.: An Introduction to Support Vector Machines. Cambridge University Press, Cambridge (1999)

Learning Human Identity Using View-Invariant Multi-view Movement Representation

Alexandros Iosifidis, Anastasios Tefas, Nikolaos Nikolaidis, and Ioannis Pitas

Aristotle University of Thessaloniki
Department of Informatics
Box 451, 54124 Thessaloniki, Greece
{aiosif,tefas,nikolaid,pitas}@aiia.csd.auth.gr

Abstract. In this paper a novel view-invariant human identification method is presented. A multi-camera setup is used to capture the human body from different observation angles. Binary body masks from all the cameras are concatenated to produce the so-called multi-view binary masks. These masks are rescaled and vectorized to create feature vectors in the input space. A view-invariant human body representation is obtained by exploiting the circular shift invariance property of the Discrete Fourier Transform (DFT). Fuzzy vector quantization (FVQ) is performed to associate human body representation with movement representations and linear discriminant analysis (LDA) is used to map movements in a low dimensionality discriminant feature space. Two human identification schemes, a movement-specific and a movement-independent one, are evaluated. Experimental results show that the method can achieve very satisfactory identification rates. Furthermore, the use of more than one movement types increases the identification rates.

Keywords: View-invariant Human Identification, Fuzzy Vector Quantization, Linear Discriminant Analysis.

1 Introduction

Human identification from video streams is an important task in a wide range of applications. The majority of methods proposed in the literature approach this issue using face recognition techniques [6], [11], [1], [12], [8]. This is a reasonalbe approach, as it is assumed that human facial features do not change in significantly small time periods. One disadvantage of this approach is the sensitivity to the deliberate distortion of facial features, for example by using a mask. Another approach, for the human identification task is the use of human motion information [9], [7], [5]. That is, the identity (ID) of a human can be discovered by learning his/her style in performing specific movements. Most of the methods that identify human's ID using motion characteristics exploit the information captured by a single-static camera. Most of these methods assume the same viewing angle in training and recognition phases which is obviously a significant constraint.

C. Vielhauer et al. (Eds.): BioID 2011, LNCS 6583, pp. 217–226, 2011.

In this paper we exploit the information provided by a multi-camera setup in order to perform view-invariant human identification exploiting movement style information. We use different movement types in order to exploit the discrimination capability of different movement patterns. A movement-independent and a movement-specific human identification scheme are assessed, while a simple procedure that combines identification results provided by these schemes for different movement types is used in order to increase the identification rates.

The remainder of this paper is organized as follow. In Section 2, we present the two human identification schemes proposed in this work. In Section 3, we present experiments conducted in order to evaluate the proposed method. Finally, conclusions are drawn in Section 4.

2 Proposed Method

The proposed method is based on a movement recognition method that we presented in [4]. This method has been extended in order to perform human identification. Movements are described by a number of consecutive human body postures, i.e., binary masks that depict the body in white and the background in black. A converging multi-camera setup is exploited in order to capture the human body from various viewing angles. By combining the single-view postures properly a view-invariant human posture representation is achieved. This leads to a view invariant movement recognition and human identification method. By taking into account more than one movement types we can increase the identification rates, as is shown in Subsection 3.3. In the remaining of this paper the term movement will denote an elementary movement. That is, a movement will correspond to one period of a simple action, e.g., a step within a walking sequence. The term movement video will correspond to a video segment that depicts a movement, while the term multi-view movement video will correspond to a movement video captured by multiple cameras.

2.1 Preprocessing

Movements are described by consecutive human body postures captured by various viewing angles. Each of the N_{t_m}, $m = 1, ..., M$ (M being the number of movement classes) single-view binary masks comprising a movement video, is centered to the human body center of mass. Image regions, of size equal to the maximum bounding box that encloses the human body in the movement video, are extracted and rescaled to a fixed size ($N_x \times N_y$) images, which are subsequently vectorized column-wise in order to produce single-view posture vectors $\mathbf{p}_{jc} \in \mathcal{R}^{N_p}$, $N_p = N_x \times N_y$, where j is the posture vector's index, $j = 1, ..., N_{t_m}$ and c is the index of the camera it is captured from $c = 1, ..., C$. Five single-view posture frames are illustrated in Figure 1.

2.2 Training Phase

Let $\mathcal{U}$ be an annotated movement video database, containing N_T C-view training movement videos of M movement classes performed by H humans. Each

Fig. 1. Five single-view posture frames

multi-view movement video is described by its $C \times N_{t_m}$ single-view posture vectors $\mathbf{p}_{ijc}, i = 1, ..., N_T, j = 1, ..., N_{t_m}, c = 1, ..., C$. Single-view posture vectors that depict the same movement instance from different viewing angles are manually concatenated in order to produce multi-view posture vectors, $\mathbf{p}_{ij} \in \mathcal{R}^{N_P}$, $N_P = N_x \times N_y \times C, i = 1, ..., N_T, j = 1, ..., N_{t_m}$. A multi-view posture frame is shown in Figure 2.

Fig. 2. One eight-view posture frame from a walking sequence

To obtain a view-invariant posture representation the following observation is used: all the C possible camera configurations can be obtained by applying a block circular shifting procedure on the multi-view posture vectors. This is because each such vector consists of blocks, each block corresponding to a single-view posture vector. A convenient, view-invariant, posture representation is the multi-view DFT posture representation. This is because the magnitudes of the DFT coefficients are invariant to block circular shifting. To obtain such a representation, each multi-view posture vector $\mathbf{p}_{ij}$ is mapped to a vector $\mathbf{P}_{ij}$ that contains the magnitudes of its DFT coefficients.

$$P_{ij}(k) = \left| \sum_{n=0}^{N_P - 1} p(n) e^{-i \frac{2\pi k}{N_P} n} \right|, \quad k = 1, ..., N_P - 1. \tag{1}$$

Multi-view posture prototypes $\mathbf{v}_d \in \mathcal{R}^{N_P}, d = 1, ..., N_D$, called dynemes, are calculated using a K-Means clustering algorithm [10] without using the labeling information available in the training phase. Fuzzy distances from all the multi-view posture vectors $\mathbf{P}_{ij}$ to all the dynemes $\mathbf{v}_d$ are calculated and the membership vectors $\mathbf{u}_{ij} \in \mathcal{R}^{N_D}$, $i = 1, ..., N_T$, $j = 1, ..., N_{t_m}$, $d = 1, ..., N_D$, are obtained:

$$\mathbf{u}_{ij} = \frac{(\| \mathbf{P}_{ij} - \mathbf{v}_d \|_2)^{-\frac{2}{m-1}}}{\sum_{d=1}^{N_D} (\| \mathbf{P}_{ij} - \mathbf{v}_d \|_2)^{-\frac{2}{m-1}}}. \tag{2}$$

where $m > 1$ is the fuzzification parameter and is set equal to 1.1 in all the experiments presented in this paper.

The mean membership vector $\mathbf{s}_i = \frac{1}{N_{t_m}} \sum_{i=1}^{N_{t_m}} \mathbf{u}_{ij}$, $\mathbf{s}_i \in \mathcal{R}^{N_D}, i = 1, ..., N_T$, is used to represent the movement video in the dyneme space and is noted as movement vector. Using the known labeling information of the training movement vectors LDA [2] is used to map the movement vectors in an optimal discriminant subspace by calculating an appropriate projection matrix $\mathbf{W}$. Discriminant movement vectors, $\mathbf{z}_i \in \mathcal{R}^{M-1}$, $i = 1, ..., N_T$, are obtained by:

$$\mathbf{z}_i = \mathbf{W}^T \mathbf{s}_i. \tag{3}$$

2.3 Classification Phase

In the classification phase single-view posture vectors consisting single-view movement videos are arranged using the camera labeling information and the multi-view posture $\mathbf{p}_j$ vector is mapped to its DFT equivalent $\mathbf{P}_j$, as in the training phase. Membership vectors $\mathbf{u}_j \in \mathcal{R}^{N_D}, j = 1, ..., N_{t_m}$ are calculated and the mean vector $\mathbf{s} \in \mathcal{R}^{N_D}$ represents this multi-view movement video in the dyneme space. The discriminant movement vector $\mathbf{z} \in \mathcal{R}^{M-1}$ is obtained by mapping $\mathbf{s}$ in the LDA space. In that space, the multi-view movement video is classified to the nearest class centroid.

2.4 Human Identification

As previously mentioned, the movement videos of the database $\mathcal{U}$ are labeled with movement class and human identity information. Thus, a classification scheme can be trained and subsequently used in order to provide the ID of a human depicted in an unlabeled movement video that depicts one of the H known humans in the database performing one of the M known movements.

In this paper we examine two classification procedures in order to achieve this. In the first one, we apply the procedure described above using one classification step. That is, the labeling information exploited by the classification procedure is that of the humans' IDs. Each multi-view movement video in the training database is annotated by the ID of the depicted human. Using this approach a movement-independent human identification scheme is devised. A block diagram of the classification procedure applied in this case is shown in Figure 3.

The second procedure consists of two classification phases. In the first phase, the multi-view movement video is classified to one of the M known movement classes. The movement classifier utilized in this phase is trained using the movement class labels that accompany the videos. Subsequently, the use of a movement-specific human identification classifier provides the ID of the depicted human. More specifically M human identification classifiers are used in this phase. Each of them is trained to identify humans using videos of a specific movement class. Human ID labels are used for the training of these classifiers. A block diagram of the classification procedure applied in this case is shown in Figure 4.

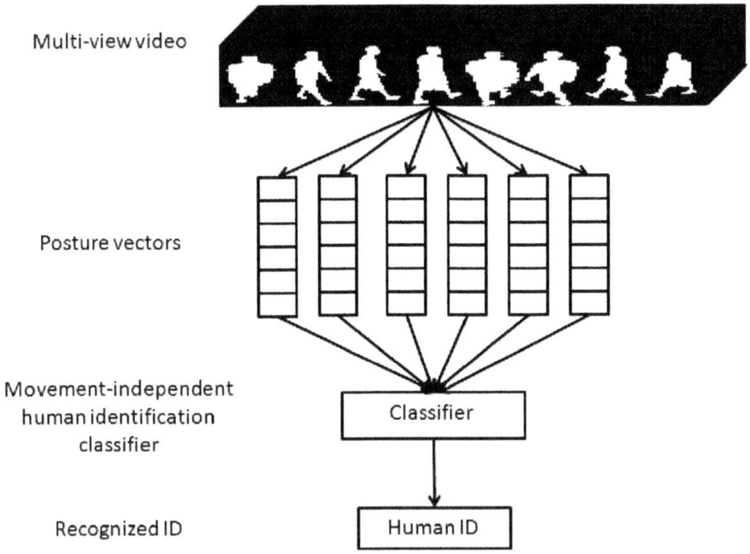

Fig. 3. Movement-independent human identification procedure

2.5 Fusion

Video segments that depict single movement periods are rare. In most real-world videos a human performs more than one movement periods of the same or different movement types. In the case where a movement video depicts N_s movement periods, of probably different movement classes, the procedures described above will provide N_s identification results. By combining these results, the human ID correct identification rates increase. A simple majority voting procedure can be used for this procedure. That is the ID of the human depicted in a video segment is set to that of the mostly recognized human.

3 Experimental Results

In this section we present experimental results in the i3DPost multi-view video database described in [3]. This database contains high definition image sequences depicting eight humans, six males and two females, performing eight movements, walk, run, jump in place, jump forward, bend, sit, fall and wave one hand. Eight cameras were equally spaced in a ring of 8m diameter at a height of 2m above the studio floor. The studio background was uniform. Single-view binary masks were obtained by discarding the background color in the HSV color space. Movements that contain more than one periods were used in the following experiments. That is movements walk (wk), run (rn), jump in place (jp), jump forward (jf) and wave one hand (wo) were used, while movements bend (bd), sit (st) and fall (fl) were not used as each human performs the movement once For each movement class

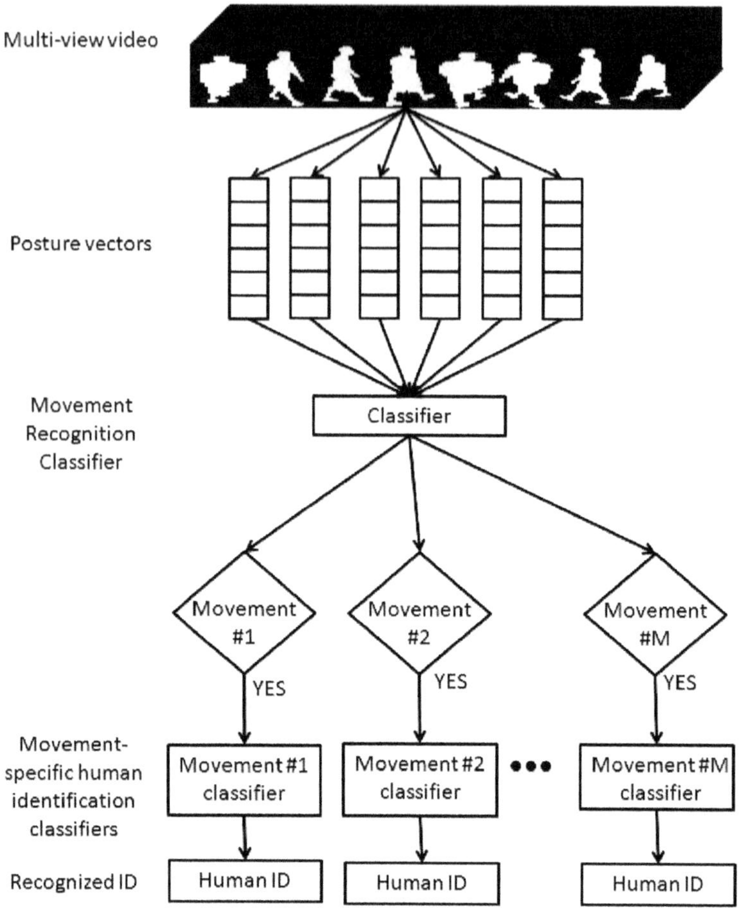

Fig. 4. Movement-specific human identification procedure

four movement videos were used in order to perform a four-fold cross-validation procedure in all the experiments presented.

3.1 Movement-Independent Human Identification

In this experiment we applied the procedure illustrated in Figure 3. In this case the multi-view training movement videos were labeled with human ID information. At every step 40 multi-view movement videos, one of each movement class (5 classes) depicting each human (8 humans), were use for testing and the remaining 120 multi-view movement videos were used for training. This procedure was applied four times, one for each movement video set. A 82.5% identification rate was obtained using 70 dynemes. The corresponding confusion matrix is presented in Table 1. As it can be seen, some of the humans are confused with others.

Table 1. Confusion matrix containing identification rates in the movement-independent case on the I3DPost database

	chr	hai	han	jea	joe	joh	nat	nik
chr	0.95			0.05				
hai		0.85		0.05	0.05		0.05	
han	0.1		0.5		0.15	0.05	0.15	0.05
jea	0.05			0.9	0.05			
joe					1			
joh					0.05	0.85	0.05	0.05
nat	0.1	0.05			0.1	0.05	0.65	0.05
nik		0.1						0.9

3.2 Movement-Specific Human Identification

In order to assess the discrimination ability of each movement type in the human identification task we applied five human identification procedures, each corresponding to one of the movement type. For example, in the case of movement walk, three multi-view movement videos depicting each of the eight humans walking were used for training and the fourth multi-view movement video depicting him/her walking was used for testing. This procedure was applied four times, one for each movement video. Identification rates provided for each of the movement types are illustrated in Table 2. As it can be seen, all the movement types provide high identification rates. Thus, such an approach can be used in order to obtain the identity of different humans in an efficient way.

Table 2. Identification rates of different movement classes

Movement	Dynemes	Identification Rate
wk	14	0.90
rn	29	0.90
jp	18	1
jf	21	0.93
wo	17	0.96

In a second experiment, we applied the procedure illustrated in Figure 4. That is, the multi-view movement videos were firstly classified to one of the M movement classes and were subsequently fed to the corresponding movement-specific classifier provided that the human's ID. An identification rate equal to 94.37% was achieved. The optimal number of dynemes, for the movement recognition classifier was equal to 25. The optimal number of dynemes for the movement-specific classifiers were 14, 29, 18, 21 and 17 for movements wk, rn, jp, jf and wo, respectively. Table 3 illustrates the confusion matrix of the optimal case. As it can be seen, most of the multi-view videos were assigned correctly to the person they depicted. Thus, the movement-specific human identification approach is more effective than the movement-independent approach.

Table 3. Confusion matrix containing identification rates in the movement-specific case on the I3DPost database

	chr	hai	han	jea	joe	joh	nat	nik
chr	1							
hai		0.9			0.05		0.05	
han			0.85				0.05	0.1
jea				1				
joe					1			
joh						0.95	0.05	
nat	0.05						0.95	
nik	0.05					0.05		0.9

Table 4. Confusion matrix containing identification rates in the movement-independent case on the I3DPost database using a majority voting procedure

	chr	hai	han	jea	joe	joh	nat	nik
chr	1							
hai		0.75		0.25				
han			0.75		0.25			
jea				1				
joe					1			
joh						1		
nat	0.25						0.75	
nik								1

Table 5. Confusion matrix containing identification rates in the movement-specific case on the I3DPost database using a majority voting procedure

	chr	hai	han	jea	joe	joh	nat	nik
chr	1							
hai		1						
han			0.75					0.25
jea				1				
joe					1			
joh						1		
nat							1	
nik								1

3.3 Combining IDs of Different Movement Types

In this experiment we combined the identification results provided the movement-independent and the movement-specific classification schemes (Figures 3 and 4). At every step 40 multi-view movement videos, each depicting one human performing one movement, were used for testing and the remaining 120 multi-view movement videos were used for training. In the movement-independent identification procedure, training multi-view movement videos were labeled with the human ID information, while in the movement-specific identification procedure the training multi-view movement videos were labeled with the movement and the human ID information. At every fold of the cross-validation procedure, the test multi-view movement videos of each humans of the database were fed to the classifier and a majority voting procedure was applied to the identification results in order to provide the final ID. Using this procedure identification rates equal to 90.62% and 96.87% were achieved for the movement-independent and movement-specific classification procedures, respectively. Tables 4 and 5 illustrate the confusion matrices of these experiments. As can be seen, a simple majority voting procedure increases the identification rates. This approach can be applied to real videos, where more than one action periods are performed.

4 Conclusion

In this paper we presented a view-invariant human identification method that exploits information captured by a multi-camera setup. A view-invariant human body representation is achieved by concatenating the single-view postures and computing the DFT equivalent posture representation. FVQ and LDA provides a generic classifier which is subsequently used in a movement-independent and a movement-specific human identification scheme. The movement-specific case seem to outperform the movement-independent one. The combination of identification results provided for different movement types increases the identification rates in both cases.

Acknowledgment

The research leading to these results has received funding from the European Community's Seventh Framework Programme (FP7/2007-2013) under grant agreement n° 211471 (i3DPost) and COST Action 2101 on Biometrics for Identity Documents and Smart Cards.

References

1. Ahonen, T., Hadid, A., et al.: Face description with local binary patterns: Application to face recognition. IEEE Transactions on Pattern Analysis and Machine Intelligence pp. 2037–2041 (2006)
2. Duda, R., Hart, P., Stork, D.: Pattern Classification, 2nd edn. Wiley-Interscience, Hoboken (2000)
3. Gkalelis, N., Kim, H., Hilton, A., Nikolaidis, N., Pitas, I.: The i3dpost multi-view and 3d human action/interaction database. In: 6th Conference on Visual Media Production, pp. 159–168 (November 2009)
4. Gkalelis, N., Nikolaidis, N., Pitas, I.: View indepedent human movement recognition from multi-view video exploiting a circular invariant posture representation. In: IEEE International Conference on Multimedia and Expo, ICME 2009, pp. 394–397. IEEE, Los Alamitos (2009)

5. Gkalelis, N., Tefas, A., Pitas, I.: Human identification from human movements. In: 2009 16th IEEE International Conference on Image Processing (ICIP), pp. 2585–2588. IEEE, Los Alamitos (2010)
6. He, X., Yan, S., Hu, Y., Niyogi, P., Zhang, H.: Face recognition using laplacianfaces. IEEE Transactions on Pattern Analysis and Machine Intelligence, 328–340 (2005)
7. Sarkar, S., Phillips, P., Liu, Z., Vega, I., Grother, P., Bowyer, K.: The humanid gait challenge problem: Data sets, performance, and analysis. IEEE Transactions on Pattern Analysis and Machine Intelligence, 162–177 (2005)
8. Turk, M., Pentland, A.: Face recognition using eigenfaces. In: IEEE Computer Society Conference on Computer Vision and Pattern Recognition, Proceedings CVPR 1991, pp. 586–591. IEEE, Los Alamitos (2002)
9. Wang, L., Tan, T., Ning, H., Hu, W.: Silhouette analysis-based gait recognition for human identification. IEEE Transactions on Pattern Analysis and Machine Intelligence 25(12), 1505–1518 (2003)
10. Webb, A.: Statistical pattern recognition. Hodder Arnold Publication (1999)
11. Wiskott, L., Fellous, J., Kuiger, N., Von der Malsburg, C.: Face recognition by elastic bunch graph matching. IEEE Transactions on Pattern Analysis and Machine Intelligence 19(7), 775–779 (2002)
12. Zhao, W., Chellappa, R., Phillips, P., Rosenfeld, A.: Face recognition: A literature survey. Acm Computing Surveys (CSUR) 35(4), 399–458 (2003)

On Combining Selective Best Bits of Iris-Codes*

Christian Rathgeb, Andreas Uhl, and Peter Wild

Department of Computer Sciences,
University of Salzburg, A-5020 Salzburg, Austria
{crathgeb,uhl,pwild}@cosy.sbg.ac.at

Abstract. This paper describes a generic fusion technique for iris recognition at bit-level we refer to as Selective Bits Fusion. Instead of storing multiple biometric templates for each algorithm, the proposed approach extracts most discriminative bits from multiple algorithms into a new template being even smaller than templates for individual algorithms. Experiments for three individual iris recognition algorithms on the open CASIA-V3-Interval iris database illustrate the ability of this technique to improve accuracy and processing time simultaneously. In all tested configurations Selective Bits Fusion turned out to be more accurate than fusion using the Sum Rule while being about twice as fast. The design of the new template allows explicit control of processing time requirements and introduces a tradeoff between time and accuracy of biometric fusion, which is highlighted in this work.

1 Introduction

The demand for secure access control has caused a widespread use of biometrics. Iris recognition [1] has emerged as one of the most reliable biometric technologies. Pioneered by the work of Daugman [2] generic iris recognition involves the extraction of binary iris-codes out of unwrapped iris textures. Similarity between iris-codes is estimated by calculating the Hamming distance. Numerous different iris recognition algorithms have been proposed, see [1] for an overview. While a combination of different biometric traits leads to generally higher accuracy (e.g., combining face and iris [16] or iris and fingerprints [6]), solutions typically require additional sensors leading to lower throughput and higher setup cost. Single-sensor biometric fusion, comparing multiple representations of a single biometric, does not significantly raise cost and has been shown to be still capable of improving recognition accuracy [11]. In both scenarios however, generic fusion strategies at score level [7] require the storage of several biometric templates per user according to the number of combined algorithms [13]. Iris recognition has been proven to provide reliable authentication on large-scale databases [3]. Particularly because it is employed in such scenarios, fusion of iris recognition algorithms may cause a drastic increase of both, required amount of storage and comparison time (which itself depends on the number of bits to be compared).

* This work has been supported by the Austrian Science Fund, project no. L554-N15 and FIT-IT Trust in IT-Systems, project no. 819382.

C. Vielhauer et al. (Eds.): BioID 2011, LNCS 6583, pp. 227–237, 2011.

The human iris has been combined with different biometric modalities, however due to reasons outlined before, we concentrate on single-sensor iris biometric fusion in this work. While the combination of iris and face data is a prospective application, see [18], still the successful extraction of high-quality iris images from surveillance data in less constrained environments is a challenging issue. In case of combining multiple iris algorithms operating on the same input instance, a couple of approaches have been published. Sun *et al.* [14] cascade two feature types employing global features in addition to a Daugman-like approach only if the result of the latter is in a questionable range. Zhang *et al.* [17] apply a similar strategy interchanging the role of global and local features. Vatsa *et al.* [15] compute the Euler number of connected components as global feature, while again using an iris-code as local texture feature. Park and Lee [11] decompose the iris data with a directional filterbank and extract two different feature types from this domain. Combining both results leads to an improvement compared to the single technique. All these techniques have in common, that they aim at gaining recognition performance in biometric fusion scenarios at the cost of larger templates or more time-consuming comparison. In contrast, the following approaches try to improve both, resource requirements (storage and/or time) and fusion recognition accuracy. Konrad *et al.* [9] combine a rotation invariant pre-selection algorithm and a traditional rotation compensating iris-code. The authors report improvements in recognition accuracy as well as computational effort. In previous work [12], we have recently presented an incremental approach to iris recognition using early rejection of unlikely matches during comparison to incrementally determine best-matching candidates in identification mode operating on reordered iris templates according to bit reliability (see [5]) of a single algorithm. Following a similar idea, Gentile et al. [4] suggested a two-stage iris recognition system, where so-called short length iris-codes (SLICs) preestimate a shortlist of candidates which are further processed. While SLICs exhibit only 8% of the original size of iris-codes the reduction of bits was limiting the true positive rate to about 93% for the overall system.

In this work we propose a fusion strategy for iris recognition algorithms, which combines the most reliable parts of different iris biometric templates in a common template. While most fusion techniques aiming to provide improvements in comparison time and accuracy operate in identification mode (e.g., [12] or [4]), our technique achieves these benefits in verification mode. In contrast to [12] our approach yields a constant number of bit tests per comparison and may more easily be integrated into existing solutions, since modules for comparison do not have to be changed. However, we adopt the analysis of bit-error occurrences in [12] for a training set of iris-codes. Thereby we can estimate a global ranking of bit positions for each applied algorithm following the observation by Hollingsworth et al. [5], that distinct parts of iris biometric templates (bits in iris-codes) exhibit more discriminative information than others. They found, that regions very close to the pupil and sclera contribute least to discrimination, i.e. the middle bands of the iris contain the most reliable information, and that masking fragile bits at the time of comparison increases accuracy. Based on obtained rankings we rearrange enrollment samples and merge them by discarding least reliable bits of extracted iris-codes. Furthermore, by introducing a ranking of bits, we can avoid keeping track of iris masks, since masked bits in typically distorted regions are most likely to be excluded from comparison by our technique. In experimental studies, we elaborate trade-offs between the accuracy and required storage by combining different iris recognition algorithms. Obtained results illustrate the worthiness of the proposed approach.

The remainder of this work is organized as follows: Section 2 introduces the architecture of the proposed system and presents necessary components for Selective Bits Fusion. Section 3 gives an overview of the experimental setup, outlines results and discusses observations. Finally, Section 4 concludes this paper.

2 Selective Bits Fusion

Selective Bits Fusion is a generic fusion technique and integrates in iris recognition systems as illustrated in Figs. 1 and 2. The following modules are involved:

- **Training Stage and Enrollment:** A training stage estimates a global ranking of bit positions, based on which given templates are rearranged.
- **Template Fusion Process:** The proposed fusion process simply extracts the most reliable parts of iris-codes from different feature extraction algorithms and concatenates relevant information, while discarding the least consistent bits.
- **Verification:** At the time of verification Selective Bits Fusion is performed at several shifting positions prior to comparison.

2.1 Training Stage and Enrollment

Following the idea in [12], we compute a global reliability mask R based on bit reliability [5] in the training stage for each feature extraction method. By assessing inter-class and intra-class comparisons, we calculate the probability of a bit-pair (for a given position) being either 0-0 or 1-1 denoted by $P_{Intra}(i)$ and $P_{Inter}(i)$ for each bit position i. The reliability at each bit position defined as $R(i) = P_{Intra}(i) + (1 - P_{Inter}(i))/2$ now reflects the stability of a bit with respect to genuine and imposter comparisons for a given algorithm. However, in order to account for inaccurate alignment, iris codes are shifted (with a maximum offset of 8) prior to evaluating $P_{Intra}(i)$ and $P_{Inter}(i)$. Reliability measures of all bit positions over all pairings define a global (user-independent) reliability distribution per algorithm, which is used to rearrange given iris-codes. Based on the reliability mask an ideal permutation of bit positions is derived for each feature extraction method and applied to reorder given samples such that the first bits represent the most reliable ones and the last bits represent the least reliable ones, respectively. At the time of enrollment preprocessing and feature extraction methods are applied to a given sample image. Subsequently, permutations derived from the previously calculated reliability masks are used to reorder iris-codes.

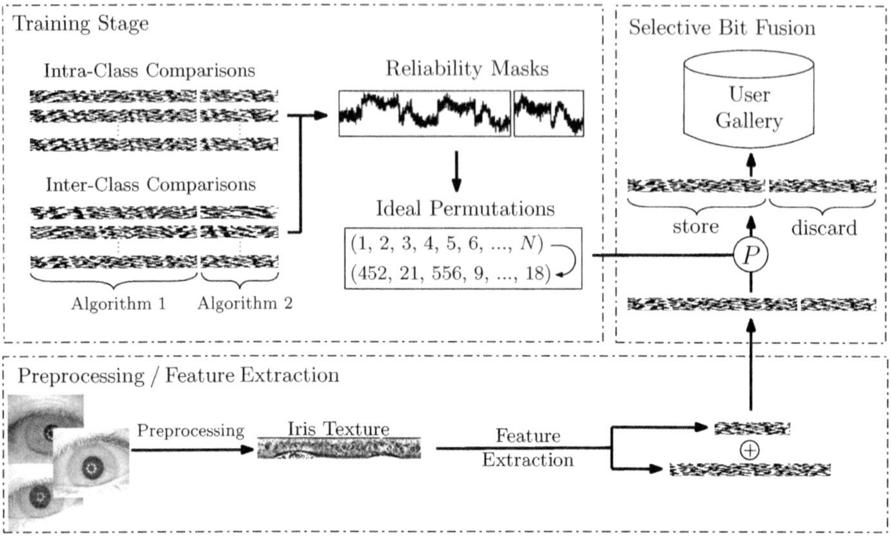

Fig. 1. Training stage and enrollment procedure of the proposed system

2.2 Template Fusion Process

The key idea of Selective Bits Fusion is to concatenate and store the most important bits only. Furthermore, since bits in typically distorted regions (close to eyelids or eyelashes) are moved backwards in the iris-code, this approach makes a storage of noise masks obsolete, i.e. their effect is less pronounced because the least reliable bits are discarded. The result of the fusion process is a new biometric template composed of the most reliable bits produced by diverse feature extraction algorithms. Focusing on recognition performance, a meaningful composition of reliable bits has to be established. In experiments this issue is discussed in more detail. Furthermore, we will show that resulting templates are at most as long as the average code size generated by the applied algorithms while recognition accuracy of traditional biometric fusion techniques is maintained or even increased.

2.3 Verification

In order to recognize subjects who have been registered with the system, in a first step feature extraction is executed for each algorithm in the combined template. Instead of comparing templates of all algorithms individually, Selective Bits Fusion combines iris-codes of different feature extraction techniques based on the global ranking of bit reliability calculated in the training stage. However, since bits are reordered, local neighborhoods of bits are obscured resulting in a loss of the property tolerating angular displacement by simple circular shifts. Instead, in order to achieve template alignment, we suggest to apply feature

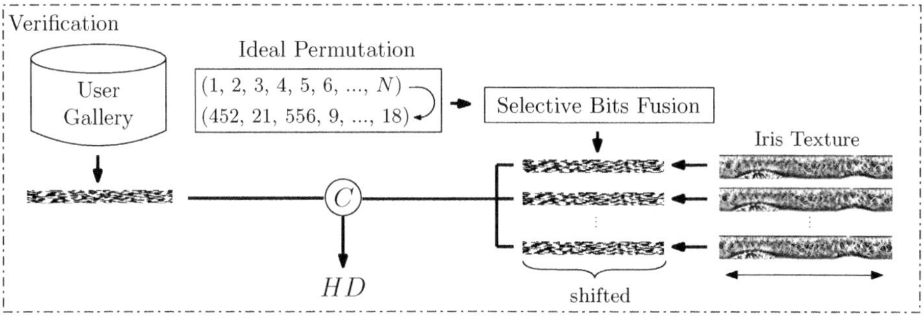

Fig. 2. Verification procedure of the proposed system

extraction methods at different shifting positions of the extracted iris texture. Subsequently, all reordered iris-codes are compared with the stored template. The minimal Hamming distance which corresponds to an optimal alignment of iris textures is returned as final comparison score (note that without loss of generality there is one optimal alignment which exhibits the best comparison scores for all feature extraction algorithms). The verification process is illustrated in Fig. 2.

3 Experimental Studies

For evaluation purposes of the proposed fusion algorithms, we employ the CASIA-V3-Interval[1] iris database. This set comprises 2639 good quality NIR illuminated indoor images of 320×280 pixel resolution from 396 different classes (eyes). Some typical input images and a resulting iris texture are given as part of the system architecture in Fig. 1. For experimental studies we evaluate all left-eye images (1332 instances) only, since the distribution of reliable bits within iris-codes will be highly influenced by natural distortions like eyelids or eyelashes and thus global reliability masks are expected to vary between left and right eyes. For training purposes of reliability masks, images of the first 20 classes are used for parameter estimation purposes.

3.1 Basic System

Selective Bits Fusion may be applied to any iris-code based biometric verification system. The tested basic system comprises the following preprocessing and feature extraction steps: At preprocessing, the pupil and the iris of an acquired image are detected by applying Canny edge detection and Hough circle detection. Once the inner and outer boundaries of the iris have been detected, the area between them is transformed to a normalized rectangular texture of

[1] The Center of Biometrics and Security Research, CASIA Iris Image Database, `http://www.sinobiometrics.com`

512×64 pixel, according to the "rubbersheet" approach by Daugman. Finally, a blockwise brightness estimation is applied to obtain a normalized illumination across the texture.

In the feature extraction stage, we employ custom implementations of three different algorithms, which extract binary iris-codes. The first one resembles Daugman's feature extraction method and follows an implementation by Masek[2] using Log-Gabor filters on rows of the iris texture (as opposed to the 2D filters used by Daugman). Within this approach the texture is divided into stripes to obtain 10 one-dimensional signals, each one averaged from the pixels of 5 adjacent rows (the upper 512×50 are analyzed). Here, a row-wise convolution with a complex Log-Gabor filter is performed on the texture pixels. The phase angle of the resulting complex value for each pixel is discretized into 2 bits. Again, row-averaging is applied to obtain 10 signals of length 512, where 2 bits of phase information are used to generate a binary code, consisting of $512 \times 20 = 10240$ bits.

The second feature to be computed is an iris-code version by Ma *et al.* [10] extracting 10 one-dimensional horizontal signals averaged from pixels of 5 adjacent rows of the upper 50 pixel rows. Each of the 10 signals is analyzed using dyadic wavelet transform, and from a total of 20 subbands (2 fixed bands per signal), local minima and maxima above a threshold define alternation points where the bitcode changes between successions of 0 and 1 bits. Finally, all 1024 bits per signal are concatenated yielding a total number of $1024 \times 10 = 10240$ bits.

The third algorithm has been proposed by Ko *et al.* [8]. Here feature extraction is performed by applying cumulative-sum-based change analysis. It is suggested to discard parts of the iris texture, from the right side [45° to 315°] and the left side [135° to 225°], since the top and bottom of the iris are often hidden by eyelashes or eyelids. Subsequently, the resulting texture is divided into basic cell regions (these cell regions are of size 8×3 pixels). For each basic cell region an average gray scale value is calculated. Then basic cell regions are grouped horizontally and vertically. It is recommended that one group should consist of five basic cell regions. Finally, cumulative sums over each group are calculated to generate an iris-code. If cumulative sums are on an upward slope or on a downward slope these are encoded with 1s and 2s, respectively, otherwise 0s are assigned to the code. In order to obtain a binary feature vector we rearrange the resulting iris-code such that the first half contains all upward slopes and the second half contains all downward slopes. With respect to the above settings the final iris-code consits of 2400 bits.

It is important to mention that the algorithms by Ma *et al.* and Masek are fundamentally different to the iris-code version by Ko *et al.* as they process texture regions of different size, extract different features and produce iris-codes of different length. Therefore, we paired up each of the two algorithms with the latter one.

---

[2] L. Masek: Recognition of Human Iris Patterns for Biometric Identification, Master's thesis, University of Western Australia, 2003.

3.2 Reliability Concentration in Early Bits

In order to be able to identify reliable bits, we assessed for each algorithm and for each bit position the probability of a bit switch. For this parameter estimation we used the inter- and intra-class comparisons of the training set. Results in form of reliability measures for each bit induced a permutation for each algorithm with the goal of moving reliable bits to the front of the iris-code while more unstable bits should be moved to the end of the iris-code. This approach is more generic than area-based exclusion of typically distorted regions as executed by many feature extraction algorithms including the applied version by Masek (e.g. by ignoring outer iris bands or sectors containing eyelids). The ability to concentrate reliable information in early bits on unseen data has been assessed for each of the applied algorithms and is illustrated in Figs. 3, 4 and 5. We found, that EER performance of Ma and Masek already tendencially increases in the original (unsorted) iris-code. This behaviour is not too surprising, since early iris-code bits correspond to the inner iris texture bands, which typically contain rich and discriminative information. However, it is clearly visible, that the second 1024-Bits block exhibits a better (lower) EER than the first block, which can be explained by segmentation inaccuracies due to varying pupil dilation. EERs for different 480-Bits blocks in the Ko algorithm do not seem to follow a specific pattern (due to the code layout grouping upward and downward slopes). As a first major result of experiments, we could verify the ability of reliability masks to really identify most reliable bits. While for Masek and Ma (see Figs. 3, 4) EERs stay low at approximately 2% for two thirds of the total number of blocks and then increase quickly, Ko's EERs (see Fig. 5) increased almost linearly for the new block order.

3.3 Selection of Bits

We use reliability masks to restrict the size of the combined template. By rejecting unstable bits we can (1) avoid degradation of results (see Figs. 6, 7 and 8) (2) accelerate comparison time and (3) reduce storage requirements. But how many bits should be used for the combination and which mixing proportion should be employed for the combined features? At this point we clearly state, that an exhaustive search for optimal parameters is avoided in order not to run into overfitting problems. Instead, we prefer an evaluation of two reasonable heuristics. Again, with this approach we alleviate a fast and almost parameterless (except for the computation and evaluation of reliability masks) integration into existing iris-code based solutions. Emphasizing the usability of Selective Bits Fusion we will show that even this simple approach will outerform traditional score-based fusion using the sum-rule. We select bits from single algorithms according to the following two strategies:

- **Zero-cost:** this heuristic simply assumes, that all algorithms provide a similar information rate per bit, thus the relative proportion in bit size is retained for the combined template. The maximum feature vector bit size is adopted

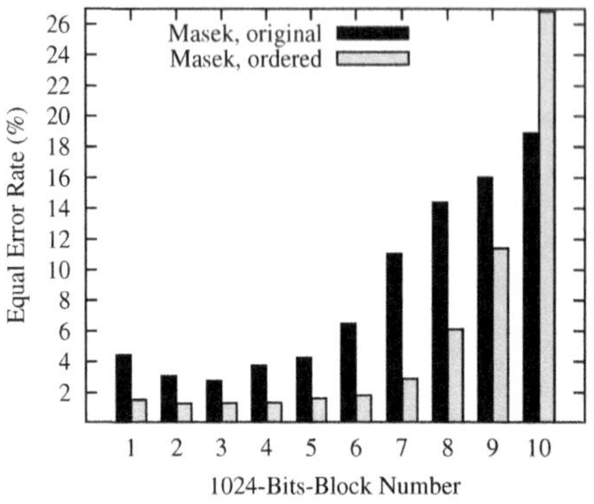

Fig. 3. EERs for Masek on 1024-Bits blocks

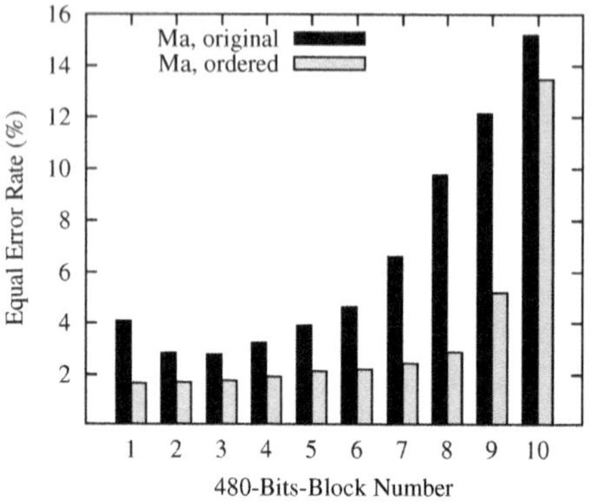

Fig. 4. EER's for Ma's on 1024-Bits blocks

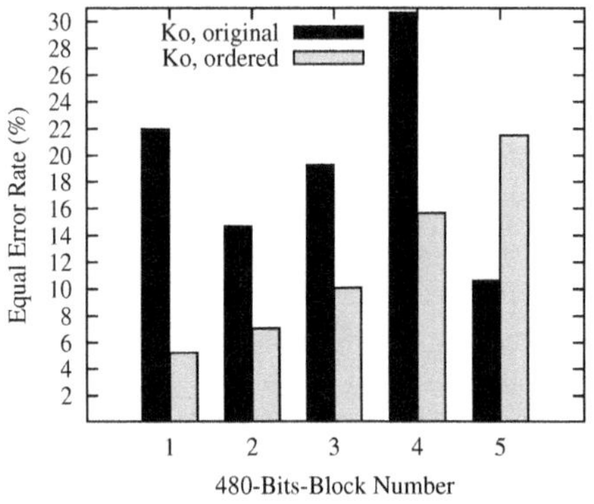

Fig. 5. EERs for Ko on 480-Bits blocks

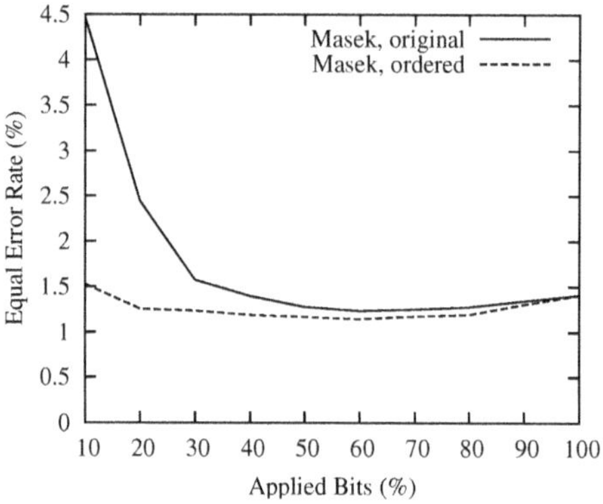

Fig. 6. EER-Bits tradeoff for Masek

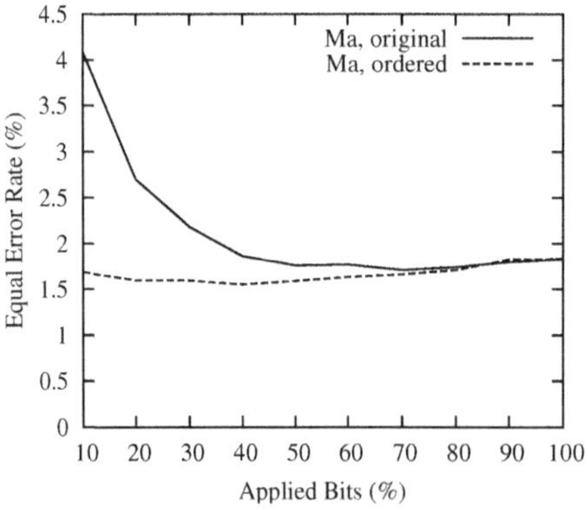

Fig. 7. EER-Bits tradeoff for Ma

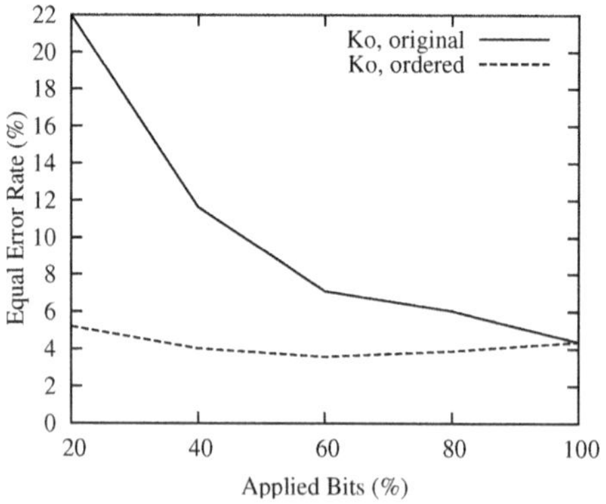

Fig. 8. EER-Bits tradeoff for Ko

Table 1. EERs of presented comparison techniques

	Original			**Sum Rule Fusion**			**Selective Bits Fusion**	
	Masek	Ko	Ma	Masek+Ko	Ko+Ma	Masek+Ma	Masek+Ko	Ko+Ma
Bits	10240	2400	10240	12640	12640	20480	6336	6336
EER	1.41%	4.36%	1.83%	1.38%	1.72%	1.54%	1.15%	1.52%

as the new template size and filled according to the relative size of the algorithm's template compared to the total sum of bits, i.e. for combining the total 10240 Masek bits and 2400 Ko bits, we extract the most reliable 8296 Masek and 1944 Ko bits and build a new template of size 10240 bits.

- **Half-sized:** when assessing the tradeoff between EER and bit count in Figs. 6, 7 and 8 we see, that for the reordered versions already very few bits suffice to obtain low EERs with a global optimum at approximately half of iris-code bits for all tested algorithms. Interestingly, even for the original (unordered) case 50% of bits seems to be a good amount to get almost the same performance like for a full-length iris-code. The new template consists of concatenating the best half-sized iris-codes of each algorithm rounded to the next 32 bits (in order to be able to use fast integer-arithmetics for the computation of the Hamming distance). This yields, e.g., 6336 bits for the combination of Masek and Ko.

3.4 Selective Bits vs. Sum Rule Fusion

Finally, we assessed the accuracy of Selective Bits Fusion in both zero-cost and half-sized configurations and compared their performance with sum rule fusion. The latter technique simply calculates the sum (or average) of individual comparison scores of each classifier C_i for two biometric samples a, b: $S(a, b) = \frac{1}{n}\sum_{i=1}^{n} C_i(a, b)$. Results of tested combinations are outlined briefly in Table 1 (Selective Bits Fusion lists results by the better half-sized variant).

First, we evaluated all single algorithms on the test set. Highest accuracy with respect to EER was provided by Masek's algorithm (1.41%) closely followed by Ma (1.83%). The almost five times shorter iris-code by Ko provided the least accurate EER results (4.36%). In experiments we tested pairwise combinations of these algorithms. It is worth noticing, that improvement in score-level biometric fusion is not self-evident but depends on whether algorithms assess complementary information. Indeed, if we combine the similar algorithms of Ma and Masek, we achieve an EER value (1.54%) right in between values for both single algorithms and at the cost of the iris-code being twice as long as for a single algorithm. For this reason we considered the combinations between the complementary algorithm pairs Masek and Ko as well as Ko and Ma only.

For the combination of Masek and Ko, sum rule yields only slightly superior EER (1.38%) than for the better single algorithm, but still despite the worse single performance of Ko, information could still be exploited and the ROC curve lies above both algorithms over almost the entire range, see Fig. 9. If we employ Selective Bits Fusion, we get a much better improvement than for the traditional combination with EERs as low as 1.15% for the half-sized version (and 1.21% for the zero-cost variant). Indeed it is even better to discard more bits, which is most likely to be caused by the fact that there is a significant amount of unstable bits present in each of the codes degrading the total result. Especially for high-security applications with requested low False Match Rates, Selective Bits Fusion performed reasonably well.

When employing fusion for Ko and Ma results indicate a similar picture. Again sum rule yields slightly better EER results than the best individual classifier (1.72%) which is beaten by Selective Bits Fusion (1.52%), see Fig. 10. Again, the zero-cost Selective Bits Fusion variant was slightly worse (1.59% EER).

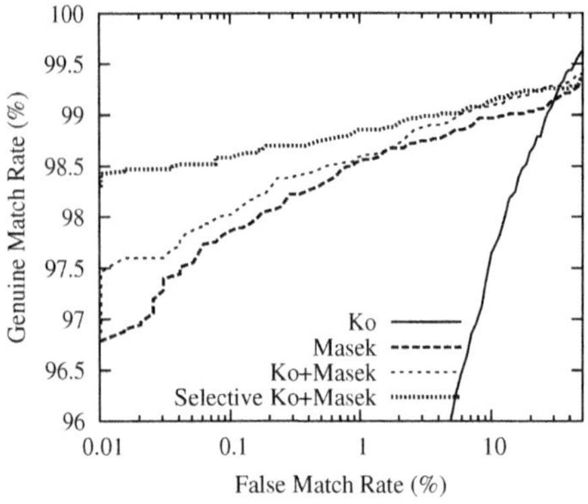

Fig. 9. Ko and Masek fusion scenario

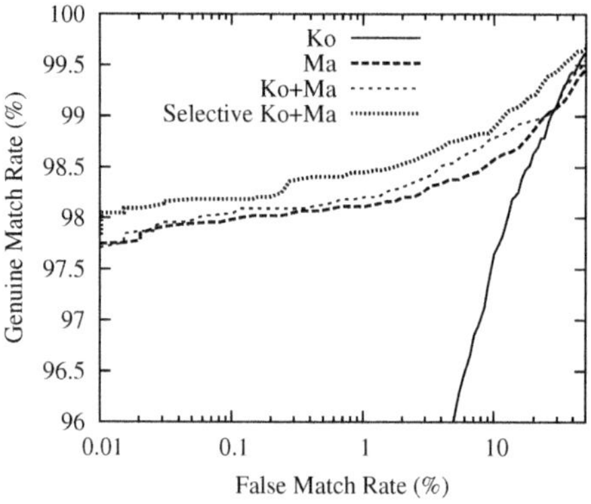

Fig. 10. Ko and Ma fusion scenario

4 Conclusion

Focusing on iris biometric fusion a reasonable combination of diverse feature extraction algorithms tends to improve recognition accuracy. However, a combination of algorithms implies the application of multiple biometric templates. That is, in conventional biometric fusion scenarios improved accuracy comes at the cost of additional template storage as well as comparison time.

In contrast, the proposed system, which is refered to as Selective Bits Fusion, presents a generic approach to iris biometric fusion which does not require the storage of a concatenation of applied biometric templates. By combining the most reliable features only (extracted by different algorithms) storage is saved while the accuracy of the biometric fusion is even improved. Experimental results confirm the worthiness of the proposed technique.

References

1. Bowyer, K., Hollingsworth, K., Flynn, P.: Image understanding for iris biometrics: A survey. Comp. Vision and Image Understanding 110(2), 281–307 (2008)
2. Daugman, J.: How iris recognition works. IEEE Trans. on Circuits and Systems for Video Technology 14(1), 21–30 (2004)

3. Daugman, J.: Probing the uniqueness and randomness of iriscodes: Results from 200 billion iris pair comparisons. Proc. of the IEEE 94(11), 1927–1935 (2006)
4. Gentile, J.E., Ratha, N., Connell, J.: SLIC: Short Length Iris Code. In: Proc. of the 3rd IEEE Int'l Conf. on Biometrics: Theory, Applications and Systems (BTAS 2009), Piscataway, NJ, USA, 2009, pp. 171–175. IEEE Press, Los Alamitos (2009)
5. Hollingsworth, K.P., Bowyer, K.W., Flynn, P.J.: The best bits in an iris code. IEEE Trans. on Pattern Analysis and Machine Intelligence 31(6), 964–973 (2009)
6. Hunny Mehrotra, A.R., Gupta, P.: Fusion of iris and fingerprint biometric for recognition. In: Proc. of the Int'l Conf. on Signal and Image Processing (ICSIP), pp. 1–6 (2006)
7. Kittler, J., Hatef, M., Duin, R., Matas, J.: On combining classifiers. IEEE Trans. on Pattern Analysis and Machine Intelligence 20(3), 226–239 (1998)
8. Ko, J.-G., Gil, Y.-H., Yoo, J.-H., Chung, K.-I.: A novel and efficient feature extraction method for iris recognition. ETRI Journal 29(3), 399–401 (2007)
9. Konrad, M., Stögner, H., Uhl, A., Wild, P.: Computationally efficient serial combination of rotation-invariant and rotation compensating iris recognition algorithms. In: Proc. of the 5th Int'l Conf. on Computer Vision Theory and Applications, VISAPP 2010, vol. 1, pp. 85–90 (2010)
10. Ma, L., Tan, T., Wang, Y., Zhang, D.: Efficient iris recognition by characterizing key local variations. IEEE Trans. on Image Processing 13(6), 739–750 (2004)
11. Park, C.-H., Lee, J.-J.: Extracting and combining multimodal directional iris features. In: Zhang, D., Jain, A.K. (eds.) ICB 2005. LNCS, vol. 3832, pp. 389–396. Springer, Heidelberg (2005)
12. Rathgeb, C., Uhl, A., Wild, P.: Incremental iris recognition: A single-algorithm serial fusion strategy to optimize time complexity. In: Proc. of the 4th IEEE Int'l. Conf. on Biometrics: Theory, Applications and Systems (BTAS 2010), pp. 1–6. IEEE Press, Los Alamitos (2010)
13. Ross, A., Nandakumar, K., Jain, A.: Handbook of Multibiometrics. Springer, Heidelberg (2006)
14. Sun, Z., Wang, Y., Tan, T., Cui, J.: Improving iris recognition accuracy via cascaded classifiers. IEEE Trans. on Systems, Man and Cybernetics 35(3), 435–441 (2005)
15. Vatsa, M., Singh, R., Noore, A.: Reducing the false rejection rate of iris recognition using textural and topological features. Int. Journal of Signal Processing 2(2), 66–72 (2005)
16. Wang, Y., Tan, T., Jain, A.K.: Combining face and iris biometrics for identity verification. In: Kittler, J., Nixon, M. (eds.) AVBPA 2003. LNCS, vol. 2688, pp. 805–813. Springer, Heidelberg (2003)
17. Zhang, P.-F., Li, D.-S., Wang, Q.: A novel iris recognition method based on feature fusion. In: Proc. of the Int'l Conf. on Machine Learning and Cybernetics, pp. 3661–3665 (2004)
18. Zhang, Z., Wang, R., Pan, K., Li, S., Zhang, P.: Fusion of near infrared face and iris biometrics. In: Lee, S.-W., Li, S.Z. (eds.) ICB 2007. LNCS, vol. 4642, pp. 172–180. Springer, Heidelberg (2007)

Processing of Palm Print and Blood Vessel Images for Multimodal Biometrics

Rihards Fuksis, Modris Greitans, and Mihails Pudzs

Institute of Electronics and Computer Science,
14 Dzerbenes Str., Riga, LV1006, Latvia
{Rihards.Fuksis,Modris.Greitans,Mihails.Pudzs}@edi.lv
http://www.edi.lv

Abstract. This paper presents a design of PC-based multimodal biometric system, where palm blood vessels and palm prints are used as the biometric parameters. Image acquisition is based on dual spectrum illumination of the palm. By using near infrared light the image of blood vessels can be obtained and using the visible light the pattern of palm print can be captured. Images are processed using gradient filtering and complex matched filtering. After filtering, most significant features from the image are extracted as a vector set, and compared later in the recognition stage. Database of palm print and blood vessel images of 50 persons have been developed for experimental evaluation. The fusion approach of the two parameters is discussed and experimental results are presented.

Keywords: Image processing, Multimodal biometrics.

1 Introduction

Multimodal biometric systems use fusion of two or more biometric parameters (e.g., fingerprint, face, iris, etc.) to increase the overall system's performance, however, it is also important to provide easy enrollment procedure for the person. Therefore, it is important to select the reliable and easy presentable biometric parameters. A number of different approaches of biometric parameter fusion are presented in last years, like hand shape and its skin texture fusion [8], fusion of palm print and hand shape [10], palm print and face [9], finger vein and finger-dorsa texture fusion [12], multispectral hand biometrics [11] etc.

In this paper we suggest to use the fusion of palm print and blood vessel patterns. Palm blood vessel pattern is a more reliable parameter for biometric systems than fingerprints and facial details due to invisibility in daylight and harder falsification [3]. The research using palm blood vessel biometrics with the results of 0.17% equal error rate (EER) is shown in [7]. It demonstrates that a secure and reliable system can be constructed using palm blood vessel pattern, however, overall systems performance could be significantly increased by adding palm prints as the second biometric parameter. Palm print image can be captured almost simultaneously with palm blood vein pattern, providing easy enrollment procedure for the person. If the image capturing procedure is done

C. Vielhauer et al. (Eds.): BioID 2011, LNCS 6583, pp. 238–249, 2011.

fast enough, person even wouldn't notice that he presented more than one parameter to the biometric system. Image acquisition specifics are explained in the Sec. 2. Parameter selection is only the first step to build a reliable biometric system, second step is to choose or develop an efficient and precise data processing algorithm. One of the popular methods is matched filtering (MF), which operates with previously known data [2]. Apart of MF, computationally improved approach called complex matched filtering [6] can be used. This approach will be discussed in detail in the Sec. 3. Finally, both parameter fusion is discussed and the evaluation of palm blood vessel pattern and palm print databases is done. Database construction and evaluation methods are discussed in the Sec. 4, following by the section which shows how the fusion of two databases significantly improves the overall results. Experimental results are presented in the Sec. 6 and conclusions are summarized in the Sec. 7.

2 Image Acquisition

The imaging of the palm is performed using dual spectrum illumination. Palm blood vessel images are captured in near infrared (NIR) spectrum, but images of palm print structure are captured in visible spectrum (white light). Infrared images of palm blood vessels can be obtained by two main approaches - reflection and transmission. In the reflection case, light source is placed in the front of the target, while in the transmission case it can be located in the back, the side, or around the target [4].

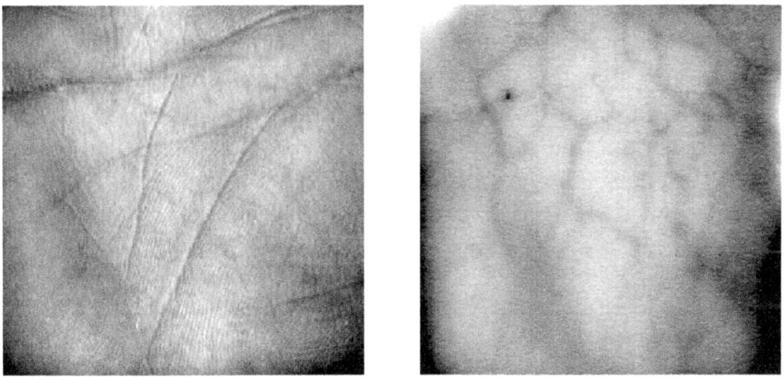

Fig. 1. One persons (left) palm print and (right) palm blood vessel images

In the reflection method palm is illuminated with IR LEDs, the reflected light is then filtered with IR filter and the image is captured by camera. In transmission method the setup remains the same, except that IR light source is located on the opposite side of the palm. In [4] it is proven that the reflection method is more suitable for compact embedded solutions. Reflection method allows to use LEDs as the light source, therefore all electronic components can be mounted on one PCB that provides the compactness of the system. Further, for image acquisition, only reflection method will be used.

We have constructed the experimental palm biometric feature acquisition prototype. It consists of low cost CCD camera module, a bank of infrared and white LEDs, IR filter, light diffuser and a palm fixing stand. First, the palm blood vessel image is captured by illuminating palm with near infrared LEDs. After the infrared illumination is switched off and the white LEDs are turned on, palm print texture is captured. Captured images are transfered to the PC for further processing. However both captured images are of poor quality, varying contrast changes and weak blood vessel and skin wrinkle intensities. Palm print and blood vessel image examples are shown in Fig. 1. Next Sec. describes the methods used for feature extraction from the acquired images.

3 Image Processing

Image processing consists of three steps: filtering of input image, most significant feature extraction and object comparison. In following two subsections all steps of acquired image processing used in our experiments are described.

3.1 Filtering

The acquired images of the palm parameters are of low quality and covered with noise. Therefore it is vital to choose the right processing approach in order to effectively extract the desired features from the images. Conventional image processing methods like histogram equalization or global thresholding [5] are not acceptable due to the irregular intensity and noisy background of the images. One of the most popular image processing techniques that involves known feature extraction is 2D matched filtering (MF). If we look at the one row of the palm blood vessel image and palm print image (Fig. 2), it can be seen, that the details are different. Intensity changes in the palm print and palm blood vessel images have a different nature, therefore two different methods have to be used to extract desired information. As it can be seen from the previous image, palm print ridge

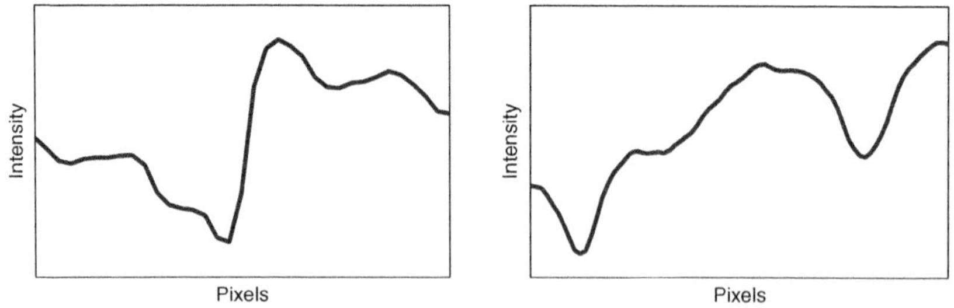

Fig. 2. Cross section of the palm print ridge (left) and two palm blood vessels (right)

has sharp intensity change. This sharp intensity change can be detected using first derivatives which are implemented using the magnitude of the gradient. For a function $g[x,y]$, the gradient of g at coordinates $[x,y]$ is defined as the two-dimensional column vector

$$\nabla g \equiv \text{grad}(g) = \begin{bmatrix} \frac{\partial g}{\partial x} \\ \frac{\partial g}{\partial y} \end{bmatrix} \tag{1}$$

Derivatives of discrete functions in particular point $[x_0, y_0]$ are calculated as the difference of nearby pixel values, for example:

$$\left.\frac{\partial g[x,y]}{\partial x}\right|_{[x_0,y_0]} = g[x_0+d, y_0] - g[x_0-d, y_0] \tag{2}$$

where d is distance between taken neighborhood pixels.

Typically the image is disturbed with noise and direct application of (2) can lead to improper result. Therefore, before calculating of the derivatives, the image $f[x,y]$ is smoothed using a Gaussian filter to reduce rapid intensity spikes that are initiated by noise.

$$g[x,y] = f[x,y] \otimes e^{-\frac{x^2+y^2}{\sigma^2}} \tag{3}$$

where σ specifies the smoothing rate, and $\otimes$ is the convolution operator.

Function's gradient vector grad(g) points at the greatest rate of change of g, which corresponds to the cross section of the skin ridge. To ease the following stage of vector set construction, the gradient vector is rotated by 90° to acquire the desired resulting matrix of vectors F_1. Since the method used to extract the blood vessels is expressed in the complex form, for convenience, we rewrite (1) using the complex notation as:

$$\underline{F}_1[x_0,y_0] = (g[x_0, y_0-d] - g[x_0, y_0+d]) + j\,(g[x_0+d, y_0] - g[x_0-d, y_0]) \tag{4}$$

Parameters σ and $d = 1.5\sigma$ were chosen empirically.

For blood vessel extraction the mask with Gaussian 2D function $G(x,y)$ can be used [2].

$$G(x,y) = \begin{cases} -exp\left(-\frac{y^2}{\sigma^2}\right), & |x| \le \frac{D}{2} \\ 0, & |x| > \frac{D}{2} \end{cases} \tag{5}$$

where D is the length of the filter in x direction. In order to detect blood vessels the filter mask must be rotated in different directions, and scaled. For convenience, rotated and scaled Gaussian 2D kernel is further referred to as:

$$G[x,y;\phi,c] \equiv G\left(\frac{x\cos\phi - y\sin\phi}{c}, \frac{x\sin\phi + y\cos\phi}{c}\right) \tag{6}$$

where c is scaling factor and ϕ is rotation angle.

The more rotation angles are used the more precise is the extraction of blood vessels. However this involves image convolution with all rotated Gaussian kernels and therefore is computationally inefficient for embedded systems. To simplify computational complexity of MF approach, an improved method of complex matched filtering (CMF), described in [6] can be used. This image processing method not only improves the computational simplicity over traditional MF approach, but also obtains additional information about the analyzed features, in our case about the blood vessels and skin wrinkles. The output of the filtering procedure is the vector set of the same size as the input image. Vectors represent the correlation with the previously defined mask representing the objects that have to be found. Instead of consecutive filtering with several differently oriented MF masks, CMF filters image only with one complex mask, which incorporates all the angles and scales. The kernel of complex matched filter is defined by the following expression:

$$\underline{M}[x,y] = \sum_{n=1}^{N}\sum_{l=0}^{L-1} exp(j2\phi_l)G[x,y;\phi_l,c_n], \tag{7}$$

where N – total number of used scales,
L – total number of used angles,
$\phi_l = \frac{l}{L}\cdot\pi$.

Image is filtered with the CMF kernel:

$$\underline{C}[x,y] = f[x,y] \otimes \underline{M}[x,y]. \tag{8}$$

Additional operation of angle decrement is performed to $\underline{\mathrm{C}}$ to acquire the CMF result.

$$\underline{F}_2[x_0,y_0] = |\underline{C}[x_0,y_0]|\, exp\left(j\frac{\mathrm{Arg}\underline{C}[x_0,y_0]}{2}\right) \tag{9}$$

Magnitudes of the vectors represent the congruence between filter mask and the object in the specific pixel of the image. Angle of the vector shows the orientation in which the congruence is found, this information is important in segmentation and recognition stage.

3.2 Vector Set Construction and Comparison

In both cases, $\underline{F}_1$ and $\underline{F}_2$ are matrices of vectors. Apart of the vectors that represent the blood vessels or skin wrinkles there are other vectors that represent noise and carry undesired information. To decrease unwanted and repetitive information about the blood vessels and skin wrinkles, only information about the significant features can be extracted from the vector matrix. The vector set construction is done similar to [7]. After the acquired image is filtered and transformed into the vector set A, recognition process begins. Vector set A is compared with the database vector sets B_n to find the best match. To compare two sets of vectors we use similar to [7] approach: Each vector $v_p(\mathrm{A})$ from the first set A is compared with each vector $v_q(\mathrm{B})$ from the second set B. Similarity of two vectors is evaluated by positive $s_{p,q}$, and is a product of three parts:

$$s_{p,q} = \mathrm{magnitudes}_{p,q} \cdot \mathrm{angles}_{p,q} \cdot \mathrm{distance}_{p,q} \tag{10}$$

These three parts evaluate the positions of two vectors (distance), the angular difference (angles), and the significance of these vectors (magnitudes). All the similarities of particular pair of vectors $s_{p,q}$ are summed together to evaluate the similarity of the vector sets in general:

$$s(\mathrm{A}, \mathrm{B}) = \sum_p \sum_q s_{p,q} \tag{11}$$

The higher is the value of particular $s_{p,q}$, the higher is their influence on the overall similarity value $s(\mathrm{A}, \mathrm{B})$. The vector magnitude is proportional to the significance of the locally extracted feature that is represented by this vector. Significant details are usually represented by vectors with high magnitudes due to their clear appearance and the large image area being occupied. Insignificant details lack either of the mentioned factors, for example, noise occupies whole image, but doesn't have any clear appearance, while artifacts occupy too small image area. For this reason, magnitudes are included into similarity evaluation (10).

$$\mathrm{magnitudes} = |v_p(A)| \cdot |v_q(B)| \tag{12}$$

For line-like object it is not important whether the vector points into its direction or the opposite. For this reason, the calculation of absolute value is included into the evaluation of angular difference of two vectors.

$$\mathrm{angles} = |\cos\angle(v_p(A) \cdot v_q(B))| \tag{13}$$

Note, that the value of (magnitudes · angles) is efficiently computable as the absolute value of vectors' scalar product. Our modification to [7] is the evaluation of distance between two vectors. Our experiments showed that due to changes of lightning conditions in the image acquisition stage, the same line-like objects appear differently on the filtered images: the positions of local maximums across the object vary. For this reason, we split the distance between vectors into parallel (to $v_p(\mathrm{A})$) and perpendicular parts, and evaluate them separately: the first mentioned is less critical for $s_{p,q}$ than the second one ($\sigma_{\parallel} > \sigma_{\perp}$).

$$\mathrm{distance} = exp\left(-\frac{d_{\parallel}^2}{\sigma_{\parallel}^2}\right) \cdot exp\left(-\frac{d_{\perp}^2}{\sigma_{\perp}^2}\right) \tag{14}$$

Both parts of the distance are found as the projections of actual distance between $v_p(\mathrm{A})$ and $v_q(\mathrm{B})$ onto the vector $v_p(\mathrm{A})$. Similarity value $s(\mathrm{A}, \mathrm{B})$ is influenced by the image contrast and the neighborhood effect of many local maximums representing one and the same line-like object jointly comparing with each other. In the evaluation stage it is normalized as described in [7].

$$S(\mathrm{A}, \mathrm{B}) = \frac{s(\mathrm{A}, \mathrm{B})}{\sqrt{s(\mathrm{A}, \mathrm{A}) \cdot s(\mathrm{B}, \mathrm{B})}} \tag{15}$$

Similarity index value $S(\mathrm{A}, \mathrm{B})$ lies in the interval of $[0; 1]$ and is used for evaluation of similarity of two images. Similarity index doesn't have commutative property, $S(\mathrm{A}, \mathrm{B}) \neq S(\mathrm{B}, \mathrm{A})$.

4 Database Construction and Evaluation

To evaluate system's performance, two databases of palm print and palm blood vessel images from 50 different persons were constructed. Each database consists of 250 images, 5 images per person. First, CMF or gradient filtering is applied on each of the database image, and most significant vector set is acquired. Next, database images are mutually compared using the vector set comparison technique shown in the previous Sec. The result of comparison is a matrix of similarity indexes $S[x, y]$, where x and y is the image number in each database. Figure 3 shows the thresholded similarity indexes matrix $S[x, y]$: black represent the values that are above the threshold level, while white below the threshold level.

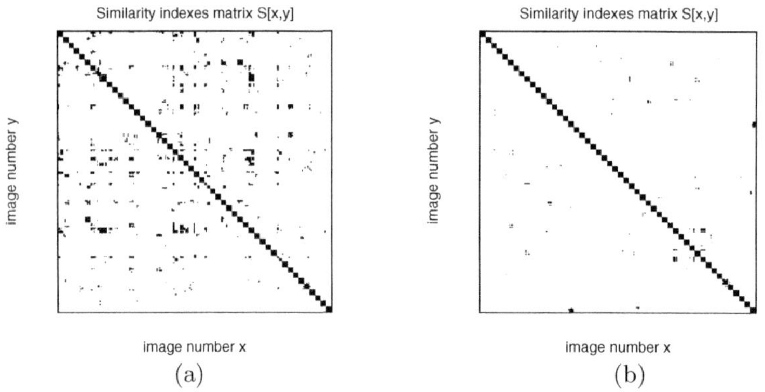

Fig. 3. S_1 and S_2; (a) for palm print database, (b) for palm blood vessel database

By analyzing each of the databases, it is possible to obtain 1000 examples of positive comparison (N_{pos}) and 61250 examples of negative comparison (N_{neg}). The diagonal values $S[x, x] = 1$ are excluded as they carry no information. Fifty black squares on the diagonal of $S[x, y]$ make the positive comparison area, where the images are mutually compared within the same person. Indexes of $S[x, y]$ outside the black squares make the negative comparison area, where the images from different persons are mutually compared. White dots in the positive comparison area and black dots in the negative comparison area indicate the errors. When the images for databases are acquired, it is not critical how much time it will take to process them, therefore, the images of the database is represented by the set of 64 vectors. On the other hand, the recognition process is time critical, since the person is waiting for an acceptance. Thus, during the recognition process, image might be processed differently, i.e. fewer vectors may be extracted. In the stage

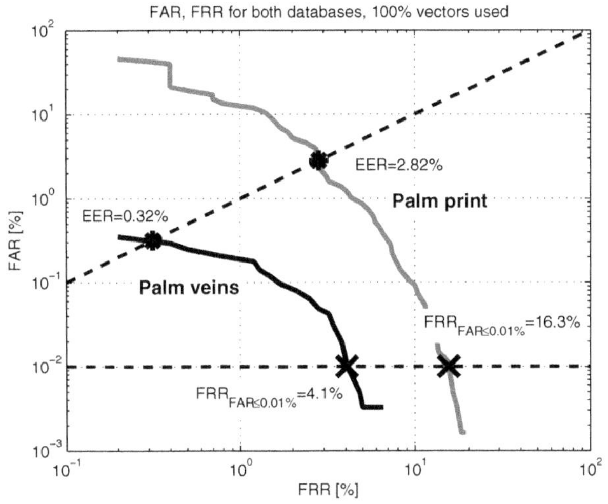

Fig. 4. FAR and FRR diagram for both databases

of the database analysis we assume that one of the compared images x belongs to the database, and the other, y, is the captured image, and simulate mentioned conditions by taking only 25%, 40%, 50%, 80% and 100% of the most significant vectors of the captured image.

To measure the performance of the biometric data evaluation method, different measures are calculated and compared, they include: False Acceptance Rate (FAR) when a person is recognized as another person within database; and False Rejection Rate (FRR) when someone within the database is not recognized as himself. We calculate FRR(T) as the number of incorrect $S[x,y]$ values (that are beyond the threshold level T) in the positive comparison area, normalized by N_{pos}. Similarly, the FAR(T) are the number of incorrect $S[x,y]$ values (that are above the threshold level T) in the negative comparison area, normalized by N_{neg}. Both of these parameters depend on the threshold level, and, by varying the threshold level, we can balance between them. Figure 4 demonstrates the FAR and FRR for both databases.

In this research, we evaluate these errors using two different approaches:

1. We measure the Equal Error Rate (EER), which is considered as a common criterion to evaluate a biometric system or algorithm. It is the rate at which both FAR and FRR are equal. The threshold level in the Fig. 3 is chosen to show the EER.
2. In practical systems we are usually concerned about the FAR, which is more important. Therefore, we evaluate $\text{FRR}_{\text{FAR}\leq 0.01\%}$ for the condition of FAR $\leq 0.01\%$.

The goal is to obtain higher overall system's performance by the fusion of both databases. Even if the difference between both database EER values is approximately 10 times greater, we search for the function that combines the similarity indexes in the way that gives minimal EER and $FRR_{FAR \leq 0.01\%}$.

5 Database Fusion

Since, for each case of the comparison we have a pair of similarity indexes, the (S_1, S_2) plane is observed, where each comparison can be represented as a mark. In Fig. 5 the black circles represent the positive comparison, while gray crosses the negative comparison. Finding the threshold level is equivalent to drawing a line, which would separate these areas to obtain minimal EER or $FRR_{FAR \leq 0.01\%}$. When operating, the system uses the chosen threshold level to decide whether to accept or to reject the person depending on which side of the separating line the current pair of similarity indexes is.

If only one biometric parameter is used, for example, S_1 in Fig. 5a, then the line that represents the threshold level is perpendicular to the S_1 axis. In this case the noticeable error is observable. Fusion of two biometric parameters increases the number of degrees of freedoms of the separating line up to two and the separation can be significantly improved as it is shown in Fig.5b. The error are minimized, if present at all.

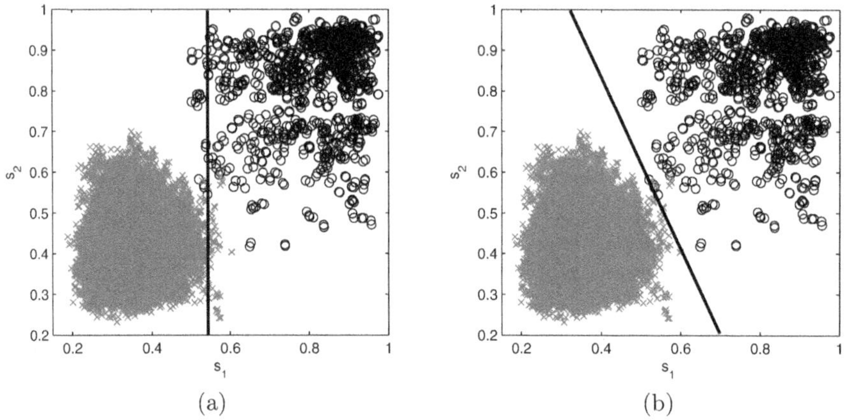

Fig. 5. Separation of similarity indexes using one biometric parameter (a) and fusion of two parameters (b)

The method, used for fusion of the biometric parameters, is similar to the support vector machines (SVM) [1]. The simplest approach for separating two data sets is the linear separation by thresholding the value S, which is equal to:

$$S = k \cdot S_1 + (1 - k) \cdot S_2, \tag{16}$$

where k adjusts the influence factor of each similarity index and defines the slope of the separating line. The threshold level $T = S$ defines offset of this line. When

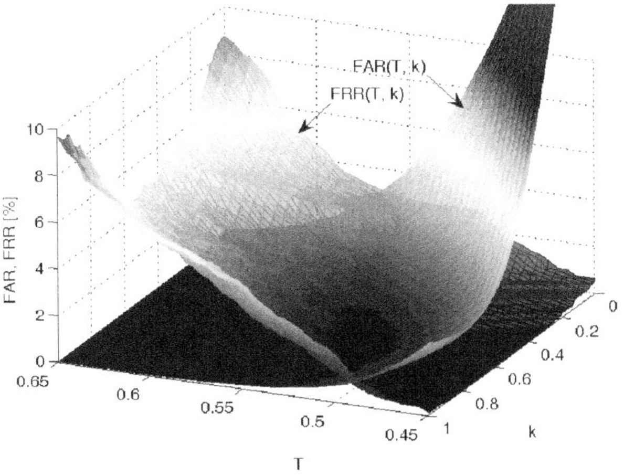

Fig. 6. FAR(T,k) and FRR(T,k) plotted as surfaces

using this method, FAR and FRR are functions of two parameters that can be plotted as surfaces shown in Fig. 6.

We search for optimal T and k, so that:

1. $\mathrm{EER}(k) \equiv \mathrm{FAR}(T,k) = \mathrm{FRR}(T,k)$ is minimized,
2. $\mathrm{FRR}_{\mathrm{FAR} \leq 0.01\%}(k) \equiv \min_T \mathrm{FRR}(T,k)|_{\mathrm{FAR}(T,k) \leq 0.01\%}$ is minimized.

6 Results

Experimental results are summarized in charts in Fig. 7: The first chart shows the evaluation of EER for palm prints, palm blood vessels and both parameter

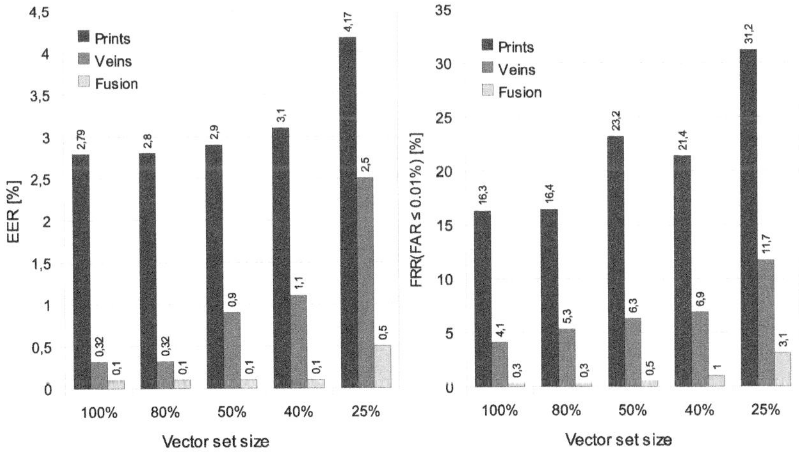

Fig. 7. Experimental results, showing the EER (left) and $\mathrm{FRR}_{FAR \leq 0.01\%}$ (right) improvement by using fusion

fusion, while the second chart shows the same parameters if the FRR at FAR $\leq 0.01\%$ is evaluated. As it can be seen, by increasing the size of the vector set, the overall precision also increases. It is obvious, because there are more parameters and fewer possibilities for different images to be evaluated as similar to each other. The results for palm blood vessels are better, since they have more unique patterns than palm prints. It is also visible that by both parameter fusion, the precision increases significantly.

7 Conclusions

This research shows that by fusion of two biometric parameters greater overall system's performance can be achieved, than when using each parameter alone. By using different data fusion methods it is possible to obtain EER less than 0.1 percent. However by using each of the databases separately the obtained EER values are 0.32 and 2.8. The observed system with FAR = 0.01% and FRR = 0.3% can be useful for the access of restricted areas if the number of persons is not greater than 50. To increase the system's precision each person must be represent with more than one image. Unlike most multimodal biometric systems, the enrollment procedure is simplified because person must provide only his palm. It is easy to acquire both parameters from the palm using one camera and only operating with the light sources. This also can seriously cut the expenses of such system's production. Complex matched filtering approach gives an opportunity to process images faster by using fewer computations and acquire vectors. By extracting the most significant vectors after filtration overall amount of information is reduced, thus reducing the memory requirements of the biometric system that is vital in embedded solutions. Future work involves the larger database construction and also algorithm implementation in embedded system with parallel computational options.

References

1. Burges, C.J.: A tutorial on support vector machines for pattern recognition. Data Mining and Knowledge Discovery 2, 121–167 (1998)
2. Chaudhuri, S., Chatterjee, S., Katz, N., Nelson, M., Goldbaum, M.: Detection of blood vessels in retinal images using two-dimensional matched filters. IEEE Transactions on Medical Imaging 8(3), 263–269 (1989)
3. Chen, H., Lu, G., Wang, R.: A new palm vein matching method based on icp algorithm. In: Proceedings of Biometric Symposium (BSYM), pp. 1–6 (2007)
4. Fuksis, R., Greitans, M., Pudzs, M.: Infrared imaging system for analysis of blood vessel structure. Electronics and Electrical Engineering 1(97), 45–48 (2010)
5. Gonzalez, R.C., Woods, R.E.: Digital image processing, 3rd edn. Prentice Hall, Englewood Cliffs (2007)
6. Greitans, M., Pudzs, M., Fuksis, R.: Object analysis in images using complex 2d matched filters. In: EUROCON 2009: Proceedings of IEEE Region 8 Conference, pp. 1392–1397. IEEE, Los Alamitos (2009)

7. Greitans, M., Pudzs, M., Fuksis, R.: Palm vein biometrics based on infrared imaging and complex matched filtering. In: MM&Sec 2010: Proceedings of the 12th ACM Workshop on Multimedia And Security, pp. 101–106. ACM, New York (2010)
8. Kumar, A., Zhang, D.: Personal recognition using hand shape and texture. IEEE Transactions on Image Processing 15(8), 2454–2461 (2006)
9. Nageshkumar, N., Mahesh, P., Shanmukha Swamy, M.: An efficient secure multi-modal biometric fusion using palmprint and face image. International Journal of Computer Science Issues, IJCSI 2, 49–53 (2009), http://cogprints.org/6696/
10. Ong, M.G.K., Connie, T., Jin, A.T.B., Ling, D.N.C.: A single-sensor hand geometry and palmprint verification system. In: WBMA 2003: Proceedings of the 2003 ACM SIGMM Workshop on Biometrics Methods and Applications, pp. 100–106. ACM, New York (2003)
11. Rowe, R.K., Uludag, U., Demirkus, M., Parthasaradhi, S., Jain, A.K.: A multi-spectral whole-hand biometric authentication system. In: ICIS 2009: Proceedings of the 2nd International Conference on Interaction Sciences, pp. 1207–1211. ACM, New York (2009)
12. Yang, W., Yu, X., Liao, Q.: Personal authentication using finger vein pattern and finger-dorsa texture fusion. In: MM 2009: Proceedings of the Seventeen ACM International Conference on Multimedia, pp. 905–908. ACM, New York (2009)

Database-Centric Chain-of-Custody in Biometric Forensic Systems

Martin Schäler, Sandro Schulze, and Stefan Kiltz

School of Computer Science, University of Magdeburg, Germany
{schaeler,sanschul,kiltz}@iti.cs.uni-magdeburg.de

Abstract. Biometric systems gain more and more attention in everyday life regarding authentication and surveillance of persons. This includes, amongst others, the login on a notebook based on fingerprint verification, controlling of airports or train stations, and the biometric identity card. Although these systems have several advantages in comparison to traditional approaches, they exhibit high risks regarding confidentiality and data protection issues. For instance, tampering biometric data or general misuse could have devastating consequences for the owner of the respective data. Furthermore, the digital nature of biometric data raises specific requirements for the usage of the data for crime detection or at court to convict a criminal. Here, the *chain-of-custody* has to be proven without any doubt. In this paper, we present a database-centric approach for ensuring the chain-of-custody in a forensic digital fingerprint system.

1 Introduction

When using physical evidence in law enforcement proceedings, a so called *chain-of-custody* has to be maintained in order for that evidence to be admissible in court. According to [19], at a crime scene evidence must be preserved for court use. Also, a documentation suitable for federal, state and local courts must be developed. It is the duty of the first responder of law enforcement to ensure that all evidence is protected and documented. Along with this, the *chain-of-custody* starts, which describes the route that evidence takes from its initial possession until its final disposition. In that process, a proper documentation process is of highest importance. It has to be proven without doubt that the evidence is *authentic* and *holds integrity*, that is, the evidence is original and has not been tampered with.

This applies also to digital evidence as used in IT-Forensic. The security aspects of *authenticity* and *integrity* have to be assured. Authenticity, according to [10], can be divided into two aspects: First, data origin authenticity is the proof of the data's origin, genuineness, originality, truth and realness. Data authenticity requirements can also be defined as prevention, detection, and recovery requirements. Second, entity authenticity is the proof that an entity, like a person or other agent, has been correctly identified as originator, sender or receiver. Hence, it can be ensured that an entity is the one it claims to be. Both, data and entity authenticity, are relevant in law enforcement proceedings. Beyond that, the security aspect of integrity (see also [3]) refers to the integrity of resources. It describes whether a resource (e.g., information) is altered or manipulated. Hence, integrity is the quality or condition of being whole and unaltered, and it refers

C. Vielhauer et al. (Eds.): BioID 2011, LNCS 6583, pp. 250–261, 2011.

to the consistency, accuracy, and correctness of the resource. Furthermore, the security aspect of *confidentiality* plays an important role in law enforcement proceedings. In detail, confidentiality refers to information that needs to be treated secret from unauthorized entities [3]. A special aspect of confidentiality is privacy, where person related data needs to be protected.

As described in [13], cryptographic mechanisms can be used to ensure the chain-of-custody and therefore, inherently, authenticity and integrity. This however, does not only apply to forensically relevant data gathered by investigating IT-based incidents. Also the traditional criminal investigation process today can be supported, e.g. by the usage of contact-less forensic fingerprint scanners as suggested in [17]. By using techniques also applied in biometric applications that allow authorization and access, digitally represented fingerprint data from a physical origin can play a very important role in law enforcement and court proceedings. For such biometric data, also a digital chain-of-custody needs to be maintained, following the same strict rules as with physical evidence. Additionally, fingerprint data are personal data, for which stringent laws exist in some countries, e.g. in Germany the federal data protection act (Bundesdatenschutzgesetz [11]). Especially for fingerprint data, the security aspect of confidentiality is very important, since such data must not be made available to unauthorized users.

In [19] it is suggested that cryptographic means are applied to data that is represented in a file system. In the approach presented in the following we investigate the appropriateness of the mechanisms provided by a database system and what extra mechanisms have to be applied.

Our contribution in this paper is as follows. Initially, we propose a database-centric chain-of-custody for relational [7] and object-relational [20] database systems. This includes a formalization of a *reliable data provenance concept* and additional requirements for an implementation of the provenance concept to ensure authenticity and integrity of the data. Furthermore, we show how the concept is integrated tightly into a fingerprint verification database to make it's circumvention as hard as possible. Finally, we exemplary show how our approach can be used to prevent malicious modification and to detect the circumvention of the chain-of-custody.

2 Problem Statement

In a current research project, we explore pattern recognition techniques for fingerprints that are captured by contact-less, optical surface sensors. To this ends, we develop a fingerprint verification database (*FiVe DB*) to support this recognition process. Although FiVe DB supports other research tasks as well, such as evaluating sensor techniques for capturing latent fingerprint, the main focus is on verifying whether a certain digital data item (captured by a sensor) contains a fingerprint or not. Since this verification process involves different transformations (e.g., for quality enhancement) of the original sensor data, the authenticity, integrity and confidentiality of the data must be guaranteed throughout the process. Otherwise, the usage of the data (e.g., as a proof at court) may cause legal problems. We conclude that our database must apply to the chain-of-custody to ensure the integrity and authenticity of the fingerprint data.

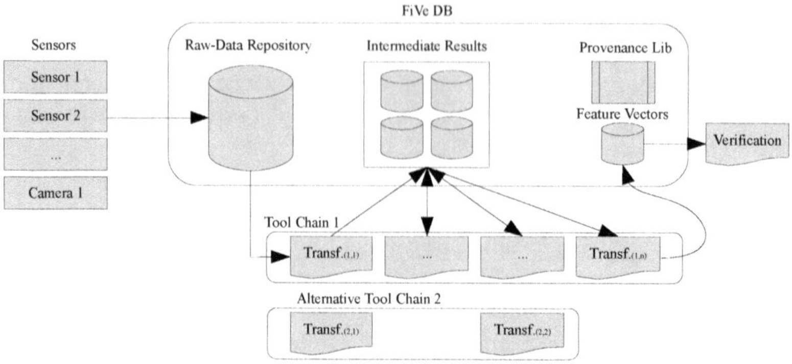

Fig. 1. Holistic Infrastructure

FiVe DB in the Center of the Global Architecture. To clarify, why the database is responsible for the chain-of-custody, we introduce a simplification of our architecture in Figure 1. The potential fingerprints are captured by some kind of sensor. That might be a simple digital camera or some other kind of scanner. We call this first digital image of fingerprint, which is stored in FiVe DB, a *raw data item*. Generally, the raw data format of two different sensors can differ, e.g., one sensor could provide additional topographic data. Furthermore, several transformations can be applied to a raw data item (or an intermediate result of a previous transformation) and thus create a new intermediate result. Each intermediate result is stored in FiVe DB persistently. Afterwards, it is possible to perform another transformation on the specified data. As a result, transformations are always performed on data items, stored in the database. Hence, we call this architecture *database-centric*. The final transformation creates a *feature vector* that allows some kind of verification to decide whether there is a fingerprint or not. Above all, a feature vector remains an image with some extracted data (e.g. material information, is there a fingerprint, is there an overlapped fingerprint etc.). Furthermore, the database contains functionality to compare different transformation chains and sensor techniques. Every piece of data in the DB is created *once* and not modified again. Here, it is worth to mention that we *do not* provide any solution of automatically identifying a suspect by its latent fingerprint.

In Figure 2, we show how the data items and its corresponding transformations are stored internally in form of tree structures. The root of a certain tree is a raw data item. The leaf is either a feature vector or some intermediate result. We call every path from the root to the leaf a *fingerprint data set (FpD)*. This serves as our central data unit for which we have to prove the chain-of-custody. The single chain links are the single data items, which are created by a sensor or quality enhancement transformations.

Relationship between Chain-of-Custody and Data Provenance. The term chain-of-custody from a biometrics point of view is highly related (but not equivalent) to data provenance in the database domain [22]. In databases, data provenance provides information about the origin of data and the transformation performed on these data items [5,6]. Although this is exactly the information we are interested in for ensuring the chain-of-custody, the mechanisms, which are usually used for data provenance, do

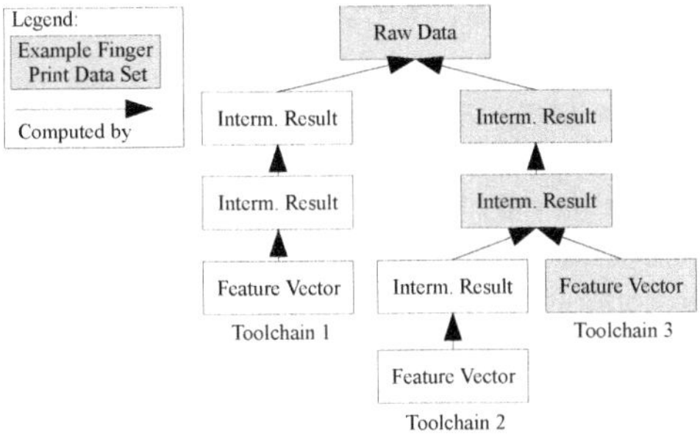

Fig. 2. Fingerprint Data Set (FpD)

not take *reliability* into account. This means that we cannot guarantee authenticity and integrity. For instance, to provide information on the original source of data, *foreign keys*, that is, referencing data by its unique identifier, can be used as a pointer to the original raw data item. Furthermore, history tables can be used to log the transformation chain. Unfortunately, foreign keys can easily be modified so that it points to the wrong original sensor image. In the same way, history and log tables can be tampered to obfuscate unauthorized or unproper changes [23]. As a result, authenticity and integrity of the data items are violated. In a real forensic scenario this may lead to devastating consequences.

Consequently, we need a *reliable data provenance approach* for relational databases that creates a chain-of-custody and thus guarantees *integrity*, *authenticity* and *confidentiality*. We must be able to prevent and detect tampering of the data that are described in the next subsection. Since no database mechanisms exist to ensure authenticity and integrity of the provenance information by our means, we have to develop additional countermeasures and integrate them into the database.

2.1 Attacker Model

To find the appropriate countermeasures, as a step of a risk analysis (see [21]) we must analyze *which* attacks are possible on our system and *how* they affect the authenticity, integrity and confidentiality of the data. According to Figure 1, we see the following threats (see [16]) of spoofing, modifying, reading or deleting data in the holistic infrastructure that we need to prevent and detect whenever the prevention was circumvented.

1. Faking a raw data item by a sensor,
2. Tampering the data send from a sensor to FiVe DB,
3. Any modification of some piece of data in FiVe DB,
4. Tampering the data send from FiVe DB to a transformation,
5. Faking an intermediate result or feature vector by a transformation,
6. Tampering a result send from a transformation to FiVe DB.

The attacks one and five try to insert unauthentic, but possibly data that hold integrity into FiVe DB. By contrast, in every other attack the integrity of the data is affected, but they may be related to an authentic fingerprint image. In the following, we discuss to which extent the mentioned threats can be addressed by the suggested concept and which possible threads cannot be addressed by our concept.

3 Formalization of the Provenance Concept

In this section we present a formalization of the *provenance concept* that lays the foundation for the chain-of-custody of our architecture. Furthermore, such a formalization is independent of a concrete implementation (i.e., how the concept is realized in a certain system). We also define further requirements that an implementation of the provenance mechanism has to fulfill so that the chain-of-custody can be proven without doubt.

3.1 Definition

First, we need to specify how a fingerprint is represented in the system to know which data items are subject to provenance information. Note that the formalization of the provenance concept can be reused in any kind of biometric application and is not limited to our system and purposes.

Definition 1. *A Fingerprint Data Set (FpD) consists of several binary data items (D). The raw data (D_{raw}) is the original data from the sensor. The sequence of intermediate results S(D_{ir}) contains the data after each transformation and the feature vector (D_{fv}) is the final result of a transformation chain.*

$$FpD = \{D_{raw}, S(D_{ir_1}, \ldots, D_{ir_n}), D_{fv}\} \tag{1}$$

Each D contains some kind of redundant structured data that allows to use them with common SQL, the query language commonly used in relational database systems. Generally, our formalization is independent of the data format, the result of a transformation or the representation of the feature vector, because we treat them as some kind of binary data. As a result, our concept is flexible regarding the structure and semantic of the data, but we cannot semantically check whether the binary data is correct on the data itself. For instance, imagine a transformation that applies a Garbor Filter to an intermediate result. In this case, FiVe DB does not check whether the result of this transformation is an image again. Particularly, FiVe DB tests whether the (trusted) transformation delivers readable provenance information that indicates *how* the transformation computed the result. Hence, we have to rely on the associated provenance information to ensure the chain-of-custody. The granularity of the transformations can be chosen as needed by the underlying system.

As an refinement of our initial definition, we define how a feature vector (the final result of a transformation chain) is calculated from the raw data by a sequence of transformations. Note that a feature vector remains an image with some extracted data as previously stated in Section 2.

Definition 2. *A Transformation is an operation which creates a new binary data item from a different one. The feature vector is calculated by a finite sequence of transformations from one raw data item. The results (if not equivalent to D_{fv}) are called intermediate results (D_{ir}) which are stored in the database.*

$$t\colon D \rightarrow D \qquad D_{fv} = t_n(\ldots(t_0(D_{raw}))) \tag{2}$$

Since our overall formalization is independent of any realization, the definition below abstracts from the semantics of a concrete transformation. Hence, we can deal with different transformations, used for different purposes such as tool chain or sensor evaluation, in the same way. However, for a concrete realization, the transformation must be certified so that we can trust its implementation, because, as previously mentioned, we cannot semantically check whether the result of a transformation is correct.

As a result of the previous definitions, we must have knowledge of the corresponding raw data item for each piece of data[1] as well as the transformation chain that lead to this item, the previous intermediate result and the meta data (e.g., the source such as a scanner, the creation date etc.) to ensure authenticity and integrity of one data item. We call this information a *ProveSet* and it is formalized as follows.

Definition 3. *A ProveSet for some piece of data D_k is defined as a tuple of a link to the raw data $L(D_{raw})$ it stems from, a sequence of transformation that created D_k from D_{raw}, a link to the previous intermediate result D_{k-1} and the meta data M that is provided by the sensor.*

$$ProveSet(D_k) = \{L(D_{raw}), S(t_0, \ldots, t_{k-1}), L(D_{k-1}), M\} \qquad D_k = t_{k-1}(D_{k-1}) \tag{3}$$

In the ProveSet of a raw data item, the sequence of transformations and the predecessor D_{k-1} is empty. In the ProveSet of a feature vector the complete transformation sequence is available.

Finally, we need to know the ProveSet for each data item of a fingerprint data set (FpD) to verify that the whole storage and transformation process performed well and to ensure that the FpD can be used in court without any doubt regarding authenticity and integrity. Therefore, we extend our ProveSet definition and define the *Complete ProveSet (CProveSet)* as follows.

Definition 4. *A Complete ProvSet (CProveSet) for an FpD exists, if for each data item D_k of the FpD the corresponding ProveSet exists.*

$$CProveSet(FpD) \leftrightarrow \forall D_k \in FpD \; \exists \; ProvSet(D_k) \tag{4}$$

A CProveSet is *correct* when there are no contradictions within the ProvSets of the single data items. With this formalization, we can track the whole history of an FpD, but to ensure authenticity and integrity we need to define additional requirements for the provenance mechanism.

3.2 Additional Requirements for the Provenance Mechanism

As mentioned before, we have to rely on the provenance information, so the mechanism has to prevent unauthorized change of the data as well as deleting or modifying the provenance information. For this reason, we define the following requirements, that

[1] This piece is either a raw data item, an intermediate result or a feature vector.

must be fulfilled by the implementation of the provenance concept. It is worth to mention that the *residential risk* of circumventing this chain-of-custody is highly dependent on its implementation and the used database system. Consequently, we eventually need an additional intrusion detection system or we have to use IT-Forensics.

Change detection. Every change in a data item must be detectable. This means that an unwanted or malicious modification (including deletion) of a data item (D_k) of an FpD must be detectable.

Tight coupling. The binary data of a data item (D_k) and the corresponding $ProveSet(D_k)$ must be tightly coupled, so that it is *practically impossible* to delete or modify the ProveSet of D_k in an *unauthorized* manner.

Applicability. We need some functionality that allows to check the ProveSet of any data item by the database itself.

Performance. The overhead of verifying the ProveSet and the additional needed disk space to store the ProveSet shall be reduced to a minimum.

Modification. A transformation t_k has to have some possibility to extend the ProveSet(D_k) of its input data D_k to create the ProveSet(D_{k+1}) of its output data D_{k+1} as follows:

$$\begin{aligned} ProveSet(D_k) &= \{L(D_{raw}), S(t_0, \ldots, t_{k-1}), L(D_{k-1}), M\} \\ ProveSet(D_{k+1}) &= \{L(D_{raw}), S(t_0, \ldots, t_{k-1}, t_k), L(D_k), M\} \end{aligned} \tag{5}$$

4 Our Solution

In this section we present a solution that integrates the provenance concept described in Section 3.1 into FiVe DB and fulfills the additional requirements from Section 3.2.

4.1 The Provenance Mechanism - Verifying Structured Data with Redundant Unstructured Data

Subsequently, we show how a data item D_k and its ProveSet(D_k) stick together, so that FiVe DB can check them. Additionally, we explain the realization of the additional requirements.

Connecting the Provenance Information in the ProveSet Tightly to the Data. As described in Section 3.2, we need a mechanism that connects the ProveSet tightly to the data. In our solution, the ProveSet is embedded into the binary data of D_k. That means that whenever a transformation requests some D_k, the corresponding ProveSet is delivered as well. This is realized by the data format illustrated in Figure 3.

Every data item D_k has a part that contains redundant structured data that makes them *applicable* with common SQL and a part, containing unstructured data including the ProveSet. Redundant in this context means that structured data, such as the foreign key of the original raw data item, is also embedded into the binary unstructured data. Due to this separation, the performance of the system is still reasonable because the ProveSet is not extracted form the binary data whenever queries are performed on the

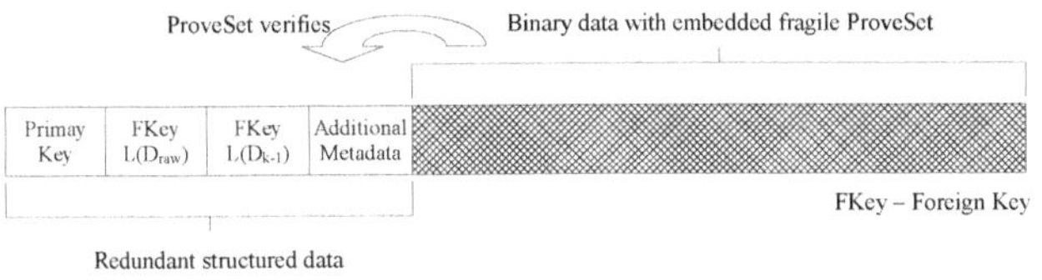

Fig. 3. Format of a data item

structured part of the data item. Additionally, we prevent from modification of the redundant data by mechanisms of the database system. It is worth to remind that the data items are inserted in FiVe DB and not modified again. When we need to verify the structured information we can do that by calling a stored procedure *check(primary_key)* from the provenance library (see Figure 1) that extracts the *fragile* ProveSet(D_k) from the binary (unstructured) data. If the *check()* function fails (i.e., it is not possible to extract the ProveSet), this indicates that the binary data has been changed unauthorized. If there are contradictions between the extracted ProveSet and the redundant structured data, the structured data has been modified unwarranted. So we can *detect* inappropriate *modification* of the data and determine that the data no longer holds integrity. We integrate the integrity checks into the system's processes that are explained in Section 4.2. Furthermore, we create internal database jobs that execute the checks continuously on the whole FiVe DB.

To realize the embedding of the fragile ProveSet into the binary data, we plan to use an invertible watermarking technique [9]. The watermark is embedded into the binary data of D_k. Furthermore, it is possible to embed the ProveSet into the watermark. Whenever an attacker modifies the data, the fragile watermark, including the ProveSet, cannot be extracted by FiVe DB. Hence, we can detect malicious data modification.

4.2 Integration of the Provenance Concept

One basic concept in designing FiVe DB is to integrate the provenance concept tightly into the system behavior to make the circumvention of this concept as hard as possible. Another important issue is to detect every inappropriate modification of an FpD or its ProveSet. As illustrated in Figure 1, there are three operations that may add data to FiVe DB: insert a new raw data item, create an intermediate result and calculate a feature vector. For each of these operations, we specify a process that ensures that the operation is well defined. We prevent every other (inappropriate) modification of the data by mechanisms of the database system itself. For example, we use a fine grained role system to specify who has access to what data. Access control is a native part of each database system following the SQL Standard [1]. Furthermore access control is one of FiVe DB's mechanisms to ensure confidentiality that is recommended for a chain-of-custody. In future we will have to define more processes for maintenance purposes where some attributes of a data item may be changed.

As an example, we will explain the process of creating a new intermediate result, because it is the most complex one and show how it fulfills the formalization presented in 3.1. The other two processes are designed in the same manner.

Example Process - Inserting a New Intermediate Result. Creating a new intermediate result consists of three steps. First, a transformation requests an intermediate result or raw data item from FiVe DB. Second, the transformation computes an new intermediate result. Finally, this result with the appropriate provenance information is inserted into FiVe DB. We illustrate the process in Figure 4 in detail and describe the particular steps in the following. Thereby, we will explain how we guarantee integrity and authenticity.

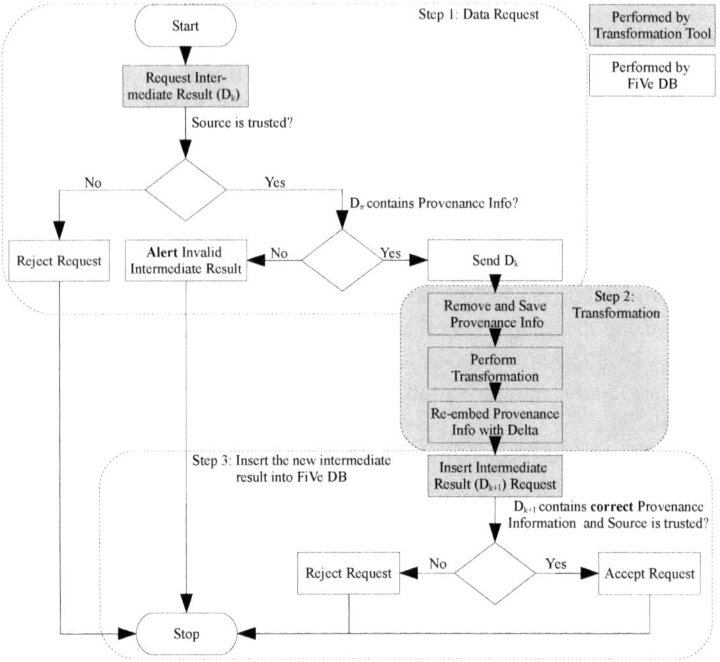

Fig. 4. Process example: Create a new intermediate result

Data request. A transformation initially triggers the process requesting the input data (D_k) from FiVe DB by calling a *stored procedure*. There is no direct way of accessing the (binary) data[2] via common SQL. This allows FiVe DB to check whether the requested data has the provenance information and to collect additional meta data.

In the case that FiVe DB trusts the transformation tool (*confidentiality*), FiVe DB checks whether the requested data D_k has a *ProveSet(D_k)*. Afterwards, the DB determines the corresponding FpD and checks *if CProveSet(FpD) is correct* using the provenance library (see Figure 1 and attack three in Section 2.1). Hence, we can guarantee that any previous transformation process from the raw data to D_k has performed well: the data holds *integrity*. This also means that FiVe DB can trace back the intermediate result to a raw data item that was inserted by a trusted sensor, so the data is *authentic*. In this way we assure that FiVe DB only sends intermediate results to a transformation tool that hold *integrity and authenticity*.

[2] The tools have read-only access to the meta data to select the right input.

Transformation. In step two, the transformation tool first checks the existence of ProveSet(D_k). If it does not exist the data has been modified during the transportation from FiVe DB to the tool (see attack four in Section 2.1). When ProveSet(D_k) exists, it has to be removed from D_k to perform the transformation. The transformation tool now creates D_{k+1} as t(D_k) and embeds ProveSet(D_{k+1}) into D_{k+1}, which allows FiVe DB to check whether this intermediate result holds *integrity* (detect attack six).

Insert new intermediate result. Finally, the transformation tool calls a different stored procedure to insert the new intermediate result D_{k+1}. Before accepting the request FiVe DB checks whether the tool is trusted, so we can assume that D_{k+1} is computed as t(D_k) and Five DB knows that D_k is authentic (prevent attack five from Section 2.1). Furthermore FiVe DB tests whether ProveSet(D_{k+1}) exists and if the CProveSet(FpD) including D_{k+1} is correct, to verify the integrity of D_{k+1}. Thus, we can detected data in this process that does not hold *integrity or authenticity*.

Rejecting request and alerts. There are several routines in the processes that detect an incorrect CProveSet or react when an untrusted transformation or sensor tries to communicate with FiVe DB.

5 Related Work

When using database systems, the security aspects of authenticity and integrity as well as confidentiality must be met (see Section 1). Especially to ensure confidentiality, it must be assured that data no longer needed is securely deleted and that the data when in use is not accessible to unauthorized users. To detect and investigate security breaches, IT-Forensics has to be applied to the mass storage, the main memory and the network data stream of a computer system. For that, the operating system, the file system, the database system and any security software as explicit means of intrusion detection as well as any scaling of methods for evidence gathering and software for data processing and evaluation will have to be investigated for the presence of forensically relevant data. In [15], Kiltz et al. show this process, using a holistic model of the forensic process that differentiates into phases, classes of forensic methods and forensically relevant data types, how main memory content can be acquired, investigated and analyzed. In [12] Fowler shows, how a database system can be forensically investigated and analyzed at the example of the Microsoft SQL Server. Here it is stated that part of potential digital evidence can be found in the main memory and in the mass storage section of a computer system but to make sense of some of the data, methods of the IT-Application (i.e., the database system) have to be used.

Ensuring the chain-of-custody in databases for forensic systems in databases is a quite new research topic. The general data provenance mechanism in databases often deal with uncertain and structured data and are not reliable [2,5,8,23]. A reliable provenance mechanism based on watermarks to guarantee the chain-of-custody for digital images, which may be used in court, is explained in [4]. This approach does not use databases and does not include quality enhancement of the original image. In [14] Hasan et al. present a secure provenance mechanism in documents, which can be interpreted as chain-of-custody. The authors concentrate on detecting unauthorized rewrites of documents and it's chain-of-custody and leave the question of efficiently tracking unauthorized reading attempts open. By contrast, we can identify unauthorized reading attempts, because of our database-centric architecture and the usage of stored procedures, which allow fine grained logging. Additionally, we can use native mechanisms of the database such as role-based access to ensure *confidentiality*. Furthermore, in our concept the provenance information (ProveSet) is tightly linked to the data, so whenever the data is send the ProveSet is delivered as well.

6 Conclusion and Future Perspectives

In this paper, we presented a database-centric chain-of-custody for databases in forensic biometric systems. First, we explained the importance of ensuring *integrity and authenticity* in forensic scenarios. We introduced FiVe DB as an example and we described an attacker model based on the architecture and the data stored in FiVe DB. To ensure the chain-of-custody, we explained that common mechanisms to track the history of a data item used in databases (data provenance) are generally *not reliable*, because they can easily be modified. Consequently, we developed a formalization of a provenance concept that provides the needed information. Additionally, we defined supplemental requirements that an implementation of this concept has to fulfill to be *reliable*. Furthermore, we explained a mechanism that allows to install our reliable provenance concept. This mechanism extends the general approach by storing redundant fragile data in the binary unstructured image of each data item. Finally, we showed how we integrate the provenance concept tightly into FiVe DB to ensure integrity and authenticity. Hence, the circumvention of the chain-of-custody is as hard as possible and we can detect malicious modification of the data (with a certain *residential risk*).

In future, we plan to evaluate different implementation of our provenance concept on different database systems according to the requirements defined in Section 3.2. Additionally, we have to extend the concept, by defining processes to modify the data for maintenance purposes, which alters the attacker model (see Section 2.1). Furthermore, we want to examine data fusion algorithms to support efficient query computation.

Acknowlegements

The work in this paper has been funded in part by the German Federal Ministry of Education and Science (BMBF) through the Research Program under Contract No. FKZ: 13N10817 and FKZ: 13N10818. We would also thank Prof. Dr.-Ing. Jana Dittmann and Prof. Dr. Gunter Saake for their support for this paper.

References

1. ANSI/ISO/IEC 9075:1999. International Standard - Database Language SQL (1999)
2. Benjelloun, O., Sarma, A., Halevy, A., Widom, J.: Uldbs: databases with uncertainty and lineage. In: Proc. Int. Conf. on Very Large Data Bases, VLDB, pp. 953–964 (2006)
3. Bishop, M.: Computer Security - Art and Science. Addison-Wesley, Reading (2003)

4. Blythe, P., Fridrich, J.: Secure digital camera. In: Proc. of Digital Forensic Research Workshop, pp. 17–19 (2004)
5. Buneman, P., Khanna, S., Tan, W.-C.: Why and where: A characterization of data provenance. In: Van den Bussche, J., Vianu, V. (eds.) ICDT 2001. LNCS, vol. 1973, pp. 316–330. Springer, Heidelberg (2000)
6. Cheney, J., Chiticariu, L., Tan, W.-C.: Provenance in databases: Why, how, and where. Foundations and Trends in Databases 1(4), 379–474 (2009)
7. Codd, E.: A relational model of data for large shared data banks. Comm. of the ACM 13(6), 377–387 (1970)
8. Cui, Y., Widom, J., Wiener, J.: Tracing the lineage of view data in a warehousing environment. ACM Trans. Database Syst. 25, 179–227 (2000)
9. Dittmann, J., Katzenbeisser, S., Schallhart, C., Veith, H.: Provably secure authentication of digital media through invertible watermarks. Cryptology ePrint Archive, Report 293 (2004)
10. Dittmann, J., Wohlmacher, P., Nahrstedt, K.: Using cryptographic and watermarking algorithms. IEEE MultiMedia 8, 54–65 (2001)
11. The Federal Commisioner for Data Protection and Freedom of Information. Federal data protection act (bdsg) in the version promulgated on 14 January 2003 (federal law gazette i, p. 66), last amended by article 1 of the act of 14 August 2009, (federal law gazette i, p. 2814), (in force from September 1, 2009)
12. Fowler, K.: SQL Server Forensic Analysis. Addison-Wesley, Reading (2008)
13. Garfinkel, S.: Providing cryptographic security and evidentiary chain-of-custody with the advanced forensic format, library, and tools. Digital Crime and Forensics 1(1), 1–28 (2009)
14. Hasan, R., Sion, R., Winslett, M.: The case of the fake picasso: preventing history forgery with secure provenance. In: Proc. Int. Conf. on File and Storage Technologies, pp. 1–14. USENIX Association (2009)
15. Kiltz, S., Hoppe, T., Dittmann, J., Vielhauer, C.: Video surveillance: A new forensic model for the forensically sound retrival of picture content off a memory dump. In: Proc. of Informatik 2009 - Digitale Multimedia-Forensik. LNI, vol. 154, pp. 1619–1633 (2009)
16. Kiltz, S., Lang, A., Dittmann, J.: Taxonomy for computer security incidents. In: Cyber Warfare and Cyber Terrorism (2007)
17. Leich, M., Ulrich, M.: Forensic fingerprint detection: Challenges of benchmarking new contact-less fingerprint scanners – a first proposal. In: Proc. Workshop on Pattern Recognition for IT Security. TU-Darmstadt, Darmstadt (2010)
18. Meints, M., Biermann, H., Bromba, M., Busch, C., Hornung, G., Quiring-Kock, G.: Biometric systems and data protection legislation in germany. In: Proc. Int. Conf. on Intelligent Information Hiding and Multimedia Signal Processing, pp. 1088–1093. IEEE, Los Alamitos (2008)
19. Newman, R.: Computer forensics: evidence, collection, and management. Auerbach (2007)
20. Stonebraker, M., Moore, D.: Object Relational DBMSs. Morgan Kaufmann, San Francisco (1996)
21. Stoneburner, G., Goguen, A., Feringa, A.: Risk management guide for information technology systems [electronic resource]: recommendations of the National Institute of Standards and Technology. U.S. Dept. of Commerce, National Institute of Standards and Technology
22. Tan, W.-C.: Provenance in databases: Past, current, and future. IEEE Data Engineering Bulletin 32(4), 3–12 (2007)
23. Zhang, J., Chapman, A., LeFevre, K.: Do you know where your data's been? - Tamper-evident database provenance. Technical Report CSE-TR-548-08, Univ. of Michigan (2009)

Automated Forensic Fingerprint Analysis: A Novel Generic Process Model and Container Format

Tobias Kiertscher[1], Claus Vielhauer[1,2], and Marcus Leich[2]

[1] University of Applied Sciences Brandenburg, Dept. of Informatics and Media, P.O. Box 2132, 14737 Brandenburg a. d. Havel, Germany

[2] Otto-von-Guericke University of Magdeburg, Dept. of Computer Science, Research Group Multimedia and Security, P.O. Box 4120, 39016 Magdeburg, Germany

{kiertscher,vielhauer}@fh-brandenburg.de, mleich@st.ovgu.de

Abstract. The automated forensic analysis of latent fingerprints poses a new challenge. While for the pattern recognition aspects involved, the required processing steps can be related to fingerprint biometrics, the common biometric model needs to be extended to face the variety of characteristics of different surfaces and image qualities and to keep the chain of custody. Therefore, we introduce a framework for automated forensic analysis of latent fingerprints. The framework consists of a generic process model for multi-branched process graphs w.r.t. security aspects like integrity, authenticity and confidentiality. It specifies a meta-model to store all necessary data and operations in the process, while keeping the chain of custody. In addition, a concept for a technical implementation of the meta-model is given, to build a container format, which suits the needs of an automated forensic analysis in research and application.

Keywords: Automated forensic analysis, automated dactyloscopy, multi-branched biometric process, forensic container format.

1 Introduction

Dactyloscopy, i.e. the recovery of latent fingerprints with a wide range of analysis methods for different kinds of surfaces is a commonly used criminal investigation technique. Currently, the recovery is a manual process, done by specialists. However, the manual processing of latent fingerprints is time-consuming and implies physical and chemical modifications of the original trace, due to vaporization, for example. Our research project [1] prospects a contactless way to recover latent fingerprints, with an optical high resolution surface scanner, which produces *topography maps*. One goal of the project is to define an automatic forensic analysis process to recover the fingerprints from a wide range of surfaces. This poses numerous research problems for example in the domains of signal processing and pattern recognition, in order to minimize detection errors. However, in this domain, an additional requirement for handling the forensic process chain has evolved, which will be addressed in this paper.

Because of the varying requirements for the pre-processing and feature extraction algorithms w.r.t. the different surfaces, our pattern recognition process is based on the

C. Vielhauer et al. (Eds.): BioID 2011, LNCS 6583, pp. 262–273, 2011.

components of a generic biometric process and embodies a *multi-branched process graph* with a number of alternative and parallel processing steps. In that multi-branched process graph it is possible to select certain algorithms based on the results of other algorithms, just like a dactyloscopy specialist selects certain methods based on his experience. And it is also possible to apply more than one algorithm in parallel and compare the results to select the best.

Integrity and *authenticity* as commonly known in IT security [2], are two important security aspects in that process graph, which is the foundation for our forensic data processing application. To assure the *chain of custody* [3], while processing the topography maps, the integrity and authenticity of the raw data from the scanner needs to be secured likewise the integrity and authenticity of intermediate and resulting data. Furthermore, a set of every algorithm and their *parameter sets*, applied in a *processing step*, needs to be kept as well to follow the Daubert standard [4], which is a set of requirements for legal relevant evidence. Since the potentially recovered fingerprints are highly sensible w.r.t. *privacy*, encryption is another important requirement, when the data is stored or transmitted.

To facilitate the chain of custody and the desired confidentiality in such an automated dactyloscopy process environment, a *forensic data container format* with sufficient support for a multi-branched process graph and the before mentioned security aspects is required. Because we have not been able to identify an existing container format which suits our needs, in our reviews, we propose a novel container format to store an evidence chain in an automated multi-branched dactyloscopy process.

This paper is organized as follows: In the first section of this paper, an introduction is given. In the second section we develop further requirements for the container format, in consideration of the multi-branched dactyloscopy process. We then review the state of the art to evaluate already introduced formats in context of the process. Following the state of the art, we describe the novel container format. Therefore, we introduce a generic process model for an automated forensic analysis of biometric trace in section 4, including a meta-model, which supports the definition of a container format to store the data and operations in each process step, while keeping the chain of custody. (The meta-model describes the logical elements without suggesting any implementation techniques.) Furthermore, we show a way to implement the meta-model with a specific forensic process in section 5. First insights in our technical implementation of the container format are given in section 6, followed by conclusion and presentation of future work in section 7.

2 Requirements of an Automated Forensic Process

As shown in the introduction, one goal of our project is to define an automated forensic analysis process for latent fingerprints. To reach this goal, we apply concepts from the field of dactyloscopy as well as from fingerprint biometrics. Dactyloscopy and fingerprint biometrics are conceptually similar w.r.t. the basic data processing steps (pre-processing, feature extraction, classification). However, there are additional requirements for dactyloscopy. The chain of custody needs to be preserved in every processing step. And due to the huge variations w.r.t. condition and environment of latent fingerprints, a broad range of algorithms for pre-processing and feature extraction is needed, and must be applied in an adaptive way. As a bridge between these two fields a forensic data container format with the capability to store the data (source, intermediate and result), algorithms and parameter sets of a multi-branched forensic fingerprint analysis process is desirable.

With respect to the chain of custody, the input and output data of each process step can be comprehended as a forensic record with a set of predecessors and an assigned processing algorithm using a parameter set. As a result the container format must support the storage of dependencies between the data, to form a multi-branched graph. The individual process steps can be distributed over network and it is necessary to be able to interrupt the process between process steps, continue later, and still keep the chain of custody. Therefore, the container format must assure integrity and authenticity of every source, intermediate and resulting data, along with the applied processing algorithms. A goal is, according to the Daubert standard, to enable the reproducibility of the whole dactyloscopy process, with the information stored in the container. In addition, the container format needs to support encryption for the data w.r.t. privacy issues.

An important additional requirement for our research is, to have easy access to the data with a broad range of programming languages and scientific tools, e.g. GNU Octave [5]. It is desirable to get at least read access to the data in the forensic container through commonly used software techniques without the need of a programming library, which restricts the retrieval of the data to a certain programming language.

3 State of the Art

The following state of the art, which is relevant to automated analysis of latent fingerprints, discusses the process model and the container format.

Process Model

Amongst the variety, a common process model for a biometric process was introduced in [6] and adopted e.g. by [7]. This process model, shown in Fig. 1, includes the three data processing steps "data acquisition", "pre-processing" and "feature extraction" for the biometric data and a classification stage, which uses a

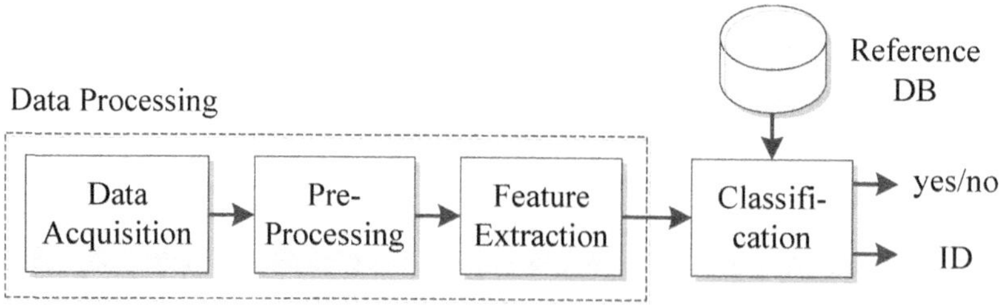

Fig. 1. A general biometric process

reference database and delivers a Boolean or an ID. This and other models have proven in a large number of biometric applications.

However, in contrast to the controlled environment in most biometric applications, forensic traces, like latent fingerprints, do have much more varying quality and characteristics. To encounter these difficulties, a process for automated dactyloscopy needs to be modular and adaptive and must support a multi-branched process graph. The whole data processing in biometrics is typically done in a trusted environment and there is no such strong need for assuring a gapless chain of custody, as with a forensic analysis in dactyloscopy, which often is distributed over a number of institutes and specialists. Therefore, we are looking for a process model to be represented by a data container format to cover the before mentioned needs.

Container Format

There are commonly used data formats in both fields, forensics and biometrics. In the field of forensics, formats, also called DEC (Digital Evidence Container) or DEB (Digital Evidence Bag), have been introduced, like the AFF (Advanced Forensics Framework) [8], and the proprietary EWF (Expert Witness Format) [9]. Both formats are specialized in storing disk images. AFF supports cryptographic methods for assuring integrity and authenticity, but since it only supports the storage of one disk image and some meta-data in a key-value manner, it is not sufficient for the needs of an automated forensic analysis of latent fingerprints. The EWF is a proprietary format with no public documentation, and is consequently not a good choice for applications in research.

An extended version of the AFF, called AFF4 and proposed in [10], is very flexible and does support multiple evidence data streams, meta-data as simple RDF triples and external references. The AFF4 is designed to support huge evidence corpuses, even if they are stored in a distributed environment. However, since AFF4 addresses the intense use of disk images in a various ways, e.g. remapping for memory analysis, it adds complexity to the format, which is not necessary in the context of a biometric process. Another problem with AFF4 is that, even though the use of hashes and signatures for data elements is possible, it is not mandatory. And there is no way specified, to put a signature of a volume into the volume to encapsulate data for verifying its own integrity.

In the field of biometrics some formats like CBEFF (Common Biometric Exchange Formats Framework) [11], developed by the NIST, and the related XCBF (XML Common Biometrical Format) [12] standardized by OASIS, have been suggested. These formats are designed to be used in biometrical applications and do support integrity and authenticity as well as confidentiality. They are using a single-file concept and their main purpose is the storage of one or multiple biometric data samples, in terms of raw data or biometric templates in a standardized format like the formats specified in [13]. This approach however, will result in a scenario with large raw data blocks (e.g. topography maps) and a couple of intermediate data with comparable size, in very large files. They do not support compression and since XCBF stores binary data with Base64 encoding, this problem increases even more.

4 Generic Process Model and Meta-model

As apparently the classic biometric process model, likewise the existing forensic and biometric file formats, do not fit the needs of an automated forensic fingerprint analysis in research and application with support for a chain of custody, we propose a generic process model along with a novel forensic container format with sufficient support for such a process.

4.1 Generic Process Model

Our generalization of the biometric process starts at the data acquisition level, by abstraction to the *initialization* of the process, because a forensic analysis can start with data acquisition, as well as with existing intermediate data. Secondly, the two steps "pre-processing" and "feature extraction" are abstracted to *transformations*, since in a multi-branched process graph for automated dactyloscopy, there are more than two fixed processing steps, which can be applied on demand. The resulting data of a step, including the used parameter set for the acquisition or transformation, is called *entity*. Every process step depends on a *provenance*: The initialization depends on a data *source* and a transformation depends on an *algorithm*. A transformation can use at least one existing entity as input and produces exactly one entity as output. The process can only be interrupted after a step is completed.

To support the chain of custody, every step ends with the signing of the resulting entity. Fig. 2 gives a brief overview to the generic process model. The classification stage of the process is not a subject of this model.

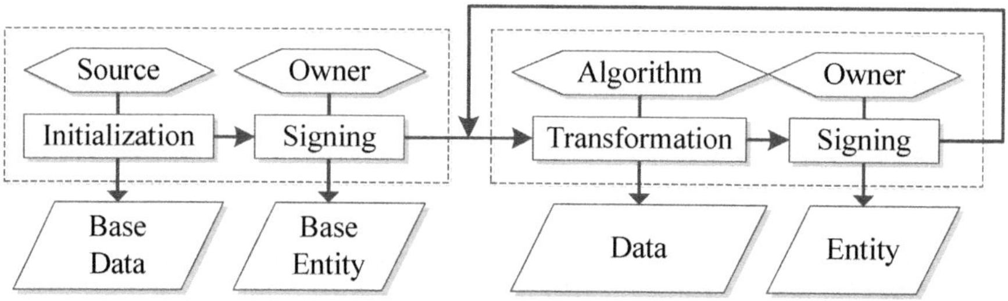

Fig. 2. Initialization and transformation in the generic process

Our assumption in this model is, that the production, transformation and signing of entities is performed in trusted environments (illustrated by dotted boxes in Fig. 2), while the container can be exchanged over untrusted channels.

4.2 Meta-model

The meta-model defines elements and their relations which are suitable to store the entities of the model introduced in 4.1, and is designed to assure integrity, authenticity and optional confidentiality.

4.2.1 Structure

The elements of the container structure are forming a tree, with the *container* element as the root. The container element is parent of a number of *editions*, one current edition and a stack of past editions. An edition contains a global unique identifier, a timestamp, the description of an authority, called *owner*, which has created or extended the container, and a list with all entities added to the container, while creation and extension, respectively. The stack of past editions is forming the *history* of the container. During the initialization of a container, the current edition is created and the history stack is empty. When the container is extended, the former current edition is wrapped into a *history item*, pushed on to the stack and a new current edition is created. Besides the current edition and the history, an *entity index*, with references to all entities stored in the container, is child of the container element too.

An entity element is the parent of an *entity header*, optionally a *parameter set* from the provenance of the entity, which can be the source or the transformation algorithm, and at least one *value*. The entity header contains a container-wide unique *id*, a list of the id's of all predecessor entities and a reference to the provenance of the entity. Furthermore the entity header references an *entity type*. The definition of the entity type describes all required and optional values of the entity along with their data types. Fig. 3 gives an overview to the meta-model.

4.2.2 Security

To assure the integrity and authenticity of the data, the provenance parameter set and all values of an entity are protected by a signature (*value signature*) as well as the whole entity (*entity signature*). In the following figures, signatures are visualized by the symbol 🖹. At the root of the structure, a *master signature* secures the whole container. Every time the container is extended, i.e. insertion of one or more new signed entities, the former master signature is integrated into the new history item and pushed on to the history stack. In the figures, a past signature is annotated by the symbol ◷. After the extension, a new master signature is created and integrated into the container element. All signatures, from the value signatures over the entity signatures up to the master signature, are implementing a hierarchical hash tree in analogy to a Merkle-Hash-Tree [14]. However, there is a difference in that every level in the tree not only uses a cryptographic hash, but uses a complete signature as well. As a result the integrity of a partial data structure, like an entity as part of the container, can be verified as well as its authenticity, even if other elements or the root in the structure are corrupted.

The hash of an entity signature does not cover the data of the child elements, like the provenance parameter set or the data of the values, but does only cover the entity header and the signatures of the child elements. The same restriction applies to the master signature. The hash of the master signature covers all child elements of the container element, including the entity signatures, but excluding the data of the entities. This way, the structure of the container can be verified, even if some child elements are corrupted. If, e.g. an entity is corrupted, the master signature is not affected directly and can still verify the history of the container and the content of the entity index. If the entity signature, covered by the master signature, is checked, it proofs the content of the entity to be corrupted. As a consequence, to proof the integrity and authenticity of a whole container, at first its master signature needs to be verified.

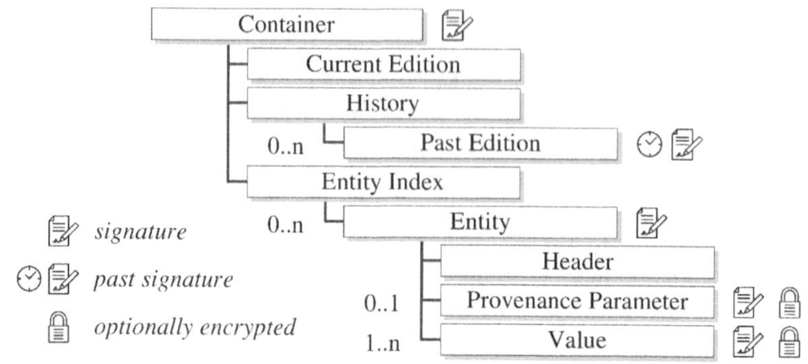

Fig. 3. Overview to the meta-model

After the master signature proofs to be correct, every entity signature needs to be verified as well. And after an entity signature proofs to be correct, the signatures of the entity's children must be verified as well.

To allow confidentiality during transmission of the container, only the parameter sets of the entity provenances and all intermediate data, in terms of entity values, need to be encrypted. Encrypted values must be decrypted prior to any transformation. If continuous confidentiality is required, resulting entity values need to be encrypted also. Respecting that the provenance parameter set and the entity values can be stored in an encrypted manner, meta-data, to describe the encryption, can be included in the entity header. In the figures, an element, which can be encrypted, is annotated with .

Our meta-model does not prescribe any cryptographic methods, like specific hash or encryption algorithms. Instead, when implementing the container format on the technical level, a catalogue with supported cryptographic algorithms needs to be embedded during application.

5 Conceptual Implementation

To map an automated analysis process of latent fingerprints to the generic process and build a process model, based on the meta-model, the following five steps are required:

Step 1 - Definition of data types for entity values. Entity values in the meta-model are treated as binary streams. To use the values in an actual process, they have to be associated with a data type, which is supported from the process. A global unique identifier is assigned to every data type to allow referencing from any number of containers. All data types have to be defined at first, to be referenced later.

Step 2 - Definition of data types for parameter sets. Equivalent to step 1, the data types for the parameter sets of the entity provenances must be defined.

Step 3 - Definition of the entity types, referencing data types for the values. Based on the data types, the entity types must be defined. Essentially an entity type is a list of property descriptions in the form (name, data type reference, use). The name is a string, unique in the context of the entity type. The data type reference points to a data type, defined in step 1. And the use can be "required" or "optional".

Step 4 - Definition of the data source interfaces, referencing an output entity type and optional a data type for a parameter set. To allow the process to start, the interfaces of all data sources, which are capable of producing entities, must be defined. A global unique identifier is assigned to every data source to be referenced from the entities in any number of containers. The output of the data source is specified by referencing an entity type, defined in step 3. Thus, the required and allowed entity values, produced by the source, are specified. If a data source is configurable by a number of parameters, its definition can reference a data type, defined in step 2, to store its configuration as provenance parameter set, along with the entity values.

Step 5 - Definition of the transformation algorithm interfaces, referencing input entity types, an output entity type and optional a data type for a parameter set. The interfaces of all transformation algorithms in the process must be defined. Therefore a global unique identifier is assigned to every transformation algorithm, accordingly to the data sources. The input of the algorithm needs to be specified in terms of a list, referencing entity types from step 3. The output type and optional a parameter set is defined in the same way as for the data sources in step 4.

Fig. 4 shows the overall method to implement an actual process model (left) and an actual container format (right) as well, which will be described later.

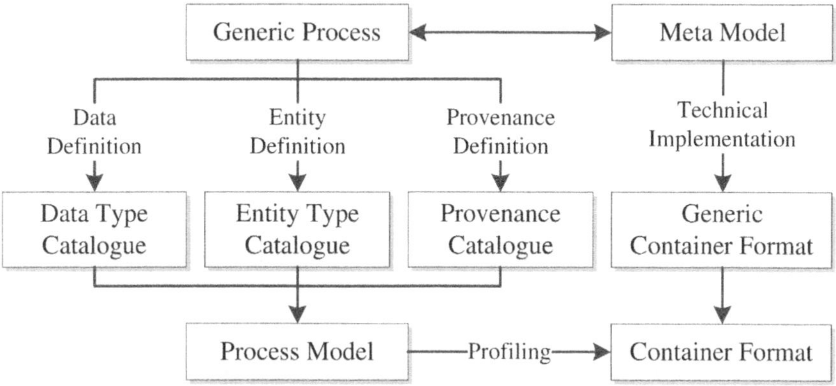

Fig. 4. Definition of an actual container format

The results are three catalogues:

Data types. This catalogue maps a global unique identifier to a data type description, which allows the interpretation of a binary data stream. The data can belong to an entity value or to an entity provenance parameter set.

Entity types. This catalogue maps a global unique identifier to a property list with references to data types, which allows the interpretation of the values in an entity.

Entity provenance interfaces. This catalogue maps a global unique identifier to an interface description of an entity provenance (sources and transformation algorithms), including input and output entity types and optional a data type for a parameter set. The relations between entity types and entity provenance interfaces are implementing the process model.

The following example illustrates an actual process model. The scenario is a fingerprint analysis process starting with a scanner, which delivers the raw image in a proprietary format. The scanner is the entity source and the proprietary raw data format is a value type, which is used by the entity type "RAW Data". There are two transformations taking "RAW Data" as input: The "Image Extraction" and the "Advanced Extraction". The algorithm for image extraction delivers an entity with the type "Bitmap"; the algorithm for advanced extraction reads the proprietary meta-data and delivers a "Physical Context" entity. In this simple example there is only one preprocessing algorithm, which takes a bitmap and delivers a bitmap. Another transformation is "Feature Extraction", which takes a "Bitmap" and a "Physical Context", and delivers a "Minutiae" entity, which encapsulates a minutiae feature vector. A possible analysis graph is shown in Fig. 5.

- Entity type catalogue: RAW Data, Bitmap, Physical Context, Minutiae
- Entity provenance catalogue
    - Scanner: input = (), output = "RAW Data"
    - Image Extraction: input = ("RAW Data"), output = "Bitmap"
    - Advanced Extraction: input = ("RAW Data"), output = "Physical Context"
    - Pre-Processing: input = ("Bitmap"), output = "Bitmap"
    - Feature Extraction: input = ("Bitmap", "Physical Context"), output = "Minutiae"

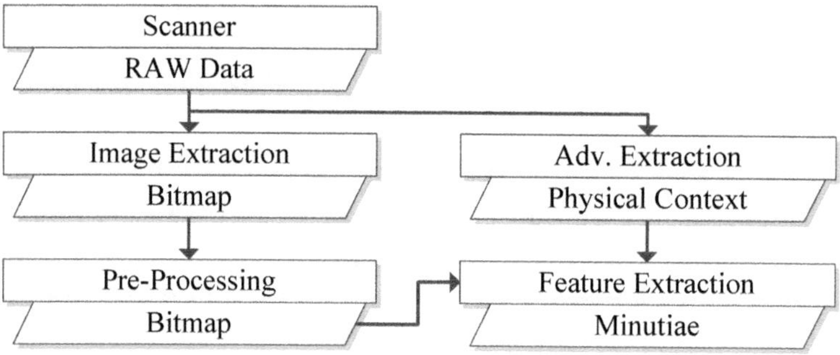

Fig. 5. Example of a multi-branched process graph

6 Technical Implementation

To build an actual container format for our concept, introduced in the previous section, a technical implementation of the meta-model is needed (see Fig. 4). In the following the basic information for a possible implementation, under use of current technologies, is given. However, this description cannot fulfill the task of a detailed technical specification.

The technical implementation stages in three levels. The first level is a storage mechanism, which can store files associated by a relative path. We suggest using the two storage mechanisms described in [10]: a directory in a file system and alternatively a

ZipFile. The storage as a directory comes with the benefit of having very easy access to all elements in the container stored as individual files, but with a lack of compression while transport, e.g. as a HTTP download. The storage as a ZipFile comes with the benefit of compression and easier handling while transport, but with the requirement to use a programming library with ZipFile parsing capability while accessing the content of the container.

The second level is to define the way of structuring and storing elements of the meta-model in files and directories. To store entity values and parameter sets according to their associated data types, we propose to store them as binary streams in a file per value or parameter set, respectively. To store the other elements of the meta-model we propose to use XML files. We suggest one XML file for the container element as root, including the current edition, the history and the entity index, but excluding the entities and their child elements. Further, every entity including header, entity signature, parameter set reference and value references, is stored in its own XML file. The entity index, however, contains copies of the signatures from every entity. This is building a three-level-hierarchy: A XML file describing the container at the root, a XML file per entity and a binary file for every value or parameter set. To simplify the identification of value and parameter set files we propose to use a sub directory for every entity (see Fig. 6). The structure of the XML files for the container and the entities is defined by a XML schema [15, 16].

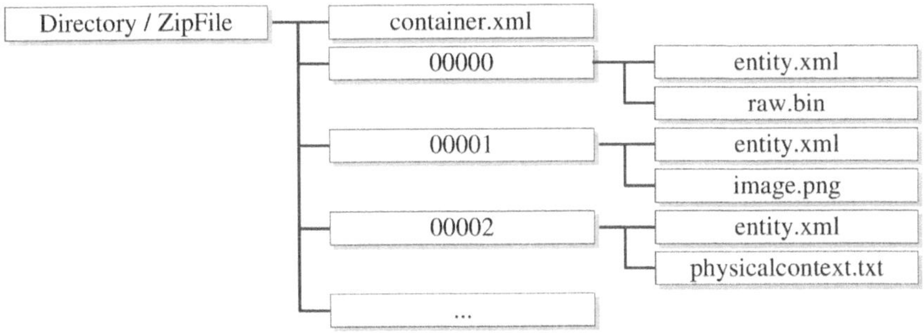

Fig. 6. Technical structure of a container

The third level of the implementation is to define the details. An important part is the design of a global unique identifier, e.g. to identify an edition. We propose to use GUID's after the scheme in RFC 4122 [17]. The signatures of the XML files, the entity signature and the master signature, should be implemented by using the W3C recommendation for signatures in XML documents [18]. To build hashes from a XML file, the canonical form without comments [19] should be used. Another important part is to implement the cryptographic aspects of the format. We propose to define a catalogue with supported cryptographic algorithms for hashing as well as for encryption. That way, the technical implementation of the container format does not need to be changed, if a better cryptographic method is going to be used after the specification of the format is completed.

7 Conclusion and Future Work

This paper motivates to the requirement of a chain-of-custody-preserving processing framework for automated forensic analysis of fingerprints. It introduces a novel process model for the automated forensic analysis of latent fingerprints and proposes a framework to specify a container format for storing all necessary data of such a process to assure the chain of custody. The framework consists of a meta-model which describes the logical elements of a container format, a description how to instantiate an actual process model based on the meta-model and a draft of a way to implement an appropriate container format on the technical level.

The meta-model further assures the authenticity and integrity of every process step, including the data from the scanner over intermediate data to the resulting biometric features. With respect to an adaptive and modular analysis process, the meta-model supports a multi-branched process graph. To suit the need for confidentiality the stored data can be encrypted. Further the draft of the technical implementation for a container format suggests the use of current technologies, like XML and ZipFiles. Following this draft, the data stored in a container can be extracted easily with a wide variety of programming languages or scientific software packages like GNU Octave and is thereby easy to use in research and application.

In future work, a detailed specification for the technical implementation needs to be devised. The implementation of the ZipFile version of the container format can benefit from the work in AFF4 [10], especially when large data values are used. Furthermore, two catalogues with standard data types and standard entity types for biometric applications are desirable. These catalogues can make benefit from the work in the CBEFF format [11], and XCBF format resp. [12]. At last a reference implementation for the container format is planned within the scope of an actual research project.

Acknowledgments

The authors want to acknowledge the support of all research partners in the project, especially Mario Hildebrand and Ronny Merkel of Otto von Guericke University.

This work is supported by the German Federal Ministry of Education and Research (BMBF), project "Digitale Fingerspuren (Digi-Dak)" under grant number 13N10816. The content of this document is under the sole responsibility of the authors.

References

1. Digitale Fingerspuren (2010), `http://omen.cs.uni-magdeburg.de/digi-dak/`
2. Bishop, M.: Introduction to Computer Security. Addison-Wesley Longman, Amsterdam (2004) ISBN 0321247442
3. Garfinkel, S.L.: Providing cryptographic security and evidentiary chain-of-custody with the advanced forensic format, library, and tools. In: IJDCF, vol. 1(1), pp. 1–28 (2009)
4. Raul, A.C., Dwyer, J.Z.: Regulatory Daubert: A Proposal to Enhance Judicial Review of Agency Science by Incorporating Daubert Principles into Administrative Law. Law and Contemporary Problems 66(4), 7–44 (2003), `http://www.law.duke.edu/shell/cite.pl?66+Law+&+Contemp.+Probs.+7+%28Autumn+2003%29`

5. Octave (2010), http://www.gnu.org/software/octave/
6. Zhang, D.D.: Automated biometrics: Technologies and systems, pp. 8–10. Kluwer, Boston (2000)
7. Vielhauer, C.: Biometric User Authentication for IT Security: From Fundamentals to Handwriting. Springer, New York (2006)
8. Garfinkel, S.L.: Afflib (2010), http://afflib.org/
9. Keightley, R.: EnCase version 3.0 manual revision 3.18 (2003), http://www.guidancesoftware.com/
10. Kohen, M., Garfinkel, S.L., Schatz, B.: Extending the advanced forensic format to accommodate multiple data sources, logical evidence, arbitrary information and forensic workflow. In: Digital Investigation, vol. 6(1), pp. 57–68. Elsevier, Amsterdam (2009)
11. Podio, F.L., et al.: Common Biometric Exchange Formats Framework, NIST IR 6529. NIST, Gaithersburg (2004), http://csrc.nist.gov/publications/nistir/NISTIR6529A.pdf
12. Larmouth, J.: XML Common Biometric Format, OASIS (2003), http://www.oasis-open.org/specs/
13. ISO/IEC 19794:2007: Information Technology: Biometric Data Interchange Formats, International Organization for Standardization, Geneva, Switzerland
14. Merkle, R.C.: A certified digital signature. In: Brassard, G. (ed.) CRYPTO 1989. LNCS, vol. 435, pp. 218–238. Springer, Heidelberg (1990)
15. W3C: XML Schema Part 1: Structures Second Edition (2004), http://www.w3.org/TR/xmlschema-1/
16. W3C: XML Schema Part 2: Datatypes Second Edition (2004), http://www.w3.org/TR/xmlschema-2/
17. Leach, P., et al.: A universally unique identifier (UUID) URN namespace. RFC 4122 (2005), http://www.ietf.org/rfc/rfc4122.txt
18. W3C: XML Signature Syntax and Processing Second Edition (2008), http://www.w3.org/TR/xmldsig-core/
19. W3C: Canonical XML Version 1.0 (2001), http://www.w3.org/TR/2001/REC-xml-c14n-20010315

Detecting Replay Attacks from Far-Field Recordings on Speaker Verification Systems

Jesús Villalba and Eduardo Lleida

Communications Technology Group (GTC),
Aragon Institute for Engineering Research (I3A),
University of Zaragoza, Spain
{villalba,lleida}@unizar.es

Abstract. In this paper, we describe a system for detecting spoofing attacks on speaker verification systems. By spoofing we mean an attempt to impersonate a legitimate user. We focus on detecting if the test segment is a far-field microphone recording of the victim. This kind of attack is of critical importance in security applications like access to bank accounts. We present experiments on databases created for this purpose, including land line and GSM telephone channels. We present spoofing detection results with EER between 0% and 9% depending on the condition. We show the degradation on the speaker verification performance in the presence of this kind of attack and how to use the spoofing detection to mitigate that degradation.

Keywords: spoofing, speaker verification, replay attack, far-field.

1 Introduction

Current state of the art speaker verification systems (SV) have achieved great performance due, mainly, to the appearance of the GMM-UBM [1] and Joint Factor Analysis (JFA) [2] approaches. However, this performance is usually measured in conditions where impostors do not make any effort to disguise their voices to make them similar to any true target speaker and where a true target speaker does not try to modify his voice to hide his identity. That is what happens in NIST evaluations [3].

In this paper, we dealt with a type of attack known as spoofing. Spoofing is the fact of impersonating another person using different techniques like voice transformation or playing of a recording of the victim. There are multiple techniques for voice disguise. In [4] authors do a study of voice disguise methods and classify them into electronic transformation or conversion, imitation, and mechanical and prosodic alteration. In [5] an impostor voice is transformed into the target speaker voice using a voice encoder and decoder. More recently, in [6] an HMM based speech synthesizer with models adapted from the target speaker is used to deceive an SV system. In this work, we focus on detecting a type of spoof known as replay attack. This is a very low technology spoof and the most easily available for any impostor without speech processing knowledge.

C. Vielhauer et al. (Eds.): BioID 2011, LNCS 6583, pp. 274–285, 2011.

The far-field recording and replay attack can be applied to text dependent and independent speaker recognition systems. The utterance used in the test is recorded by a far-field microphone and/or replayed on the telephone handset using a loudspeaker.

This paper is organized as follows. Section 2 explains the replay attack detection system. Section 3 describes the experiments and results. Finally, in section 4 we show some conclusions.

2 Far-Field Replay Attack Detection System

2.1 Features

For each recording we extract a set of several features. These features have been selected in order to be able to detect two types of manipulations on the speech signal:

- The signal have been acquired using a far-field microphone.
- The signal have been replayed using a loudspeaker.

Currently, speaker verification systems are mostly used on telephone applications. This means that the user is suppose to be near the telephone handset. If we can detect that the user was far of the handset during the recording we can consider it as an spoofing attempt. A far-field recording will cause an increment of the noise and reverberation levels of the signal. This will have as consequence a flattening of the spectrum and a reduction of the modulation indexes of the signal.

The simpliest way of injecting the spoofing recording into a phone-call is using a loudspeaker. Probably, the impostor will use a easily transportable device, with a small loudspeaker, like a smart-phone. This kind of loudspeaker presents bad frequency responses in the low part of the spectrum. Figure 1 shows a typical frequency response of a smart-phone loudspeaker. We can see that the low frequencies are strongly attenuated.

Following, we describe each of the features extracted.

Spectral Ratio. The spectral ratio (SR) is the ratio between the signal energy from 0 to 2 kHz and from 2 kHz and 4 kHz. For a frame n, it is calculated as:

$$SR(n) = \sum_{f=0}^{NFFT/2-1} \log\left(|X(f,n)|\right) \cos\left(\frac{(2f+1)\pi}{NFFT}\right) . \quad (1)$$

where $X(f, n)$ is the Fast Fourier Transform of the signal for the frame n. The average value of the spectral ratio for the speech segment is calculated using speech frames only. Using this ratio we can detect the flattening of the spectrum due to noise and reverberation.

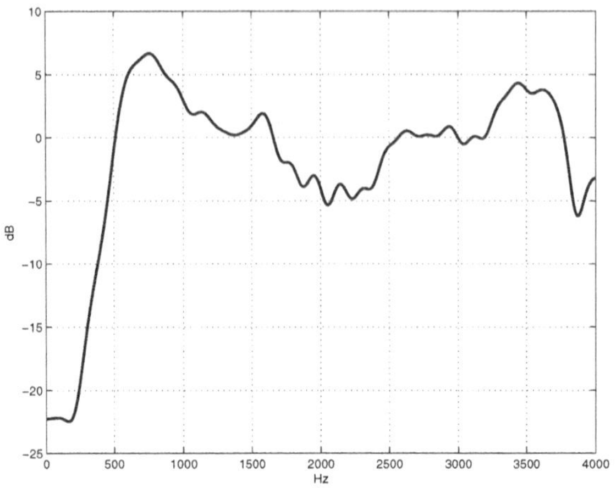

Fig. 1. Typical frequency response of smartphone loudspeaker

Low Frequency Ratio. We call low frequency (LFR) ratio to the ratio between the signal energy from 100Hz to 300Hz and from 300Hz to 500Hz. For a frame n, it is calculated as:

$$LFR(n) = \sum_{f=100\text{Hz}}^{300\text{Hz}} \log\left(|X(f,n)|\right) - \sum_{f=300\text{Hz}}^{500\text{Hz}} \log\left(|X(f,n)|\right) . \tag{2}$$

where $X(f,n)$ is the Fast Fourier Transform of the signal for frame n. The average value of the low frequency ratio for the speech segment is calculated using speech frames only. This ratio is useful for detecting the effect of the loudspeaker on the low part of the spectrum of the replayed signal.

Modulation Index. The modulation index at time t is calculated as

$$Indx(t) = \frac{v_{max}(t) - v_{min}(t)}{v_{max}(t) + v_{min}(t)} . \tag{3}$$

where $v(t)$ is the envelope of the signal and $v_{max}(t)$ and $v_{min}(t)$ are the local maximum and minimum of the envelope in the region close to time t. The envelope is approximated by the absolute value of the signal $s(t)$ down sampled to 60 Hz. The mean modulation index of the signal is calculated as the average of the modulation index of the frames that are above a threshold of 0.75. In Figure 2 we show a block diagram of the algorithm. The envelope of the far-field recording has higher local minimums due, mainly, to the additive noise. Therefore, it will have lower modulation indexes.

Sub-band Modulation Index. If the noise affects only to a small frequency band it could not have a noticeable effect on the previous modulation index. We calculate the modulation index of several sub-bands to be able to detect far-field recordings with coloured noises. The modulation index of each sub-band is

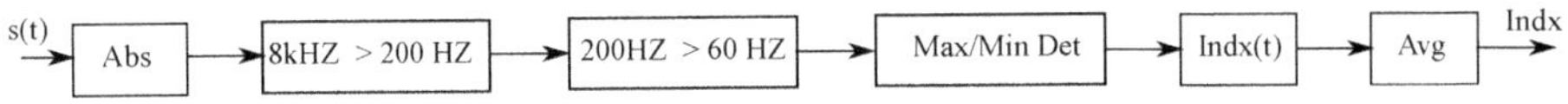

Fig. 2. Modulation index calculation

calculated filtering the signal with a pass-band filter in the desired band previous to calculating the modulation index. We have chosen to use indexes in the bands: 1kHz-3kHz, 1kHz–2kHz, 2kHz–3kHz, 0.5kHz–1kHz, 1kHz–1.5kHz, 1.5kHz–2kHz, 2kHz–2.5kHz, 2.5kHz–3kHz, 3kHz–3.5kHz.

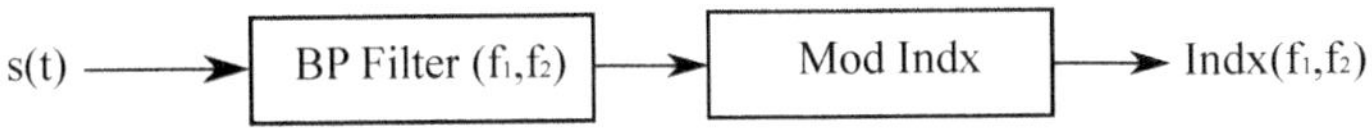

Fig. 3. Sub-band modulation index calculation

2.2 Classification Algorithm

Using the features described in the previous section we get a feature vector for each recording:

$$x = (SR, LFR, Indx(0, 4kHz), \ldots, Indx(3kHz, 3.5kHz)) . \quad (4)$$

For each input vector x we apply the SVM classification function:

$$f(x) = \sum_i \alpha_i k(x, x_i) + b . \quad (5)$$

where k is the kernel function, and x_i, α_i and b are the support vectors, the support vector weights, and the bias parameter that are estimated in the SVM training process. The kernel that best suits our task is the Gaussian kernel.

$$k(x_i, x_j) = exp\left(\gamma \left\|x_i - x_j\right\|^2\right) . \quad (6)$$

For each input vector x we apply an SVM classifier with a Gaussian kernel. We have used the LIBSVM toolkit [7]. For training the SVM parameters we have used data extracted from the training set of the SRE08 NIST database:

- Non spoofs: 1788 telephone signals of NIST SRE08 train set.
- Spoofs: synthetic spoofs made using interview signals from NIST SRE08 train set. We pass these signals through a loudspeaker and a telephone channel to simulate the conditions of a real spoof. We have used two different loudspeakers: a USB loudspeaker for a desktop computer and a mobile device loudspeaker; and two different telephone channels: analog and digital. In this way, we have 1475x4 spoof signals.

3 Experiments

3.1 Databases Description

Far-Field Database 1. We have used a database consisting of 5 speakers. Each speaker has 4 groups of signals:

- Originals: Recorded by a close talk microphone and transmitted by telephone channel. There are 1 train signal and 7 test signals. They are transmitted through different telephone channels: digital (1 train and 3 test signals), analog wired (2 test signals) and analog wireless (2 test signals).
- Microphone: Recorded simultaneously with the originals by a far-field microphone.
- Analog Spoof: The microphone test signals are used to do a replay attack on a telephone handset and transmitted by an analog channel.
- Digital Spoof: The microphone test signals with replay attack and transmitted by a digital channel.

Far-Field Database 2. This database has been recorded to do experiments with replay attacks on text dependent speaker recognition systems. In this kind of system, during the test phase, the speaker is asked to utter a given sentence. The spoofing process consists of manufacturing the test utterance by cutting and pasting fragments of speech (words, syllables) recorded previously from the speaker. There are no publicly available databases for this task so we have recorded our own one. The fragments used to create the test segments have been recorded using a far-field microphone so we can use our system to detect spoofing trials.

The database consists of three phases:

- Phase 1 + Phase 2: it has 20 speakers. It includes landline (T) signals for training, non spoof tests and spoofs tests; and GSM (G) for spoofs tests.
- Phase 3: it has 10 speakers. It includes landline and GSM signals for all training and testing sets.

Each phase has three sessions:

- Session 1: it is used for enrolling the speakers into the system. Each speaker has 3 utterances by channel type of 2 different sentences (F1,F2). Each sentence is about 2 seconds long.
- Session 2: it is used for testing non spoofing access trials and has 3 recordings by channel type of each of the F1 and F2 sentences.
- Session 3: it is made of different sentences and a long text that contain words from the sentences F1 and F2. It has been recorded by a far-field microphone. From this session several segments are extracted and used to build 6 sentences F1 and F2 that will be used for spoofing trials. After that, the signals are played on a telephone handset with a loudspeaker and transmitted through a landline or GSM channel.

3.2 Speaker Verification System

We have used an SV system based on JFA [2] to measure the performance degradation. Feature vectors of 20 MFCCs (C0-C19) plus first and second derivatives are extracted. After frame selection, features are short time Gaussianized as in [8]. A gender independent Universal Background Model (UBM) of 2048 Gaussians is trained by EM iterations. Then 300 eigenvoices v and 100 eigenchannels u are trained by EM ML+MD iterations. Speakers are enrolled using MAP estimates of their speaker factors (y,z) so the speaker means super vector is given by $M_s = m_{UBM} + vy + dz$. Trial scoring is performed using a first order Taylor approximation of the LLR between the target and the UBM models like in [9]. Scores are ZT Normalized and calibrated to log-likelihood ratios by linear logistic regression using the FoCal package [10] and the SRE08 trial lists. We have used telephone data from SRE04, SRE05 and SRE06 for UBM and JFA training, and score normalization.

3.3 Speaker Verification Performance Degradation

Far-Field Database 1. We have used this database to create 35 legitimate target trials, 140 non spoof non target, 35 analog spoofs and 35 digital spoofs. The training signals are 60 seconds long and the test signals 5 seconds approximately. We have got an EER of 0.71% using the non spoofing trials only. In Figure 4 we show the miss and false acceptance probabilities against the decision threshold. In that figure, we can see that, if we would choose the EER operating point as the decision threshold, we would accept 68% of the spoofing trials.

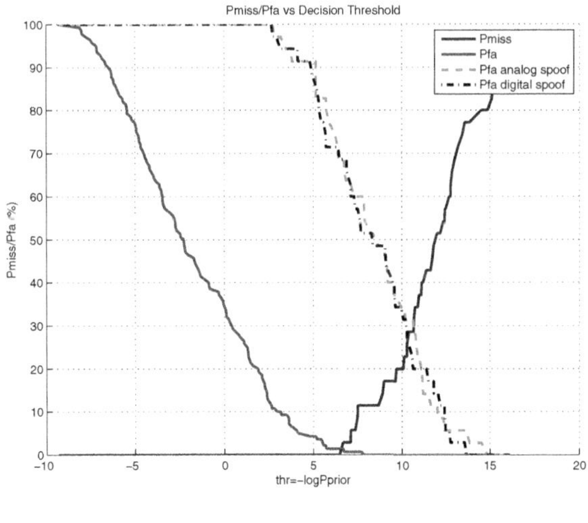

Fig. 4. Pmiss/Pfa vs decision threshold of the far-field database 1

In Figure 5 we show the score distribution of each trial dataset. There is an important overlap between the target and the spoof dataset. Table 1 presents the

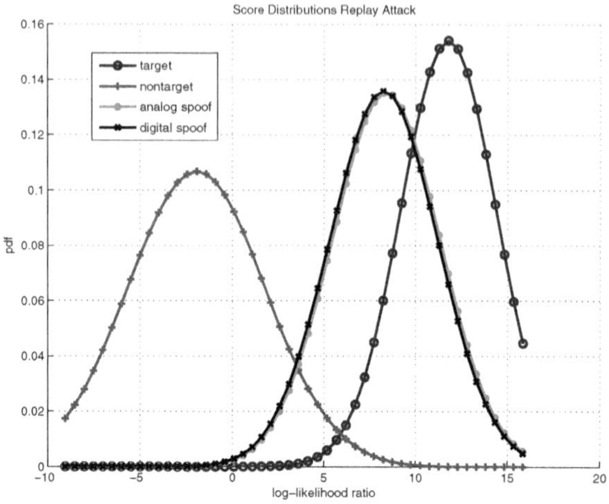

Fig. 5. Speaker verification score distributions of the far-field database 1

Table 1. Score degradation due to replay attack of the far-field database 1

		Mean	Std	Median	Max	Min
Analog	Δscr	3.38	2.42	3.47	9.70	-1.26
	Δscr/scr (%)	29.00	19.37	28.22	70.43	-10.38
Digital	Δscr	3.52	2.30	3.37	9.87	-1.68
	Δscr/scr (%)	30.29	18.92	29.52	77.06	-16.74

score degradation statistics from a legitimate utterance to the same utterance after the spoofing processing (far-field recording, replay attack). The average degradation is only around 30%. However, it has a big dispersion with some spoofing utterances getting a higher score than the original ones.

Far-Field Database 2. We did separate experiments using phase1+2 and phase3 datasets. For phase1+2, we train speaker models using 6 landline utterances, and do 120 legitimate target trials, 2280 non spoof non target, 80 landline spoofs and 80 GSM spoofs. For phase 3, we train speaker models using 12 utterances (6 landline + 6 GSM), and do 120 legitimate target trials (60 landline + 60 GSM), 1080 non spoof non target (540 landline + 540 GSM) and 80 spoofs (40 landline + 40 GSM).

Using non spoof trials we have got and EER of 1.66% and EER of 5.74% for phase1+2 and phase3 respectively. In Figure 6 we show the miss and false acceptance probabilities against the decision threshold for phase1+2 database. If we choose the EER threshold we have 5% of landline spoofs passing the speaker verification which is not as bad as in the previous database. None of the GSM spoofs would be accepted.

Figure 7 shows the score distributions for each of the databases. Table 2 shows the score degradation statistics due to the spoofing processing. The degradation

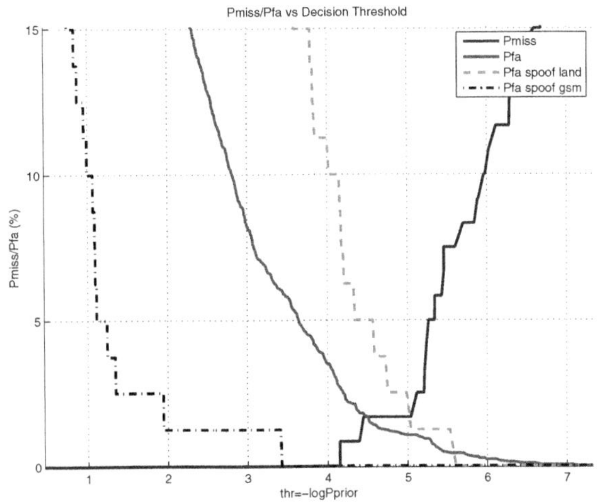

Fig. 6. Pmiss/Pfa vs decision threshold of far-field database 2 phase 1+2

is calculated by speaker and sentence type, that is, we calculate the difference between the average score of the clean sentence Fx of a given speaker and the average score of the spoofing sentences Fx of the same speaker. As expected, the degradation is worse in this case than in the database with replay attack only. Even for phase 3, the spoofing scores are lower than the non target scores. This means that the processing used for creating the spoofs can modify the channel conditions in a way that makes the spoofing useless. We think that this is also affected by the length of the utterances. It is known that when the utterances are very short, Joint Factor Analysis cannot do proper channel compensation. If the channel component were well estimated the spoofing scores should be higher.

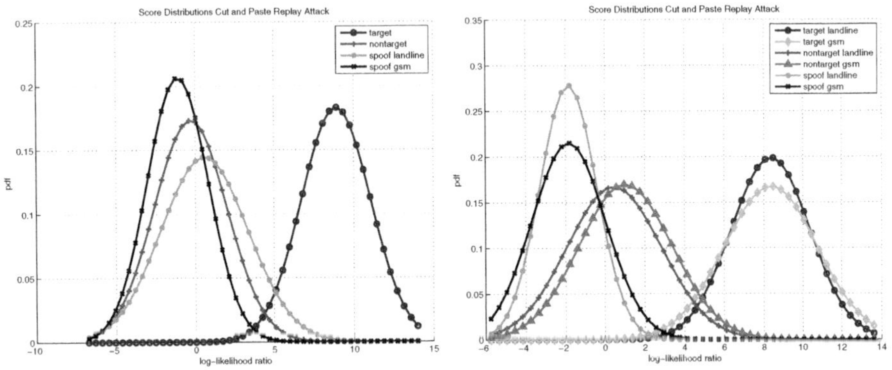

Fig. 7. Score distributions of far-field database 2 phase1+2 (left) and phase3 (right)

Table 2. Score degradation due to replay attack of the far-field database 2

			Mean	Std	Median	Max	Min
Phase1+2	T	Δscr	8.29	3.87	7.96	17.89	1.41
		Δscr/scr (%)	90.53	31.64	90.72	144.88	27.46
	G	Δscr	9.98	2.96	9.56	18.517535	5.40
		Δscr/scr (%)	111.94	18.03	109.437717	159.69	80.41
Phase3	T	Δscr	10.21	2.51	9.76	17.78	6.86
		Δscr/scr (%)	123.06	18.47	117.54	180.38	95.60
	G	Δscr	10.21	3.32	10.19	18.36	4.65
		Δscr/scr (%)	121.63	19.50	119.39	167.15	92.67

3.4 Far-Field Replay Attack Detection

Far-Field Database 1. In Table 3 we show spoofing detection EER for the different channel types and features. The LFR is the feature that produces better results getting 0% of error in the same channel condition and 7.32% in the mixed channel condition. The spectral ratio and modulation indexes do not achieve very good results separately but combined can be near the results of the LFR. Digital spoofs are more difficult to detect than analog with the SR and modulation indexes. We think that the digital processing mitigate the noise effect on the signal. The LFR is mainly detecting the effect of the loudspeaker. To detect spoofs where the impostor uses another mean to inject the speech signal into the telephone line we keep the rest of features. Using all the features, we achieve similar performance than using the LFR only.

Figure 8 shows the DET curve for the mixed channel condition using all the features.

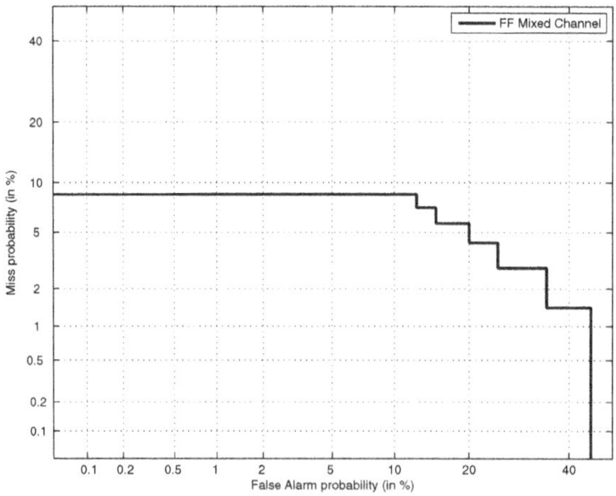

Fig. 8. DET spoofing detection curve for the far-field database 1

Table 3. Spoofing detection EER for the far-field database 1

Channel	Features	EER(%)
Analog Orig. vs. Analog Spoof	SR	20.00
	LFR	0.00
	MI	30.7
	Sb-MI	10.71
	(SR,MI,Sb-MI)	0.00
	(SR,LFR,MI,Sb-MI)	0.00
Digital Orig. vs. Digital Spoof	SR	36.07
	LFR	0.00
	MI	30.7
	Sb-MI	14.64
	(SR,MI,Sb-MI)	10.71
	(SR,LFR,MI,Sb-MI)	0.00
Analog+Dig Orig. vs. Analog+Dig Spoof	SR	37.32
	LFR	7.32
	MI	31.9
	Sb-MI	12.36
	(SR,MI,Sb-MI)	8.03
	(SR,LFR,MI,Sb-MI)	8.03

Far-Field Database 2. In Table 4 we show EER for both databases for the different channel combinations. The nomenclature used for defining each condition is: NonSpoofTestChannel_SpoofTestChannel. Phase1+2 database has higher error rates which could mean that they have been recorded in a way that produces less channel mismatch. That is also consistent with the speaker verification performance, the database with less channel mismatch has higher spoof acceptance. The type of telephone channel has little effect on the results. Figure 9 shows the spoofing detection DET curves.

Table 4. Spoofing detection EER for the far-field database 2

		EER(%)
Phase1+2	T_T	9.38
	T_G	2.71
	T_TG	5.62
Phase3	T_T	0.00
	G_G	1.67
	TG_TG	1.46

3.5 Fusion of Speaker Verification and Spoofing Detection

Finally we are going to fuse the spoofing detection and speaker verification systems. The fused system should keep similar performance for legitimate trials to the original speaker verification system but reduce the number of spoofing trials that deceive the system. We have done a hard fusion in which we reject the trials

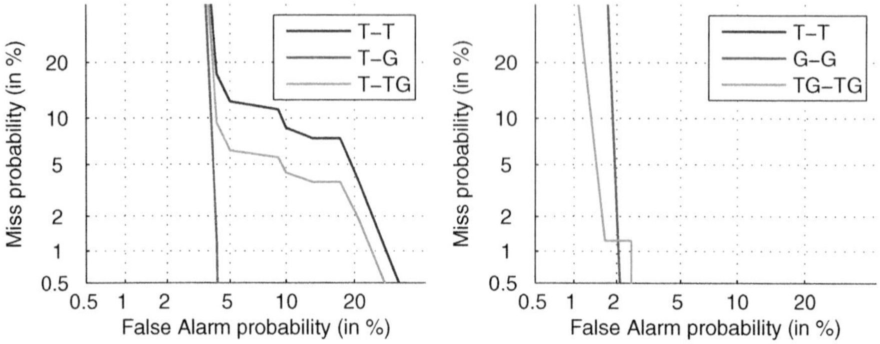

Fig. 9. DET spoofing detection curves for the far-field database 2 phase1+2 (left) and phase 3 (right)

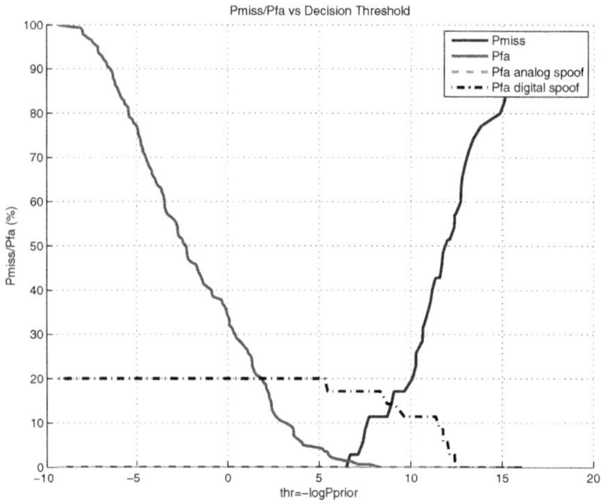

Fig. 10. Pmiss/Pfa vs. decision threshold for a speaker verification system with spoofing detection

that are marked as spoof by the spoofing detection system; the rest of trials keep the score given by the speaker verification system. In order to not increase the number of misses of target trials, which would annoy the legitimate users of the system, we have selected a high decision threshold for the spoofing detection system.

We present results on the far-field database 1 because it has the higher spoofing acceptance rate. Figure 10 shows the miss and false acceptance probabilities against the decision threshold for the fused system. If we again consider the EER operating point we can see that the number of accepted spoofs has decreased from 68% to zero for landlines and 17% for GSM.

4 Conclusions

We have presented a system able to detect replay attacks on speaker verification systems when the recordings of the victim have been obtained using a far-field microphone and replayed on a telephone handset with a loudspeaker. We have seen that the procedure to carry out this kind of attack changes the spectrum and modulation indexes of the signal in a way that can be modeled by discriminative approaches. We have found that we can use synthetic spoofs to train the SVM model and yet, we can get good results on real spoofs. This method can significantly reduce the number of false acceptances when impostors try to deceive an SV system. This is especially important for persuading users and companies to accept using SV for security applications.

References

1. Reynolds, D.A., Quatieri, T.F., Dunn, R.B.: Speaker Verification Using Adapted Gaussian Mixture Models. Digital Signal Processing 10(1-3), 19–41 (2000)
2. Kenny, P., Ouellet, P., Dehak, N., Gupta, V., Dumouchel, P.: A Study of Interspeaker Variability in Speaker Verification. IEEE Transactions on Audio, Speech, and Language Processing 16(5), 980–988 (2008)
3. `http://www.itl.nist.gov/iad/mig/tests/sre/2010/NIST_SRE10_evalplan.r6.pdf`
4. Perrot, P., Aversano, G., Chollet, G.: Voice disguise and automatic detection: review and perspectives. Lecture Notes In Computer Science, pp. 101–117 (2007)
5. Perrot, P., Aversano, G., Blouet, R., Charbit, M., Chollet, G.: Voice Forgery Using ALISP: Indexation in a Client Memory. In: Proceedings (ICASSP 2005). IEEE International Conference on Acoustics, Speech, and Signal Processing, pp. 17–20. IEEE, Los Alamitos (2005)
6. De Leon, P.L., Pucher, M., Yamagishi, J.: Evaluation of the vulnerability of speaker verification to synthetic speech. In: Proceedings of Odyssey 2010 - The Speaker and Language Recognition Workshop, Brno, Czech Republic (2010)
7. Chang, C.-C., Lin, C.-J.: LIBSVM: a library for support vector machines (2001)
8. Pelecanos, J., Sridharan, S.: Feature warping for robust speaker verification. In: Oddyssey Speaker and Language Recognition Workshop, Crete, Greece (2001)
9. Glembek, O., Burget, L., Dehak, N., Brummer, N., Kenny, P.: Comparison of scoring methods used in speaker recognition with Joint Factor Analysis. In: ICASSP 2009: Proceedings of the 2009 IEEE International Conference on Acoustics, Speech and Signal Processing, Washington, DC, USA, 2009, pp. 4057–4060. IEEE Computer Society, Los Alamitos (2009)
10. Brummer, N.: `http://sites.google.com/site/nikobrummer/focalbilinear`

Privacy Preserving Challenges: New Design Aspects for Latent Fingerprint Detection Systems with Contact-Less Sensors for Future Preventive Applications in Airport Luggage Handling

Mario Hildebrandt[1], Jana Dittmann[1], Matthias Pocs[2], Michael Ulrich[3], Ronny Merkel[1], and Thomas Fries[4]

[1] Research Group on Multimedia and Security, Otto-von-Guericke University Magdeburg, Universitaetsplatz 2, 39106 Magdeburg, Germany
{hildebrandt,dittmann,merkel}@iti.cs.uni-magdeburg.de
[2] Projektgruppe verfassungsverträgliche Technikgestaltung (provet), Universität Kassel, Wilhelmshöher Allee 64-66, 34109 Kassel
matthias.pocs@uni-kassel.de
[3] State police headquarters Saxony-Anhalt, Luebecker Str. 53, Magdeburg, Germany
michael.ulrich@polizei.sachsen-anhalt.de
[4] FRT, Fries Research & Technology GmbH, Friedrich-Ebert-Straße, 51429 Bergisch Gladbach, Germany
fries@frt-gmbh.com

Abstract. This paper provides first ideas and considerations for designing and developing future technologies relevant for challenging privacy-preserving preventive applications of contact-less sensors. We introduce four use-cases: preventive detailed acquisition of fingerprints, coarse scans for fingerprint localisation, separation of overlapping fingerprints and age determination for manipulation detection and automatic securing of evidence. To enable and support these four use-cases in future, we suggest developing four techniques: coarse scans, detailed scans, separation and age determination of fingerprints. We derive a new definition for the separation from a forensic approach: presence detection of overlapping fingerprints, estimation of the number of fingerprints, separation and sequence (order) detection. We discuss main challenges for technical solutions enabling the suggested privacy-preserving use-cases combined with a brief summary of preliminary results from our first experiments. We analyse the legal principles and requirements for European law and the design of the use-cases, which show tendencies for other countries.

Keywords: latent fingerprints, preventive application, contact-less fingerprint acquisition, legal requirements.

1 Motivation

The detection of latent fingerprints with new contact-less sensors is a new challenge in forensics when investigating crime scenes (e.g. see [1]). Those sensors are recently investigated (not yet applied in the field) and allow new application areas by a faster

C. Vielhauer et al. (Eds.): BioID 2011, LNCS 6583, pp. 286–298, 2011.

and more detailed and non-destructive acquisition. Before such sensors can be used practically several aspects need to be investigated. The overall research questions are for example related to the quality of fingerprint acquisition and detection on different surfaces. As future applications might include the usage in crime prevention scenarios, additional questions of privacy preserving technologies and application approaches arise. They include, but are not limited to, challenging research questions by having to consider data minimality need to be answered before the release of such applications. This becomes a necessity because fingerprint data is personal data and subject to privacy and data protection laws [2]. Stringent precautions need to be taken since traces of innocent people are scanned a priori.

The scenarios include, but are not limited to, large crime scenes, dangerous environments or security checks of luggage and freight. The technology of high quality contact-less scans might enable scenarios, which include automatic verification or even identification of latent fingerprints. However, due to high error rates (reported in the range of 93.4% accuracy for the verification in [3]) an automatic identification of potential "endangerers" is not considered, yet. Therefore, the traditional subjective assessment of the fingerprints by a dactyloscopic expert remains the recommended approach. Furthermore, an automatic verification or authentication gathers data about innocent people and increases risks of misuse. Hence, such scenarios are not regarded due to legal, ethical and societal reasons. However, today fingerprints are taken often anyway at border controls where potential "endangerers" could be identified with the help of their exemplary fingerprints and their photograph. Therefore our goal is to introduce first ideas and considerations for designing and developing future technologies relevant for challenging privacy-preserving preventive applications and their legal requirements for European law. These are used to show tendencies for European and other countries. Therefore, we provide preliminary approaches and results by showing tendencies and potential future technical possibilities. However, our focus for experiments is limited in this paper.

Our idea is to divide the acquisition into *coarse scans* for the manipulation detection (if someone touched the luggage without permission) and *detailed scans* of fingerprint for further manual investigations (if there is any indication of a malicious activity) in an airport luggage-handling use-case. We suggest that *coarse scans* are used for the automatic localisation of fingerprints on a particular surface (Regions-of-Interest). The advantage of such a coarse scan is that no visible fingerprint patterns allowing for a verification of the fingerprint are present in the acquired data; thus they preserve privacy. We suggest *detailed scans* by capturing at a much higher resolution, depending on the particular surface and the quality of the latent fingerprint even level 3 features [5], such as pores on the ridge lines, can be detected. We show first tendencies towards those techniques, too. Furthermore, we suggest using the *Separation of overlapping fingerprints* to analyse multiple fingerprint patterns on the same position. Derived from a forensic approach, we define four phases of the separation: *detection of the presence of overlapping fingerprints*, *estimation of the number of involved fingerprints*, *separation of overlapping fingerprint patterns* and *sequence (order) detection*. The sequence detection is a first *age detection* and we propose to use further *absolute age detection* to estimate the point in time a particular fingerprint was left on the surface. First results provide promising data; however, the feasibility of the short term age detection has to be evaluated in large scale tests in future work. In the following, we introduce the basic technologies of our suggested *coarse scans* for fingerprint position determination and verification, *detailed scans* to support forensic investigations, *separation of overlapping fingerprints* and *age detection* of latent fingerprints, as fundamentals for the four basic privacy-preserving use-cases *coarse detection, detailed detection, separation and age detection* and *securing of evidence*.

We analyse the legal requirements for privacy and data protection for each use-case. The European privacy and data protection principles are lawfulness, purpose limitation, necessity and proportionality, data minimality, data accuracy, data sensitivity, transparency (that is, participation and accountability), supervision by data protection authorities, data security, and privacy by design [2]. The results of a preventive collection of latent fingerprint data that enables an identification or verification have to be earmarked on storage. Access to the stored data should be highly restricted and an automated secure deletion must be performed if the data is no longer needed.

This paper is structured as follows: Section two provides an overview of currently available contact-less sensors actually considered in research for forensic investigations, which are capable of capturing latent fingerprints from surfaces. Section three summarises the legal principles. Section four introduces our ideas towards basic technologies as fundamentals for the four use-cases and shows first tendencies for the localisation of fingerprints using *coarse scans*, as well as for *detailed scans* of the detected fingerprints and first results of the *age detection*. In section five our ideas for the design of the potential fingerprint detection systems for the four new use-cases are introduced. The legal requirements for the use-cases are analysed in section six for the European legislation to show tendencies for other countries. Section seven summarises the content of this paper and provides an outlook to the future work.

2 State of the Art of Contact-Less Fingerprint Acquisition Devices

The contact-less acquisition of latent fingerprints without any treatment, which is used in crime scene investigation, is a challenging problem. From several known approaches, see e.g. [4, 8, 9, 10, 11], in this paper we currently use a FRT MicroProf200 equipped with a chromatic white light (CWL) sensor [11], which captures intensity and topography data of the surface. Different contact-less sensors are currently researched in more detail.

The approach from [4] uses a digital camera with a polarisation filter to reduce the specular component of the reflected light of the fingerprint residue while still capturing the specular component of the surface reflection for the contrast enhancement. However, the exact positioning of the light source, the camera and the polarization filter angle is necessary to get a usable result. The CWL sensor uses a beam of white light and the effect of chromatic aberration of lenses. The wavelength with the focal length exactly matching the distance to the surface is reflected most; this enables an exact determination of the distance to the surface by the sensor. Additionally the amount of reflected light is recorded for each point. We use differential images of one area with and without a fingerprint to determine which information is visible to the sensor. Engel and Masgai use a FRT MicroProf with CWL sensor [7] for the acquisition of latent fingerprints in 2004. In 2008 the technique of optical coherence tomography is adopted by Dubey et al. [8] for the detection of latent fingerprints under a layer of dust. Other sensors include [9], where 2D fingerprints are lifted from curved surfaces and [10] where fingerprints on absorbing surfaces should be ascertainable.

For the evaluation of our first approaches in this paper, we use a MicroProf200 with CWL 600 sensor [11], since it is commercially easily available and provides topography data, which might be useful for the separation and age detection. Furthermore, this device is a multi-sensor device and can be tuned for higher scan speeds and different surfaces. It is used to show first tendencies for the utilisation of contact-less fingerprint scanners. In theory this technique allows for an automatic identification of fingerprints. However, even the verification of latent fingerprints with exemplary fingerprints has been reported in the range of 93.4% accuracy (see [3]). Hence, the current algorithms must be improved to enable a reliable identification of fingerprints. Additionally, an automatic identification without a particular suspicion is not necessary. Thus we introduce four new promising use-cases for the application of such sensors in section 5; they are designed to be privacy-preserving and compatible with ethical and legal requirements.

3 Legal Principles

This section outlines the legal principles in relation to the fundamental rights of persons whose fingerprints are scanned. By deploying the fingerprint scanning system, fundamental rights of individuals may be interfered with [22]. If personal data is collected, the deployment interferes with the right to privacy and data protection [15]. This interference triggers protection under the European privacy and data protection principles (see section 1). According to the principle of privacy by design, the interference can be qualified on the basis of the application design. Thus, design proposals could establish the legality of the preventive application of the fingerprint scanner. In particular, the legal assessment in this paper focuses on the use-case 5.2 (detailed detection) for securing evidence for future criminal prosecution. The goal is to draft legally relevant elements of technology design.

The detailed scan (5.2 to 5.4; see section six for the coarse scan) aims at identifying persons no later than on criminal prosecution. With access to these data the police can identify persons subject to AFIS (automated fingerprint identification system) and other reference databases. However, also the data about persons that are not subject to AFIS are personal because they represent "factors specific to [the data subject's] physical identity" according to Article 2(a) Data Protection Directive and the detailed scan allows to distinguish one from the other [16] [17]. In addition, these data are unique and lifelong valid so that relating data to an identifiable person is more likely. Besides, identifiability may also derive from extra information; for example, from the time of leaving a fingerprint and the working schedule one might relate the fingerprint to an employee [17]. The interference can be justified by purposes that serve public interests if the interests pursued with the use-cases are proportionate to the gravity of the interference. In section six the proportionality is analysed.

4 Our Design Approach

In our paper we focus on the acquisition of fingerprints with the FRT MicroProf 200 using a CWL sensor to show tendencies for preventive fingerprint acquisition systems. In the actual settings of our test, we consider a working distance of 6.5mm [11]. In particular first results for the coarse and detailed fingerprint detections as the fundamental requirement for such systems are shown. The overall technical solution is future research work. In this section we discuss and introduce four basic technologies as fundamentals for the privacy-preserving use-cases in section 5.

4.1 Design of Coarse Scan for Fingerprint Detection and Localisation

In our setting used, the CWL is a point sensor; the amount of points for measuring significantly affects the total acquisition time. Our idea of a first approach of coarse scans with this CWL is a trade-off between acquisition time and result quality. Our first results indicate that a point distance of 400µm (63.5dpi) is sufficient for the localisation of fingerprints. Using the CWL sensor fingerprint residue usually appears darker than the surface material (Fig. 1). Hint: this effect is not or not as obvious on absorbing surfaces with our actual CWL setup, but can be achieved with enhanced sensor settings, which are considered in our further research.

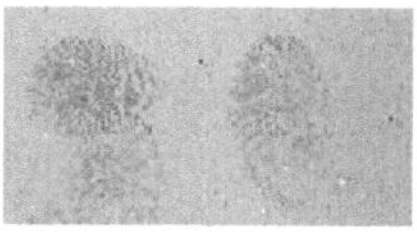

Fig. 1. Coarse scan of smooth black plasic surface with fingerprints

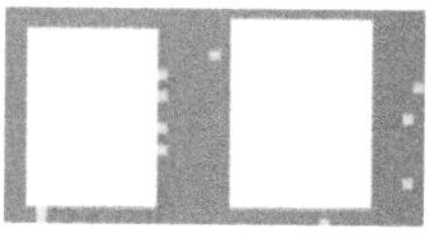

Fig. 2. Automatically identified fingerprint positions

Our idea generally is to determine the variance of the intensity within segments to a global mean of the complete surface. In the first step segments with variances exceeding a surface dependent threshold are marked as possible Regions-of-Interest (see the small grey squares in Fig. 2). In a second step, nearby regions are combined to bigger Regions-of-Interest. If a region exceeds the size of 5x5mm it is automatically marked as a possible latent fingerprint location (see white rectangles in Fig. 2). As evaluated in first tests, this approach currently works on non-absorbing smooth surfaces, such as various hardtop cases (e.g. plasic or polished metal); a section of 10x10cm can be currently acquired and analysed within 10 minutes. With enhanced sensor settings, appropriate algorithms for different surface materials need to be investigated. This is necessary for a reliable detection of fingerprint positions on every kind of luggage. Our experimental work shows here already very good indications.

4.2 Design of Detailed Scan for Fingerprint Verification and Identification

Our idea of detailed scans is to support further investigations of the fingerprint patterns for verification, and in theory identification, of the particular fingerprint on all three feature levels (see [5]). They require a much higher acquisition resolution compared to coarse scans. Our exemplary first tests are performed at a distance of 10µm between two measured points (2540dpi), which enables, depending on the fingerprint pattern and the surface material, a detection of pores (level 3 features in [5]). The fingerprint ridgelines are visibly darker than the surface material; the pores on them are visible as brighter spots. From our first tests, the overall quality of the acquired data is dependent to the surface material. The first test set is limited to smooth, non-absorbing surface materials, which provide the best results with our current algorithm.

4.3 Definition and Design of Overlapping Fingerprint Detection

The separation of overlapping fingerprints is a challenge to our current research. It is mostly an enhancement for the detailed scan, since the coarse scan does not provide enough data for the separation. Regarding overlapping fingerprint detection from a forensic point of view, we divide it into four different objectives: *detection of the presence of overlapping fingerprints, estimation of the number of involved fingerprints, separation of overlapping fingerprints, sequence (order) detection.* The detection and separation of overlapping fingerprints is necessary for the discrimination between multiple fingerprint patterns at the same position on the luggage, e.g. on the locks or handle. In respect to the state of the art, there is several works on separation of overlapping fingerprints such as [12] or [13]. Singh et al. [12] use independent component analysis to separate overlapping fingerprints. In [13] an approach to separate two overlapping fingerprints under ideal conditions is introduced, requiring a significantly different angle, to be able to determine the different orientation fields. However, the used fingerprints are developed, e.g. by carbon black powdering. Work in respect to sequence detection can be found in [14]; here it is observed that the first fingerprint pattern is interrupted by the overlaying one. However, different residues are applied to the fingers prior to imprinting the fingerprints to the surface to enable the separation and sequence detection. The sequence detection is a special form of the age detection, which determines the *relative age* between multiple fingerprints; it does not determine the *absolute age* of each fingerprint. To our knowledge, there is currently no work in respect to all four different objectives of overlapping latent fingerprints for contact-less acquisition, supporting different kinds of surfaces (e.g. rough, absorbing or textured) without pre-processing such as carbon black powdering.

4.4 Design of Fingerprint Age Detection

The age detection is necessary to estimate a certain point in time, when a particular fingerprint was left on the surface (*absolute age*). This allows for the selection of only the relevant fingerprints, avoiding the storage of fingerprint data of uninvolved or innocent people. Prior work discovered a degeneration of features and ridge line width as aging effects and that closed pores might merge or become open pores [6]. They investigate aging effects of latent fingerprints over a time frame of two years for relative age detection. It is highly dependent on the original pattern, since, to our knowledge, without the information of the initial ridge line width and pore size and distribution the estimation of the fingerprint age with optical sensors is not possible, yet. The possibility of the age detection for very small time intervals with contact-less sensors should be evaluated in future work in more detail. Our first experiments with the CWL (3x3mm, 3-10µm) use a *differential age detection* approach to investigate

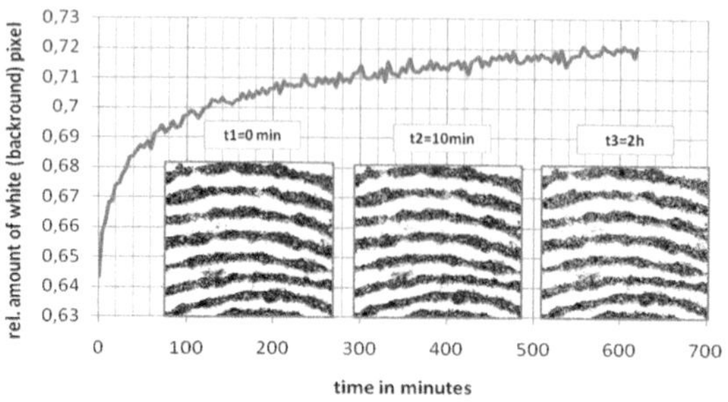

Fig. 3. The increase of the white (background) pixel of a binarised fingerprint image part (3x3mm, 300x300 pixel) in relation to the time passed. In the right corner the binarised fingerprint is shown at three points in time (t1=0 min; t2=10min; t3=2h).

the aging of the residue. Therefore, multiple scans of the same area of a fingerprint are performed in short intervals for a time span of ten hours using a test set of four fingerprints (one of which is exemplary shown in Fig. 3).

To our knowledge, most curves of natural processes are either logarithmic, exponential, or, in some cases, linear. Our idea is to study the amount of changes within the captured image caused by water evaporating from the print involved when a fingerprint trace is left on a surface. A possible way of measuring this fact is counting the black/white pixels in a scanned and binarised fingerprint intensity image, representing the amount of residue which is present. The curve of such an aging-feature is logarithmic over time, as shown in Fig. 3 for an exemplary fingerprint part (3x3 mm, 10μm).

4.5 Overall Perspective for the Design Approaches and Their Technical Challenges

From the overall perspective, the localisation of fingerprints using a coarse scan is our first step for the fingerprint acquisition. The second step is the detailed scan of each identified position. If an overlapping fingerprint pattern is detected in the detailed scan, the number of patterns is determined and all fingerprints have to be separated. Subsequently, the order of overlapping fingerprints (*relative age*) and the *absolute age* for each fingerprint should be determined. We are currently able to successfully locate the fingerprint positions with our experimental CWL setting on smooth surfaces; the detailed acquisition of fingerprints is possible on such surfaces, too. Research questions are here how to improve the acquisition of fingerprint patterns from rough, textured and/or absorbing surfaces. First tests indicate that the approach can be modified to work on textured veneers or brushed metal. The evaluation of short term age detection using contact-less optical scanners in large scale tests to confirm our first results remains future work. The *absolute age* detection can reduce the number of fingerprints that are acquired in detail; thus, non relevant fingerprints are not captured, which supports the privacy preserving application. This also applies for *relative age* detection where only the overlaying pattern is necessary in most cases. Currently, *differential age detection* using multiple scans can be performed. Furthermore, other sensors like digital cameras should be evaluated for a localisation of fingerprints on bigger areas. All four aspects of the separation of overlapping fingerprints on various surfaces remains future work for contact-less scans of latent fingerprints.

5 Design of Preventive Applications to Enhance Airport Luggage Handling Security Systems

Based on our approaches introduced in section 4, the fingerprint acquisition can be integrated into the available luggage handling systems. Potential applications are derived and illustrated in the use-cases *coarse detection*, *detailed detection*, *separation and age detection*, as well as *securing of evidence* (all shown in Fig. 4). We show exemplary implementations for these use-cases in the following subsections.

5.1 Coarse Scan System for Fingerprint Location Verification (*Coarse Detection*)

The idea of *coarse scans* supports the detection of the fingerprint positions. From the first experimental setup, our current algorithms only work on smooth, non-absorbing surfaces. A possible system for fingerprint location and position verification is shown in Fig. 4(a). Our objective is to use such a system for the detection of the manipulation of the luggage during the automatic luggage processing by detecting changes of the number and positions of fingerprints. After the check-in an initial coarse scan is performed. It determines the locations of all fingerprints and stores only a bounding box for each position (see Fig. 2). Afterwards, the usual automatic luggage handling with the security scans takes place. Before the luggage is prepared for the manual loading to the airplane, a new coarse scan is performed.

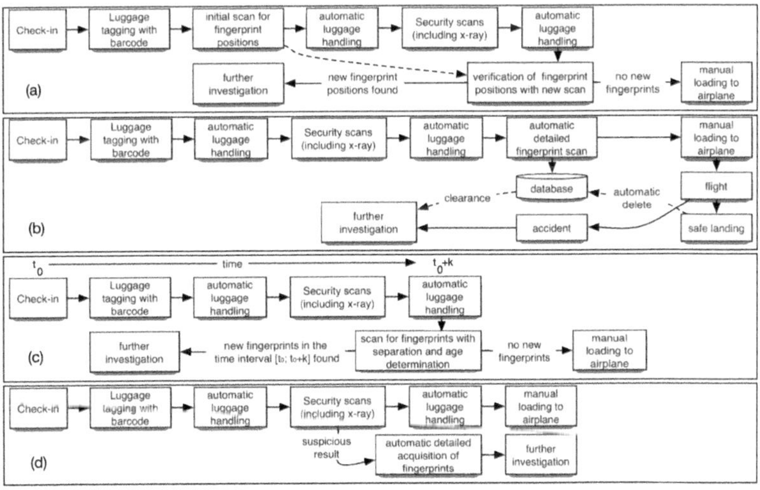

Fig. 4. Illustration of use-cases: (a) coarse detection, (b) detailed detection, (c) separation and age detection, (d) securing of evidence

If new fingerprint positions are found during the verification of positions, the particular piece of luggage is separated for further investigation. This might include a detailed scan of the additional fingerprint positions for the purpose of securing of evidence. However, no detailed fingerprints are acquired and stored a priori; only the new fingerprints are acquired, fulfilling the minimality principle (Section 1).

5.2 Scan System for Detailed Fingerprints (*Detailed Detection*)

Our proposed *detailed scans* of fingerprints on luggage can be a useful preventive use-case. However, the access to the acquired data should be highly restricted and as soon as possible unneeded data must be securely deleted automatically. Our general idea for such a system (see Fig. 4(b)) is to perform a *detailed scan* of fingerprints prior to the manual luggage loading and to keep them until the airplane has landed safely. Then the acquired fingerprints are automatically securely deleted from the database. However, the secure deletion from databases remains future work. If an accident or serious incident happens during the flight, the acquired data for this particular flight is cleared for further investigations. The fingerprint data should only be used earmarked for this particular case.

5.3 Scan System with Detection of Fingerprint Age and Overlapping Fingerprints (*Separation and Age Detection*)

Our idea is to use the *separation, sequence and age detection* of fingerprints to reduce the number of necessary scans of the luggage to one. This might be possible if the *absolute age* of the fingerprint can be determined and overlapping fingerprints can be separated. The Fig. 4(c) shows the modified system. Here our idea is to locate and acquire fingerprints prior to the manual loading of the luggage to the airplane. If new fingerprints that are applied in the time frame between the check-in time t_0 and the scan time t_0+k are found, a further investigation is performed. The separation and age determination of fingerprints most likely requires a detailed scan (although, a very small area of the fingerprint might be sufficient for the age detection). In this case, the acquired data must be securely deleted instantly, if no trace of new fingerprints is found in the timeframe between t_0 and t_0+k. However, if new fingerprints are detected, those particular fingerprints newer than t_0 can be used earmarked for further investigation. This implements the stated goal of the minimality principle (section 1). However, to our knowledge, the determination of the *absolute age* is currently not feasible. Therefore, we suggest performing a *differential age determination*. From the curve shape (see Fig. 3 in section 4.4), we can derive, that there is the tendency of water evaporating from the print within the first hours, which gives us the possibility for our considered privacy preserving use-case. For this purpose a small portion of the fingerprint must be scanned two times t_0+k-t_Δ and t_0+k shortly before being loaded onto the aircraft with an exemplary time span, such as $t_\Delta=10min$ in between these two scans $((t_0+k-t_\Delta)-(t_0+k)=10min)$. The white pixels of both scans can then be counted and their difference calculated. Since the aging curve is logarithmic, a high difference-value accounts for an early stage in the run of the curve and therefore a young age ($age < k$) of the print. This can be considered suspicious, since nobody should have touched the luggage since the check-in. In such a case the suspicious fingerprint can then be investigated further with the help of a detailed scan.

5.4 Automatic Securing of Evidence (*Securing of Evidence*)

In this case our idea is to connect the fingerprint acquisition system with the existing security scans. If one of the present security scan systems detects something suspicious, e.g. possible drug smuggling, the fingerprints on the particular piece of luggage are acquired in detail for the securing of evidence. Hence, this use-case, as shown in Fig. 4(d), differs from the prior use-cases; it relies on a precisely defined suspicion. This exemplary system separates the suspicious luggage directly after the security scan that initiated the investigation and acquires the fingerprints with a separate contact-less latent fingerprint acquisition device. The automatic securing of evidence is very useful, since the fingerprints are preserved prior to the further investigation. This is beneficial if the original fingerprint patterns are destroyed due to the investigation. However, the acquired data should be used earmarked and should be securely deleted if the initial suspicion could not be approved.

6 Analysis of Legal Issues for the Defined Use-Cases

In this section, we show potential legal challenges for the use-cases. Particular attention is drawn to the use-case "detailed detection" (5.2), in order to establish and optimise legal compatibility. Regarding the coarse scan (5.1), no personal data is collected if single fingerprints cannot be distinguished from a sufficiently large number of other fingerprints [17]. This inability also excludes the assertion of other legal violations (e.g., discrimination). However, this exclusion presupposes that individual scans are not otherwise related to specific passengers. For example, video and audio material of surveillance cameras or working schedules must not reveal such a relationship. In the application scenario this is not the case. Therefore, coarse scans can even serve as privacy-enhancing technology if they limit detailed scans to manipulated or dangerous luggage.

The interference (see section 3) caused by the detailed scans (5.2 to 5.4) can be justified if the use-cases answer a "pressing social need" [18]. They answer such a need because they enable the police to take purpose-specific measures and allow for a new reach of police observation (e.g., in Germany [19]). However, the principle of proportionality requires that the use-cases be proportionate to the gravity of the interference with the fundamental rights to privacy and data protection. Where manipulation or dangerous luggage content indicates a source of danger (5.1, 5.3 and 5.4), the interference is proportionate since the data subject has given a reason for the police to act and the luggage is examined immediately after capturing the fingerprints and the captured data is deleted securely without further use if the result is negative.

In the use-case "detailed detection" (5.2), proportionality of the interference has to be assessed in detail. To this end, the European privacy and data protection principles give guidance: a) the interference is grave because the data subject has not given a reason (e.g., suspicion) for the capture of his fingerprints (purpose limitation); b) due to the secretive nature of the fingerprint capture, citizens might feel like being watched and therefore not exercise their rights freely (transparency; in Germany, e.g. [20]); c) unique data with lifelong validity facilitate connecting different databases (purpose limitation); d) sensitive data may be extracted from fingerprints (sensitivity; hence, minimising sensitive data for comparison with AFIS and other reference databases should be object of future research). There is also the societal dimension of privacy and data protection: the number of citizens that are subject to interference without having given a reason for it, may be significantly large and therefore create the risk of abuse of political power (societal data protection [21]).

In contrast, secondary use of fingerprint data is avoided by technology design and organisational measures. The data is secured from access for purposes other than those specified (see below), the data accessed are the ones relating to the flight in question (data accuracy), and all data related to other flights are automatically deleted when the airplane has landed. It does not allow human interaction like CCTV cameras. If only the data related to a flight where an accident occurs are accessed, the interference is similar to that at conventional crime scenes. Overall the gravity of the interference depends on whether or not the number of citizens is significantly large.

On the other hand, the more important the goal pursued by the use-case is, the more grave interferences it can justify. This "preventive use-case" aims at facilitating investigations of an accident or other serious incidents by securing evidence beforehand. The goal has to be further specified (purpose limitation). For example, it could be required that the incidents put at risk the security of the state or individuals' lives, bodies or freedom, or constitute a crime specified due to its range of penalties and the extent of wrongdoing in the particular case is taken into account. Further, passengers of the flight in question may not be suspects. The importance of the pursued goal depends on whether or not there is suspicion (based on facts and criminalistic experience), and whether or not the suspicion is still valid (erasing data about others as soon as the offender has been found).

In order to justify the capture of fingerprint data for which the individuals have not given reason, the system design can be optimised. In the case of the Data Retention Directive 2006/24/EC, it is accepted to store data for future crimes because numerous companies control smaller databases, avoiding a centralised database (societal data protection), and the data controllers are not the executing police authorities which creates transparency of data access (transparency). Consequently, the legislator should also provide that the captured data is controlled by several police (or even non-police) authorities. Regarding the large number of citizens at airports, such system architecture optimises compatibility with the fundamental rights to privacy and data protection (privacy by design).

The overall interference is grave for both citizens that are not subject to further use as well as those who are. Therefore, the legal, organisational and technical guarantees for both groups are subject to particularly strict requirements. These requirements can only be fulfilled if not only legal but also organisational and technical guarantees are laid down in a legally binding manner (data security; see, e.g. [23]). Finally, the deployment of the technology (5.2 to 5.4; except for the coarse scan) has to be provided for by law (lawfulness). Concerning the use-cases where the manipulation or the dangerous content of the luggage indicates a source of danger (5.3 and 5.4), specificity and safeguards of the legal basis do not have to meet high standards. Therefore, general provisions about police data collection and use suffice. Concerning the capturing of fingerprints without suspicion in order to obtain evidence for future prosecution (5.2), general police provisions on data processing do not suffice. Hence, a legal basis needs to be introduced that specifically lays down this use-case. Depending on the interference with the societal dimension of data protection, clarity of the purpose specification, technology design, and organisational safeguards, introduction of a legal basis may also be in line with the fundamental rights to privacy and data protection.

7 Summary and Future Work

This paper provides a first exemplary design of preventive applications utilising contact-less fingerprint acquisition sensors for four exemplary use-cases. We show first tendencies for the localisation of fingerprints and their detailed acquisition as part of the basic technologies representing the fundamentals for the use-cases. The legal assessment suggests that there are design approaches that may be decisive to avoid that the highest courts in Europe veto the preventive application of the fingerprint scanner. Future work should concentrate on the improvement of the available sensors and algorithms to improve the quality of the results and to reduce the surface material dependency to fit the requirements of a preventive application and further specification of the application to prepare legal instruments. Furthermore, the basic technologies of separation of overlapping fingerprints including the relative age detection and the absolute age detection of fingerprints have to be researched in detail. First evaluations of the differential age detection show already promising results that should be confirmed using large scale tests.

Acknowledgments. The work in this paper has been funded in part by the German Federal Ministry of Education and Science (BMBF) through the Research Programme under Contract No. FKZ: 13N10818, FKZ: 13N10820, FKZ: 13N10822 and FKZ: 13N10821.

References

1. Leich, M., Ulrich, M., Hildebrandt, M., Kiltz, S., Vielhauer, C.: Forensic fingerprint detection: Challenges of benchmarking new contact-less fingerprint scanners – a first proposal. In: Pattern Recognition for IT Security, TU-Darmstadt, Darmstadt (2010)
2. Data Protection Directive 95/46/EC, Council of Europe Convention ETS no. 108; also OECD Guidelines 1980, UN Guidelines 1990; in Germany, since BVerfGE 65, 1
3. Jain, A., Feng, J., Nagar, A., Nandakumar, K.: On Matching Latent Fingerprints. In: IEEE Computer Society Conference on Computer Vision and Pattern Recognition Workshops, CVPRW 2008, pp. 1–8 (2008)
4. Lin, S.-S., Yemelyanov, K.M., Pugh, E.N., Engheta, N.: Polarization- and Specular-Reflection-Based, Non-contact Latent Fingerprint Imaging and Lifting. Journal of the Optical Society of America A 23(9), 2137–2153 (2006)
5. Jain, A., Chen, Y., Demirkus, M.: Pores and Ridges: fingerprint Matching Using Level 3 Features. In: 18th International Conference on Pattern Recognition, ICPR 2006, pp. 477–480 (2006)

6. Popa, G., Potorac, R., Preda, N.: Method for fingerprints age determination. Romanian Journal of Legal Medicine 18(2), 149–154 (2010)
7. Engel, A., Masgai, G.: Detektion von Fingerspuren und Windows-Fingerprint-GINA. Entwurf, Implementierung und Evaluierung, Bachelor Thesis, Otto-von-Guericke-University of Magdeburg (2004)
8. Dubey, S.K., Mehta, D.S., Anand, A., Shakher, C.: Simultaneous topography and tomography of latent fingerprints using full-field swept-source optical coherence tomography. Journal of Optics A: Pure and Applied Optics 10(1), 015307–015315 (2008)
9. Kuivalainen, K., Peiponen, K.-E., Myller, K.: Application of a diffractive element-based sensor for detection of latent fingerprints from a curved smooth surface. Measurement Science and Technology, vol 20(7), 77002 (2009)
10. EVISCAN by cote:m (2010), `http://www.cotem.de/eviscan_web/index.html`
11. Chromatic White Light Sensor CWL - Fries Research & Technology - FRT GmbH (2010), `http://www.frt-gmbh.com/en/products/sensors/cwl/`
12. Singh, M., Singh, D.K., Kalra, P.K.: Fingerprint separation: an application of ICA. In: Proc. SPIE 6982, 69820L (2008)
13. Chen, F., Feng, J., Zhou, J.: On Separating Overlapped Fingerprints, Biometrics: Theory Applications and Systems (IEEE BTAS 2010), pp. 1–6 (2010)
14. Tang, H.-W., Lu, W., Che, C.-M., Ng, K.-M.: Gold Nanoparticles and Imaging Mass Spectrometry: Double Imaging of Latent Fingerprints. Anal. Chem. 82(5), 1589–1593 (2010)
15. Art. 16 Treaty on the Functioning of the EU; in Germany lately, BVerfG, 2 BvR 1372/07 (Mikado), para. 18
16. Article 29 Data Protection Working Party of the EU: Biometrics (WP80), p. 5 (2003), `http://ec.europa.eu/justice_home/fsj/privacy/docs/wpdocs/2003/wp80_en.pdf`
17. Article 29 Data Protection Working Party of the EU: Concept of personal data (WP136), `http://ec.europa.eu/justice/policies/privacy/docs/wpdocs/2007/wp136_en.pdf`
18. European Court of Human Rights, S and Marper v. UK (30562/04, 30566/04), para. 101
19. BVerfGE (Collection of Federal Constitutional Court descisions) 120, 378 (428), `http://www.servat.unibe.ch/dfr/`
20. BVerfGE 120, 378 (402); BVerfG, 2 BvR 1345/03 (IMSI-Catcher), Abs. 65; BVerfGE 115, 320 (342); BVerfGE 115, 166 (188); BVerfGE 113, 29 (46); BVerfGE 65, 1 (42)
21. Dix in: Roßnagel, Handbuch Datenschutzrecht, München 2003; Bygrave para. 20; Regan: Legislating Privacy, University of North Carolina Press, pp. 230ff.; Steinmüller, Informationstechnologie und Gesellschaft, Darmstadt, p. 671; Podlech in: Brückner/Dalichau, Festgabe für Hans Grüner, Percha, pp. 452ff.; BVerfGE 65, 1 (43); "scatter," BVerfGE 120, 378 (402 f.) w. f. r (1995), `http://www.austlii.edu.au/au/journals/UNSWLJ/2001/6.html`
22. Hornung/Desoi/Pocs in: Brömme/Busch, BIOSIG, Proceedings of the Special Interest Group on Biometrics and Electronic Signatures, Bonn, p. 83 (2010)
23. BVerfG 1 BvR 256/08, para. 224 (English press release under "Data Security") (March 2, 2010), `http://www.bverfg.de/pressemitteilun-gen/bvg10-011en.html`

Author Index